TEMPLES AND TEMPLE-SERVICE IN ANCIENT ISRAEL

TEMPLES AND TEMPLE-SERVICE IN ANCIENT ISRAEL

An Inquiry into the Character of Cult Phenomena and the Historical Setting of the Priestly School

BY

MENAHEM HARAN

OXFORD
AT THE CLARENDON PRESS
1978

Oxford University Press, Walton Street, Oxford OX2 6DP

OXFORD LONDON GLASGOW
NEW YORK TORONTO MELBOURNE WELLINGTON
KUALA LUMPUR SINGAPORE JAKARTA HONG KONG TOKYO
DELHI BOMBAY CALCUTTA MADRAS KARACHI
NAIROBI DAR ES SALAAM CAPE TOWN

British Library Cataloguing in Publication Data
Haran, Menahem
Temples and Temple-Service in Ancient Israel.
1. Judaism 2. Temples – Israel
I. Title
296.6 BM655 77-30069
ISBN 0-19-826318-X

Printed in Great Britain
at the University Press, Oxford
by Eric Buckley
Printer to the University

PREFACE

I HAVE attempted in this work to synthesize studies of biblical cult and related fields that I have undertaken and put forward in various publications for about twenty-five years and some of which are accessible only to the Hebrew reader. As explained in the Prologue, the work bears upon three levels of concern, which will account for its somewhat lengthy sub-title. The first of these is the direct examination, from a morphological point of view, of cultic and social phenomena connected with the temple and deriving from its essential nature—an examination which illuminates at least some aspects of the biblical cult, important enough in and of themselves. It should be noted that 'cult' is taken here as denoting mainly the activities connected with the temple's inner sphere and belonging to the priestly circle. So far as the public was concerned, these activities would be expressed for the most part in offering sacrifices; other activities such as prostrations, prayer, processions, or dances, belonged to the periphery of the cult and in Old Testament times were considered a kind of substitute for, or supplement to, the offering of sacrifices.

The second level is an attempt to demonstrate the antiquity of all the material embodied in the Pentateuchal priestly source (P). Contrary to the opinion predominant in modern biblical research, it is contended here that this material derives from conditions that prevailed in the pre-exilic, not the post-exilic, period of ancient Israelite history. Had time and space permitted, the demonstration suggested here could profitably have been extended to themes other than those covered in this book, but I believe that even within its present scope it is enough to establish the thesis. The third level is an attempt to show that even the literary crystallization of P must have taken place in pre-exilic times—though I do not deny that it was only in the days of Ezra, when the Law was canonized and became the corner-stone of Jewish communal life, that P's presence became perceptible in historical reality and began to exercise its influence on the formation of Judaism.

It goes without saying that some of these problems are of great importance for biblical research as a whole, just as some of the conclusions arrived at here, in particular those of the third level, are likely to have significant implications for the correct understanding of ancient Israelite history. This inquiry may thus be said to contain somewhat more than its title, 'Temples and Temple-Service', would indicate (and only its sub-title alludes to the more significant aspects dealt with here). I hope that the reader will find himself convinced at least as far as the first level of discussion is concerned. Acceptance of the conclusions of the second and third levels may be more difficult, but here too I hope I have managed to express my thoughts and arguments cogently enough to persuade anybody who considers them in the most careful manner, and approaches them with an open mind, unimpeded by fixed, preconceived notions. The dictum of one of the greatest minds of our century may be applied to our field no less than to natural science: 'There are no eternal theories in science . . . Every theory has its period of gradual development and triumph, after which it may experience a [rapid] decline . . . Nearly every great advance in science arises from a crisis in the old theory, through an endeavor to find a way out of the difficulties created.'[1]

I have tried to make use of most of the sources of thought, early or late, which have contributed to the understanding of the Old Testament, and as far as my knowledge goes I have ascribed any idea, comment, or opinion mentioned in the discussion, first of all to the first authority to suggest it. To this end I have used, among other things, the medieval Jewish exegetes, whose perception of the literal meaning of the biblical text (in contradistinction to its elucidation by means of literary and historical criticism) was quite often incisive and worthy of admiration, and in which regard the moderns have no advantage over them. If the reader feels that, in quoting modern critical scholars, I have perhaps given too much weight to J. Wellhausen and his contemporaries, this is indeed not accidental. It results simply from the rule that when referring to any view one ought, as a matter of fairness, to make mention of the first authority to express that view. However, it also reflects the unique importance to biblical research of that brilliant systematizer, whose long shadow still stretches over the field. For it can hardly be contested that virtually all the schools of thought in biblical research that have arisen since his time, on

[1] A. Einstein and L. Infeld, *The Evolution of Physics* (New York, 1938), p. 77.

both sides of the Atlantic (in this regard, even the Scandinavian school is not a real exception), have attempted not so much to replace the postulates of his system as to build and refine upon them, to sharpen and develop or, alternatively, to moderate them in some way. Leaving aside the Hegelian dialectic and the principle of evolution, which by themselves have evoked much disputation, the fact remains that the basic historical sequence of the Pentateuchal sources, as advocated by Wellhausen, has in effect endured to this day.[2] From this perspective the conception suggested in this inquiry may mark a change of direction, a switch to another course, from the point where he stood. The great, inescapable debate should begin at that point.

The subject-matter dealt with here, even though based mainly on the study of the Pentateuch, has connections with several other areas of biblical research, and in particular relates to the question of the composition of the Former Prophets. My own opinions on the basic problems of these areas (such as the character of the Pentateuchal sources and the questions of their scope—whether they are limited to the Tetrateuch, or to the Hexateuch, or whether they extend into the Books of Kings) are indicated in several places throughout this book or explained more fully in Hebrew publications; and my somewhat more detailed treatments of some of the problems that belong to the body of this book were likewise published in Hebrew. I have therefore had to refer the reader to some of these publications and occasionally also to other Hebrew works, mostly by Israeli scholars. I hope that, even though not all these references may be of help to the reader who has no access to modern Hebrew scholarly literature, he will at least be able to infer that those problems have not been left unconsidered, and at any rate I expect that my own standpoint will be found to have been presented here in sufficient clarity.

Chapter and verse references are to the Massoretic Bible. In quoting the biblical text in English I have mainly followed the RSV, but in certain places I have preferred other English versions, and in some have had to diverge from all of them. References to the treatises of Maimonides' Code, *Mišnēh Tôrāh*, are made directly

[2] I have been told that W. F. Albright used to quote A. Alt, an outstanding initiator of a more recent school of biblical criticism, as saying that 'we all are but children of Wellhausen'. Though I have not come across such a statement in the writings of either of them, it sounds authentic and is also true.

from the Hebrew original. If need arises, the reader can locate them in the English translation published by the Yale Judaica Series (New Haven and London, 1949–). References to the Ugaritic texts are to C. H. Gordon's *Ugaritic Textbook* (Rome, 1965). To find the corresponding reference according to A. Herdner's system in his *Corpus des Tablettes en Cunéiformes Alphabétiques* (Paris, 1964), the reader should consult M. Dietrich and O. Loretz, *Konkordanz der ugaritischen Textzählungen* (Neukirchen-Vluyn, 1972), pp. 230–6.

The first draft of this book was submitted towards the end of the academic year 1972–3, which I had the pleasure of spending in Cambridge, England. Even at that point, however, I felt it necessary to round off this inquiry by the addition of certain chapters and some other material; and several matters, such as those connected with archaeological findings, had to wait until the results of certain excavations which had been undertaken in Israel could take shape. The completion of this work thus extended over a somewhat longer time.

I am grateful to the editorial boards of *HUCA*, *IEJ*, *JBL*, *JSS*, *Scripta Hierosolymitana*, and *VT*, for allowing me to use freely material that previously appeared in their pages—to re-write and modify it, to bring it up to date, and to incorporate it into this book (several of these studies were intended from the very beginning to be parts of a broader project, while the material of other parts of the book has not yet been published anywhere). The Revd. John A. Emerton, Regius Professor of Hebrew at the University of Cambridge, who afforded me his hospitality in 1972–3, showed me further kindness in undertaking the task of reading the proofs of this book in page form. I am also indebted to the Delegates of the Oxford University Press and to the members of their staff for their patient and scrupulous treatment of this book during all the stages of its publication. Finally I wish to express my gratitude to my students, Mr. Meir Paran and Mr. Raymond Edge, who put much effort into the preparation of the glossary and the indexes.

והאמת יוֹרֶה דרכו (Ibn-Ezra on Prov. 9: 1)

The Hebrew University,
Jerusalem M. H.

CONTENTS

LIST OF MAPS AND FIGURES

ABBREVIATIONS

PERIODICALS

AASOR	*Annual of the American Schools of Oriental Research*, New Haven, Conn.
AcOr	*Acta Orientalia*, Kopenhagen
ARW	*Archiv für Religionswissenschaft*, Leipzig–Berlin
ASTI	*Annual of the Swedish Theological Institute* (at Jerusalem), Leiden
BA	*The Biblical Archaeologist*, New Haven, Conn.
BASOR	*Bulletin of the American Schools of Oriental Research*, Baltimore, Md.
BIES	*Bulletin of the Israel [Jewish Palestine] Exploration Society* (Hebrew), Jerusalem
CBQ	*Catholic Biblical Quarterly*, Washington, D.C.
EI	*Eretz-Israel*, Archaeological, Historical and Geographical Studies, Jerusalem
EsBi	*Estudios Biblicos*, Madrid
HThR	*Harvard Theological Review*, Cambridge, Mass.
HUCA	*Hebrew Union College Annual*, Cincinnati, Ohio
IEJ	*Israel Exploration Journal*, Jerusalem
JAOS	*Journal of the American Oriental Society*, New Haven, Conn.
JBL	*Journal of Biblical Literature*, Philadelphia, Pa.
JCS	*Journal of Cuneiform Studies*, New Haven, Conn.
JJS	*Journal of Jewish Studies*, London
JNES	*Journal of Near Eastern Studies*, Chicago, Ill.
JPOS	*Journal of Palestine Oriental Society*, Jerusalem
JSS	*Journal of Semitic Studies*, Manchester
OTS	*Oudtestamentische Studiën*, Leiden
PEQ	*Palestine Exploration Quarterly*, London
PJB	*Palästinajahrbuch (des deutschen evangelischen Instituts für Altertumswissenschaft des heiligen Landes zu Jerusalem)*, Berlin
RB	*Revue Biblique*, Paris
RHR	*Revue de l'Histoire des Religions*, Paris
SVT	*Supplements to Vetus Testamentum*, Leiden
TA	*Tel-Aviv*, Journal of the Tel-Aviv University Institute of Archaeology, Tel-Aviv

Tarbiẓ	*Tarbiẓ*, A Quarterly for Jewish Studies (Hebrew), Jerusalem
Textus	*Textus*, Annual of the Hebrew University Bible Project, Jerusalem
ThLZ	*Theologische Literaturzeitung*, Leipzig–Berlin
ThZ	*Theologische Zeitschrift*, Basel
VT	*Vetus Testamentum*, Leiden
WdO	*Die Welt des Orients, Wissenschaftliche Beiträge zur Kunde des Morgenlandes*, Göttingen
ZAW	*Zeitschrift für die Alttestamentliche Wissenschaft*, Berlin
ZDMG	*Zeitschrift der Deutschen Morgenländischen Gesellschaft*, Wiesbaden
ZDPV	*Zeitschrift des Deutschen Palästina-Vereins*, Wiesbaden
Zion	*Zion*, A Quarterly for Research in Jewish History (Hebrew), Jerusalem

SERIES OF COMMENTARIES AND ENGLISH VERSIONS OF THE BIBLE

AB	The Anchor Bible, Garden City, N.Y.
AT	American Translation, Chicago, 1931
ATD	Das Alte Testament Deutsch, Göttingen
BK	Biblischer Kommentar AT, Neukirchen
CBSC	Cambridge Bible for Schools and Colleges, Cambridge
EVV	English Versions
GHK	(Göttinger) Handkommentar zum AT, Göttingen
HAT	Handbuch zum AT, Tübingen
ICC	The International Critical Commentary, Edinburgh and New York
JB	The Jerusalem Bible, London, 1968
KAT	Kommentar zum AT, Leipzig
KEH	Kurzgefasstes Exegetisches Handbuch zum AT, Leipzig
KHC	Kurzer Hand-Commentar zum AT, Freiburg i. Br.–Leipzig–Tübingen
KJV	King James Version, 1611
NEB	The New English Bible, Oxford–Cambridge, 1970
NJPS	New Translation, Jewish Publication Society of America, Philadelphia, 1962–
OTL	Old Testament Library, London
RSV	Revised Standard Version, 1952
RV	Revised Version, 1881
SAT	Die Schriften des AT, Göttingen
WC	The Westminster Commentaries, London

OTHER BOOKS

ANEP	*The Ancient Near East in Pictures Relating to the OT*², Ed. J. B. Pritchard (Princeton, N.J., 1969)
ANET	*The Ancient Near Eastern Texts Relating to the OT*³, Ed. J. B. Pritchard (Princeton, N.J., 1969)
ARI	W. F. Albright, *Archaeology and the Religion of Israel* (Baltimore, 1946; 1953)
CAD	*The Assyrian Dictionary of the Oriental Institute of the University of Chicago* (Chicago, 1956–)
DB	*A Dictionary of the Bible*, Ed. J. Hastings, i–v (Edinburgh, 1898–1904)
EB	*Encyclopaedia Biblica*, Ed. T. K. Cheyne, i–iv (London, 1899–1903)
EM	אנציקלופדיה מקראית = *Encyclopaedia Biblica*, i–vii (Jerusalem, 1950–76)
ERE	*Encyclopaedia of Religion and Ethics*, Ed. J. Hastings, i–xii (Edinburgh, 1908–21)
IDB	*The Interpreter's Dictionary of the Bible*, i–iv (Nashville–New York, 1962); Supplementary Volume (Nashville, 1976)
ILC	J. Pedersen, *Israel, its Life and Culture*, i–iv (London–Copenhagen, 1926–40)
KAI	H. Donner and W. Röllig, *Kanaanäische und aramäische Inschriften*², i–iii (Wiesbaden, 1966–9)
KS	A. Alt, *Kleine Schriften zur Geschichte des Volkes Israel*, i–iii (München, 1953–9); *or*: O. Eissfeldt, *Kleine Schriften*, i–v (Tübingen, 1962–73)
PGI	J. Wellhausen, *Prolegomena zur Geschichte Israels*; unless otherwise indicated, cited from the sixth edition (Berlin, 1905; 1927)
THH	Y. Kaufmann, תולדות האמונה הישראלית i–iv (Tel-Aviv, 1937–56); [Abridgement and translation of vols. i–iii by M. Greenberg, *The Religion of Israel from its Beginnings to the Babylonian Exile* (Chicago and London, 1961); translation of vol. iv by C. W. Efroymson, *History of the Religion of Israel* (New York, 1977)]
ThWAT	*Theologisches Wörterbuch zum AT*, Ed. G. J. Botterweck and H. Ringgren (Stuttgart etc., 1972–)
UT	C. H. Gordon, *Ugaritic Textbook* (Rome, 1965)

VARIA

AT	Alte (Alten, Altes) Testament
Bab. Tal.	The Babylonian Talmud

D, E, J, P	The Pentateuchal Sources
H	The Holiness Code (main part of Lev. 17–26)
Jer. Tal.	The Jerusalemite (Palestinian) Talmud
LXX	The Septuagint Version
MT	The Massoretic Text
OT	Old Testament

I

PROLOGUE

I

THE temple is the most conspicuous and prominent of all cultic institutions in ancient Israel and, for that matter, in the ancient Near East as a whole. The primary object of this study is to define its essence and to describe various phenomena connected with it. To set forth the true character of the temple and the exact distinction between it and other cultic institutions is a task important enough in itself, as a prerequisite for a proper understanding of cultic phenomena in general. But it can also shed some light, as the following chapters will show, on other matters of crucial importance: the antiquity of the priesthood and the course of some of its main lines of development in ancient Israel; the real nature of the pilgrim-feasts; or the intimate connection between the temple and the Passover offering—perhaps the most remarkable of all the sacrifices of the yearly cycle.

The basic distinction between the temple and all other cultic institutions will underlie the ensuing discussion as it comes to deal with the nature of cultic activity in each of its possible dimensions. These are at the most four in number: place (or institution), time (or occasion), act (or ceremony) performed, person (or personnel) performing it—and no description of cult is complete unless it embraces them all.[1] Though it is not the intention of this inquiry,

[1] Wellhausen, with his feeling for perfection, is still the only one to have come close to an all-embracing description of the biblical cult in its four dimensions (and, of course, from a certain specific point of view). The first part of *PGI*, entitled *Geschichte des Kultus*, falls into five chapters, the first four of which correspond to those dimensions: 'Der Ort des Gottesdienstes', 'Die Opfer', 'Die Feste', and 'Die Priester und Leviten' (the dimension of time comes third with him). The fifth chapter, 'Die Ausstattung des Klerus', is intended to round off the description by discussing the priesthood's economic existence and sources of income.

nor is it possible within the present framework, to exhaust the subject and to say the last word on all of the many problems connected with these cult dimensions, the discussion will none the less treat at least the principal aspects of all four (though not necessarily in the afore-mentioned order).

Place and institutions. An explanation will be given, in the first place, of the temple's unique position among the cultic establishments, and the distribution of temples in ancient Israel will be outlined (Chapters II–III). Later on the following points will be discussed: the cult reforms which put an end to all sites of worship outside Jerusalem (Chapter VII), P's conception of the temple as rooted in extremely ancient patterns (Chapters VIII–IX), and the relationship of P's tabernacle to the actual temple that existed in Jerusalem (Chapter X).

Personnel. The basic character of the priesthood and the non-priestly Levitical status will be described, together with their historical setting (Chapters IV–VI).[2]

Acts. The ritual complex relating to the interior of the temple will be described, and its significance will be explained (Chapters XI–XIII). In this connection a definition will be called for of the exact character of E's tent of *môʿēd* ('tent of meeting'), although in fact it was an institution of prophetic–ecstatic activity and had nothing to do with the priestly cult (Chapter XIV). From among the varied array of sacrifices associated with the altar in the temple court, just one outstanding example will be examined, the Passover offering (Chapter XVII).

Occasions. A description will be given only of the pilgrim-feasts, which will be distinguished on the one hand from other set occasions of sacred character (such as New Year, Day of Atonement, New Moon days, and Sabbaths) which involved no obligation of pilgrimage, and on the other hand from the non-national, familial festivities which constituted a lower category (Chapter XVI). The examination of the Passover offering which concludes this inquiry (Chapter XVII) also has a bearing on the dimension of time, since, as will be shown, in the Old Testament this offering is already connected with the Feast of Unleavened Bread.

[2] For various reasons, mainly connected with the line of argument, the chapters dealing with the dimension of personnel intersect those dealing with that of place.

2

The attempt to define the cultic–institutional and social phenomena connected with the temple and its service, and the morphological description of them, constitute just one level of the discussion in the subsequent chapters. Another level, certainly of no less importance, is that of the historical implications. For the inquiry, consistently and from any direction, leads to what appears to be the inevitable conclusion that the priestly source—the copious, overflowing treasure trove of information about Israelite temple ideology and temple service in biblical times—rests on historical conditions that prevailed not in the post-exilic but in the pre-exilic period. The significance of this result is that the data available from this source—when stripped of the utopian mask with which they are disguised, and when their ideological bent is taken into account—can properly serve as direct, substantial testimony to the cultic mannerisms, temple procedures, and priestly concepts that obtained in and around the First Temple during the last third of its existence.

At this level, too, the discussion will be concerned with the four cult dimensions.

Personnel. An attempt will be made (in Chapter V) to show that P's distinction between the priesthood and the Levites is not to be explained as a development of Ezekiel's prescriptions (Ezek. 44: 1–14) and that its historical context is earlier than Ezekiel. Though it is true that after Ezra's activities this distinction became a dogmatic principle founded on the canonized Law, it was not constitutionally based on the conditions prevailing in that period, but is the product of the realities of First Temple times.

Place and institutions. It will be demonstrated (in Chapter X) that the priestly tabernacle is merely a utopian reflection of Jerusalem's First Temple. To be sure, in post-exilic times attempts were made to adjust some of the temple's details and components to the mythic–ideal pattern as represented in the image of the tabernacle, which at that time was already 'found written in the Law' (in the words of Neh. 8: 14). Nevertheless, in other essential details the gap could not be bridged, and the lack of correlation between the Second Temple and the tabernacle remained clear. Suffice it to mention that the Babylonian exiles who returned to Jerusalem had neither the intention nor the ability to reinstitute the ark and the cherubim, or the Urim and Thummim (cf. Ezra 2: 63; Neh. 7: 65), or the anointing oil, together with the idea of contagious holiness which, according to P, is attributed to the tabernacle and all its paraphernalia. In P, however, all these are indispensable tenets.[3] In passing it may be remarked that the post-exilic community was, in fact, unable to put into practice —according to their genuine meaning—many other concepts and rites which belong to the bedrock of P's world.

Acts. It will be pointed out (in Chapter XI) that in P's writings one can discern a complex of rites which was regularly performed inside the temple and the antiquity of which cannot be questioned. Its relevance to the First Temple practice should be accepted as indubitable at least because the post-exilic priests could hardly have invented it; and, moreover, in the Second Temple period it could have led only a shadowy existence (in the absence of ark and cherubim it did not even have a centre of gravity). It will also be demonstrated (in Chapter XVII) that the principal features of the Passover sacrifice, as described in great detail by P (Exod. 12: 1–14, 43–50), were in existence well before the end of the pre-exilic period and are indeed compressed into succinct injunctions occurring already in the Books of the Covenant (Exod. 23: 18; 34: 25).

Occasions. As for the pilgrim-feasts we shall see (in Chapter XVI) that P conceives of them in a way that is practically equivalent to that of the ancient sources. (In a way, the examination of the pilgrim-feasts, as well as that of the Passover sacrifice in Chapter XVII, can here be regarded as in the nature of sample studies of the method put forward in this inquiry.)

Let it be added that, even though the themes which it will be possible to cover in the present inquiry are certainly central and weighty enough in their bearing on each of the four dimensions of cult, in no case should the historical inferences be supposed to be limited to these themes alone. Were such the case, the evidence, owing to the special significance and great import of these themes, would still suffice to point to the correct answer as to the historical

[3] On P's conceptions of contagious holiness see below, pp. 176–7. Even the talmudic sages were compelled to admit that lacking the above-mentioned constituents the Second Temple was dissimilar to the First (Bab. Tal. Yoma, 21*b*). As for the anointing oil, they assumed that it was hidden away together with the ark, when the jar of manna and Aaron's rod (cf. Exod. 16: 33–4; Num. 17: 25–6) were also hidden away (Bab. Tal. Horayoth, 12*a*; Yoma, 52*b*).

position of all of the material embodied in P. All the more so when I am firmly convinced that a direct examination of any other sector or topic embraced by P will lead to the self-same results. For lack of space, however, if for no other reason, the discussion will be focused here on the subject-matter of temples and temple-service.

3

The determination of the historical setting of P's material in its entirety, however important this may be, is perhaps not altogether new. A drift in this direction may even be found in the works of representatives of orthodox research, which for more than a century has accepted as a matter of doctrine that P is the product of post-exilic times. Nevertheless, exponents of this school are at times prepared to admit that certain ancient relics are still discernible within P, or that the priestly writers sometimes engaged in 'archaisms', or that old and quasi-pagan concepts which had been suppressed in the pre-exilic period occasionally resumed the foreground in P, since by then they were no longer considered 'dangerous'.[4] In the light of these opinions, the view presented here might perhaps seem to be a mere broadening of a characteristic already recognized as existing in P—albeit occasionally and to only a limited extent—by applying it to the whole of P's scope. The truth is, however, that what is here suggested is of a more fundamental nature. For a close examination of the qualities of P's material and of its historical position tends to show that P's literary crystallization itself had already occurred in pre-exilic times. This is yet another level of historical inference resulting from the present inquiry, and its implication is certainly no less significant.

The profound conviction underlying this inquiry is that P is

[4] See, e.g., A. Kuenen, *The Religion of Israel*, ii (London–Edinburgh, 1875), p. 255; S. R. Driver, *Introduction to the Literature of the OT*[9] (Edinburgh, 1913), pp. 142–5; R. Kittel, *Geschichte des Volkes Israel*, i (Gotha, 1921), pp. 322–8; R. H. Pfeiffer, *Introduction to the OT* (New York, 1948), pp. 255–6, 266–8. Similar views will be also found in scholarly literature in connection with specific points such as the New Moon day—known in P and not infrequently mentioned in the Former Prophets, as it is indeed an institution of remote antiquity, though it does not occur in the Pentateuchal non-priestly sources (which in fact had no occasion to deal with it)—and rites of purification and of apotropaic character mentioned in P, in particular the unique ceremony of purging the temple of any possible impurity as described in Lev. 16, or certain priestly narrative sections which have a flavour of antiquity.

the literary product of circles of the Jerusalemite priesthood of the First Temple, not of the Second Temple period. This implies, among other things, that not only P's material, but even its literary form, together with the ideology embodied in it and the particular disposition typifying it, are monuments to the contemplations and aspirations of the First Temple priesthood at a certain point in time. It is maintained here, therefore, that all the sources of the Pentateuch—the most sacred part of the Old Testament canon—did in fact attain literary crystallization during the First Temple period, differing from each other only in character and dates of composition. P, written in the form of a treatise which covers the whole span of time from the primordial age until after the conquest of Canaan, actually parallels J and E, though it is later than them, while D is exceptional among them all in that it is cast in a rhetorical mould. In its pragmatic character and ideological bent P bears a resemblance to D, and both of them, in favouring the idea of cult centralization (although in various styles, corresponding to the different ways in which they conceive the idea itself), are in sharp contrast to the two earlier, 'epic' sources.[5] However, in its manifestly priestly character P differs from all the other sources, all three of which are indeed non-priestly in their evident features.[6]

In assigning P to the post-exilic period orthodox research bases itself on the Hegelian principle of dialectic and historic evolution. Indeed it uses this principle to try to explain almost all of the spiritual phenomena of ancient Israelite life, including the supposed emergence of the monotheistic idea itself as a direct development out of the pagan conception of the world. Naturally enough, by an application of the same principle to the suggested historical order of the biblical literature, the appearance of P is taken as a direct dialectic development out of the stage represented by D.[7] However, the Hegelian principle of evolution itself need not be

[5] The designation 'epic' for these sources has been coined by F. M. Cross, *Canaanite Myth and Hebrew Epic* (Cambridge, Mass., 1973), p. 6 and *passim*.

[6] Other aspects of the crossing relationships between the sources will be dealt with at appropriate points in the subsequent discussions (see pp. 92, 334). For the relationship between P and Ezekiel's constitution (chaps. 40–8) see below, p. 147; also especially pp. 102, 125–8, 187, 193–4, 225, 288, 296–7.

[7] The first to suggest the principle of Hegelian dialectic as the basis for biblical criticism was W. Vatke, *Die Biblische Theologie wissenschaftlich dargestellt*, i (Berlin, 1835). In the preceding year E. Reuss had come to a similar idea, but his work (*Geschichte der heiligen Schriften AT*, Braunschweig, 1881) was published a long time after Vatke's.

considered an ultimate, irreplaceable truth.[8] Even if it were, one might still doubt, in the specific case of P, whether this source can really be explained as a dialectic 'reaction' or as an advanced stage of development as against D. It is incontestable that the two are different from each other in a good few respects, but the question is whether we are really faced by an inescapable necessity, by a methodical inevitability of acknowledging their suggested historical relation. Moreover, in the whole corpus of P there are no 'kernels' that might be traced back to D, either in the legal and narrative material or in stylistic elements, so much so that one can be sure that the priestly writers did not ever have access to D (which cannot be said about the relation between D and the early, 'epic' sources, especially E). What distinguishes P from D (as well as from J and E) is not necessarily its alleged place at the end of a dialectic evolutionary scale, but its remarkably *priestly* character, which places it apart as a distinct element among the Pentateuchal sources. This distinctiveness is obviously rooted in a particularity of social background and creative milieu, and in the spiritual

[8] Thus, Kaufmann's approach (in *THH* and earlier publications) is directly opposed to the Hegelian thinking. He defines paganism as a mythological, pantheistic religion which views the divine being as part of a settled cosmic order, while monotheism is a non-mythological religion conceiving of the deity as an absolutely sovereign entity not subject to limitations of nature or any system of laws. There can be therefore no direct transition between these two types of faith; the Israelite religion had no pagan origins whatsoever, and is the outcome of an original, intuitive spark of creative genius (Kaufmann does not deny that this religion did inherit certain mythological 'shells' which, however, lost their innate spirit after having been taken up by the new faith). In his definition of monotheism Kaufmann comes close to the neo-Kantian philosopher from Marburg, Hermann Cohen, in the first chapters of whose posthumous work *Religion der Vernunft aus der Quellen des Judentums* (Leipzig, 1919) one can find somewhat similar statements (some seeds of Kaufmann's system of comprehending Judaism are already recognizable in one of his publications from 1914). In addition, Kaufmann argues that P preceded D, but his reasoning here, for the most part, is unconvincing. He tries, for example, to define P as the 'law code for worship at the high-places' and to claim that P does not actually demand cult centralization, on the ground that for P this idea has only conceptual and symbolic significance without practical implications—an interpretation which can by no means be adopted. Though Kaufmann admitted P's general antiquity, he did not attempt to fix the limits of the period to which it could belong, and consequently in later publications went too far in attributing to P an antiquity which is beyond the boundaries of critical caution. In dating P, I am prepared, then, to concur with Kaufmann's view not more than in some degree, and not exactly for his own reasons. As regards the early dating of P, I have also chanced upon R. Abba's noteworthy observations in the last section of 'Priests and Levites', *IDB*, iii. 886–9 (several of his points, quite reasonable and proper in themselves, can already be found in Kaufmann's work).

idiosyncrasy which marked the priesthood. However, such a distinctiveness should not be removed from the typological–social context and made mainly a matter of historical–chronological sequence. P received its particular character not because the priesthood gained ascendency in the Second Temple theocracy, at which time P's concepts were supposedly formed as an evolutionary outcome of the previous historical stages, but simply because this source is a product of priesthood. In pre-exilic times, no less than later, the priesthood was certainly remarkable for its unique quality and characteristics, and as a distinctive, semi-esoteric group it certainly found a place beside other groups which existed at the same time. If P does contain a hierocratic ideal then this only proves that such an ideal was already harboured in the First Temple Jerusalemite priesthood.

The idea that P is a post-exilic work becomes even less plausible when we consider the additional fact that there is no basic, primary correspondence between this source and the actual conditions of that time. This fact, which will be confirmed in the course of further discussions, has already been mentioned as an indication that all of P's material and traditions must be pushed back to the pre-exilic period. But it also has a decisive bearing on the question of the date of P's literary crystallization. For it is much simpler and more direct to accept that a literary corpus, the whole content of which rests on pre-exilic conditions, is a product of that same time than to assume that it is a late work in which the presence of features more suited to the First Temple period has to be explained as a restoration of archaic 'relics'.

How much more so when the relation perceptible in P's material to the pre-exilic period is not just general and indefinite. An ideological and pragmatic work of the sort of P needs, as its background, a 'critical point' in history which would stimulate its coming into being—some irregular situation accompanied by upheavals and significant changes—and indeed, in P's case there seems to have been one. The discussion in the subsequent chapters will show that, beyond the general connection of P's material to the pre-exilic period as a whole, there are some indications, positive and palpable enough, of that special historical 'critical point' in the background of P's formation. This was, it is suggested, the period of Hezekiah and the time immediately preceding it, a period of severe historical tremors, which saw the decline and fall of the

Northern Kingdom and presaged noteworthy changes in the stature of the Jerusalem temple. This direction is pointed to, in an entirely independent manner, by various considerations connected with, for example, the separation of the Levitical class from the priesthood (Chapter V), Jerusalem's position as a place of worship (Chapter VII), and by various data appertaining to the temple (Chapters X, XV).

4

In the interest of clarity let it be added that no one will deny Ezra's decisive role in the formation of Judaism. The solemn ceremony performed under his inspiration and leadership, that is, the declaration of the '*amānāh*, 'pact', and the public undertaking of the duty to fulfil all the Law's commandments from that time on (Neh. 8–10),[9] is certainly a watershed in the history of Israel and even overshadows its forerunner, the covenant-making in the time of Josiah (2 Kgs. 22: 3—23: 24). As a result of Ezra's activity the Law, in its entirety, becomes the normative document in the life of Israel, and the first phase of Judaism as a denominational community, as an *ecclesia*, begins (even so, religious conversion, one of the essential hallmarks of a denominational group, was not yet invented and its introduction would have still to wait until the Hasmonean period).

It is beyond all question that from then on P, too, being now an integral part of the canonized Law, emerges as an effective factor in the life of Israel, and in this regard there is indeed general consent in modern scholarship.[10] However, ever since K. H. Graf,

[9] The references to Nehemiah the governor [the son of Hacaliah] in Neh. 8: 9; 10: 2 are merely insertions; cf. commentaries and most recently also F. M. Cross, *JBL* 94 (1975), 8. The personality dominating the activities described in Neh. 8–10 is only Ezra's. (The section Neh. 8–10 is a particular source that was incorporated into the Chronistic composition; it speaks of Ezra in the third person and is not identical with his memoirs.)

[10] There has, it is true, been no consensus on the question whether the book promulgated by Ezra encompassed the entire Law or whether it contained only P. Wellhausen (*PGI*, pp. 407–8) advocated the former possibility (in this section Wellhausen made extensive changes in later editions of *PGI*, but even in the earlier editions his position was no less firm on this point; in the second edition, of 1883, for example, he says in this context on p. 434: 'dass das Gesetz Esra's der Ganze Pentateuch gewesen ist, unterliegt keinem Zweifel'). The chief exponent of the latter possibility was A. Kuenen, *Historisch-kritische Einleitung in die Bücher des AT* i. 1 (Leipzig, 1887), pp. 211–14. See also H. Holzinger, *Einleitung in den Hexateuch* (Freiburg, 1893), pp. 430–1. Most recently a tendency in this direction can be noticed in, for example, K. Koch's statements in

A. Kuenen, and J. Wellhausen the assumption has prevailed that this abrupt intrusion of P into Israel's life coincided with its formation as a literary work. Of course, as far as details are concerned scholars feel themselves free to move about within the given framework. For it makes no substantial difference whether it is suggested that P was composed in Babylonia after the Exile or in Palestine after the Return, or that Ezra really brought it with him on his arrival in Jerusalem, when the basic assumption remains that its composition was but a preparatory step towards its ensuing promulgation in public. It is precisely on this point that the present inquiry ventures to deviate from the prevalent assumption and to claim that P's composition as a literary work on the one hand, and its canonization and publication on the other, are not coincidental; these are two distinct events rather widely separated in time.

The reasoning of the orthodox school implies a belief that a literary composition with the scope of P, and, what is more, so highly pragmatic and ideological in character, could not have been in existence without having an impact on the historical realities. But that is just the point: such a state of affairs is by no means impossible, especially when it has to do with a work of a remarkably utopian content in which conspicuous sectarian traits are also apparent—another respect in which P very much differs from all the remaining Pentateuchal sources. For P's unbending legalistic

JSS 19 (1974), 180–2, 194–5; or, for that matter, in the assumption underlying J. G. Vink's (to my mind rather problematical) study, 'The Date and Origin of the Priestly Code in the OT', *OTS* 15 (1969), 1–144. In this point, however, I am definitely prepared to accept Wellhausen's assertion. The main reasons are: (1) after D, or its main edition, was canonized and made known in Josiah's time, it never again went off stage, and Ezra's action could be expressed only by tacking P on to the already existing sources; (2) we have no record of, nor any allusion to, a third act of canonization, after those of Josiah and Ezra, when presumably the fully consolidated Law would have appeared; (3) the obligations mentioned as concluding the pact (Neh. 10: 30–40) are based not solely on P but also on D (as Wellhausen rightly pointed out), and also on the Books of the Covenant—while some of them have no direct basis in any Pentateuchal passage, being 'synthetic' innovations which resulted from the demands of life and were deduced by way of halachic exposition (such as presenting annually a third of a shekel for the temple service, or casting lots for a wood offering). A few quite sound observations against Kuenen's position on this point may even be found in D. Hoffmann, *Die wichtigsten Instanzen gegen die Gruf-Wellhausensche Hypothese*, i (Berlin, 1904), pp. 65–9 (though this author's general stand is non-critical, he is not lacking in acuteness). Be it as it may, no one will deny that P's actual emergence proceeded from Ezra's activity.

rigidity gives at least a large portion of its laws an idealistic cast which was never translated into reality—not even in the Second Temple period.[11] A literary work of such content—which, as we shall see further on (in Chapter VII), far from being committed to writing at a single stroke, is the fruit of collective labour—could have well remained guarded property within the initiated circle of the priesthood without making any impression on the 'outside', that is, on the matter-of-fact reality of communal life which, by the nature of things, cannot accord with idealistic patterns. I believe that if we do not take account of this special quality immanent in P, which permitted this literary work to exist as if in the back-stage of history, if we put P, in this respect, on a par with the other Pentateuchal sources, we cannot hope to give a satisfactory answer to the problem of its date.[12] This means

[11] Examples: One of P's central laws postulates that the major sources of impurity—any leper, anyone suffering a flux, and anyone who has touched a corpse—must be removed from the camp, that is, away from a place of settlement (Num. 5: 1–4). Where lepers were concerned this law certainly had some basis in reality, though even in this case observance was not always strict (cf. Num. 12: 14–15; 2 Kgs. 5: 1, 27; 7: 3; 15: 5). However, in the case of those suffering a flux, which includes menstruant women, or those who have touched a corpse, there is not the slightest hint or possibility that in biblical society such a law was ever put into practice. The talmudic sages, for their part, were forced to soften this law (as they also did with many others) by distinguishing, on the one hand, between grades of the sanctity of camps (the camp of the Shechinah, i.e. the Divine presence, which is the temple and the adjoining area; the camp of Levites, being the temple mount; the camp of Israel—from the entrance to Jerusalem towards the inside of the city) and, on the other hand, between grades of impurity in the principal sources (most severe in the leper, less severe in men and women with a flux, and milder still in those defiled by a corpse and even in the corpse itself, those in the latter class being permitted to enter the temple mount). See Maimonides, הלכות ביאת המקדש iii. 1–4. The tabernacle itself, in whose holy of holies the cloud of glory was believed to be ever present (Exod. 25: 22; 29: 42–5; Lev. 16: 2), is held in P as a 'law' which, as it were, must be enacted in existence—only it is an altogether utopian existence (cf. below, pp. 203–4). The law of the jubilee year (Lev. 25: 8–55), during which, according to P, fields revert back to their owners, and which serves in P as a major means for preserving the attachment of an *'ezrāḥ* ('citizen', 'free tribesman') to his portion of land, is conditional upon a continuous, unbroken count of years and therefore could not actually be practised before the Hellenistic period (cf. below, pp. 123–4).

[12] This also applies to the approach of Kaufmann (above, n. 8) who advocates the early date of P without taking into account its special utopian nature. My position may be said to be midway between the orthodox view that P is late and Kaufmann's attempt to regard P as an early work. My contention is that P is both early and late—early (though existing at first only within a semi-esoteric circle) and late (though only in the date of its 'discovery', not that of its formation).

that even those who consider P a pre-exilic work must concede that before Ezra it led only a quasi-sectarian existence and could hardly be discerned against the visible course of history.

The major premise adopted in this inquiry is, therefore, that Ezra's activity was the moment of P's exposure to the public view, not the moment of its composition. When Ezra turned the canonized Torah into the foundation-stone of Jewish life, he included in this Torah 'hidden scrolls'—priestly writings which by then had already been in existence for almost three centuries. Consequently, these writings entered into the arena of history, and in becoming part of the Torah they began to contribute to the shaping of Judaism—not always in accordance with their original meaning, but usually through secondary interpretation and by way of *midrash*. It is a good general rule that the canonization of the Torah brings about the birth of *midrash*, the harmonistic and homiletic exegesis of the Scriptures; even the very act of assembling various and contradictory sources into one framework is enough to call it into being. To put it in Wellhausen's terms one may say: P is the creation not of Judaism but of ancient Israel, of the people which characterized the pre-exilic period. Yet the real historical presence of this source began to be felt only with the foundation of Judaism.

II

THE ISRAELITE TEMPLES

I

THE word 'temple', derived from the Latin *templum*, serves in EVV as a rendering of the biblical Hebrew word *hêḵāl*, which is also found in Canaanite and Ugaritic (being based on the Akkadian *êkallu* which in turn stems from the Sumerian *ê-gal* meaning 'big house'). Since the combination *hêḵal Yahweh*, 'Yahweh's palace', is used in the Old Testament as one of the epithets of the building erected in Jerusalem by King Solomon, the word temple (sometimes spelt with a capital letter, Temple) became reserved in EVV, and consequently in the English language in general, as principally the name of that particular cultic institution. Other cultic institutions of the same category, which historically preceded the Jerusalem temple and had existed in Israel ever since the settlement in Canaan, are not usually called temples in English but are given other designations such as 'shrines' or 'sanctuaries'. However, in biblical Hebrew itself the basic term, which defines and specifies the building erected by Solomon in Jerusalem, as well as other buildings of the same category found in Israel in other places, is *bêt Yahweh*, 'house of Yahweh', or *bêt 'ᵉlōhîm*, 'house of God'. This name arises from the concept of divine residence and expresses the intrinsic nature of the institution, which was primarily conceived as the god's dwelling place. It is this institution which is the main subject of the discussions in the following chapters and is implied in the title of this inquiry. Nevertheless, for the sake of simplicity and uniformity, and in order not to deviate too far from common English usage, the term 'temple' rather than 'house of God' (but neither 'sanctuary' nor 'shrine') will be used throughout this inquiry, even when referring to pre-Jerusalemite representatives of this category.

The designations applied in the Old Testament to this institution, other than *bêt Yahweh* (*'ᵉlōhîm*), are relatively rare and their basic meaning relates to other concepts, while in reference to the temple they are only used secondarily. Conspicuous among these is the one already mentioned, *hêkal Yahweh* (Jer. 7: 4; 24: 1; Ezek. 8: 16; Jonah 2: 5, 8 *et al.*). However, the noun *hêkāl* itself is a non-sacral term meaning any large, luxurious house (1 Kgs. 21: 1; 2 Kgs. 20: 18; Isa. 13: 22; 66: 6;[1] Amos 8: 3; Hos. 8: 14 *et al.*), while in the form *hahêkāl*, with the definite article, it sometimes serves to designate not the temple as a whole but only a part of it—the outer sanctum, that is, the large ante-chamber in front of the holy of holies (1 Kgs. 6: 5, 17; 7: 21; Isa. 6: 1; Ezek. 41: 1 *et al.*).[2]

In the Psalms the temple is sometimes called Yahweh's *'ōhel*, 'tent' (Ps. 15: 1; 27: 5–6; 61: 5; cf. Isa. 33: 20) and *miškānôt*, 'tabernacles', in the plural only (Ps. 43: 3; 84: 2; 132: 5, 7), both these appelations reflecting the conditions of life of prehistoric Israel. A similar term is *nāweh*, 'abode (of shepherds or flocks)', which is also poetically applied to the temple (2 Sam. 15: 25; cf. Isa. 33: 20: *nāweh ša'anān*, 'quiet abode'; Jer. 31: 22: *newēh ṣedeq har haqqōdeš*, 'abode of righteousness, holy hill'; also Exod. 15: 13; Jer. 50: 7). Other poetic terms for temple are *bêt zebûl*, 'lofty house' (1 Kgs. 8: 13; cf. Isa. 63: 15), and Yahweh's 'fixed place for sitting', *mākôn lešibtô* (Exod. 15: 17; 1 Kgs. 8: 13), which seem to be based on Canaanite stereotypes; Yahweh's 'habitation', *mā'ôn* or *me'ônāh*, which sometimes comes in construct state with an inflected noun, as *me'ôn bêtô*, 'habitation of his house', *me'ôn qodšô*, 'his holy habitation' (Ps. 26: 8; 68: 6; 76: 3; 2 Chron. 36: 15 *et al.*); *miškān* in the general sense of 'dwelling place', when it does not imply the form of 'tabernacle', and which may likewise come in construct state with an inflected noun, as *miškan kebôdô*, *miškan šemô*, 'place where his glory, his name, dwells' (Ps. 26: 8; 74: 7),[3] and the like.

The noun *miqdāš*, which the dictionaries usually render as

[1] Here too the word *hêkāl* means just 'a palace', as it is not here in a construct state with the name of God, nor does it have a definite article, and, moreover, its parallel in this verse is *'îr*, 'a city' (cf. Hos. 8: 14). EVV, however, render it here as 'the temple'.

[2] There are, of course, some variations as well. Thus, in 1 Kgs. 6: 3 the outer sanctum is called *hêkal habbayit*, 'nave of the house'. In Isa. 44: 28 the Jerusalem temple is referred to as *hêkāl*, where it is not in a construct state with the name of Yahweh and without the definite article (but cf. commentaries).

[3] In P's style the word *miškān* denotes 'tabernacle' only. Elsewhere than in P it sometimes also has the specific meaning (cf. below, pp. 195–6), but it may occur with the general, non-technical meaning of 'dwelling place', 'abode'. See, e.g., Lev. 26: 11 (H): Isa. 22: 16; 32: 18; Ezek. 37: 27 (apparently, following H's usage).

'sacred place', 'sanctuary', does not necessarily refer to a house of God. In the priestly terminology it indicates any article or object possessing sanctity. Thus it is used as a designation of the 'tithe of the tithe', which is the tithe's hallowed part handed over by the Levites to the priests (Num. 18: 29). It also denotes the tabernacle vessels carried and guarded by the Kohathites (ibid. 3: 38; 10: 21; 18: 1; also 1 Chron. 28: 10). The phrase *miqdaš haqqōdeš* may indicate, in the priestly style, the inner sanctum, that is, the holy of holies (Lev. 16: 33; cf. v. 16). In the warning of the Holiness Code: 'you shall keep my sabbaths and venerate my *miqdāš*' (Lev. 19: 30; 26: 2) *miqdāš* appears to indicate the entire complex of sancta (cf. Isa. 8: 13–14). There are even cases when it is applied to the temple in the plural, thereby pointing at the temple's various structures and appurtenances, all of which were considered holy (Ezek. 21: 7; also Ps. 68: 38; 73: 17; cf. Jer. 51: 51: *miqdᵉšê bêt Yahweh*, 'the sacred objects [or buildings] of Yahweh's house'; also Lev. 21: 23). At the same time, the word *miqdāš* comes to be also used as a designation of the entire temple compound—for instance, the entire area of the tabernacle described in P (Exod. 25: 8; Lev. 12: 4; 21: 12 *et al.*), the entire district of the temple described in Ezekiel's code (Ezek. 43: 21; 44: 1, 5, 7–8 *et al.*)—as well as a term for all temples within Israel (Amos 7: 9, 13) and outside (Isa. 16: 12), and the great temple of Jerusalem (Isa. 63: 18; Ezek. 5: 11; 9: 6; Ps. 74: 7; 96: 6; Lam. 1: 10; 2: 7, 20 *et al.*). The phrase *bêt miqdāš*, which conveys approximately the idea of 'house of holiness', with the component *bêt* in the construct state, occurs in the Old Testament only once (2 Chron. 36: 17), but in post-biblical Hebrew it became the prevalent term for temple.

TEMPLES AND ALTARS

2

For a proper understanding of the nature of cultic practices in Israel, as well as the history of cult in general, it is essential to make a clear distinction between the temple, as the house of God, and the altar. A house of God, to begin with, as even the name implies, was a building, a roofed edifice, while an altar, upon which sacrifices were offered up (in contrast to the incense altar, which is a separate matter) was found only in the open. The two institutions also differed in function. Since, by its very nature, a temple was considered to be a divine dwelling-place it was equipped with furnishings that would symbolize the divine presence in that house (such as the ark, the cherubim, on rare occasions even a statue of Yahweh) and with objects used in God's service (such as the table of shewbread, a lampstand, an ephod). On an altar, however, virtually nothing but sacrifices could be offered up. Any temple would be accompanied by an altar placed in the adjoining court, but not every altar would necessarily be attached to a temple. Those who officiated in a temple, or at an altar adjoining a temple, were exclusive functionaries from priestly families, while at solitary altars, as we shall see later on, any Israelite could serve. The solitary altars were numerous and scattered throughout the country; there was probably no settlement without its altar, and altars could even be found outside cities, in the countryside. The number of temples, on the other hand, was quite limited and the Old Testament attests, or alludes, to only about a dozen of them, as will be shown below.

Furthermore, since an altar at a temple would usually be considered as of higher standing than a solitary altar, not every type of sacrifice would be deemed suitable for the solitary altars. Many offerings were held to be reserved for the temple, and it was obligatory to take them exclusively to a temple altar. Such were the firstlings of cattle and sheep, thanksgiving sacrifices, offerings in fulfilment of vows, including tithes,[4] *ḥērem* offerings, and even free-will, *n^e^dāḇāh* offerings, and others.[5] Similarly, the first fruits and first crops of the soil were brought solely to the temples

[4] For the tithe as, in the first place, a votive offering (excluding D's conception, where it was transformed into an annual obligation), cf. below, pp. 109 (n. 36), 116–17 (n. 8).

[5] For instance, in Deut. 12: 17, 26, in a warning not to slaughter temple offerings profanely or eat them in the provinces, mention is made of *qodāšîm*, 'sacred donations' (apparently a comprehensive term for all those offerings which may not be desanctified and made profane), and then grain and fruit tithes, first-born of cattle and sheep, vows, free-will offerings, and *t^e^rûmat yādeḵā*, 'contribution(s) of your hand(s)'; cf. also vv. 6, 11, 13 and commentaries. Analogy and reason suggest that D must have permitted profanation of only those sacrifices that could be offered upon solitary altars, whereas sacrifices and dedications which were originally brought to a temple were not altered in status, and should continue to be brought to the temple (of which, in D's view, there ought to be only one). That the sacrifices mentioned by D, as well as others not mentioned by him (such as thanksgiving offerings and *ḥērem* donations), were indeed of the temple variety may be further verified by an examination of each category by itself. Cf. my observations on this matter in *EM* v. 323–4.

(Exod. 23: 19; 34: 26; Deut. 26: 1–11). The three major seasonal feasts were celebrated by making a pilgrimage to one of the temples and sacrificing there; the obligations of these feasts could not be fulfilled by sacrificing at a high-place or at a local altar, as will be shown in Chapter XVI.

3

Both the altar, along with the sacrificial system connected with it, and the temple, which was considered in essence as a divine dwelling-place, preceded Israel's *début* on the stage of history, and both are rooted in the pagan cultures of the ancient Near East. For the sacrifices, which in the fossilized routine terminology are still referred to in the Old Testament as 'God's food' (Lev. 3: 11; 21: 21–2; Num. 28: 2), the altar, which is still called 'the Lord's table' (Ezek. 41: 22; 44: 16; Mal. 1: 7), and the temple, where the cultic activities seek to provide, as if it were, for God's household necessities, are clearly based on a very ancient and elementary conception of the world and could not possibly be the products of Israel's own cultural *milieu*.[6] In fact, there is no doubt that Israel absorbed these self-same institutions ready-made.

Yet the admittance of these institutions to Israel took place only gradually, with the altar preceding the temple. The altar has an almost universal dispersion and is not unknown even in nomadic or semi-nomadic societies. The temple, on the other hand, is found only among sedentary societies in which the fixed dwelling-place is the accepted form of living. Thus biblical tradition takes for granted that the Patriarchs, who lived a semi-nomadic existence, built altars and offered sacrifices (Gen. 12: 7–8; 13: 4, 18; 22: 9, 13; 26: 25; 31: 46–54 *et al.*). Temples, however, are still beyond the ken of the Patriarchs, as is also priesthood, since in semi-nomadic societies both temples and priesthood usually have no place.[7] Temples make their appearance in Israel's life only

[6] On the concept of the temple as a divine abode in the ancient Near Eastern religions cf., e.g., H. H. Nelson, A. L. Oppenheim *et al.*, 'The Significance of the Temple in the Ancient Near East', *BA* 7 (1944), 42, 44, 58–9, 66–8.

[7] This is the straightforward reason for the absence of temples in the Genesis stories and in the social background of the Patriarchs—viz. that the society of the Patriarchs still lives under nomadic or semi-nomadic conditions. Alt, in his study 'Der Gott der Väter' (*KS* i. 1–67), suggests that the religion of the pre-conquest Hebrew tribes was marked by a special cult of 'gods of the fathers' and that these were not worshipped in temples. One who would not agree with this

after the settlement in Canaan. This is the assumption of the biblical tradition itself, as explicitly set forth in the Song at the Sea (Exod. 15: 17). Indirectly, but none the less in a clear manner, D also assents to it when he states that the chosen place will be established only after the Israelites have crossed the Jordan, while until then every man is 'doing whatever is right in his own eyes' (Deut. 12: 8–11). Undoubtedly this assumption reflects the historical truth, since the semi-nomadic period actually ended in Israel with the settlement in the land. Yet the biblical tradition, especially in its priestly manifestation, also reports the existence of a temple even before the entry into the land. This is none other than the tabernacle which P describes in minute detail (Exod. chaps. 25–31, 35–40). It was a portable temple which, as the legend has it, was erected at the foot of Mount Sinai and wandered with the Israelites until they crossed the Jordan and conquered the promised land. A portable temple in the form of a tabernacle is, in itself, quite feasible in a semi-nomadic group and, as we shall see in the following chapters, this tradition, too, contains a certain kernel of truth.

THE HIGH-PLACES

4

Among the altars, one can single out a distinct type which was given the name *bāmāh* (plural *bāmôt*), rendered by EVV mostly as 'high-place' ('high-places'), with the exclusion of NEB which mostly has it as 'hill-shrine(s)'. What distinguishes this type from other altars, and why it received its name, are still open questions. However, the fact itself that the 'high-places' are included in the category of altars is beyond any doubt.

The word *bāmāh* presents itself in the Old Testament in three meanings. One is 'mountains, hills, heights'; in this sense it comes only in the plural, as it does in the Akkadian *bāmātu* which has approximately the same connotation. This meaning is attested in the Old Testament only seldom: 'and the temple-mountain as wooded heights, *bāmôt ya'ar*' (Jer. 26: 18; Mic. 3: 12); apparently also '(lies) slain upon thy heights', *'al bāmôtêḵā ḥālāl* (2 Sam. 1:

theory may claim that the reason for the absence of temples among those tribes has nothing to do with the conjectured content of their religion but is to be sought merely in the sociological conditions of their existence. In any case, this reason seems to be somewhat simpler and more applicable.

19, 25). Another meaning is 'trunk, torso', possibly also 'back (of an animal)', whose cognates will be the Akkadian *bām(a)tu*, *bāntu*, and the Ugaritic *bmt* (*bāmatu*). With this meaning the word appears in the Old Testament as an object of the verbs *drk* (stride, trample), *rkb* (ride) or *'lh 'al* (ascend upon), while the relevant passages contain mythological overtones: 'he made him ride on the "back", *bmwty* (*legendum*: *bām^{o}tê*) of the earth' (Deut. 32: 13; cf. Isa. 58: 14), 'and treads on the "back", *bām^{o}tê* of the earth' (Amos 4: 13; cf. Mic. 1: 3), 'and trampled the "trunk", *bām^{o}tê* of the sea-dragon' (Job 9: 8), 'I will ascend above the "torso", *bām^{o}tê* of a cloud' (Isa. 14: 14);[8] also 'and you shall trample *bāmôtêmô*, their bodies' (Deut. 33: 29). In two other cases: 'and sets me secure upon my *bāmôt*' (2 Sam. 22: 34; Ps. 18: 34), 'he makes me tread upon my *bāmôt*' (Hab. 3: 19), the word may carry either the first or the second meaning.[9]

In the third meaning—which is the important one for our discussion—the word denotes an object similar in structure to an altar and identical with it in function. With this meaning the

[8] Note that in the passages cited for this meaning, the MT has *bām^{o}tê*, sometimes as the *q^{e}rê* (*legendum*) but for the most part as both *q^{e}rê* and *k^{e}tîḇ* (*scriptum*). On this reading, which looks like a combined form of two plural terminations, the second of which is in construct state, see Gesenius–Kautzsch–Cowley, *Grammar*, §§ 87*s*, 95*o*. The context, however, calls for a meaning in the singular. Possibly the MT conceals behind it a reading which was singular even in its grammatical form, such as the one which could end with *ḥireq compaginis* (cf. ibid., § 90*l*), or an archaic form which was forgotten and distorted. In contrast with these cases, in Deut. 33: 29, mentioned further, MT reads *bāmôtêmô*, both in *q^{e}rê* and *k^{e}tîḇ*, the form being an obvious plural and not in construct state with another noun, since the text here speaks of Israel's numerous enemies.

[9] For these two meanings of *bāmāh*, cf. the discussions of W. F. Albright, 'The High-Place in Ancient Palestine', *SVT* 4 (1957), 242, 249–50, 255–6; N. H. Tur-Sinai, הלשון והספר, iii (Jerusalem, 1955), pp. 235–41; also *CAD* ii, s.v. *bamâtu*, *bamtu*B, pp. 76a, 78a; W. F. Albright, *Yahweh and the Gods of Canaan* (London, 1968), p. 177; and S. E. Loewenstamm and J. Blau, *Thesaurus of the Language of the Bible*, ii (Jerusalem, 1959), s.v. במה. Tur-Sinai totally denies that the first meaning is found in the Bible. And all these scholars are inclined to interpret the passages in 2 Sam. 22: 34 (= Ps. 18: 34); Hab. 3: 19 according to the second meaning only. This, however, is far from certain. For one who says 'and sets me secure upon *bāmôtay*, my *bāmôt*', 'he makes me tread upon *bāmôtay*, my *bāmôt*', with the pronominal suffix of the first person, can hardly be referring to the bodies of his adversaries; were that the case, he would have said *bāmôtêhem*, 'their *bāmôt*'. A comprehensive examination of these meanings is now available in P. H. Vaughan, *The Meaning of 'Bāmâ' in the OT* (Cambridge, 1974), pp. 4–12. In this monograph the author also deals adequately with the other aspects discussed below, though I would not accept his position in every detail.

bāmāh serves, then, as a concept synonymous to altar, actually indicating a special kind of altar. This is its sense in the Mesha' inscription: *w''ś hbmt z't lkmš*, 'I made this *bmt* for Chemosh'.[10] In the Pentateuch the word occurs quite rarely with this meaning and then only in the Holiness Code (Lev. 26: 30; Num. 33: 52).[11] The pre-Deuteronomistic sources of the Former Prophets know of this *bāmāh*, mentioning it as a commonplace matter, a part of every-day reality, and they display no negative attitude towards it (1 Sam. 9: 12–25; 10: 5; 1 Kgs. 3: 4). As an accessible and legitimate institution it is also mentioned by some of the prophets, sometimes in parallel with *miqdāš*, i.e. a sacred area or temple, and again with no negative sentiments being disclosed towards the *bāmāh* as such—either when it is referred to in connection with other people (Isa. 15: 2; 16: 12) or when included among the Israelite cultic sites doomed for destruction (Amos 7: 9).[12] In the Deuteronomistic redaction of the Book of Kings, however, this *bāmāh* features more prominently and is considered an absolutely illegitimate, detestable object.[13]

[10] Donner-Röllig, *KAI*, no. 181, l. 3.

[11] The passage in Num. 33: 50–6 incorporates elements of H (vv. 52–3, 55–6), being one of the spatterings of H material to have found its way out of the main corpus in Lev. 17–26 (such as Exod. 31: 13–17; Lev. 11: 2–45 [see especially vv. 43–5]; Num. 15: 38–41). That the verses Num. 33: 52–3, 55–6 belong to H is indicated by the appearance of words and expressions that are otherwise found only in the main corpus of the Holiness Code, or that are found nowhere else in P, or that approximate to the tenor of D's style (of all parts of P, H somehow is the closest in character and flavour to D); cf. also commentaries. In Num. 21: 28; 22: 41; Josh. 13: 17, the word *bāmôt* appears as a component in toponyms. In the Mesha' inscription, l. 27, the combination *bt bmt* turns up, apparently as a place name (cf. Num. 21: 19–20).

[12] See also Hos. 10: 8, where *bāmôt* is mentioned in parallelism to *mizbeḥôt*, 'altars'. The '*bāmôt* of Aven', spoken of in this verse are the *bāmôt* of Bethel, since *bêt-'āwen*, in Hosea's diction, is only a derogatory name for Bethel (4: 15; 5: 8; 10: 5; cf. Amos 5: 5). Hosea, too, certainly does not mean to imply that the 'high-places' as such are not legitimate institutions for cultic use, since he pronounces destruction not only upon them but upon all of Israel's places of worship (cf. Hos. 3: 4; 10: 2). Even when he calls the *bāmôt* of Beth-aven *ḥaṭṭa't yiśrā'ēl*, 'the sin of Israel' (10: 8), the sin is, in his opinion, an all-inclusive one, one of its aspects being the very fact that the cultic institutions are overabounding; cf. 4: 7; 8: 11; 10: 11 and the remarks of H. W. Wolff, *Dodekapropheton l, Hosea* (BK, 1961), pp. 99, 185. Micah 1: 5 should be read ומי חטאת יהודה, 'and what is the sin of Judah', rather than ומי במות יהודה, 'and what are the high-places of Judah', as is evident from LXX's reading as well as from the first half of this verse (cf. commentaries).

[13] Again, in the interest of simplicity and not to diverge from the terminology accepted in EVV, in the following discussions the term 'high-place' will be

5

Bible study is still not in a position to determine how the *bāmāh*, as a cultic institution, fits into the archaeological context and with which of the types of structures unearthed in excavations it can be identified. One of the paradoxes of Biblical Archaeology is the fact that, despite the frequent references to the high-places in the Old Testament, no archaeological structure has yet been found which could seriously be considered a candidate for recognition as one. This is perhaps not as paradoxical as it seems, since the Bible itself informs us that well before the end of the First Temple period all of the high-places in the country were destroyed, never again to be rebuilt (below, Chapter VII).

The only archaeological structures that have so far been claimed as *bāmôt* with any degree of plausibility are those found at Megiddo and Nahariyah: both of these are in the form of round heaps of unhewn stones, not fastened to each other, some encrusted with a dark substance which has hardened with time. The two heaps were found in the vicinity of buildings which the excavators thought to be 'temples'. None the less, it must be pointed out that these two finds, at the least, have nothing to do with the biblical period and that their definition as *bāmôt* is no more than a conjecture.[14] Other candidates for identification as *bāmôt* were believed, for a while, to be found in mysterious stone cairns which

retained for *bāmāh* in this third meaning. In reality, though, such a 'high-place' (or 'hill-shrine', as rendered by NEB) might sometimes be located down in a valley. See, e.g., Jer. 7: 31; 19: 5–6; 32: 35 (also 2: 23).

[14] On the supposed 'high-place' of Megiddo see G. Loud, *Megiddo II: Seasons of 1935–1939* (Chicago, 1948), pp. 73–84; also Claire Epstein, 'An Interpretation of the Megiddo Sacred Area During Middle Bronze II', *IEJ* 15 (1965), 204–21. On the one in Nahariyah see M. Dothan, *EI* 4 (1956), 41–6; idem, *IEJ* 6 (1956), 16–25. As reported by the excavators, the cairn at Megiddo was in use from the middle of the third millennium until the eighteenth century B.C., the one in Nahariyah from the middle of the eighteenth century until the end of the sixteenth century B.C. It should be noted that beside the 'high-place' in Nahariyah the excavators found another small structure, partly enclosed by flat, erect stones, which they took to be an altar. Yet, at least according to biblical concepts, there would be no reason to set up a high-place and an altar next to each other, as both of them serve the same function (see also further, sect. 6). Vaughan, op. cit., pp. 40–3 adds to the questionable 'high-places' of Megiddo and Nahariyah the sacred area of Ein-Gedi, which belongs to the Chalcolithic Age, and the 'high-place' of Arad, which preceded the (supposed) temple erected there (on which see below, sect. 9) and relates to Level XII (eleventh century B.C.). However, to the reservations expressed by Vaughan himself, several others may well be added.

were observed on one of the ridges west of Jerusalem; they have a conical shape which emphasizes them against their surroundings. About twenty such cairns were remarked on that ridge, and potsherds discovered in those loci pointed to the second half of the eighth century or to the seventh century B.C. In the summer and autumn of 1953 some of the cairns were excavated, and it turned out that they usually covered a piece of ground encircled by a low polygonal ring-wall. On the ground, under one of the cairns that was completely uncovered, there were noted a rampart, slightly raised above ground level, and a pavement. In the middle there was a small hexagonal pit, at the side of which there were remnants of fire, broken pieces of charcoal, and ashes.[15] Yet, despite the appearance of cultic activity, neither the conical cairns nor the areas buried beneath them can positively be identified as *bāmôt*.[16]

Just as the architectural form and the archaeological identity of the high-places have eluded us, so no reason has yet been found for their distinction as a particular form of cultic facility. The conjecture that they were originally burial places and served as sites for worshipping the dead is totally unfounded.[17]

[15] See Ruth Amiran, 'The Excavations in the Cairns to the West of Jerusalem' (Hebrew), *BIES* 18 (1954), 45–59; idem, 'The Tumuli West of Jerusalem', *IEJ* 8 (1958), 205–27. A trial digging in one of these cairns was carried out some thirty years earlier by W. F. Albright (*BASOR* 10 (1923), 1–3).

[16] Despite the relative frequency of high-places in the biblical period, it is improbable that about twenty of them would have been packed together in such a small area: these cairns are all in three compact concentrations, to the north and south of Ein Karim, forming a triangle whose area does not exceed 3–4 square miles (one of the concentrations comprises seven cairns and is confined to the summit and slopes of one hill). The excavator herself wondered to which settlement they all belonged. In addition, it is unlikely that so many high-places would suddenly crop up together and lead such an ephemeral existence. Nor is it likely that high-places would be obliterated in such a 'monumental' fashion as piling conical cairns on top of them.

[17] This conjecture was attractive to Albright ('The High-Place in Ancient Palestine', pp. 242–58) and Tur-Sinai in their above-mentioned studies (n. 9). Albright tried to support his position by extracting references to *bāmôt* and a connection of them with the dead from verses which are either obscure or definitely can bear another interpretation without entailing emendation (Isa. 53: 9; Job 27: 16; Ezek. 43: 7; also Isa. 6: 13). Tur-Sinai sought support in the other meaning of the word *bāmāh*—that implying 'corpse, body'—and believed that there was a semantic transition from it to the connotation of grave (he also cited some of the verses mentioned above). Both of them, however, seem to have ignored the fact that the pre-Deuteronomic (and pre-priestly) layers of biblical literature find no fault in the *bāmāh* as such, although it is inconceivable that they would have granted such an unconditional legitimation to a worship of the dead. It should further be remembered that in the cairns excavated to the west

6

At the same time it cannot be doubted that the high-places fall within the general category of altars and have nothing to do with temples. Several unmistakable signs will illustrate this point.

The idea of destroying high-places is frequently expressed in the Old Testament by the verbs *sār*, 'was taken away', *hēsîr*, 'removed, took away' (1 Kgs. 15: 14; 22: 44; 2 Kgs. 12: 4; 14: 4 *et al.*; cf. 2 Kgs. 18: 4, 22). In biblical idiom these verbs cannot appropriately be applied to a building, and they indicate that the *bāmôt* were simple, solid, and exposed constructions, located in the open. In one case the high-places are even mentioned in explicit contrast to 'a *house* for the name of the Lord' (1 Kgs. 3: 2), implying that a *bāmāh* does not fall under the definition of 'house'. It would be certainly wrong to suppose that the high-places referred to in the Books of Kings and disapproved by the Deuteronomistic redaction were not used for the worship of Yahweh; the cult was obviously that of the God of Israel except that the Deuteronomistic redaction considered them illegitimate just because they contradicted its principle of cult centralization. (There were, of course, also *bāmôt* to foreign gods, such as those which Solomon set up for his wives, as mentioned in 1 Kgs. 11: 7–8; 2 Kgs. 23: 13).

Furthermore, the major, if not the only, cultic activity which, according to the biblical evidence, took place at the high-places was that the people, or one of the kings would perform the acts denoted by the verbs *zbḥ* and *qṭr* in the *piʿēl* conjugation (1 Kgs. 22: 44; 2 Kgs. 12: 4; 14: 4 *et al.*; cf. 1 Kgs. 3: 2–3); that is, they

of Jerusalem Mrs. Amiran found no graves—a fact that did not hinder Albright from considering these cairns as *bāmôt*. Mrs. Amiran herself, who at first (in the Hebrew report) also thought that the cairns were *bāmôt*, changed her opinion and in the English report (above, note 15) called them tumuli (as Albright had done originally), that is, grave mounds, similar to the ones in Anatolia, assuming that in the tumuli of Anatolia, too, the burial site might sometimes be found outside the tumulus itself. But west of Jerusalem graves were not found even outside the stone cairns, and just as these are not *bāmôt* so one may scarcely consider them to be tumuli in the proper sense of the word. A geographer has suggested that they may be 'mere depositories for surplus stones, appearing only in quarriable soft rock areas', while the polygonal low ring-wall was only 'destined to prevent dispersal of the piled stones' (Z. Ron, *IEJ* 16 (1966), 48–9). For a detailed and incisive criticism of Albright's view as to the supposed origin of the *bāmôt* see now also W. Boyd Barrick, 'The Funerary Character of "High-Places": A Reassessment', *VT* 25 (1975), 565–95.

would offer up *z^eḇāḥîm*, animal sacrifices (which were eaten by the sacrificer) and grain-offerings.[18] These are rites which were performed only at an altar, and the Old Testament mentions no other rite performed on the *bāmôt* which would be connected with temples (what the temple rites are will be discussed below, especially in Chapter XI). In like manner, the story in 1 Sam. 9: 11–25, which describes a festival day at a high-place in Samuel's city and considers the high-place itself as a holy and honoured institution, clearly shows that the activities at that particular high-place were limited to sacrificing and to a gathering of invited notables to eat the sacrificial flesh.[19] This implies that the *liškāh*, 'chamber', where the invited persons had their meal (ibid., v. 22), is regarded as one of the auxiliary structures which in the course of time could be put up beside the high-place to provide comfortable quarters for gatherings and overnight visits—but nothing in the nature of the *liškāh*, or any other annex, need obscure the fact that, by its basic character, the high-place was only a large altar.[20] Likewise, of the great high-place in Gibeon it is said that all Solomon did there was to offer sacrifices and burnt-offerings (1 Kgs. 3: 4), while the dream and divine revelation (ibid., vv. 5–14) could well have occurred to him in an adjoining chamber.[21]

[18] For the exact meaning of the verb *qṭr* in the *pi'ēl* conjugation, to wit, bringing a grain-offering, not an incense-offering—see below, pp. 233–4. It is difficult to explain why the offering of animal- and grain-offerings is said to have taken place '*in* the *bāmôt*' and not '*on* the *bāmôt*', as in all these cases the text has the prefixed *b* instead of the preposition *'al* (as would be demanded). The reason seems to be connected with certain architectural details of the *bāmāh* the knowledge of which has been lost.

[19] The nature of this offering and the procedures of the accompanying meal will be discussed below, pp. 309–11.

[20] 'Chambers' could naturally be found in the court of a temple as well, and there too they had no essential and determinative function, serving merely as auxiliary structures around the site of cultic sanctity. In the court of the Jerusalem temple these chambers made a relatively late appearance, apparently in the days of Hezekiah and later; see 2 Chron. 31: 11 and 2 Kgs. 23: 11; Jer. 35: 2, 4; 36: 10, 12 *et al.*, where the same substantive, *liškāh*, is used. According to LXX, *liškāh*, κατάλυμα is also mentioned in connection with the Shiloh temple (1 Sam. 1: 18). It is not impossible that the *liškāh* of 1 Sam. 9: 22, as well as the κατάλυμα of 1 Sam. 1: 18, are just projections into the past of conditions which actually existed in the Jerusalem temple (cf. below, pp. 201–2).

[21] Note, in addition, the phraseology applied in the text: 'And the king went to Gibeon . . . for that was the great *bāmāh*, high-place; a thousand burnt-offerings did Solomon offer upon that *mizbē^aḥ*, altar' (1 Kgs. 3: 4). The second half of the verse is in the nature of an explanation of the first half, which implies that *bāmāh* is just another name for *mizbē^aḥ*, altar, and the two are actually alike. A similar relationship between the concepts *mizbē^aḥ* and *bāmāh* finds expression

Since a high-place is essentially just a large altar, it need not surprise us that in no case is the name *bāmāh* applied to any of the temples. For this purpose, the Deuteronomistic redaction coined the term *bêt bāmôt*, 'house of high-places', which serves perhaps as a derogatory designation for Jeroboam's temple in Bethel (1 Kgs. 12: 31; LXX has it here in the plural), apparently also for certain temples—or what looked like temples to the Deuteronomistic redactors—'in the cities of Samaria' (ibid. 13: 32; 2 Kgs. 23: 19) and for the temples which the new inhabitants of Samaria are said to have set up to their gods (ibid. 17: 29–32). According to Jer. 7: 31 there were high-places (or rather a high-place, following LXX) of Topheth in the Valley of Ben-hinnom, where the Molech cult was practised.[22] Indeed, it seems likely that there was no temple there but only an open-air altar (cf. Isa. 30: 33).

It should be added that both formally and by the nature of the institution the temple was accorded more honour and respect than the altar and the high-place. However, even within these two categories there was an order of status, sanctity, and prestige, so that a large, well known high-place could overshadow a modest, out-of-the-way temple (as a senior official in the consular service may exceed in importance a low-ranking official in the diplomatic corps, even though the latter belongs to a higher category of service). A high-place like the one in Gibeon, where King Solomon himself is said to have offered up 'a thousand burnt-offerings' (1 Kgs. 3: 4), or the one in Beer-sheba (2 Kgs. 23: 8)[23] might possibly have been of no lower status than Micayehu's private temple in the hill-country of Ephraim (Jud. 17: 5), even though the temple was in a higher category. As we shall see in Chapter III, there were to be found some cultic places of the open type whose *hieroi logoi* connected them with the figures of the Patriarchs and lent them a very great prestige.

in 2 Kgs. 23:15 (even if we assume that the *wāw* copulative in *w*^{e}*'et habbāmāh* is original), but this verse was expanded by the Deuteronomistic redactors and has also suffered textual mishaps.

[22] Cf. also Jer. 2: 23, where 'the valley' (*gay'*) undoubtedly refers to the Valley (*gay'*) of Ben-hinnom; also 2 Kgs. 23: 10 and above, n. 13. In Jer. 19: 5; 32: 35, as a result of Deuteronomistic blurring, the reference is to 'high-places of Baal'. For the identity of 'the valley' in Jer. 2: 23 cf. also J. Alberto Soggin, *OT and Oriental Studies* (Rome, 1975), pp. 79–81.

[23] Concerning this high-place cf. below, pp. 55–6.

THE DISTRIBUTION OF THE ISRAELITE TEMPLES

7

If we leave aside for the moment the Jerusalem temple, the direct and explicit biblical testimony about ancient Israelite temples is quite limited. The existence of some temples, however, may be inferred indirectly from references to certain cultic acts carried out in particular places when those acts are of a kind performed only in temples, such as the fulfilment of a vow (above, sect. 2), or the community's entering into a covenant 'before the Lord', *lip̲nê Yahweh*. In general, any cultic activity to which the biblical text applies the formula 'before the Lord' can be considered an indication of the existence of a temple at the site, since this expression stems from the basic conception of the temple as a divine dwelling-place and actually belongs to the temple's technical terminology.[24] Archaeological finds, on the other hand, have so far offered very little in the way of traces of Israelite temples, possibly because most of the excavations have so far been carried out at sites where there were simply no Israelite temples—or because several Israelite temples may have been wiped out leaving no archaeological traces (as happened to Solomon's temple itself, and even to the Second Temple). Speculation apart, the only archaeological find which may perhaps provide evidence of an

[24] Out of about 230 occurrences of this expression in the Old Testament, 58 of which are in the Book of Leviticus alone, the overwhelming majority are found in clear temple contexts, where the expression means 'before the ark' (see, e.g., Exod. 16: 33–4; Num. 17: 19, 22, where *lip̲nê Yahweh* interchanges with *lip̲nê hāʿēdût*, 'before the testimony'), or 'in the (outer) sanctum before the *pārōk̲et*-veil', or 'in the court before the tabernacle' (in which the ark is found, symbolizing Yahweh's presence), or 'in the temple court' in general (the temple being the 'house of Yahweh'). The expression can, understandably, be used in connection with the ark even when it is found outside the temple (for example, 2 Sam. 6: 5, 14, 16–17, 21). Consequently, the trans-Jordanian tribes are said to have 'passed over' the river, armed 'before the Lord for battle' (Num. 32: 20–2 *et al.*; Josh. 4: 13), since the ark was supposed to be found within the war camp. Also to be reckoned with are anachronistic ways of expression which envision a temple situation, or employ temple terminology, outside the appropriate framework. For instance, David's words 'may they be cursed before the Lord' (1 Sam. 26: 19) seem to be phrased as if they were said in the temple, 'before the Lord', at a place where curses were customarily pronounced in order to enhance their effectiveness; see 1 Kgs. 8: 31. The same exposition would also apply, then, to the wording of Josh. 6: 26. For the technical significance of this expression, cf. N. Rabban, 'Before the Lord', *Tarbiẓ* 23 (1952), 1–8 (Hebrew). Certain modifications are necessary to the meaning Rabban attributes to this expression.

Israelite temple is the one in Arad; but even this is by no means certain.

The following list comprises the Israelite temples from the Old Testament period which are attested explicitly or indirectly.

1. The most prominent temple of the pre-monarchic period is the one which stood at Shiloh. It was from here that Solomon's temple inherited its most sacred cultic object, the ark (1 Sam. 4: 3–7: 1; 2 Sam. 6: 1–19; 1 Kgs. 8: 1–9); and it was from the ark that the house built by Solomon apparently acquired its sanctification. It is also possible that along with and in the wake of the ark some other doctrines and cultic concepts found their way from Shiloh to Jerusalem. The memory of the Shiloh temple has been preserved in the Bible in different forms. In the background of the opening story in the first Book of Samuel where it is related how, in the shadow of the temple of Shiloh, Samuel rose to his position of leadership while Eli's priestly dynasty declined, the temple is depicted as 'the palace of the Lord', *hêḵal Yahweh* (1 Sam. 1: 9; 3: 3), making it the only house of God outside Jerusalem to merit this epithet in the Bible (and, as a result, it also earned the designation 'temple' in EVV). The priestly tradition, however, assumes that it was the tabernacle that was installed at Shiloh after the conquest (Josh. 18: 1; 19: 51; 22: 19, 29). Which of the two postulates approximates the historical truth more closely is still a problem that will be discussed in the following chapters.

It is clear that after the ark was removed from the temple of Shiloh, never to return, the temple was destined to decline and lose importance. The carrying away of the ark is described in 1 Sam. 4: 17–22 as a fatal, irreparable disaster, and it certainly ought to have involved the temple's extinction. The removal of the ark from the temple of Shiloh is also mentioned in Ps. 78: 60–1. Yet our sources say nothing about the destruction of the city of Shiloh or of its temple by the Philistines. If the temple was not actually destroyed by the Philistines it certainly declined and fell out of use some time later (cf. Judg. 18: 31), while the overthrow of the Northern Kingdom ought to have brought about a destruction of the city of Shiloh (though it could have continued to exist in the form of a tiny settlement; cf. Jer. 41: 5). The excavations carried out by the Danish expeditions during some seasons between 1915 and 1932 and again in 1963 at the tell beside Khirbet Seilûn, the site of biblical Shiloh, lend support to this general impression, even though their results did not leave the excavators with clear-cut and definite conclusions.[25]

2–3. The temples of Dan and Bethel also existed from remote times, their origins being rooted almost in the beginning of the period of the Judges. The temple of Dan was founded when the tribe of this name settled in that city, and according to the polemical story that has come down to us the temple housed a statue, or statuette, of Yahweh which the Danites had found along their way through the hill-country of Ephraim (Judg. 18: 28–31). The story of the founding of Bethel's temple has not been preserved, but its antiquity is also unquestionable.[26]

When Jeroboam the son of Nebat set up the golden calves in these two temples (1 Kgs. 12: 28–9) they became royal temples (cf. Amos 7: 13), but it would be quite inaccurate to claim that the Bethel temple was first established by him.[27] Neither was the

[25] For the results of the first seasons, during which W. F. Albright served as an archaeological adviser, see the provisional reports by H. Kjaer in *PEQ* 59 (1927), 202–13; *JPOS* 10 (1930), 87–174; *PEQ* 63 (1931), 71–88. Kjaer concluded that the city was destroyed in the middle of the eleventh century B.C. and remained in ruins until the beginning of the Hellenistic period. The final results of all the seasons were published by M. L. Buhl and S. Holm Nielsen, *Shiloh, The Danish Excavations at Tall Sailun, Palestine, in 1926, 1929, 1932, and 1963: The Pre-Hellenistic Remains* (Copenhagen, 1969). Their main conclusion is that the Philistines did not destroy Shiloh, which was ruined only by the Assyrians at the end of the eighth century B.C. (that the place was still inhabited after the eleventh century has been confirmed by the discovery, after 1967, of Iron Age II pottery at the tell). Y. Shiloh, however, in his article 'The Camp at Shiloh' (Hebrew), *Eretz Shomron, The Thirtieth Archaeological Convention* (Jerusalem, 1973), pp. 10–18, and also B. Mazar, apparently revert to Albright's view that Shiloh was destroyed in the middle of the eleventh century B.C., but with the modification that the site was not abandoned and a small village existed there during Iron Age II. Cf. also below, p. 200.

[26] The story in Gen. 28: 10–12, 16–22 does not belong here, as it refers only to the erection of a pillar, not to the founding of Bethel's temple, and the expression *bêt 'ᵉlōhîm*, 'God's house' is used (vv. 17, 22) as an appellation for the pillar which Jacob set up in what later became an open cultic place in the vicinity of Bethel. See below, p. 52.

[27] The Deuteronomistic remark in 1 Kgs. 12: 31: 'He also made *bêt bāmôt*, house of *bāmôt*', even if left unamended and not read *bātê bāmôt*, 'houses of *bāmôt*', following LXX's version, is not enough to prove that it was Jeroboam who built the temple at Bethel. The mention of *bêt* (or *bātê*) *bāmôt* has probably arisen here in anticipation of, and as a background for, the subsequent reference to the 'priests from among all the people'—one of the other transgressions which the Deuteronomistic redaction ascribes to Jeroboam. The antiquity of the temple at Bethel is indirectly attested in, e.g., 1 Sam. 10: 3, where a pilgrimage to this temple is implied.

placing of a golden calf in the Dan temple inconsistent with the presence there already of a silver statue of Yahweh. For the calf is one of the external court symbols, standing visible to the public eye, while the statue is a symbol of the divine presence belonging to the internal priestly circle, and its place is in the innermost, inaccessible point of cultic sanctity (the temple of Bethel certainly had some symbol equivalent to this, but we do not know what it was). Thus the calf in the Dan temple need not have replaced the statue of Yahweh (nor did the calf of the Bethel temple take the place of a statue or some other symbol of Yahweh's presence).[28]

[28] That the calves belonged to the court (not to the temple's interior) is indicated by the declaration accompanying them: 'These are [Behold] your gods, O Israel, who brought you up out of the land of Egypt' (Exod. 32: 4; 1 Kgs. 12: 28), where the crier surely assumes that his audience set their eyes on the object. The joyous voices and dancing around the calf, as they are described in Exod. 32: 17–19, also seem to reflect an activity that must have taken place in the temple courts. Still a further indication may possibly be found in the allusion in Hos. 13: 2 to the popular custom of kissing the calves. Certain scholars have been attracted to the opinion first expressed by K. Th. Obbink, 'Jahwebilder', *ZAW* 47 (1929), 264–74, that the calves symbolized Yahweh's seat or pedestal, and that they were the Northern equivalent of what the cherubim, or the ark, were in the Jerusalem temple. So, e.g., W. F. Albright, *From the Stone Age to Christianity* (Baltimore, 1940), pp. 228–30; Kaufmann, *THH*, ii. 259–61; and in a somewhat different manner also Eissfeldt, *KS*, ii. 282–305; R. de Vaux, *Bible et Orient* (Paris, 1967), pp. 155–6. More acceptable, in my opinion, is the alternative suggestion that the calves themselves were held to be a symbol of Yahweh. So H. Gressmann, *Mose und seine Zeit* (Göttingen, 1913), pp. 207–8; also M. Weippert, 'Gott und Stier', *ZDPV* 77 (1961), 93–103; H. J. Kraus, *Gottesdienst in Israel*[2] (München, 1962), pp. 176–7, and others. This interpretation is supported, as some have already remarked, by the proclamation mentioned above: 'These are [Behold] your gods, O Israel, etc.', which implies that the calves themselves were regarded as embodiments of Yahweh. Likewise, in Ps. 106: 19–20 the Israelites are said to have exchanged God's glory 'for the image of an ox that feeds on grass', viz., the image of the ox took the place of the Glory itself. Moreover, in Exod. 32: 31 the golden calf is referred to as *'ᵉlōhê zāhāḇ*, 'god of gold' ('gods' being here only an abstract plural transferred, in this case, to the divine image; cf. Gesenius-Kautzsch-Cowley, *Grammar*, § 124*g*), an appellation which relates to the prohibition in Exod. 20: 23, and would have been entirely out of place if the calf were to symbolize a seat or pedestal (indeed, such an appellation is nowhere applied to the cherubim). The testimony of the divine iconography of the ancient Near East, as well as that of epigraphy, may lend support to either position and therefore need not deter us from adopting the second. On this view the proper Jerusalemite equivalent of the calves was not the cherubim and the ark; rather it was the bronze serpent (Num. 21: 6–9; 2 Kgs. 18: 4) which, like the calves, was placed in the court and belonged to the 'popular' cult. Just as in the Jerusalem temple the cherubim were found within and the bronze serpent outside, so in the Dan temple a statue of Yahweh (apparently of anthropomorphic features) could have been found within while the golden calf would have stood in the court. However, according to Judg. 18: 31 the statue vanished in a relatively early period.

In addition to setting up the calf, it seems that Jeroboam enlarged the altar in the temple of Bethel (1 Kgs. 12: 32–3), and in the time of Josiah, who took over most of the Northern Kingdom's territory, all that remained of the temple was this altar with an adjoining Asherah. Josiah pulled down and defiled this altar, together with the rest of the high-places in the provinces, and burned the Asherah (ibid. 13: 1–5; 2 Kgs. 23: 15). It seems that the temple of Bethel had been destroyed previously, when the Northern Kingdom fell to Assyria in 721 B.C., and the Dan temple somewhat earlier still, with the exile of the land of Naphtali by Tiglath-pileser III in 732 B.C. (2 Kgs. 15: 29; cf. Judg. 18: 30).

Archaeological excavations near the village of Beitin, the site of biblical Bethel, about ten miles north of Jerusalem, encountered neither an Israelite temple nor any cultic remains from the Israelite period. To be sure, at the site's north-east corner the excavators came upon what appeared to be a place of sacrifice, with stains of blood in the soft chalk stone (*ḥuwar*) and signs of fire-hollows, which led them to conclude that it was a 'high-place'; but it belongs to a Middle Bronze I complex. In the unearthed corner of a building which looked like a temple, animal bones and cultic pottery were found, but this find, too, belongs to a period no later than the other.[29]

In the excavations at Tel Dan (Tell el-Qadi) in 1968 a mysterious structure was uncovered. It has the shape of a gigantic quadrilateral measuring 60 by 62 feet, whose side walls have the immense thickness of five to seven feet, the space between the walls being filled with basalt stones so that it looks like a flat platform. Ascending to this platform from the southern edge was a monumental flight of steps, and pottery collected at the site pointed to the period of Israelite monarchy in two stages of building—the tenth and the middle of the ninth centuries B.C. Though the excavators decided to label this place a *bāmāh*, this can at most be taken here as a figurative use, as an application of an archaeological technical term, and not of the authentic, biblical one. Moreover, even if it were a real *bāmāh* in the biblical sense it would still have nothing to do with the biblical temple of Dan.[30] In the summer of 1974

[29] See J. L. Kelso, 'The Fourth Campaign at Bethel', *BASOR* 164 (1961), 5–15.

[30] See A. Biran, 'Tel Dan', *BA* 37 (1974), 40–3; cf. *IEJ* 19 (1969), 240–1; 20 (1970), 118. Supposing that this structure really had a sacral-cultic character, it would have been better to be content with the designation 'an open-air sanctuary' (also mentioned in the report). In the summer of 1977, however, the seventh

a horned altar was found here, almost square in form, measuring about 16 inches on each side and 14 inches in height, with a calcined top surface. It was found lying at the foot of the stairway on the earthen floor of the courtyard. Since it may have been brought here from another location, no one can say with certainty whether it is actually of an earlier or somewhat later date than the 'high-place'.[31] Neither does this find, however interesting in itself, tell us anything of the temple of Dan (while it only serves to eliminate finally the identifying of the site as a 'high-place' in the biblical sense). So the temples of Bethel and Dan must still be discussed on the basis of information preserved in the Old Testament alone.

8

4. Another temple which had its origins in the period of the Judges was the one which stood at Gilgal. This, together with Bethel and Mizpah, was one of the places where Samuel administered justice (1 Sam. 7: 16). Here Saul was made a king 'before the Lord' (ibid. 11: 14–15), and Israel mustered for war with the Philistines (ibid. 13: 4–15). Here, after his war with the Amalekites, Saul brought the best of the *ḥērem*, i.e. those parts of the spoil devoted to be sacrificed (ibid. 15: 12–21), and it was here that Samuel hewed Agag in pieces 'before the Lord' (ibid., v. 33). The temple of Gilgal is also referred to in the reproofs of Amos (4: 4; 5: 5) and Hosea (4: 15; 9: 15; 12: 12), who frequently mention it alongside of Bethel. It seems that all these references are to Gilgal in the hill-country of Ephraim, which was close to Bethel but higher up (see 2 Kgs. 2: 1–2).[32] As for other places to

season of excavations at the site has shown that the upper four rows of the steps leading to the platform belong to the Roman period; thus, the above statement will have to be modified at least in some respects.

[31] On this altar see A. Biran, *BA* 37 (1974), 106–7; *IEJ* 24 (1974), 262.

[32] As stated here, Elijah and Elisha 'went down' to Bethel. To be sure, LXX reads in 2 Kgs. 2: 2 *καὶ ἦλθον εἰς Βαιθήλ*, 'and they came (instead of "went down") to Bethel', but this reading is not to be preferred, and in any case the Gilgal mentioned here cannot be the one on the Jordan. Had Elijah and Elisha gone from Gilgal on the Jordan to Bethel, what reason could they have had for turning back from there to Jericho and going on to the Jordan (vv. 3–8) when the narrative itself makes no mention that they are returning? Nor does the statement in 1 Sam. 10: 8, 'And you shall go down before me to Gilgal', prove that the one referred to there is the Gilgal on Jordan, as it is presupposed there that Saul had to reach Gilgal from Gibeah of Saul, which was higher than the Gilgal in mount Ephraim. The latter statement can be supported by the fact that we are

which the name Gilgal was affixed and most of which were certainly also of cultic nature, we have no proof that they had temples. The Gilgal on Jordan in the vicinity of Jericho, which, according to the biblical tradition, was Israel's first encampment after the crossing of the Jordan, is the most prominent of these other places, but all that could be found there was a group of pillar-stones or an ancient, prestigious altar (Josh. 4: 19–24; 5: 8–12; 9: 6 *et al.*).

5. Still another temple which certainly originated in the period of the Judges was the one at Mizpah in Benjamin, Samuel's third place of judgement (1 Sam. 7: 16). Here the tribes of Israel assembled 'to the Lord' for war against Benjamin and cast lots to pick out the warriors among them (Judg. 20: 1–3, 8–10) and here they went up 'to the Lord' to swear oaths (ibid. 21: 1, 5, 8). Here they gathered for prayer, fasting, and a water libation 'before the Lord' as a preliminary to going out to war against the Philistines (1 Sam. 7: 5–11). This was also one of the places connected with Saul's appointment as king: the people were summoned hither and cast lots 'before the Lord' in order to choose the king (ibid. 10: 17–24), and Samuel wrote 'the rules of kingship' in a scroll which was deposited 'before the Lord', that is, in the temple (ibid., v. 25). After the Babylonians destroyed Jerusalem, Mizpah became the temporary centre for the remaining Judean inhabitants in the country and the seat of Gedaliah, the son of Ahikam, whom the Babylonians appointed as governor (2 Kgs. 25: 23–6; Jer. 40: 7—41: 18). But by that time there was no longer any temple standing at the site, since Josiah had already wiped out all cultic places outside Jerusalem (as will be described in Chapter VII). It seems that the location of this Mizpah is the village en-Nabi Samwîl, on the highest summit north-west of Jerusalem.[33]

told of Saul's return home from Gilgal: 'and Saul went up to his house in Gibeah of Saul' (1 Sam. 15: 34). The topographical relationship between Gilgal in mount Ephraim and points higher up will also explain the statements in 1 Sam. 13: 12 ('Now the Philistines will come down upon me at Gilgal', that is, from Michmash; cf. vv. 5, 11); 15: 12 ('and he turned, and passed on, and went down to Gilgal', that is, from the Carmel in the hills of Judah at the place where Saul had set up a monument). Thus there is no justification for taking the Gilgal referred to in these passages to be the one on Jordan, as various scholars did. The exact location of the Gilgal in the hill-country of Ephraim has not been established. In any case, it is not to be connected with the Gilgal beside the terebinth of Moreh (Deut. 11: 30) in the vicinity of Shechem (Gen. 12: 6), where there was a cultic open area (cf. below, p. 49).

33 This is the opinion of W. F. Albright, 'The Site of Mizpah in Benjamin', *JPOS* 3 (1923), 110–21; idem, *BASOR* 35 (1929), 4; H. W. Hertzberg,

From the story of Jephthah one might be lead to conclude that there also was a temple in the Mizpah of Gilead. For as the story has it, at Mizpah of Gilead Israel appointed Jephthah as their head and commander, with the formula 'before the Lord' being used in the text (Judg. 11: 11), and, moreover, the story implies that at this place Jephthah also made and carried out his vow (vv. 30–1, 34, 39). Other biblical evidence attests the existence in this Mizpah of a cultic place of the open type, whose foundation-legend goes back to the Patriarchal age.[34] True, this fact in itself does not make it impossible for the city to have had a temple as well, just as cultic institutions of various types coexisted in other cities too. Yet, if in this respect the story of Jephthah does indeed convey a historical fact, this would be the one and only piece of evidence for the existence of a temple on the other side of the Jordan. It is therefore only proper to consider the possibility that because of the identity of names there occurred in the story of Jephthah what might be called a geographical shift by which a certain feature of one city (Mizpah in Benjamin, which really was a temple city) was attributed to another city bearing the same name (Mizpah of Gilead).[35]

'Mizpah', *ZAW* 47 (1929), 161–3, 181–95; and to a certain extent also A. Alt, in one of his latest articles: 'Neue Erwägungen über die Lage von Mizpa, Ataroth, Beeroth und Gibeon', *ZDPV* 69 (1953), 15–16. This identification had already been suggested by E. Robinson, *Biblical Researches in Palestine*, i (Boston, 1856), pp. 457–60 and F. Buhl, *Geographie des alten Palästina* (Freiburg, 1896), p. 168. Others contend that Mizpah should be looked for at Tell en-Nasbeh, about eight miles north of Jerusalem (where in 1926–35 excavations were carried out which uncovered the site almost in its entirety, but without finding a temple). This is, e.g., the opinion of C. C. McCown, *Excavations at Tell en-Nasbeh I* (Berkeley–New Haven, 1974), pp. 57–9; and most recently Z. Kallai, *EM*, v. 238–41.

[34] See below, pp. 56–7.

[35] As another example of this rule I would cite the reference to Kedesh in Naphtali in Judges 4. According to the narrative, Barak mustered ten thousand men in Kedesh in Naphtali and led them to Mount Tabor near which the battle with Sisera's army was waged. However, in order to do this he had to march his men past Hazor, the city of Jabin, since Kedesh in Naphtali (apparently Tell Qadis on the western edge of the Hullah Valley, near the Lebanese border) is situated north of Hazor. Furthermore, Sisera flees to the Kenite camp near Kedesh, and on his way he does not even consider the possibility of seeking refuge in Hazor. Even if we remove Jabin and Hazor from the story—as various critics have suggested, not without some justification—the location of Kedesh in Naphtali will still remain problematic as it is not suited to be the rallying place of ten thousand men who wish to 'go up' to Mount Tabor (vv. 10, 12), thirty miles to the south as the crow flies. Again, it seems clear that Jael's tent, where Sisera fled, was not far from the battlefield (vv. 17, 20, 22), but the

9

6. In the ancient temple of Hebron David was anointed as King of Judah (2 Sam. 2: 4), and later on as king over all of Israel, when he made a covenant there with the elders of Israel 'before the Lord' (ibid. 5: 3). It was this temple that Absalom, according to the story, visited in order to pay his vow when there was still no temple in Jerusalem (ibid. 15: 7).

7. There seems to have been a house of God in Bethlehem, which enabled Jesse's clan to offer their yearly sacrifice there (1 Sam. 20: 6; cf. vv. 28–9), just as Elkanah's family was wont to offer its yearly sacrifice in Shiloh (1 Sam. 1: 3; 2: 19).[36] Perhaps this temple is the one referred to when the Levite from the far side of the hill-country of Ephraim says to his elderly host in Gibeah: 'I went to Bethlehem in Judah and it is to the house of the Lord that I was going' (Judg. 19: 18).[37] By claiming that his going to Bethlehem was a pilgrimage to a temple-city he thus tries to account for his trip to Bethlehem—from which he is now returning—and to satisfy his host's curiosity while avoiding the embarrassment of having to relate the unpleasant incident of his concubine's behaviour (cf. v. 2). It is true that LXX read ביתי, my home ('and I am going to my home') instead of בית יהוה, the house of the Lord. But though this reading, too, makes reasonable sense, there is no justification for preferring it to the MT reading.[38]

Kenite camp, in whose midst Jael dwelt, spread out to Kedesh (v. 11). Thus, we are forced to conclude that this Kedesh, which had to be located near the battlefield, was not the one in Galilee. It seems to have been the one in the territory of Issachar mentioned in 1 Chron. 6: 57 (in Josh. 21: 28 Kishion appears in its place), and also in Josh. 12: 22 along with Taanach, Megiddo, and Jokneam in Carmel. It is not even impossible that it is the one with which the list of Tuthmosis III commences and there as well it is mentioned alongside Megiddo (J. Simons, *Handbook for the Study of Egyptian Topographical Lists Relating to Western Asia* (Leiden, 1937), pp. 35, 115). In Judges 4 it is switched to Kedesh in Naphtali, since Barak really came from there (see v. 6; in the continuation of the chapter Kedesh is mentioned alone without the qualification 'Naphtali'). Be it as it may, it cannot be denied that not even the biblical writers were immune to geographical inaccuracies.

[36] Cf. below, p. 308 (and what is said there about Samuel's arrival in Bethlehem in order to 'sacrifice to the Lord' according to 1 Sam. 16: 2–5).

[37] ואלך עד בית־לחם יהודה, ואת בית יהוה אני הולך. The participle of הולך can here be taken as indicating the perfect tense (cf. Gesenius–Kautzsch–Cowley, *Grammar*, § 116*d*).

[38] As a matter of fact, it is rather more likely that in LXX's reading the tetragrammaton has been abbreviated into a single *y* and subsequently mistaken for the suffix of the singular first person than that in MT the pronominal suffix has

8. There is evidence in 1 Sam. 21: 1–10 of the existence of a small temple in Nob. Mention is here made of the shewbread (vv. 5–7) and an ephod (v. 10), and it is remarked that even the sword of Goliath was kept in this temple (ibid.). It seems that the temple of Nob was destroyed, or abandoned, when, by order of Saul, the city with all its priests were exterminated (ibid. 22: 16–19), except Abiathar who rescued the ephod and brought it to David's camp (ibid. 23: 6). The exact location of this city is not clear, but from the description in Isa. 10: 32 it seems as if it was very close to, and to the north of, Jerusalem.

9. In Micayehu's small temple in the heart of the hill-country of Ephraim, as it looms in the background of the story of Judges 17–18, there is mention of a statue of Yahweh,[39] an ephod, teraphim, and also a priest from the tribe of Levi. All of these, according to the story, were stolen by the Danites and carried away to the temple set up in the city of Dan.

10. In Ophrah in the territory of Manasseh there seems also to have been a small temple, inasmuch as it was there that Gideon set up an ephod (Judg. 8: 27)—a most distinctive temple appurtenance, though, like the ark, it could be carried and used outside the temple as well.[40] This temple was apparently the property of Gideon and his family, just as the one in the hill-country of Ephraim was the property of Micayehu. The exact location of this Ophrah is still unclear. It is usually taken to be on the south side, or on the fringes, of the ridge of Samaria. Perhaps it should be located, following one suggestion, at the village of eṭ-Ṭayibeh in the Sharon Valley, four miles south of Ṭul-Karm.

11. From the narrative in 2 Sam. 21: 1–14 we may infer that Gibeah of Saul, too, was the site of a temple, apparently in the

been erroneously expanded into the tetragrammaton. Cf. the observation on this point made by G. R. Driver, in *Textus* 1 (1960), 119–20, who indeed preferred MT's reading in Judg. 19: 18. This observation notwithstanding, the NEB, like most EVV before it, still follows LXX's reading here. The possibility itself that in LXX's reading of Judg. 19: 18 as well as in other places the tetragrammaton is simply abbreviated into a *y*, was already suggested by Driver *père*; see S. R. Driver, *Notes on . . . the Books of Samuel*[2] (Oxford, 1913), p. xlix, n. 2.

39 The expression *pesel ûmassēḵāh*, which recurs in this story, is a hendiadys meaning a statue poured from a single casting, in contrast to a statue put together from pieces. See E. Z. Melamed, 'Break-up of Stereotype Phrases as an Artistic Device in Biblical Poetry', *Studies in the Bible*, ed. Ch. Rabin = *Scripta Hierosolymitana*, viii (Jerusalem, 1964), pp. 125–6.

40 On the nature of Gideon's ephod, which was not a statue but also seems to have been a priestly vestment, see below, pp. 167–8 (and n. 42).

possession of Saul's family. As stated there, the Gibeonites impaled seven of Saul's sons 'on the mountain before the Lord' (v. 9).[41] This mountain is also meant in v. 6, where MT has בגבעת שאול בחיר יהוה, 'in Gibeah of Saul, the chosen of Yahweh', but LXX read בגבעון בהר יהוה, 'in Gibeon, on the mountain of Yahweh', a reading the end of which appears preferable. Most moderns also adopt the first part of LXX's reading, 'in Gibeon' instead of 'in Gibeah of Saul', which would imply that a temple stood at Gibeon. However, this is hardly conceivable, since Gibeon could have only a high-place. Had there also been a temple in Gibeon, it would have been unseemly for Solomon to display a preference towards the local high-place (1 Kgs. 3: 4). In the time of Saul the Gibeonites could have no reason to wreak their vengeance upon him and impale his sons in Gibeon rather than in any other place, for, as the narrative itself admits, at that time they were already scattered throughout 'all the territory of Israel' (v. 5) and Gibeon was no longer inhabited by them.[42] And by any logic of revenge or cultic reasoning, Gibeah, as Saul's city, was certainly no less suitable a place for fulfilling their desire than Gibeon. Furthermore, the status of Gibeah of Saul, as the place of his patrician family's residence, and especially afterwards, as his royal city, called by his name, serves to strengthen the probability that there was a house of God in that city, which was a kind of royal temple.[43]

[41] Impalement, as a legal-cultic form of execution, is mentioned once more in Num. 25: 4 and there too it is carried out at a high place ('in face of the sun', *neged haššāmeš*). The act itself, expressed in biblical Hebrew by means of the verb *yq'* in the *hip̄'îl* conjugation, means neither 'to hang up' (KJV, RSV) nor 'to hurl down' (NEB), but only 'to impale', as correctly rendered by NJPS and JB, and it seems to have been done after the victim was already executed. For the significance of this act cf., for the present, S. E. Loewenstamm, *EM* ii. 798–800, s.v. הוקעה. Impalement is mentioned in the Code of Hammurapi, § 153 and in the Middle-Assyrian Laws, § 53. See also G. R. Driver–J. C. Miles, *The Babylonian Laws*, i (Oxford, 1952), pp. 313–14.

[42] Therefore, in 2 Sam. 21: 1–9 they are called גבעונים, 'Gibeonites', after their city *of origin*. Were they still thought of as dwelling in Gibeon, they would have been called יושבי גבעון, 'the inhabitants of Gibeon', as in Josh. 9: 3; 10: 1; 11: 19 *et al.*

[43] Even so, it should be admitted that the title 'mountain of Yahweh' (2 Sam. 21: 6, following LXX) seems excessive for Gibeah of Saul (all the more so for Gibeon), seeing that it was commonly used for the temple mount of Jerusalem (Gen. 22: 14; Isa. 2: 3; 30: 29; Ps. 24: 3 *et al.*). It is therefore quite probable that its occurrence here is a mere projection of Jerusalemite reality. Yet the existence of a temple in Gibeah of Saul is still indicated by the use of the expression 'before Yahweh' in 2 Sam. 21: 9 as it is also borne out by reason.

The location of Gibeah of Saul seems to be Tell el-Fûl, about three miles north of Jerusalem, by the road leading to Shechem. Here, in 1922–3, 1933, and 1964, excavations were carried out, but the archaeologists' spades came across no Israelite temple.[44]

12. At the end of the second season of excavations at Arad, in the summer of 1963, in the north-west corner of the citadel situated at the top of the mound, certain remains were uncovered which the excavators defined as the remnants of a temple. This temple was thus supposed to have been part of the royal citadel. Inner and outer sanctums were descried in it, the latter being contiguous with a courtyard. Three steps led from the outer to the inner sanctum, but the latter was far smaller than the former:

[44] On the identification of Gibeah of Saul see, e.g., S. Linder, 'Sauls Gibea—tell el-fûll', *PJB* 18–19 (1923), 89–99. On the excavations at Tell el-Fûl see W. F. Albright, *Excavations and Results at Tell el-Fûl* (*Gibeah of Saul*) = *AASOR* 4 (1924); idem, *BASOR* 52 (1933), 6–12; A. Alt, *PJB* 30 (1934), 8–9; L. A. Sinclair, *AASOR* 34–5 (1960), 1–52; idem, *BA* 27 (1964), 52–64; P. W. Lapp, *BA* 28 (1965), 2–10. *Pace* Albright, the biblical evidence demands that a distinction be made between Gibeah of Saul and that of Benjamin. Gibeah of Benjamin, which is also called simply Gibeah, was the residence of the Philistine governor, and immediately after he was killed the city became Israel's rallying place against the Philistines who gathered at Michmash (1 Sam. 13: 2–3, 15–16; 14: 16). However, before that killing took place, the messengers of Jabesh-gilead had come to Gibeah of Saul, where Saul was aroused to call up all the people against the Ammonites without being disturbed by the Philistines and their governor (11: 4–9). Since according to 1 Sam. 10: 5 a Philistine governor (singular, as in LXX) sat in *Giḇʿat hāʾᵉlōhîm*, the 'Gibeah of God', it follows that this is just an alternative name for Gibeah of Benjamin (but not for Gibeah of Saul). To this Gibeah of Benjamin Saul comes when he returns from Samuel, and here one of the three signs predicted by Samuel occurs to him (10: 10–16), but his home is not here—even though he is known to the local populace, some probably being relatives—since here he relates his adventures to his uncle and not to his father, who has already started worrying about his son (this point has been duly noted by Qimḥi in his commentary). Gibeah of Benjamin might be identical with Geba (Josh. 18: 24; 2 Sam. 5: 25; 1 Kgs. 15: 22 *et al.*), which was one of the priestly cities (Josh. 21: 17), and it also stands at the focus of the story in Judges 19–20 (cf. also Hos. 9: 9; 10: 9). Its location is apparently the Arab village Jabaʿ, which stands on the ruins of the ancient settlement. Gibeah of Saul, on the other hand, which also is sometimes called simply 'the Gibeah' (1 Sam. 10: 26; 15: 34; 22: 6; 23: 19; 26: 1) cannot be identical with Geba (in Isa. 10: 29 they are mentioned as two cities). Criticism of Albright's view, but from a different position from the one expressed here, has most recently been voiced by J. Maxwell Miller, 'Geba/Gibeah of Benjamin', *VT* 25 (1975), 145–66. Gibeah of Benjamin, then, was the site of a prominent high-place, and apparently for this reason it was given the epithet the Gibeah of God (1 Sam. 10: 5); the high-place seems to have remained in existence until the time of Josiah (2 Kgs. 23: 8). Gibeah of Saul, however, was possibly a temple city, though the temple was definitely a modest one and probably did not continue to exist after Saul's dynasty was finally eradicated.

the outer sanctum was an oblong room laid out on a north–south axis, while the inner, the 'holy of holies', looked like an adjacent side-chamber or a large recess in the west wall of the outer sanctum. At the ends of the second of the steps leading from the outer to the inner sanctum were found what seemed to be two stone altars, without horns and with slightly concave tops. In the far corner of the inner sanctum, on the floor, was found a small flat bed of stones, rising above ground level to the height of a single stone, while nearby were found remnants of three stelae. A small part of the courtyard was separated from the rest in such a way that the outer sanctum was directly connected with the 'great' court, and in one of the latter's corners was a supposed altar, built of small unhewn stones and clay, covered with plaster and without horns. Out of the various levels distinguished at the mound, the temple belongs to those bearing the numbers XI to VII, which date from the tenth to the end of the eighth centuries B.C.[45] If the doubts accompanying the identification of these remains as a temple do not suffice to undermine the identification from the very start, then this is the single example of an Israelite temple provided for us by archaeology.

13. The largest and by far the most important temple to exist in Israel was the one erected in Jerusalem and served as the royal temple of the Davidic dynasty. Historically speaking, this is the most recent of the temples attested in the Old Testament—and it is also the only one of the Israelite temples about which the Bible provides us with tangible historical evidence concerning its construction and even the details of its architecture.[46] Nevertheless, in

[45] See the reports and articles by Y. Aharoni: 'Excavations at Tel Arad', *IEJ* 17 (1967), 247–9; 'Arad: Its Inscriptions and Temple', *BA* 31 (1968), 19–21; 'The Israelite Sanctuary at Arad', *New Directions in Biblical Archaeology*, ed. D. N. Freedman and J. C. Greenfield (Garden City, N.Y., 1969), pp. 29–36. It must be emphasized that if this really is a temple (some doubts have already been voiced as to this definition), it is one with some surprising features that cannot be reconciled without the help of tortuous explanations. Interestingly enough, one of the inscribed potsherds discovered at Arad contains an explicit mention of *byt yhwh*, 'house of the Lord'; however, even the excavators are of the opinion that this has nothing to do with the temple in Arad (but apparently refers to the one in Jerusalem), since the potsherd in question dates from around 600 B.C., when what is taken to be the temple in Arad was already in ruins.

[46] The other temple about whose erection we have a biblical account is the one in Dan (Judg. 17–18). However, the story is rather vague and indistinct, and in addition it is preserved in a polemical version (most probably southern in provenance) which reveals a most ironical attitude to that temple. The attitude is not that of a redactor, Deuteronomistic or other, but is indigenous to the story

its fundamental institutional nature it is no different from the temples which preceded it. More will be said about this temple in the following chapter.

10

In addition to the twelve or thirteen temples listed so far, ancient Israel may have known some other temples which have left no trace whatsoever in the Old Testament. Nevertheless, it is a reasonable assumption that any addition to this list (which would have to be based on new, extra-biblical evidence) would be insignificant, and that the total number of Israelite temples can not have been much greater than that which emerges from the biblical records.

At the same time, it is worth noting the interesting fact that—apart from the isolated case of the temple in Mizpah of Gilead mentioned in the story of Jephthah, which we have already suspected (above, sect. 8, no. 5) of being a fictitious projection of the one at Mizpah in Benjamin—all the temples known to have existed in ancient Israel were in cities to the west of the Jordan (see Map 1). This fact may have something to do with the idea of the sanctity of the land of Canaan, whose eastern border ran along the Jordan (see Num. 34: 2, 11–12). At any rate, the idea itself finds an explicit expression in the Old Testament. In one of P's narratives, the land east of the Jordan is described as 'unclean', and its inhabitants must refute the claim that they 'have no share in the Lord', while the land to the west of the Jordan is 'the Lord's possession' and the tabernacle stands there (Josh. 22: 19, 25, 27). From David's claim we learn that one driven out of the land of 'the Lord's heritage' is as if doomed to worship other gods (1 Sam. 26: 19). It is from this land that Naaman the Aramean requests to take some soil in order to build an altar to Yahweh in his own country (2 Kgs. 5: 17); to set up a temple of Yahweh in the land of Aram—or, to all appearance, in any place outside the land of Canaan—even this measure would be insufficient, since temples

itself and seems to be based on the isolated character of that temple, which was far away from the heart of settlement, at the outskirts of the country. I cannot concur with the opinion of M. Noth, *Aufsätze zur biblischen Landes- und Altertumskunde*, i (Neukirchen, 1970), pp. 141–5, that the polemic is here directed against a supposed opposition to the innovations introduced by Jeroboam I into the temple at Dan. The account of the erection of the tabernacle (Exod. 25–31, 35–40) is in fact the foundation-legend of the temple of Shiloh, but its character is indeed strictly imaginary, as will be explained in Chapter X (sects. 8–10).

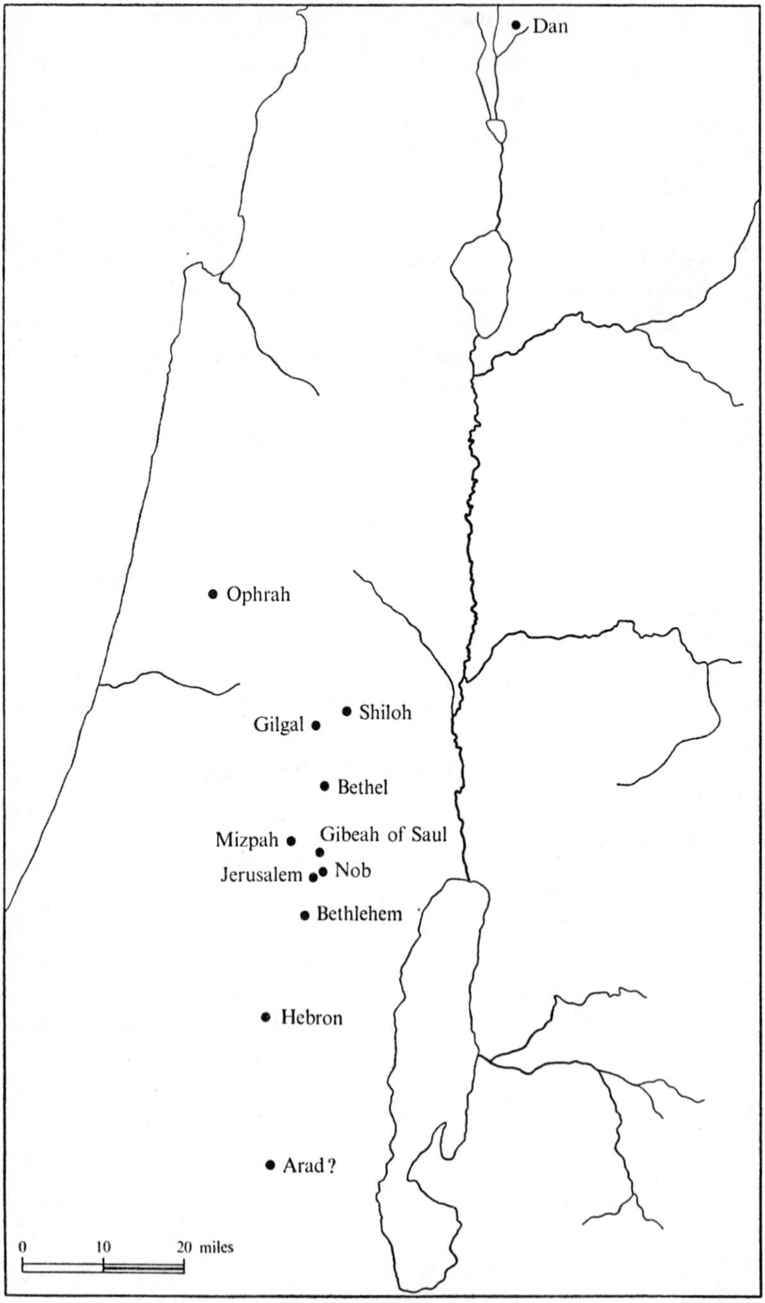

MAP 1. The Temple Cities

can be found only in the country of 'the Lord's heritage'.[47] Another expression of the sacral uniqueness of the land of Canaan is the priestly 'legal' stipulation—however ideal and speculative its character may be—that all tribal possessions to the west of the Jordan must be portioned out by casting lots (Num. 26: 55–6; 33: 54; Josh. 14: 1–2; 18: 6–10 *et al.*), while in trans-Jordan, which was not considered to be a part of the land of promise and was believed to have been conquered with no preconceived intent, Moses gave the tribes their portions without the procedure of casting lots (Josh. 13: 15–32; 14: 3; 18: 7). Likewise, in Ezekiel's visionary programme all the tribal territories stretch from the Great Sea to the Jordan only (Ezek. 47: 13–21; 48: 1–29) and are thus bounded by the eastern border of the land of Canaan.

Furthermore, the geographical distribution of Israelite temples shows that rather than being spaced evenly over the entire land of Canaan the vast majority of them are concentrated in one continuous block between Shiloh and Hebron (or, if preferred, between Shiloh and Arad). This block stretches over the territories of Judah, Benjamin, and Ephraim, and the chain of temples here forms a kind of backbone along the mountainous massif in the southern part of the country. In fact, outside this block we find only Gideon's family temple in Ophrah in the territory of Manasseh (possibly even this is not very far from the main block) and the temple of Dan. But the foundation legend of the Dan temple in Judges 17–18 has it that the first sacral 'spores' of this temple

[47] The ceremonial impurity of foreign lands in general is also hinted at in the words of Amos to Amaziah, the priest of Bethel: 'you yourself shall die in an unclean land' (Amos 7: 17). From the words of Hosea we learn that outside 'Yahweh's land' it is impossible to offer him sacrifices and libations and, consequently, food is considered impure there (9: 3–4). Cf. also Ezek. 4: 13. The assumption that it is impossible to worship Yahweh outside his land is also expressed in Deut. 4: 28; Jer. 16: 13. The psalmists go even further with their claim that it is impossible to 'sing a song of the Lord on alien soil' (Ps. 137: 4). It has been properly emphasized by Kaufmann that all these assumptions are drawn from the popular religion, with which on this point the prophets (as well as the Deuteronomists and psalmists) were in agreement. In this matter Kaufmann also distinguished between Yahweh's 'province of dominion' which actually knows no territorial bounds, and the province of Yahweh's 'favour' where he chooses to reveal himself to his select and lays out his cultic sanctity, which is confined to the land of his 'heritage'. The territorial circumscription of the 'province of favour' is not exactly a sign of polytheism or monolatry, rather it is a characteristic of the primary phase of 'national-territorial monotheism' already perceptible in the earliest strata of the Old Testament (*THH*, i. 606–8, 612–23).

which gave it its legitimacy (the statue of Yahweh, the ephod and the teraphim) were transferred from the hill-country of Ephraim—just as the principal sacral object of the Jerusalem temple (the ark) had its origin in Shiloh. It is therefore quite probable that the marked concentration of temples in the block extending from the territory of Judah to that of Ephraim is no mere coincidence. This block apparently extends over the area of the earliest Israelite settlement in the country. It may be conjectured that after the first wave of settlement ebbed and the Israelite population began to expand to other parts of Canaan—not to mention, to the other side of the Jordan—the primary momentum of temple founding spent itself. (The founding of the temple in Jerusalem, the last event of that kind in the biblical period, was not a direct continuation of the original momentum, but a separate initiative after a long interval of time; when Solomon built his temple, some other temples had already declined and disappeared.) In any case, it seems that the territories of Judah and Benjamin (and Ephraim) were considered to be the area where the most ancient and authentic manifestations of the worship of Yahweh were to be found—and in subsequent chapters we shall arrive at the same conclusion from some other directions. This is apparently why it was in this area that there was found the main concentration of temples in ancient Israel.

III

TEMPLES AND OPEN SACRED PLACES

1

THE building of Solomon's temple in Jerusalem lasted seven years and was completed in the eleventh year of his reign (1 Kgs. 6: 1, 37–8). The blueprint of this temple is set out in 1 Kgs. 6: 2–36; 7: 13–51, with parallels in 2 Chron. 3: 3—5: 1 containing certain changes and adaptations from the earlier description. Substantial repairs were made in this temple at least twice, during the reigns of Jehoash (2 Kgs. 12: 5–17) and Josiah (ibid. 22: 3–9), while some other changes and renovations were made on various occasions (cf. 1 Kgs. 14: 27–8; 2 Kgs. 15: 35; 16: 11–18), and thus it stood for nearly four centuries. In 597 B.C., at the end of the siege of Jerusalem and the termination of Jehoiachin's brief reign, Nebuchadnezzar King of Babylon broke into the temple and plundered it of all the vessels which Solomon had installed (ibid. 24: 13).[1] For the remaining eleven years of its existence, it stood bare, stripped of most of its cultic implements, until in the month of Ab 586 B.C., it was finally destroyed in the devastation of the city by Nebuchadnezzar's general, Nebuzaradan (ibid. 25: 8–21; Jer. 39: 8–10; 52: 12–27).

THE TEMPLES OF JERUSALEM AND LATER TEMPLES

2

By the time of its destruction Solomon's temple had achieved a stature far exceeding that of any of the previous temples. Its extraordinary status as the royal temple of the Davidic dynasty, the prestige of being the largest, best adorned, and most glorious temple in both Kingdoms, the extreme attributes of sanctity ascribed to it in the strains of the psalmodic poetry which blossomed in its courts, the massive religious and literary activity which took

[1] On the nature of this assault and the resultant loss caused to the temple, see below, pp. 286–8.

place around it and found its way into the Old Testament—all combined to transform this temple eventually into a religious symbol in itself. The reforms of cult centralization carried out in the eighth and seventh centuries B.C., and especially the second decisive reform enacted by Josiah, as will be described in Chapter VII, made it the only Israelite place of worship throughout the country. These circumstances brought it about, among other things, that all pre-Jerusalem temples—which, being pre-monarchic, did not even attain the clear light of tangible historical testimony—faded from view, though not from memory, and nearly all present knowledge of the form of an Israelite temple and the service performed in it is for the most part filtered through a Jerusalemite lens. Inasmuch as the Jerusalem temple became one of the cornerstones of biblical religion and of its cultic manifestation, its destruction by the Babylonians created a void which, at the time of the Return from the Exile, had to be filled as soon as possible. A sign of the lofty position attained by the Jerusalem temple in the Old Testament religion is the fact that even after the destruction of the Second Temple, when Judaism had already long been sufficiently mature to do without the institution altogether, it continued to hold on to it, turning the temple's restoration into an eschatological expectation. That is to say, the religious symbol which was shaped in the image of the First Temple did not lose vitality and had not totally passed out of existence even a millennium later.

After the Return from the Exile, and through the permission granted in the Decree of Cyrus (Ezra 1: 2–6; 2 Chron. 36: 22–3) as well as in the memorandum which was deposited in the archives of Ecbatana the capital of Media (Ezra 6: 3–12), the Second Temple was built on the site of that of Solomon. Its foundations seem to have been laid by Sheshbazzar, the leader of the initial wave of repatriates to arrive in Palestine (ibid. 5: 16; cf. 1: 4–11; 5: 14–15; 6: 5, 8–9), but the opposition of the local population and rulers disturbed and repeatedly interrupted the building, so that the temple took over twenty years to reach completion in the sixth year of Darius I, 515 B.C. (ibid. 6: 15–18). Even so, by the time it was destroyed by Titus' soldiers in A.D. 70 it had been in existence for an even longer period than the previous temple. Moreover, the grandeur attained by this temple, through the repairs done by the Hasmonean kings and especially after Herod's construction projects and in the wake of Judaism's expansion outside the confines of Palestine, actually surpassed that of the First Temple. One can therefore say that Haggai's prediction in 2: 9, 'The glory of this latter house shall be greater than that of the former', was amply fulfilled.

The Second Temple of Jerusalem was a direct successor of the First and also served as an expression of the vitality and indispensibility of the institution in that stage of biblical history which preceded the rise of the Jewish Church. At the same time, however, it already shows signs of entirely new principles while the earlier features of the institution of the house of God are fading away. It marks a stage of transition to a new period which was preparing to give up this institution altogether in practice—even while clinging to it as an eschatological symbol. For this reason, and because of its relative lateness in history, the Second Temple of Jerusalem will be for the most part beyond the scope of the present inquiry.

3

Solomon's temple provided the background for two literary monuments in which its image is reflected. One is the temple depicted at the centre of Ezekiel's constitution (chaps. 40–8). In the form in which this temple is outlined there (chaps. 40–4) it certainly never existed in reality but is merely an imaginary construction. Yet there is no doubt that at the root of Ezekiel's visions lies the real profile of the Jerusalem temple (of which Ezekiel himself was one of the priests) as it was towards the end of its existence, during the last eleven years following the deportation of Jehoiachin, when it had been despoiled of most of its vessels. Its likeness, however, is reshaped in the spirit of the priestly school of which Ezekiel was a disciple. In accordance with the peculiar predilection of that school its plan is excessively schematized: its surfaces are rectangular, its courts are square, and the gates, along with the kitchens and chambers, are arranged with painstaking symmetry. The school's influence is also discernible in certain changes and adjustments made in the real Jerusalem temple in order to bring it into line with the priestly requirements, as, for example, by separating the temple compound from the royal palace (43: 7–9) and placing it far away from the city; confining the slaughter of burnt-offerings to the north gate (40: 42); setting up separate tables for slaughtering burnt-offerings, sin- and guilt-offerings in one place and peace-offerings in another (40: 39–41); and turning the inner court into an area accessible only to the priests.[2]

The second literary monument displaying a connection with the Jerusalem temple is the image of the tabernacle depicted at the centre of P and described in striking detail in Exod. 25–31, 35–40. This image too is highly fictitious, and it too has grown and crystallized as one of the scholastic–literary products of the Jerusalem priesthood—even more remarkable a product than Ezekiel's temple. However, the ascertained principle underlying the present work is that the real prototype of the image of the tabernacle is historically older than that of Ezekiel's vision of the temple. In the course of the following chapters we shall illustrate and support this statement.

4

If only for the sake of completeness and as mere curiosities of later history mention should be made here of two other temples set up by Jews in Egypt, and also of the Samaritan temple on Mount Gerizim.

A temple of *Yhw* was erected in the Jewish colony in Elephantine apparently some time after the Babylonians destroyed Jerusalem. At any rate it was already there when Cambyses conquered Egypt in 525 B.C. It was ruined in 410 B.C. Expeditions which have carried out excavations at the place have not been able to agree about the site of this temple, but its existence is undeniable, as it is mentioned in letters, and details of its form are implied in some deeds of conveyance uncovered in those excavations.[3]

Much later, in the middle of the second century B.C., a temple was set up in Leontopolis in Lower Egypt by Onias IV, who was son of the High Priest Onias III and escaped from Jerusalem to enter the service of Ptolemy VI Philometor. From several references by Josephus it seems that the Jews of Egypt who offered sacrifices in it did not consider it of equal value to, still less a substitute for, the temple in Jerusalem. It is also referred to in the talmudic literature where it is regarded ambivalently—some sages say that the sacrifices offered there were considered idolatrous,

[2] These aspects have been treated by me in detail in *EM* v. 353–6.

[3] The principal papyrus mentioning the temple and its destruction is the one preserved in two copies, Nos. 30–1 in the edition of A. Cowley, *Aramaic Papyri of the Fifth Century B.C.* (Oxford, 1923), pp. 108–22. For a discussion of the topic see B. Porten, *Archives from Elephantine* (Berkeley and Los Angeles, 1968), pp. 109–16, 119–22.

while others claim that they were intended, albeit illegitimately, for the God of Israel. It continued to stand for a short while after the destruction of the Second Temple, finally being shut down in A.D. 73 by order of Vespasian.[4] An analogy has been suggested between this temple and the palace Qaṣr el-ʿAbd near ʿArâq el-Emîr in trans-Jordan, built between 182 and 175 B.C. by Hyrcanus son of Joseph and grandson of Tobias, after he fled there from Jerusalem, and an attempt made to label this palace as a temple. But this is just a bold speculation, totally out of harmony with the historical conditions known to have prevailed at that time.[5]

As for the Samaritan temple on Mount Gerizim, it seems likely since the discovery of the Wadi Dâliyeh papyri that we can rely on Josephus' testimony on this matter. He relates that Sanballat the governor of Samaria married off his daughter Nikaso to Manasseh, the brother of the High Priest Jaddua, as a result of which Manasseh was expelled from the Jerusalem priesthood. Subsequently, Manasseh accepted the invitation of his Samaritan father-in-law to be High Priest in the temple which the latter had set up on Mount Gerizim some time after Alexander's appearance in Palestine. This temple stood for two centuries, until it was destroyed in 128 B.C. by John Hyrcanus when he conquered Shechem and subdued the Samaritans.[6] During the persecutions

[4] See Josephus, *Wars* i. 1. 1; vii. 10. 2–4; *Antiquities* xii. 9. 7; xiii. 3. 1–3; 10. 4; xx. 10. 3; Mishnah Menaḥoth xiii. 10; Bab. Tal. Menaḥoth, 109*b*; Megillah, 10*a*. The talmudic sages report that this temple was in Alexandria but this is only an inaccuracy in the tradition of the academy. Philo does not mention it at all. For a discussion of the subject cf. V. Tcherikover and A. Fuks, *Corpus Papyrorum Judaicarum*, i (Oxford, 1957), pp. 44–6, 52, 80; V. Tcherikover, *Hellenistic Civilization and the Jews* (Philadelphia, 1959), pp. 276–81, 392–4.

[5] The suggestion was made by P. W. Lapp, 'The Second and Third Campaigns at ʿArâq el-Emîr', *BASOR* 171 (1963), 27–32. Without going into details it should be emphasized that the features pointed to in Qaṣr el-ʿAbd—a stairway, terrace, and tower—can by no means be accepted as indications of a Jewish temple. Furthermore, temples erected for Jewish colonies in the Nile Valley, far away and isolated from Palestine, are not to be likened to a palace built by a Jerusalemite nobleman a few miles east of Jericho. Again, even if this palace does contain certain architectural features of a Hellenistic–pagan temple, they still should not be taken as an actual proof of the palace's function. It is a fact that in the literary evidence concerning this palace—evidence the like of which few archaeological sites in the Near East enjoy—it is called not a 'temple' but *βᾶρις*, i.e. large house, fortress (Josephus, *Antiquities*, xii. 4. 11). Lapp, therefore, had no reason for surprise that, for example, H. C. Butler and R. Amy (whom he mentions) were not lured by appearances into considering this palace a temple.

[6] On its foundation see Josephus, *Antiquities*, xi. 7. 2; 8. 2–7. On the identity of this Sanballat, apparently the third (as opposed to Sanballat, Nehemiah's

of Antiochus IV Epiphanes it seems to have acquired a Hellenistic flavour either with the consent of the Samaritans, as Josephus claims, or against their will.[7]

THE CULTIC OPEN AREAS

5

In addition to temples and solitary altars (and *bāmôt*) there were found during the Old Testament period open, unenclosed cult areas. These were located in the vicinity of some cities and could comprise several objects of the non-temple category—altar, pillar, sacred tree (Asherah would be the name of such a tree when dedicated to the worship of Baal)—or at least two such components could occur in the same place. Clusters of such objects might indeed also be found in the court of a temple, but those now under discussion stood in the open and were apparently grouped into a special cultic area, a kind of unenclosed temenos. Some of these places attained a high degree of fame and prominence and made a noticeable impact on ancient Israelite cultic life. Nevertheless, it would be wrong to confuse them with temples—not only on account of the essential difference in the character of the institutions, but also because they were found by and large outside the built-up areas of cities, in spots which were as if designed for the accommodation of wayfarers or the encampment of nomads. In fact, the

contemporary, who was the first) and on the reliability of Josephus' account in general see F. M. Cross, 'Papyri of the Fourth Century B.C. from Dâliyeh', *New Directions in Biblical Archaeology*, ed. D. F. Freedman and J. C. Greenfield (Garden City, N.Y., 1969), pp. 53–7; cf. also idem, in *Discoveries in the Wâdī ed-Dâliyeh*, ed. P. W. Lapp and N. L. Lapp = *AASOR* 41 (1974), 20–2; and in *JBL* 94 (1975), 5–7. On the destruction of this temple, see Josephus, *Antiquities*, xiii. 9. 1; cf. *Wars* i. 2. 6. Its remains were probably excavated in the lower layer (Building B) of Tell er-Râs, the northernmost peak of Mount Gerizim; see R. J. Bull, *BASOR* 180 (1965), 37, 41; ibid. 190 (1968), 18; *BA* 38 (1975), 57–9.

[7] According to Josephus, *Antiquities*, xii. 5. 5, the Samaritans, in a letter addressed to Antiochus, denied their relationship to the Jews and asked for permission, among other things, to call their temple after *Ζεὺς Ἑλλήνιος*, which Antiochus granted in his letter of reply. To be sure, scholars are divided as to the authenticity of these letters. Among those accepting it is E. Bickermann, 'Un document relatif à la persécution d'Antiochos IV Epiphane', *RHR* 115 (1937), 188–223. Those who reject it include G. Alon, in *Tarbiẓ* 18 (1947), 149, 154–6 = *Jews, Judaism, and the Classical World* (Jerusalem, 1977), pp. 360, 369–72, who does not assent to Bickermann's arguments. In 2 Macc. 6: 2 it is remarked that Antiochus decreed that the temple on Mount Gerizim be called after *Ζεὺς ξένιος*, in accordance with the manner (or the wish) of the local residents.

foundation-legends of those places are for the most part associated with the figures of the Patriarchs and are embedded in the Book of Genesis.

As to the environs of Shechem, the ancient sources have at least three descriptions of such places. J refers to the terebinth of Moreh, close to which there was an altar built by Abraham after Yahweh appeared to him there and promised the land to his descendants (Gen. 12: 6–7; for the terebinth[s] of Moreh cf. also Deut. 11: 30). E tells of the 'strip of field' which Jacob bought from the sons of Hamor, Shechem's father, and where he built an altar which he called *'El 'ᵉlōhê yiśrā'ēl*, 'El, the God of Israel' (Gen. 33: 18–20).[8] In this field, too, Joseph's bones were believed to have been interred after being brought up from Egypt (Josh. 24: 32; cf. Gen. 50: 25–6; Exod. 13: 19). It seems that the 'oak [or terebinth] that was by Shechem', under which, according to E, Jacob buried the foreign gods and the rings which the members of his household had removed (Gen. 35: 2, 4) was also found close to that field and near that altar.

A third account of such a cultic area near Shechem shows up in the background of Joshua's covenant-making in Josh. 24, which also belongs to E (or, as many scholars will say, E_2), except for a few Deuteronomistic expansions. The event described is so extraordinary that some scholars have been led to conjecture that what we have here is an echo of an annually (or otherwise periodically) recurring ceremony, preserving a memory of the adoption by Israelite tribes of the faith of Yahweh in the land of Canaan. Others have added that the place of the ceremony in Shechem was the earliest amphictyonic centre of the Israelite tribes—even earlier than that of Shiloh.[9] Without entering into these weighty problems we can at least point out that the scene of the narrative

[8] Israel here refers rather to the Patriarch than to the people bearing this name. Cf. the comments of Rashi, Ibn-Ezra, Rashbam, and others ad loc.

[9] See E. Sellin, 'Seit welcher Zeit verehrten die nordisraelitischen Stämme Jahwe?', *Oriental Studies Dedicated to Paul Haupt* (Baltimore, 1926), pp. 126–8; idem, *Geschichte des israelitisch-jüdischen Volkes*, i² (Leipzig, 1935), pp. 97–9, 101; M. J. Bin Gorion, *Sinai und Garizim* (Berlin, 1926), pp. 311–25. For the application of the theory of the amphictyonic organization of the Israelite tribes see M. Noth, *Das System der Zwölf Stämme Israels* (Stuttgart, 1930), pp. 65–74; *Geschichte Israels*³ (Göttingen, 1956), pp. 89–90. A. Alt agreed with him (*KS* i, pp. 191–2, 325; cf. pp. 81–2). See also G. von Rad, *Gesammelte Studien zum AT* (München, 1958), p. 44; W. Beyerlin, *Herkunft und Geschichte der ältesten Sinaitraditionen* (Tübingen, 1961), pp. 137–8.

in Josh. 24 is laid not in some temple within the city of Shechem but in a cultic site in the open country outside the city. The term '*miqdāš* of Yahweh' mentioned in this narrative does not mean a temple but only a 'holy place', that is, a cultic area where there stood an oak (or a terebinth)[10] under which Joshua set up a big stone, which, for its part, signified either an altar or a pillar (vv. 26–7). In any case, owing to the topographical circumstances, a gathering of 'all the tribes of Israel', which, according to the story, was the framework for the event described here, is inconceivable unless carried out in the valley of Shechem. A large crowd, let alone the whole of Israel, cannot possibly assemble within the walls of a tiny city.[11]

It is difficult to decide whether these traditions, recorded as they are by different sources, refer to a single place (with the figures of Abraham, Jacob, and Joshua being interchanged, as in part of the narratives is also the case with the trees named *'allôn* and *'ēlāh*) or to two or three distinct sites near Shechem.[12] On the other hand, there is clear evidence of the existence of a temple within the city of Shechem; this comes in the story of Abimelech, where it is entitled ***bêt ba'al berît***, 'the house of Baal-berith' and ***bêt 'ēl-berît***, 'the house of El-berith' (Judg. 9: 4, 46; cf. v. 27). It would appear that its location was in the city's most strongly fortified section,

[10] MT has here (v. 26) *'allāh*, which is rather curious and perhaps should be read *'ēlāh* (cf. dictionaries and commentaries).

[11] Therefore, the expression 'and they presented themselves before God, *lip̄nê hā'elōhîm*' seems to be employed somewhat loosely in Josh. 24: 1. Possibly, however, the use of this expression implies that the ark was then for a time in that place near Shechem (cf. above, p. 26, n. 24). In connection with Josh. 24, both Alt and Noth speak, and rightly so, of the cultic site 'near Shechem'—not within the city (see Noth, *Das System der Zwölf Stämme*, pp. 92–3, 140). Others have overlooked this nicety; cf. also below.

[12] Besides the three accounts already referred to, mention should be also made of *'Ēlôn muṣṣāḇ*, 'the oak of the pillar'(?), next to which the masters of Shechem made Abimelech king (Judg. 9: 6). Possibly this site too had something to do with the cultic areas, or with some of them, spoken of in connection with the Patriarchs (cf. also the commentaries ad loc.). The possibility that all four of these places are just different names for a single site near Shechem has already been considered by, e.g., E. Meyer, *Die Israeliten und ihre Nachbarstämme* (Halle a.S., 1906), pp. 542–3. At the same time I see no justification for identifying the terebinth of *me'ônenîm*, 'soothsayers', which according to Judg. 9: 37 stood at the side of one of the roads leading to Shechem, with J's terebinth of Moreh. Still another cultic open area near Shechem was found on the slopes of Mount Ebal; it contained a group of pillars, or a particular altar made of stones, which were coated with plaster and bore signs of inscriptions. The aetiological tale of this site has been assimilated into Deut. 27: 1–8; see my observations in 'Shechem Studies' (Hebrew), *Zion* 38 (1973), 6–15.

which is called in the story *migdal šᵉḵem*, 'the tower of Shechem', and served as a sort of acropolis (ibid. vv. 46–9). An enormously massive structure of such an acropolis was discovered in the summer of 1926 at the excavations of Tell Balâṭah, the site of ancient Shechem, and the directors of the expedition were inclined to see in it (at least in its final phase, rebuilt with a slight change in orientation) the temple of Baal-berith itself.[13] They may be right and their claim may certainly be supported by some arguments. However, it would be a complete mistake to identify either the cultic places connected with the Patriarchs or the place of the covenant in Josh. 24 with the temple mentioned in Judg. 9 or with the structure uncovered in the excavations.[14] To do so would be to ignore the difference between two institutions which are dissimilar to each other in character, function, and even in location relative to the city. Furthermore, such an identification is invalidated by the simple fact that until nearly the end of the period of the Judges Shechem was Canaanite and so was the temple of Baal-berith within it, as the narrative of Judg. 9 really implies. Along with the city of Shechem, Abimelech destroyed the temple of Baal-berith (Judg. 9: 46–9), and there is no indication that the latter was ever rebuilt either in Canaanite or Israelite form. The excavations in Tell Balâṭah have also demonstrated that after the destruction of the massive structure, apparently at the end of the twelfth century B.C., its site was not used again for cultic purposes.[15]

[13] See in the reports of E. Sellin: *ZDPV* 49 (1926), 309–11; ibid. 64 (1941), 18–20; subsequently, G. E. Wright's comments: *Shechem—The Biography of a Biblical City* (New York, 1965), pp. 80–7; *BASOR* 144 (1956), 9–10; also L. E. Toombs and G. E. Wright, ibid. 169 (1963), 18–26, 28; R. J. Bull, *BA* 23 (1960), 100–19. Gabriel Welter, who headed the German expedition in Tell Balâṭah during the seasons of 1928–32, refused to identify the massive edifice with the temple of Baal-berith, but in this he has been followed by only a few scholars. See also J. A. Soggin's résumé in 'Bemerkungen zur alttestamentlichen Topographie Sichems mit bezonderem Bezug auf Jdc. 9', *ZDPV* 83 (1967), 186–8.

[14] One who fell into such an error is G. E. Wright, *Shechem*, pp. 132–8; *BASOR* 169 (1963), 30–2; see also E. F. Campbell and J. F. Ross, *BA* 26 (1963), 14.

[15] Upon the ruins of the massive, supposedly cultic structure an Israelite house was subsequently built (E. Sellin, *ZDPV* 49 (1926), 309–10), which the American excavators defined as a storage-house, *מִסְכֶּנֶת, for grain, wine, and oil collected as taxes to the government. See G. E. Wright, *Shechem*, pp. 145–9; *BASOR* 148 (1957), 23–4; ibid. 161 (1961), 13–15; R. J. Bull, *BA* 23 (1960), 113–14.

Consequently, so far as Shechem was a temple-city it was one in its Canaanite stage only. We have no knowledge whether there was ever a temple built in Shechem after it became, in the period of the United Monarchy, an Israelite city. Even the fact that it is listed among the cities of refuge (Josh. 20: 7) and the Levitical cities (Josh. 21: 21) is irrelevant to this point, since, as will be shown in Chapter VI, these two kinds of cities should not be considered in the same category as temple-cities.

6

A cultic area similar to those mentioned as existing near Shechem was also to be found in the vicinity of Bethel. According to the E narrative, Jacob once happened upon what later came to be the '(holy) place' near Bethel, rested his head on one of the stones lying there, and after he dreamt on the stone, seeing divine visions, he set the stone up as a pillar (Gen. 28: 10–12, 16–22). Deviating somewhat here from regular biblical usage the text attaches the title *bêt 'ᵉlōhîm*, 'house of God' to the stone itself, regarding it as a kind of mysterious receptacle of divine powers, as a *βαίτυλος*. This somewhat irregular treatment of the expression also serves here as an aetiological explanation of the name *bêt 'ēl*, Bethel (vv. 17, 19, 22). However, all this has nothing to do with the temple of Bethel, since the Patriarchs, being tent-dwelling semi-nomads (cf. Gen. 13: 12, 18; 18: 1–10; 24: 67; 26: 25; 33: 19 *et al.*), did not found temples, and Jacob's dream is explicitly stated to have taken place in the open countryside outside the city of Luz, which is Bethel, somewhere along the road from Beer-sheba to Haran. Later on Jacob returns to the same place, sets up an altar there and calls the place *'ēl bêt 'ēl*, 'El (God) of Bethel' (Gen. 35: 1, 7; cf. 31: 13). It is likewise possible that the *'allôn bāḵût*, 'the oak of weeping', 'below Bethel', under which Deborah, Rebekah's nurse was buried after the altar was set up (35: 8), was also nearby.

According to J, however, there was an altar east of Bethel, in the place where Abraham encamped when he first arrived in the land of Canaan, and it was he who set up the altar after he was given divine promises there (Gen. 12: 8; 13: 4). There is also an isolated verse, apparently of J, which relates how Jacob set up a pillar in Bethel (35: 14).[16] Once again, we cannot tell whether E and J took down variant traditions on the same matter, referring to the same place, or whether they allude to different sites in the vicinity of Bethel; but again it is clear that these have nothing to do with the temple of Bethel.

Similarly, near Hebron there was the cultic area of *'ēlōnê mamrē'*, 'the oaks (or the terebinths) of Mamre', where, according to J, Abraham encamped and built an altar (Gen. 13: 18) and God appeared to him in the form of three angels with tidings of Sarah's pregnancy (18: 1–15). The narrative in Gen. 14 (E?) also reports that Abraham dwelt at a place with this name, but it takes Mamre to be the name of an Amorite local lord, one of Abraham's allies (v. 13).[17] P, for his part, cannot connect the figure of Abraham with holy trees or an altar, since in his view these are strictly prohibited, and thus for him the name Mamre becomes a title of Hebron. However, he knows of the existence of the field of Machpelah outside the city, which Abraham bought from the inhabitants of Hebron and which included the cave where the Patriarchs and their wives were buried (Gen. 23: 8–20; 25: 9–10;

[16] This verse cannot belong to P, which knows of no pillars, nor, for that matter, of any cultic activity prior to Mount Sinai. At the same time, the event has already been related by E in Gen. 28: 18. It is therefore likely that this is a J fragment. So, e.g., S. R. Driver, *Genesis*[12] (WC, 1926), ad loc.

[17] From the statement that Abraham 'came to dwell at the terebinths of Mamre which are in Hebron' (Gen. 13: 18) some commentators have mistakenly concluded that J located these terebinths within the city itself. In fact, the expression *b^eheḇrôn*, 'in Hebron', indicates here the district around the city, and the reference is to a place close by the city but not within the walls. Similarly, Joshua's covenant is said to have been made *biš^eḵem*, 'in Shechem' (Josh. 24: 25), and the tribes of Israel are spoken of as gathering *š^eḵemāh*, 'to Shechem' (ibid., v. 1), though the reference is, as we have seen, to a certain place in the valley of Shechem (these two readings in MT are preferable to LXX's: 'in Shiloh before the tabernacle of the God of Israel', 'to Shiloh', as many have admitted; cf. A. Geiger, *Urschrift und Übersetzungen der Bibel*[2] (Frankfurt a. Main, 1928), p. 81). In just the same manner, Jacob's sons are said to have been pasturing *biš^eḵem*, 'in Shechem' and, following them, Joseph too comes *š^eḵemāh*, 'to Shechem' (Gen. 37: 12–14), even though only the area outside the city is meant. Jacob is likewise said to have arrived *'îr š^eḵem*, 'in the city of Shechem' but encamped 'before the city' (Gen. 33: 18). As for the terebinths of Mamre there can be no doubt that they were located outside the city since, after the regular fashion of the Patriarchs, Abraham is said to have dwelt there in tents (13: 18; 18: 1, 6, 9–10), which is not a proper way of staying within the city. Furthermore, in Gen. 14: 13 it is explicitly said of Abraham that he 'was "tabernacling", *šōḵēn* at the terebinths of Mamre the Amorite'; for the meaning of the verb *škn* and the nature of the tabernacle see below, pp. 195–6. From the description of the theophany in Gen. 18: 1–8 it is also clear that the scene takes place out in the open.

49: 29–32; 50: 13; cf. 35: 27). There may actually have been such a cave close to the cultic site, but the site itself was certainly outside the city and is not to be identified with the temple of Hebron.[18]

7

In the patriarchal narratives, Beer-sheba appears not as a city but merely as a well and encampment site, and the popular etymologies of its name are based on the number seven or on an allusion to an oath supposedly taken in that place (Gen. 21: 22–31; 26: 26–33), as both seven (in Hebrew *šeḇaʿ*) and the idea of oath (in Hebrew expressed by the root *šbʿ*) appear to be cognate with the site's name. The fact that the place was not settled until after the Israelite possession of the land is indeed verified by the excavations carried out in 1969 and annually thereafter in Tel Beer-sheba (Tell 'es-Sabaʿ, east of the modern city). The results have shown that there was no settlement here during the Bronze Age (previously, in the Chalcolithic Age, there was a small, unwalled hamlet), that in the Iron Age the site became populated, and that only in the tenth century B.C. was it surrounded by a wall so as to become a real city.

In any case, in the patriarchal narratives the cultic site of Beer-sheba is clearly depicted as an open area: Abraham plants a tamarisk in Beer-sheba (Gen. 21: 33) and Isaac builds an altar there (26: 25; cf. 46: 1), and both these traditions apparently refer to the same place.[19] A temple could have been built in Beer-sheba only during the period of the monarchy, but there is no proof, either from the Old Testament or from the archaeological find, that this did actually happen. Samuel, we are told, appointed his sons as judges in Beer-sheba (1 Sam. 8: 2), but apart from the

[18] On which see above, p. 34.

[19] On the slope of the mound, before the city-gate, the excavators found a well which is possibly the one whose digging was attributed to Abraham according to Gen. 21: 22–32 (E) and to Isaac according to Gen. 26: 25–33 (J). The city itself, the street layout of which indicates intentional planning, was not built until the time of David or Solomon, but near the well were found remnants of three levels of solid building which apparently belong to the twelfth or eleventh centuries B.C., 'and the possibility of . . . going back to the thirteenth century B.C. should not be excluded'. See Y. Aharoni, 'Excavations at Tel Beer-sheba, 1973–1974', *TA* 2 (1975), 148–51; also *IEJ* 25 (1975), 170. The well's location on the slope of the mound distinguishes it from the other wells of the biblical period, which were usually found at a low ground level.

doubtful character of this remark, which relates Samuel's sons, during their father's lifetime, to a city at the end of the country,[20] it is not enough to prove the existence of a temple at that place. A place of judgement is certainly expected to be a site of cultic activity and sacredness, but it need not be a temple only; (in Samuel's city, Ramah, where he judged Israel [1 Sam. 7: 17], as well as in Deborah's seat of judgement in the hill-country of Ephraim [Judg. 4: 5], for instance, there were no temples). In the time of Josiah, Beer-sheba is mentioned as one of the cities of high-places (2 Kgs. 23: 8). Amos mentions it as a well-known cultic centre which attracted northerners to 'pass on' to it (Amos 5: 5) and as the geographical opposite of the temple-city of Dan (8: 14), but even this need not be taken as suggesting that, just as in Dan, there was necessarily a temple in Beer-sheba too, and not a 'simple' cultic site—which could also achieve great fame. Nor do we have any means of determining whether that high-place, or whatever similar cultic site it was that made Beer-sheba still remarkable at the end of the monarchy (2 Kgs. 23: 8), is the same spot with which the patriarchal traditions are connected, or some high-place within the city which in the course of time attained prominence, or both of these possibilities.

In the summer of 1973, the excavations at Tel Beer-sheba unearthed a horned altar, large enough to be suitable for animal sacrifices (and not for incense), whose ashlar blocks had been separated and built into the walls of a large store-house near the city-gate. The excavators were able to piece the blocks together and restore the altar practically in its entirety. They supposed that the store-house was destroyed at the end of the eighth century B.C., and thus conjectured that the repairs in the walls of the store-house that coincided with the dismantling of the altar were done somewhat earlier, that is, in the days of Hezekiah, who, according to the biblical testimony, removed the high-places (2 Kgs. 18: 4, 22). It goes without saying that this is quite an interesting discovery, as it bears out the cultic character of Beer-sheba, and may even cast light on a cultic object whose existence is indirectly attested in the Old Testament.[21] Yet it still does not

[20] Josephus (*Antiquities*, vi. 3. 2) states that one son judged in Bethel and the other in Beer-sheba. It is difficult to tell whence he derived this detail, which has no support in the Versions.

[21] On the altar found at Tel Beer-sheba see Y. Aharoni, *BA* 37 (1974), 2–6; idem, *TA* 2 (1975), 154–6. However, according to Yadin's interpretation, which

demonstrate the existence of a temple in Beer-sheba, which the biblical evidence does not indicate either.[22] Until more substantial proof of the existence of a temple in this city is found, it is better not to read into the evidence more than it can actually sustain.

8

Cultic sites of the type discussed here were also found in some other places—either in the vicinity of cities, be they temple-cities or otherwise, or far away from any city. Thus, for instance, E knows of an altar set up by Moses at the foot of Mount Sinai (Horeb) along with 'twelve pillars, according to the twelve tribes of Israel'. Upon descending from the mountain Moses performed there a covenant ceremony between Yahweh and the people (Exod. 24: 3–8). In Gen. 31: 44–54, the J and E accounts, intertwined in such a way that it is already difficult to separate them, tell of a heap of stones, which by every indication functioned as an altar, and also of a pillar, both of which were found on Mount Gilead or nearby (see vv. 23, 25, 54). Both sources provide popular

seems much more convincing, the store-house with the whole city was destroyed in the seventh or the beginning of the sixth centuries B.C., while the dismantling of the altar must be ascribed to King Josiah; see Y. Yadin, 'Beer-sheba: The High-Place Destroyed by King Josiah', *BASOR* 222 (1976), 5–7. He also maintains that, originally, the altar stood to the left of the city-gate as one enters the city, and was part of the *bāmāh* referred to in 2 Kgs. 23: 8 (that is, in the second half of this verse), and, moreover, the *bāmāh* can be exactly identified in one of the buildings (no. 430) uncovered in the excavations (ibid. 8–14).

22 Aharoni has somehow been caught up in the peculiar theory that the border-cities of a state can be expected to contain royal temples, and that the kings of Israel and Judah presumably built temples, mostly if not only along the boundaries of their domains, thereby designating, as it were, the area of their and their God's dominion. See Y. Aharoni, 'Arad: Its Inscriptions and Temple', *BA* 31 (1968), 32; idem, 'Israelite Temples in the Period of the Monarchy', *Proceedings of the Fifth World Congress of Jewish Studies*, i (Jerusalem, 1969), pp. 69–74; idem, in: *New Directions in Biblical Archaeology* (n. 6), pp. 36–8. This theory was one of his motives for undertaking excavations in Beer-sheba, in the hope of finding an Israelite temple there, and it was not given up even in the face of the archaeological results. However, the whole theory is entirely incompatible both with the institutional character of the temples and with their geographical distribution as reflected in the Old Testament. Aharoni's conjecture in *IEJ* 24 (1974), 271; ibid. 25 (1975), 170; *TA* 2 (1975), 162, that the 'basement house' found in the north-western corner of Tel Beer-sheba, with a row of cellars and walls built on the *bedrock*, took the place of some temple, is only a vain attempt to compensate for the lack of actual remnants (cf. also Yadin's remarks, art. cit., 7–8).

etymologies of the name of the heap-altar, called here *gal'ēd*, 'heap of witness'—a form which is akin to *gil'ād*, Gilead. Since the name Mizpah is also mentioned and given a popular-etymological explanation (vv. 49–50) it should not be denied that the allusion here is to Mizpah of Gilead, which also was the site of an important open-type cultic area, but apparently not of a temple.[23]

Against a background of a later period, a cultic area of this type is depicted in the parallel commission-stories of Gideon: one (Judg. 6: 11–24) refers to an altar set up by Gideon and to a terebinth tree, while the other (ibid., vv. 25–32) speaks of an altar which Gideon built on the site of an altar of Baal and of a felled Asherah-tree. To all appearance, these two cultic features were to be found near Ophrah of the Abiezrites in the territory of Manasseh. However, as was said above (Chapter II), the fact that Gideon placed an ephod in Ophrah (ibid. 8: 27) leads one to suppose that it was also a temple-city.

[23] Cf. above, p. 33.

IV

THE PRIESTHOOD AND THE TRIBE OF LEVI

I

THE main characteristic of a cultic activity is permanence. This is manifest in all the four dimensions by which the cult can be described. The cult enjoys permanence of place—irrespective of whether there are many places or just one (in theory or in practice) centralized place. In certain circumstances, particularly in nomadic societies, the 'places' might be movable, but this does not annul their permanent character. The cult enjoys permanence of time—for the cultic activity does not take place continuously and without interruption, nor at random, but with cyclic and temporal regularity, when the religious experience which accompanies the cult is also renewed. It enjoys permanence of ceremony. And it has regular personnel—for the main cultic tasks are not performed by just anyone but are the prerogative of particular circles of functionaries (though in the course of time certain forms of democratization might occur).[1] In all these aspects the cultic manifestations are also stamped with the impression of sanctity—of places, times (the feasts and the appointed seasons), ceremonial acts, and men (the priestly personnel).

At this juncture let us take up another dimension of the four—that of the men dedicated to the priesthood. We shall have to reflect on theories that have been put forward and suggest an interpretation which seems to us the most acceptable.

THE PREROGATIVE OF PRIESTHOOD AND THE LEVITICAL STATUS

2

Who is entitled to officiate in the priesthood? P's answer to this question is absolutely clear: Aaron and his sons, who constitute

[1] Cf. above, pp. 1–2.

a single and singular family within the tribe of Levi. In order to carry out their cultic functions they are dressed in priestly vestments, which are considered an inseparable part of the tabernacle appurtenances (Exod. 28; 39: 1–31), and they are anointed with the sacred oil, as are all the tabernacle vessels (ibid. 30: 26–30; 40: 9–15). Henceforth, Aaron and his sons are integrated into the concrete, contagious holiness of the tabernacle (as will be described in Chapter IX). Within the family of priests Aaron and the first-born of his descendants are set apart and given the high priesthood. The high priest is accorded a higher rank of sanctity and the most exalted cultic position as against his brethren. Yet all the priestly males are alike separated from the rest of the tribe of Levi, who according to P can never attain priesthood. In P, the ordination of Aaron and his sons for the priestly service (Exod. 29; Lev. 8) accompanies the story of the construction of the tabernacle itself, for there can be no tabernacle in existence without priests to attend to it.

In its essence this view is also that of Ezekiel's code, except that Ezekiel substitutes the sons of Zadok for the sons of Aaron (Ezek. 40: 46; 43: 19; 44: 15–16; 48: 11). In addition, Ezekiel does not recognize—at least, no mention of them is made in his code—either anointing with oil or even the institution of the high priesthood. However, he does make a definite distinction between one priestly family, which according to him is that of Zadok, and all the other members of the Levitical tribe, and he too emphasizes that the priests are distinguished by special vestments (Ezek. 44: 17–19) and are obliged to refrain from touching other people while officiating in the temple or partaking of sacrifices of the most holy order (ibid. 42: 13–14; 44: 19; 46: 19–20; cf. 46: 2). In his view too Levites can never attain the office of priesthood (ibid. 44: 13).

Although according to both P and Ezekiel the status and functions of the Levites are invested with a certain sanctity, it is a sanctity of minor degree: it does not embody substantial, material 'power', neither is it cultic in nature. It is simply an expression of ritual purity. In P's account, the Levites were dedicated to God when they were substituted for the first-born (Num. 3: 40–5). Later, a ceremony of purification was performed over them and they were 'offered as a wave offering before the Lord' (ibid. 8: 5–22). During the wanderings in the desert they had two tasks:

first, the 'work', *ʿᵃḇôḏāh*, and the portage of the tabernacle, that is, its dismantling, carrying, and reassembling in a new station; second, the guarding of the tabernacle and its appurtenances, by forming a barrier between the priestly holiness and the people, so as to prevent the Israelites from approaching too closely and from coming into contact with this holiness. The former task was reserved for males between the ages of thirty and fifty (Num. 4), or, according to another account of P, between the ages of twenty-five and fifty (Num. 8: 23–6), whereas the second task devolved upon every male Levite from a month upwards (ibid. 3: 14–39) and also upon all those of fifty and upwards who 'withdraw from the service of the work' and join their brethren 'to keep the guard' (ibid. 8: 25–6).[2] The general body of Levites is also under an obligation to be attached to the priests and assist them (Num. 18: 2, 4) as well as 'to stand before the congregation to serve them' (ibid. 16: 9), that is to say, to serve the priests and the people by performing acts which do not appertain directly to the altar, such as slaughtering the sacrifices, or preparing the sacrifices for consumption after the fats had been burned in the fire.

Of the two main functions, Ezekiel's code stresses the second one, the keeping of the guard. In fact, he calls the Levites: 'The keepers of the guard of the house', שומרי משמרת הבית (Ezek. 40: 45; 44: 14)—*bayit* being employed here in its wider connotation, to include the temple's courts and chambers; in this respect the Levites are distinguished from the priests, the sons of Zadok, who 'come near to Yahweh to serve him' and are called 'the keepers of the guard of the altar' (ibid. 40: 46), or 'those who kept the guard of my sanctity', אשר שמרו את משמרת מקדשי, 'those who kept my guard', אשר שמרו משמרתי (ibid. 44: 15–16; 48: 11).[3] To be sure, the prophet also tries to attach the term *ʿᵃḇôḏāh*, 'work' to his description of the Levites and in one instance he dwells upon the point at some length, calling them: 'Keepers of the guard of the house (the temple), with all its work (*lᵉḵol ʿᵃḇôḏātô*), and with all that is to be done in it' (ibid. 44: 14).

[2] For these two tasks of the Levites cf. also below, pp. 181–3.

[3] It must again be borne in mind that in biblical Hebrew the word *miqdāš* does not necessarily mean a house of God. It can mean any place or object to which holiness is attached (cf. above, pp. 14–15; also below, p. 172, n. 50). Access to the altar and to the holiness is thus accorded to the priests alone. 'The guard of the altar' or of God's 'sanctity', *miqdāš* is, then, more exalted than 'the guard of the house'.

However, *ʿaḇôdāh*, as used in its technical sense in P to mean the dismantling and reassembling of the tabernacle at the camping sites is irrelevant in Ezekiel's code, since a solid building cannot be moved about. But the obligation to maintain a barrier between the cultic holiness and the people remains valid and Ezekiel gives it strong emphasis. The Levites' third task, as described in P, is also to be found in Ezekiel's code. He calls them 'the servants of the temple', *mᵉšārᵉtê habbayit* (Ezek. 45: 5; 46: 24; cf. 44: 11), and in this capacity they slaughter the burnt- and the peace-offerings for the people (ibid. 44: 11),[4] they boil the peoples' sacrifices (ibid. 46: 24), and 'stand before them to serve them' (ibid. 44: 11)—on this point the wording is reminiscent of P (cf. Num. 16: 9). Hence, according to the priestly school (that is, P and Ezekiel 40–8 taken together) all the functions of the Levites are performed outside the cultic sanctity. The Levites have no place inside the priestly circle.

3

Who, according to D, is entitled to officiate in the priesthood?

Here the answer is also clear-cut: Every male member of the tribe of Levi, or, more precisely, every male member of the tribe of Levi may become a priest if he is in the 'chosen place', since D admits the validity of a cult which is only performed in the chosen place (Deut. 12: 5–18 *et al*). A Levite who lives in the provinces and wishes 'with all the desire of his soul' to come to the chosen place may do so and become in every respect a priest, 'like all his brethren the Levites who stand there before the Lord' (Deut. 18: 6–7). According to D, the lack of inheritance and the dependance on *'iššê Yahweh*, 'offerings of the Lord [made] by fire', characterize the position of 'the Levitical priests, all the tribe of Levi' (ibid., v. 1), that is to say, the Levitical priests can actually be found in any part of the tribe of Levi, as the entire tribe is one of potential priests. Hence the recurring formula, applied to the tribe of Levi:

[4] The slaughtering of a burnt-offering or of a *zeḇaḥ* (which is the ordinary sacrifice, identical with the peace-offering), is certainly valid if done by a layman (Lev. 1: 5, 11; 3: 2, 8 *et al.*) and this is how the talmudic sages decided for every sacrifice (Bab. Tal. Yoma, 27*a*; Zabaḥim, 32*a et al.*). This slaughtering performed by the Levites is described in Ezekiel's code as a kind of service which they render to the people, like the 'standing before the congregation to serve them' in Num. 16: 9 (and in similar wording also in Ezek. 44: 11).

'he shall have no inheritance among his brothers; the Lord is his inheritance' (ibid., v. 2; cf. Josh. 13: 14; 18: 7; also Deut. 10: 9), since Levi is, so to say, a tribe of priests. The expression 'the Levitical priests', *hakkōhᵃnîm halᵉwiyyim* or 'the priests the sons of Levi', *hakkōhᵃnîm bᵉnê lēwî* is characteristic of D (Deut. 17: 9, 18; 21: 5; 24: 8; 27: 9 *et al.*) as well as of the Deuteronomistic school as a whole (Josh. 3: 3; 8: 33; 1 Kgs. 12: 31; Jer. 33: 18, 21 *et al.*), and its precise meaning is: the priests from any family of the tribe of Levi, the priests who put into practice the tribal prerogative of priesthood.[5]

Levites living in the provinces take no part in the cultic activities, and are thus unable to share in 'the offerings of the Lord made by fire'. For them, the rule 'the Lord is their inheritance' remains merely an abstract promise and their economic and social position is therefore difficult. In D's system they join well-to-do citizens on feasts and festive occasions and partake of sacrificial meals with the owners, their families, and slaves (Deut. 12: 12, 18–19; 14: 27; 16: 11, 14). They are mentioned in one breath with the sojourner, the fatherless, and the widow (ibid. 14: 29; 16: 11, 14; 26: 11–13). In such circumstances they might be better off if they moved to the chosen place and officiated as priests. However, prevailing circumstances call for a balance between supply and demand, and if all Levites were to exercise their right to the priesthood, it would become worthless. D himself does not encourage the provincial Levite to exercise his prerogative. He simply permits him to do so when he is forced to come to the chosen place, *bᵉḵol 'awwat napšô*, 'with all the desire of his soul' (Deut. 18: 6), that is, when he is driven by dire necessity and has no alternative but to come.[6] At any rate, D allots no function whatsoever to the Levite who lives in the provinces. In fact, outside the chosen place the Levite is considered by D an ordinary layman.[7]

[5] An additional shade of meaning perhaps implied in this expression is noted below, sect. 15.

[6] The expression בכל אות נפשו, 'with all the desire of his soul' occurs again in D in connection with eating animals slaughtered for non-sacrificial purposes (Deut. 12: 15, 20–1). D does not encourage this practice either, but only permits a person to eat if he very much wants to. Similar expressions also occur in 1 Sam. 23: 20; Jer. 2: 24, where the meaning is close to the above. See also dictionaries.

[7] G. E. Wright, 'The Levites in Deuteronomy', *VT* 4 (1954), 325–30 conjectured that according to D only the Levitical priests were destined to officiate at the altar, whereas all the rest of the tribe were client-Levites and should

According to P and Ezek. 40–8 a Levite can never become a priest—but even when he occupies a sub-priestly rank he is present at the place of worship, he has his own tasks, and a certain sanctity of his own. According to D every Levite has the right to become a priest—but so long as he has not done so he is far away from the place of worship and there is no real difference between him and any ordinary Israelite. The phrase 'the Levitical priests' is characteristic of D, whereas the mention of Levites in contradistinction to priests, or in contradistinction to Aaron, or the combination 'the priests *and* the Levites' as an expression of two categories of status and function will only occur within the framework of the priestly doctrine or when describing a reality based upon this doctrine (Exod. 38: 21; Num. 3: 9; 4: 18–19; 18: 6, 26–8; 1 Kgs. 8: 4; Ezek. 45: 4–5; 48: 13 *et al.*; cf. Ezra 1: 5; 2: 70; 3: 8 *et al.*). It might be said that the conjunctive *waw* appearing between the priests and the Levites constitutes the firm and concrete line of differentiation between P's and D's views.

4

Who, according to J and E, is entitled to officiate in priesthood?

It is commonly held that according to these sources any Israelite has this right, and on the face of it there is ample evidence to support such an opinion. The archaic law of the Book of the Covenant states clearly that every Israelite is entitled to sacrifice burnt- and peace-offerings on an altar, where no mention whatsoever of priests is made (Exod. 20: 24, 26). Similarly, as it has already been remarked in Chapter II, J and E relate that the Patriarchs set up altars on which they made sacrifices (Gen. 12: 8; 13: 18; 22: 9 *et al.*). J carries the notion that someone who is not a priest may build an altar and sacrifice on it as far back as the time of Noah after the flood (Gen. 8: 20–1), while, on the other hand, J and E carry it forward to the time of Moses (Exod. 17: 15; 18: 12; 24: 4). This view also seems to characterize the pre-Deuteronomistic sources of the Former Prophets (which are at least close to, if not identical with, J and E in quality and form),

teach the law to the people, in a way which did not make them very much different from the Levites as conceived of in P. It is, however, far from likely, and cannot really bridge the gap between the two sources. Wright's suggestion has been acutely refuted by J. A. Emerton, *VT* 12 (1962), 129–38. Of late, R. Abba, *VT* 27 (1977), 257–67 has tried to corroborate Wright's suggestion, but his arguments on that score are still not enough to prove his case.

and it also appears to reflect actual historical circumstances. One is no longer surprised, therefore, at the many examples to be found in these sources of people unconnected with the priesthood using altars and sacrificing. Thus, Gideon in Ophrah (Jud. 6: 20–8), Manoah in Mahaneh-dan (ibid. 13: 15–23), the men of Beth-shemesh on the great stone in the field (1 Sam. 6: 14–15), and Elijah on Mount Carmel (1 Kgs. 18: 30–8). Some scholars have gone so far as to claim that the early layers of JE, or J, which is the earlier of the two sources, do not even mention priests. If Aaron is mentioned there by name (e.g., Exod. 15: 20; 24: 9; Num. 12: 1–6) it is in the role, not of priest, but of prophet or of one of the elders of Israel.

These data, most of which are indisputable, have been taken in biblical criticism as a decisive starting-point for any description of the Israelite priesthood in its earliest stages. The historical aspect of the problem will be dealt with further on. At first we must restrict ourselves to J's and E's understanding of the priestly institution. Do they really fail to recognize the distinctiveness of this institution, or do they ignore its confines to the extent of blurring the difference between a priest and an ordinary Israelite?

THE VIEWPOINT OF J AND E

5

Here we must recall the iron rule that there is a fundamental institutional difference between the altar and the temple.[8] For it must always be borne in mind that in Israel, as in the entire ancient Near East, the priest's place was in temples, in the houses of God. On solitary altars every Israelite could make his offerings without the help of intermediaries, but cultic officiation in the temples and at the altars attached to temples was in Israel (as everywhere else) the prerogative of established families of priests only.[9] One

[8] Cf. above, pp. 15–16.

[9] This fact accords with the conventional priestly epithet fossilized in the biblical language, *m^e šāret Yahweh*, 'the Lord's servant' (Isa. 61: 6; Jer. 33: 21–2; Joel 1: 9, 13; 2: 17 *et al.*). In the same manner the priestly officiation in the temple is referred to as 'to serve in the holy place' (Exod. 28: 43; 29: 30 *et al.*), the priests 'stand before the Lord to serve him' (Deut. 10: 8; cf. 17: 12; 18: 5, 7 *et al.*), 'come near to him to serve him' (Ezek. 40: 46; 43: 19; 44: 15), 'approach his table to serve him' (ibid. 44: 16) and the like—in all these cases the verb

must, therefore, not be misled by the contrary impression given by J and E, for their narratives are concerned with individual, provincial altars, which were to be found almost everywhere. Had they been dealing with the houses of God and the altars attached to them, the assumptions of these self-same sources would undoubtedly have differed and their account would have taken a different form.

J's and E's limited concern with temples results, first of all, from the non-priestly character of these sources. This is one of the reasons why the exploits they describe take place in the popular, 'secular' sphere, which is remote from the temple and where provincial altars still exist. In their accounts it is therefore quite impossible to find evidence of the circumstances and rules of conduct which characterize priestly sanctity within the temple, and indeed it is possible that most of those rules were not even sufficiently clear to these writers. J's and E's limited concern with the priesthood is also connected with their presupposition that, historically, houses of God did not make their appearance in Israel until after the settlement in Canaan, while before that only solitary altars had been put up. This presupposition is expressed, as it has already been said, in the Song of the Sea (Exod. 15: 17), and D also subscribes to it (Deut. 12: 8–11). If houses of God were not established until after the time of Joshua, then J and E would obviously be unable to mention either the institution itself or the priestly personnel attached to it in their accounts of that period, except by using anachronistic phraseology. However, as they do occasionally lapse into such anachronisms we can infer that the existence of houses of God and of priests was not unknown to the writers of these sources.

A mention of the house of God is made in one of the laws recurring in the Books of the Covenant (Exod. 23: 19; 34: 26) and here it is not in fact an anachronism. In other cases this institution

šrt being used. Likewise, the name denoting priest in Egyptian, for instance, is *ḥm-nṯr*, which means literally 'god's servant'. And it is only natural that, before anywhere else, the servant should be present at the master's residence. The conventional epithet of a prophet, however, is *'eḇed Yahweh*, 'the Lord's slave' (2 Kgs. 9: 7; 17: 13, 23; Jer. 7: 25; 25: 4; 26: 5 *et al.*; 1 Kgs. 14: 18; 15: 29; 2 Kgs. 9: 36; 10: 10; 14: 25; Isa. 20: 3 *et al.*; on Moses: Num. 12: 7–8; Deut. 34: 5; Josh. 1: 1–2, 7 *et al.*). This epithet, which surely originated in prophetic circles, seems to have been also applied to non-prophetic figures (on Abraham: Gen. 26: 24; Caleb: Num. 14: 24; David: 2 Sam. 7: 5, 8; 1 Kgs. 8: 66; 14: 8 *et al.*; Job: Job 1: 8; 2: 3; 42: 7–8; and others).

826318X D

was referred to in spite of the unsuitability of the background: in the account of the battle of Jericho, because silver, gold, and vessels of bronze and iron were consecrated and presumably put in the temple treasury (Josh. 6: 19, 24 [even if the word *bêt* is deleted in the last verse, following LXX, the reference would still be to the temple treasury]), and in the narrative about the Gibeonites, because they were designated to be temple slaves (ibid. 9: 23)—even though these narratives presuppose that the Israelites were at that time still in camp.[10] In one passage the term 'kingdom of Priests' is employed as a synonym or as a complementary concept, of 'a holy nation' (Exod. 19: 6), while in the first chapters of the Book of Joshua, not necessarily in the Deuteronomistic layer, frequent mention is made of priests carrying the ark (Josh. 3–6), a task which according to both J, E, and D is one of their specific prerogatives (cf. Deut. 10: 8; 31: 9, 25; Josh. 8: 33; and below, sect. 12). Priests are also mentioned at the revelation on Mount Sinai (Exod. 19: 22–4). This is simply an anachronism of the type common in the Pentateuchal stories, and the proposal to delete the priests from this passage, or to consider Exod. 19: 6 as a late accretion, influenced by Deuteronomic style, seems quite unnecessary.

6

Moreover, J and E clearly take it for granted, exactly as D does, that priesthood is given to the tribe of Levi alone. This is stated explicitly in the J fragment Exod. 32: 25–9, which is embedded in the narrative about the golden calf.[11] Here we read that after the

[10] However, for the sake of accuracy it must be recalled that the text in Gen. 28: 22 refers only to a stone-pillar, not to a temple (cf. above, p. 52). This story, then, portrays Jacob not as a founder of a temple, as a number of commentators assumed, but as setting up the pillar and initiating the cultic place of the open type which was located by that city.

[11] The fragment Exod. 32: 25–9, which is inserted into E's narrative about the golden calf (Exod. 32: 1–24, 30–5), is, as most critics agree, incompatible with the narrative. Earlier on we are told that, when Moses had descended from the mountain and seen the calf, he broke the tables, burned the calf, ground it into powder, and rebuked Aaron. Later, he ascends to Yahweh to request that the people's sin be forgiven (vv. 30–2). But if the people have already been punished with the death of all the transgressors, as we read in vv. 25–9, then Moses' request is pointless. In fact, only after Moses' entreaty, at the end of the chapter, do we read that Yahweh sent a plague upon the people 'because they made the calf' (v. 35), this being a doublet to the story of the killing by the sons of Levi. Again, the description itself: 'The people were broken loose, for Aaron had let them break loose' (v. 25) and the mention of thousands being killed by the sons

sons of Levi had revealed their zeal for Yahweh and for Moses and had put down the rebels by force of arms, Moses told them: 'Fill [LXX: you have filled] your hand today for the Lord' (ibid., v. 29). 'To fill one's hand' is the usual term for consecration for the priesthood (cf. Exod. 28: 41; Num. 3: 3; Judg. 17: 5, 12 *et al.*), which implies that priesthood was given to this tribe as a reward for its faithfulness at a moment of crisis.

Levi is likewise described as a tribe of priests in Moses' blessing (Deut. 33: 8–11), which apparently belongs to J.[12] The passage there devoted to Levi describes him as Yahweh's 'devout' upon whom the Urim and Thummim—one of the most outstanding priestly appurtenances—were bestowed (cf. Exod. 28: 30; Lev. 8: 8; Num. 27: 21 *et al.*). The continuation of Levi's blessing, namely, that he made himself a stranger to his father and mother, 'he disowned his brothers, and ignored his children' because of an abundant zeal for his Lord (Deut. 33: 9), is a somewhat exaggerated poetic rendering of the events described in the passage inserted into the narrative of the golden calf that the Levites passed through the camp and killed 'every man his brother, and every man his companion, and every man his neighbour' (Exod. 32: 27). Thus this blessing too assumes that the Levites were given the priesthood as a reward for their devotion to Yahweh. The members of the tribe of Levi are then described as priests by mentioning three of their typical functions: to instruct the people

of Levi do not seem to make sense after Moses had made the Israelites drink the water on which the powdered remains of the calf had been scattered (v. 20). It was A. Dillmann's attractive suggestion, with which a number of scholars have agreed, that basically this fragment is meant to describe not the punishment for the transgression over the calf, but rather for some rebellion against Yahweh. It might be added that the calf was taken as a symbol for Yahweh and in connection with it Aaron proclaimed a 'feast to Yahweh' (v. 5). But according to the J fragment, Israel's rebellion implied a rejection of Yahweh himself, and this is echoed in the call: 'Whoso is on Yahweh's side, let him come to me' (v. 26). There is also an affinity of language between the end of v. 27 and Num. 25: 5, which concludes the fragmentary J account of the Baal of Peor. It may be that our fragment of Exod. 32: 25–9 also referred to a transgression like attachment to Baal. In any event, P's account of the Baal of Peor (Num. 25: 6–13) also recounts that after Phinehas had revealed his zeal for Yahweh by the use of arms, he was given 'a perpetual priesthood', which recalls what is told here concerning the Levites. The argument that Exod. 32: 25–9 belongs to J can itself be substantiated by further considerations.

[12] Though the Book of Deuteronomy overlaps with D, they are not synonymous. D ends, as we know, at Deut. 32: 47. The remainder of the Book (Deut. 32: 48—34: 12) is a combination of material from J, E, and P.

in the law, to put incense in the Lord's 'nostrils', and to sacrifice a burnt-offering upon the altar (Deut. 33: 10).[13]

In addition, in J's account we find that, when God addresses Moses, Aaron is called 'your brother, the Levite' (Exod. 4: 14). A number of scholars have expressed surprise that the text should distinguish Aaron from his brother in this manner since they both, after all, belonged to the same tribe. The simple truth is that this phrase is based upon the assumption that priesthood is in principle the privilege of the tribe of Levi, so much so that the appellation 'the Levite' becomes synonymous with a priest. Since of the two brothers only Aaron is considered to have become a priest, the epithet 'the Levite' is applied only to him, which gives the impression that Moses is not a Levite (and, in fact, he is not a Levite in the sense that he is not a priest). Needless to say, the use of this epithet here too is anachronistic in character.

Scholars who subscribed to the prevalent theory on the history of the Israelite priesthood tried, quite unjustifiedly, to depreciate the importance of these pieces of evidence.[14] J's understanding of the right to officiate in priesthood is perfectly clear in these texts, and is the same as we have already found in D. E probably shared this view, but this source is one of those which have come down to us in fragmentary form. If we add the passage Deut. 10: 6–9, which is embedded in Moses' discourse and seems to be a remnant of E,[15] the evidence gains additional force—if such were still needed.

7

There should be no doubt that the realization of the privilege of priesthood, too, is understood by J and E in exactly the same

[13] The noun *kālîl*, used in this verse, is an appellation for burnt-offering, *'ôlāh* (cf. 1 Sam. 7: 9; Ps. 51: 21 *et al.*). It is also to be found in the Phoenician inscriptions (Donner–Röllig, *KAI*, iii, Glossar, s.v. כלל).

[14] As for Exod. 32: 29, Wellhausen claims that it is based on D, whereas Exod. 19: 22 does not belong to the story in its original form (*PGI*, 134). As regards Exod. 4: 14 it was argued that the term 'the Levite' refers here not to the tribe, but to the professional order (already alluded to by Wellhausen, loc. cit.; cf. also, e.g., the commentaries to Exodus by A. H. McNeile (WC, 1908) and S. R. Driver (CBSC, 1918), ad loc.). The blessing in Deut. 33: 8–11 was explained by Wellhausen as referring to the priestly class in the Northern Kingdom, not to the tribe of Levi (cf. below, n. 22).

[15] This fragmentary passage, apparently consisting of two pieces (vv. 6–7, 8–9), has a narrative, not a rhetorical, form, and it breaks the continuity of Moses' oration; cf. commentaries (and below, n. 25).

manner as by D, to wit, all the sons of Levi are potential priests and all they have to do to attain the actual priesthood is to be present at a temple. For he who refers to '*all* the sons of Levi' as being consecrated to the priesthood (Exod. 32: 26, 29) and describes the entire tribe of Levi as being engaged in this function (Deut. 33: 8–10 and 10: 8–9), cannot possibly restrict the priesthood to one of the tribe's families—but neither can he imagine that the priesthood extends to the whole tribe, except in that any member of the tribe has the right to become a priest should he so desire. In this respect, the only difference between D and J or E is the matter of the centralization of the cult—whereas D acknowledges the legitimacy of only one temple, one place of worship, this being the only place where the Levites can exercise their right to the priesthood, J and E assume that there are many houses of God, where various Levitic families have already become priests and where every Levite has the option to take the holy orders.

There is no point in claiming that in the early layers of J and E Aaron was not considered a priest. As we have already mentioned, precisely the opposite transpires from the epithet 'your brother, the Levite' (Exod. 4: 14). The J passages relating to the revelation at Sinai even mention Nadab and Abihu by name (Exod. 24: 1, 9), while the wording of the text: 'Moses and Aaron, Nadab and Abihu, and seventy of the elders of Israel' implies that Aaron and his two sons are not included in the seventy elders. Nor can we see any justification for the claim that the names of the sons were added to these verses.[16] In E's account of the golden calf Aaron appears as the leader of the cultic activity, displaying the features of a priest (Exod. 32: 1–5, 21–4; this is also referred to in Deut. 9: 20). At the same time, one must not forget the basic rule that according to both J, E, and D Aaron's priesthood could not manifest itself during the period of bondage in Egypt and the wanderings in the wilderness, when no houses of God were existent and therefore any description of Aaron as a priest had to be anachronistic in character. If, nevertheless, one reads in Deut. 10: 6 that after Aaron's death at Moserah 'Eleazar his son officiated as priest in his stead', this can be taken as decisive proof of how

[16] The absence of Nadab and Abihu from the preceding passage of J (Exod. 19: 20–5) might be explained, for instance, by features of elliptic style, which omits some details in one place to supply them later on in the continuation of the story (some additional remarks on this point may be found in my book תקופות ומוסדות במקרא (Tel-Aviv, 1972), pp. 147–8).

the non-priestly sources conceive of Aaron's image, which is fundamentally not unlike the way P conceives of it. Even if it were claimed that Deut. 10: 6 is part of D, not a remnant of E, this would scarcely reduce the force of the evidence. Aaron, Eleazar, and even Phinehas are further mentioned in Josh. 24: 33, a verse which has no connection with P; it sets the seal upon the pre-Deuteronomistic narrative which starts at the beginning of that same chapter.[17]

8

All the sources agree, therefore, that from the very beginning the priesthood was given to the tribe of Levi alone, but they differ as to how it functions within the tribe. According to the priestly school (P and Ezek. 40–8) the priesthood is restricted to one family of the tribe: according to P to the sons of Aaron, according to Ezekiel's code to the sons of Zadok. All the rest of the tribe are subordinate to the priests and cannot ever become priests, even if they are present at the place of worship; yet, a certain sanctity—below that of priests and above that of Israelites—is delegated to them (above, sect. 2). According to the non-priestly sources the priesthood is vested in the entire tribe and can be realized at one of the temples: according to J and E in one of the existing temples, according to D in the one chosen temple. Provincial Levites who did not attain the priesthood are devoid of any degree of sanctity and in this respect do not differ from ordinary Israelites.

The sources are also at variance in their attitude to the solitary altars, those which are not connected with temples. J and E acknowledge the legitimacy of such altars, where any Israelite can make his sacrifices (which created the impression that Israelites officiated in the priesthood). D demands the abolition of those altars, along with all cult institutions apart from the chosen place. P, which is

[17] This narrative, which the Deuteronomistic edition has touched upon but lightly (the ending is not theirs), belongs to E; cf. commentaries (especially G. A. Cooke, *Joshua* (CBSC, 1918), pp. 223–4). Incidentally, the statement made in this verse, that Phinehas was given an inheritance of his own in the hill country of Ephraim, a place which bore his name (Gibeah of Phinehas) and where Eleazar and apparently Phinehas himself were buried, is highly significant; it displays a unique tradition which claims that there was a special connection between the Aaronic clan and this part of the country. The relation of the Aaronites to the southern part of the country, particularly to the territories of Judah and Benjamin and as reflected mainly in P's tradition, will be described in the following chapter.

also based on the idea of the centralization of the cult (but in a different manner from D), grants these altars no right of existence in his utopian accounts of the desert period. Accordingly, only on this point does D dissent from J and E and is linked to P.

Nevertheless, *in practice*, one can discern considerable agreement between all the sources, for not only do they all admit that no priesthood exists outside the tribe of Levi, but they all acknowledge that, practically speaking, the priesthood is carried out only by certain families of that tribe—by that of Aaron, or of Zadok, or by families who have attained the priesthood at the temples. Moreover, since according to P the Aaronites were given thirteen cities out of the total of forty-eight which were allotted to the whole tribe of Levi (Josh. 21: 1–40), it becomes obvious that the concept 'sons of Aaron' comprises a sizable group of the tribe, and was therefore likely to constitute a significant number of priests. The numerical size of such a group might well equal all that part of the tribe of Levi which according to J and E graduated to priesthood in the temples.

THE HISTORICAL ASPECT

9

Let us now turn to the historical reality and try to draw its main outlines. We will then be in a position to attempt to reconcile it with the various interpretations of the prerogative of priesthood as given in the sources.

According to the theory established by classical Old Testament scholarship, a theory which still has considerable influence today, the priesthood in Israel had its beginnings with the establishment of the monarchy.[18] The early, pre-monarchic priesthood was mantic rather than cultic, and to some extent also apotropaic in nature. That priesthood is felt to be represented in the Old Testament by the figures of Eli in Shiloh and Ahimelech in Nob. The

[18] The foremost proponent of this theory was Wellhausen (*PGI*, 115–45). Alongside him mention may be made of the following: A. Kuenen, *Gesammelte Abhandlungen zur biblischen Wissenschaft* (Freiburg, 1894), pp. 465–500 (in a criticism of earlier studies, in particular that of W. W. Baudissin); W. Robertson Smith and A. Bertholet, *EB* iii, 3837–47; I. Benzinger, *Hebräische Archäologie*[3] (Leipzig, 1927), pp. 341–58; R. Kittel, *Geschichte des Volkes Israel*, i[3] (Gotha, 1916), pp. 340–9. Pedersen (*ILC* iii–iv, 150–97) was in fact of the same opinion though he was also influenced by Meyer (see below).

ancient priests acted as doorkeepers at the sanctuaries and their task was to guard the divine images from harm, somewhat in the manner of the Arabic *ḥājib* and *sādin* of the pre-Islamic period. It is also believed that they were engaged in divination, as was the ancient Arab *kāhin*, while the cultic functions could be performed by anyone as described in J and E who, as the theory assumes, do not acknowledge the separate existence of priesthood (above, sect. 4).

With the establishment of the monarchy public life became more pompous and cultic functions more onerous, so that the kings were obliged to appoint special officials to deal with the large numbers of sacrifices. This marked the supposed beginning of the priesthood in Israel as a cultic class. The early priests were considered to be the king's servants. They officiated at his sanctuary and the whole of their authority derived from him. They were not necessarily of the tribe of Levi. Thus we find that David's sons were priests (2 Sam. 8: 18), Ira the Jairite was also David's priest (ibid. 20: 26), and it is taken for granted that Zadok did not belong to the tribe of Levi either. It has even been suggested that Zadok was of the Jebusite priesthood of Jerusalem and was attached to David's court after the city had been conquered.[19] In Solomon's entourage we find Zabud the son of Nathan 'priest and king's friend' (1 Kgs. 4: 5), while Jeroboam selected his priests from amongst the whole people (ibid. 12: 31; 13: 33). The descendants of the royally appointed priests clung to their office, arguing their traditional right to the priesthood, and in the course of time became an established class.

The destruction of Samaria put an end to the northern sanctuaries. Later on Josiah's cult reform abolished all cult places outside Jerusalem, and all the priests from the cities of Judah were brought to Jerusalem. They were not allowed to come up to the altar (2 Kgs. 23: 8–9) and this marked the beginning of the separation of the priestly family from the 'tribe' in general. According to the theory, the First Temple priesthood had no connection with the

[19] This is the suggestion made by H. H. Rowley, 'Zadok and Nehushtan', *JBL* 58 (1939), 123–32. S. Mowinckel and A. Bentzen preceded him somewhat in this opinion, as Rowley indicates, and a number of scholars (such as Ch. E. Hauer, Jr., 'Who was Zadok?', *JBL* 82 (1963), 89–94; S. Terrien, 'The Omphalos Myth and Hebrew Religion', *VT* 20 (1970), 320–1) followed him. The suggestion has been acutely refuted by F. M. Cross, *Canaanite Myth and Hebrew Epic* (Cambridge, Mass., 1973), pp. 209–11.

tribe of Levi. In former times this had been a secular tribe of warriors, which eventually disappeared from the scene. Equating the professional priestly class with the tribe of Levi was an innovation, first made by D and repeated with emphasis in Ezekiel's code and in P. Beyond the tribal fiction, the separation between priests and Levites became progressively more decisive. Following Ezekiel's demand, the priests brought to Jerusalem from the high-places were downgraded to the rank of Levites (Ezek. 44: 10–14). In P, the division between priests and Levites became an absolute principle and was pushed back in time to the revelation at Sinai, while the sons of Aaron replaced the sons of Zadok.

10

The above-mentioned theory has, as a whole, some questionable points, which groups of scholars have used to challenge it in their efforts to find alternative solutions to the historical problem of the Israelite priesthood.

On the one hand, there is scarcely any evidence for stating that the ancient Israelite priesthood was only mantic and apotropaic. It is difficult to show that there was any substantial difference between Eli and Ahimelech in Shiloh and Nob and the priests of the First Temple (though nobody would deny that in the course of time the character of the priesthood became more intricate and its duties increased). The analogy with the pre-Islamic priesthood can easily be disposed of, while the background of the ancient Near East clearly indicates that in its cultic form the institution is very ancient. This accounts for one of the motives which led some scholars to emphasize the antiquity of the Israelite priesthood and admit that its actual existence dates back to the period of the Judges.[20]

[20] Among those holding this view may be mentioned: R. Brinker, *The Influence of Sanctuaries in Early Israel* (Manchester, 1948), pp. 65–88; Th. J. Meek, *Hebrew Origins*[2] (New York, 1950), pp. 119–47 (a mixture of correct details and unfounded assumptions); and, in particular, Albright, *ARI*, 107–10. Kaufmann's view in this matter seems rather peculiar; yet he sharply and incisively rejected Wellhausen's theory of the history of the priesthood in Israel, as well as the hypothesis (see below) that the Levites were primarily an order (*THH*, i. 160–76). The argument in favour of the antiquity of the priesthood in Israel has found expression in recent monographs: A. H. J. Gunneweg, *Leviten und Priester* (Göttingen, 1965) and A. Cody, *A History of the Old Testament Priesthood* (Rome, 1969). The former, arguing for the antiquity of the Aaronites, but not of the Levitical tribe, tries to base his theory on an analysis of the traditions

On the other hand, if the tribe of Levi was as secular as any other Israelite tribe, one can ask what made D and P graft upon the priesthood of their time fictitious descent from this tribe, particularly as the tribe had already faded out of existence. It has been claimed that the priestly families wished to attach themselves to Moses, the founder of the belief in Yahweh,[21] but this argument is rather strained, as in the case of most of the known priestly families it has no foundation. Furthermore, it is invalid in face of the fact that the relatively late sources themselves hold that the priesthood was in no way linked to the descendants of Moses, but was given to the whole tribe (according to D) or restricted to a certain family and definitely forbidden to Moses' descendants (according to P and Ezekiel's code). This accounts for one of the motives which led scholars to admit that from the outset there was a certain sanctity in the status of the Levites, as the main disseminators of Yahwism, or that in one of their metamorphoses (at first, or at some later stage) they were not a tribe, but an order of professional cult functionaries.[22] However, the order hypothesis

rather than of the sources. One of the cornerstones of his study is his use of the concept of amphictyony and of G. von Rad's view of the Levites as the amphictyonic tradition bearers. Cody, on the other hand, though arguing for the early participation of members of the tribe of Levi in priestly functions, betrays, especially in the first part of his work, ostensibly Wellhausenian traits in some of his basic assumptions as well as in general outlook.

[21] This is Wellhausen's conjecture (*PGI*, 135–6), which has been repeated by many scholars; most recently, and with a somewhat individual slant, by Cross, op. cit., pp. 189–206.

[22] Of those holding this view we may mention E. Meyer, *Die Israeliten und ihre Nachbarstämme* (Halle, 1906), pp. 51–6, 82–9; and also the following: A. Menes, *Die vorexilischen Gesetze Israels* (Giessen, 1928), pp. 7–11; A. Causse, *Du groupe ethnique à la communauté religieuse* (Paris, 1937), pp. 67–8; M. Weber, *Ancient Judaism* (New York, 1952), pp. 170–4; E. Nielsen, *Shechem* (Copenhagen, 1955), pp. 264–83; idem, 'The Levites in Ancient Israel', *ASTI* 3 (1964), 16–27 (in *Shechem* Nielsen speaks, though, of Levitic priesthood connected mainly with the North, without committing himself to the order theory). Wellhausen's thought also tended in this direction, and he even sought to found an explanation of Deut. 33: 8–11 on the order theory (*PGI*, 128–30, 135–7; in the latter pages of the sixth edition of *PGI* a few sentences in which the order theory was expressed more clearly were omitted). In Wellhausen's view the blessing in Deut. 33: 8–11 refers to the priestly class in its professional form, which it achieved at the beginning of the Northern Kingdom, not to the tribe of Levi. The explanation, to which Meyer and others assented, that the priests (or the Levites) used to leave their families and hire themselves out for professional duties, hardly fits the simple meaning of the text. As we have already said (above, sect. 6) this text is only meant to describe what is related in Exod. 32: 25–9—as others have already suggested.

also seems far-fetched, for there is no solid support for it in the sources. The evidence deduced from the term *lawi'u*, *lawi'atu* mentioned in the Dedanite inscriptions of North Arabia (the *el-'ula* oasis), is rather weak[23] and cannot really bear the weight of this hypothesis.

One can further question the prevailing theory from the point of view of the supposed connection between the sons of Zadok and the Aaronites. If P came into being after Ezekiel demanded that cultic service be restricted to the Jerusalem priests and if P's view developed from this demand, one wonders how the Aaronites could have replaced the sons of Zadok, since according to P Aaron left two sons, Eleazar and Ithamar (Exod. 6: 23; Lev. 10: 1–2 *et al.*), both of whom were qualified for priesthood, whereas Zadok can be held to be a descendant of only one of them. In other words, according to P the priesthood family actually has two branches, one of which must of necessity exclude Zadok and his descendants. To overcome this difficulty it was suggested that after Ezekiel's time a number of non-Jerusalemite groups joined the priesthood, finally gaining recognition and claiming they were descended from Ithamar.[24] Yet it still remains unexplained how the latter were able to join the priesthood since, as the theory will have it, Josiah's reform and Ezekiel's demand served only to divide the Jerusalem priests from the rest of the Levites, the division becoming increasingly pronounced until in P it turned to an unshakable tenet. Nor must we forget that even Eleazar and Zadok are not exactly the same and a distance of many generations lies between them, so that if Aaron and Eleazar are put in Zadok's place, it could only mean that in P's own view the sons of Zadok do not cover the whole range of legitimate priesthood—even disregarding Ithamar's branch for the moment. It goes without saying that the Chronicler

[23] These inscriptions which date from the Persian period and after are in South Arabic. N. Rhodokanakis and H. Grimme were the first to consider the meaning of the concepts *lawi'u*, *lawi'atu* mentioned in them, and the latter suggested that the Levites were descendants of the *lawi'atu*. Albright sought to connect these terms with the Late Babylonian *lawûtânu*, *lamûtânu*, meaning apprentice, clerk (*ARI*, 204–5). On the supposed 'Levites' of the *el-'ula* oasis cf. also R. de Vaux, ' "Levites" minéens et lévites israélites', *Bible et Orient* (Paris, 1967), pp. 277–85; Cody, op. cit., pp. 30–2.

[24] Kuenen (op. cit. (note 18), pp. 488–91) already thought along these lines, following the criticism of previous scholars (especially of H. Oort). See further, e.g., G. A. Cooke, *Ezekiel* (ICC, 1936), pp. 482–3; Pedersen, *ILC* iii–iv. 186; W. Eichrodt, *Ezekiel* (OTL, 1970), p. 566.

was forced to accept P's view, since P had in the meantime become part of the canonized Pentateuch, which henceforward constituted the basic document of Jewish communal life. In the Chronicler's mirror Zadok could therefore be placed among Eleazar's descendants (1 Chron. 6: 35–8; 24: 3) while Abiathar became an offspring of Ithamar (ibid. 24: 1–6). But the idea of two sons remaining to Aaron after his older sons, Nadab and Abihu, had passed away was not in itself created in order to explain post-exilic conditions and in no way results from Ezekiel's demand. Suffice it to recall that the names Nadab, Abihu, Eleazar, and even Phinehas occur, in fact, in J and E (above, sect. 7), so that the relative antiquity of these concepts cannot be denied.

The inadequacies of the prevalent theory become no less evident when it is examined so far as it relates to the views of J and E. This theory bases its entire *raison d'être* on the conjecture that the Israelite priesthood had its beginnings in the royal administration, that originally every Israelite was entitled to offer up sacrifices, and that no special priestly class existed. It is assumed that this is the state of affairs which lies at the background of J and E. But we have already shown that according to both J and E the priesthood is taken to be restricted to the tribe of Levi and that all the Pentateuchal sources basically agree on this point (above, sects. 6, 8). If that is not enough, let us add that on this point J and E's view corresponds even with the historical reality—that same reality which, as we shall see immediately, is reflected in the pre-Deuteronomistic sources of the Former Prophets.

THE LEVITICAL PRIESTS IN HISTORICAL REALITY

11

In the Old Testament only a few of the Israelite priestly families are identified and their tribal genealogies traced. Nevertheless, fragmentary as our information is, we can reasonably assert that as a general rule the priestly families considered themselves as belonging to the tribe of Levi.

Eli, whose family officiated in Shiloh and Nob (1 Sam. 1–4; 14: 3; 21: 1–10; 22: 9, 11), is described as one whose father's house was chosen 'out of all the tribes of Israel' after the Lord had revealed himself to them, and this event took place as early as 'when they were in Egypt subject to the house of Pharaoh' (ibid. 2: 27–8). This is in accord with the story occurring in the Pentateuchal sources of Moses and Aaron who from amongst the tribes of Israel came in the name of the Lord to speak with Pharaoh.[25] The priests of the house of God in Dan traced their genealogy to a young Levite who had come there in the wake of the conquerors of the city (Judg. 18: 3–27), or to Jonathan the son of Gershom the son of Ma(n)asseh (ibid., v. 30).[26] If the suspended *nun* indicates that the reading *mōšeh* is the correct one here, then we are faced with a unique piece of evidence that one of the priestly families actually traced its ancestry to Moses. At the very least, it is obvious that this family too considered itself as belonging to the tribe of Levi.

It seems that even Zadok, the founder of the Jerusalemite

[25] We do not know exactly when, according to J, E, and D, Aaron was chosen for the priesthood, as only fragments of the J and E material have been preserved (as it has been remarked, the phrase 'your brother, the Levite' in Exod. 4:14 and likewise the mention of priests in the Sinai pericope are just anachronistic modes of speech), while D does not relate anything about this. At any rate, it is the assumption of these sources that the tribe of Levi was not appointed to the priesthood until after Aaron had been chosen: according to J the Levites were given the priesthood after demonstrating their zeal for Yahweh by force of arms (Exod. 32: 25–9); according to E (or D) apparently at Aaron's death at Moserah (see Deut. 10: 6–9), or, as seems much more plausible, under exactly the same circumstances as in J (that is, after the affair of the golden calf), since in Deut. 10 verse 8 refers back to verse 5, as has been noted by scholars; see, e.g., S. R. Driver, *Deuteronomy* (ICC, 1902), p. 121 (this point was already observed by B. de Spinoza in *Tractatus Theologico-Politicus*; see his *Opera*, edited by C. Gebhardt, iii (Heidelberg, 1925), p. 127). Likewise according to P Aaron and his house were chosen for the priesthood (Exod. 28–9; Lev. 8) before the Levites were appointed to their functions (Num. 3–4). However, Yahweh's revelation to Moses and Aaron took place while they were still 'in Egypt, subject to the house of Pharaoh', for they came to Pharaoh in the name of Yahweh (Exod. 5: 1). In 1 Sam. 2: 27–8, it is stated not that Eli's father's house was chosen for the priesthood in Egypt, but only that Yahweh revealed himself to them in Egypt—and afterwards, apparently after the Exodus, Eli's father's house was chosen 'out of all the tribes of Israel for me as priest'. It is clear that this passage is completely in accord with the spirit and the assumptions of the J and E narrative. See also below, p. 87.

[26] Verse 30 is clearly a doublet of v. 31. Inasmuch as the whole chapter deals with an anonymous Levite, the mention of the priest by name and genealogy in v. 30 seems sudden and entirely unexpected. It is probable, therefore, that this verse, and perhaps the fragment constituting vv. 29–30, came from a parallel story; cf. commentaries (however, I am not persuaded that the whole story consists of two strands, one supplementing the other, as J. Wellhausen, A. Kuenen, and others claimed, or that it consists of two independent strands, as K. Budde, K. Kautzsch, G. F. Moore, R. Kittel, and others thought; the presence of doublets due to textual accidents cannot be denied).

priesthood, belonged to the tribe of Levi. When, after Absalom's revolt, David's supporters prepare to move the ark from the city, it is carried by Zadok accompanied by a group of Levites—that is, Levites acting as priests (2 Sam. 15: 24). This gives the impression that Zadok is considered to be one of them, and there can be no justification for deleting the words וכל הלוים אתו, 'and all the Levites with him' from the text. Zadok appears in David's entourage unexpectedly and officiates in the priesthood together with Abiathar (ibid. 8: 17; 15: 24–9, 35; 20: 25) until in Solomon's time he alone is firmly established as priest (1 Kgs. 2: 35; cf. 1 Sam. 2: 35). We do not definitely know whence he came to David's court, but it seems likely that he originated from one of the Levitical families of Judah.[27] This can be substantiated by the fact that Ezekiel at least, using D's terminology, calls the sons of Zadok 'the priests the sons of Levi', 'the Levitical priests' (Ezek. 40: 46; 43: 19; 44: 15), which means that he clearly considered them to be descendants of that tribe.

We possess no evidence of the tribal affinity of the priests of Bethel, one of whom, Amaziah, is referred to by Amos (7: 10), yet it would be unfair to assume that they necessarily were non-Levites. In Micayehu's remote temple in the hill-country of Ephraim, the master of the house could authorize one of his sons to officiate in the priesthood, but even he prefers a Levite to undertake this function (Judg. 17: 5, 13).

12

We further find that as a rule only Levites carry the ark, the most outstanding temple appurtenance which, according to J, E, and D (and the non-priestly parts of the Former Prophets), may be removed from the house of God but must be returned to its place afterwards. According to these sources the ark-bearing Levites are performing a priestly task.[28]

[27] Cf. below, p. 88.

[28] Cf. above, sect. 5. But according to P, the ark must on no account be removed from the inner sanctum, and when the camp travels the whole tabernacle is carried, with the ark and all the other accessories; the bearers of the *tabernacle* are the Levites—the priests never do this (as will be explained in Chapters VIII and IX). The permissive viewpoint of J, E, and D, who allow the ark to be removed from the house of God, makes it possible for them to imagine the existence of the ark in the desert period (Num. 10: 33–6; 14: 44; Deut. 10: 1–5, 8), even though they themselves acknowledge that Israel had no temple at that time. The Israelite camp in the desert was also a war-camp (cf. Num. 10:

When the ark was taken from Shiloh to the battlefield near Ebenezer, Hophni and Phinehas, the sons of Eli (1 Sam. 4: 4, 11), whose tribal origin has already been discussed, accompanied it. When it was returned from the Philistine country to Beth-shemesh it was taken down from the cart and placed on the large stone by Levites—that is, Levites who were thus engaged in a priestly task (1 Sam. 6: 15). When David's supporters wished to take the ark out of the city it was carried by Zadok and 'all the Levites' (2 Sam. 15: 24). Similarly, it is said that Abiathar, Eli's descendant, 'bore the ark', that is to say, he used to be one of the ark-bearers in battles, before David (1 Kgs. 2: 26), and we see no reason to substitute 'ephod' for *'ᵃrôn 'ᵃdōnāy Yahweh*, 'the ark of the Lord God' in this verse. When the ark was in Saul's war-camp, Ahijah the priest, Eli's great grandson, was at its side (1 Sam. 14: 18); only here the LXX read 'ephod' instead of 'the ark of the Lord' and it is difficult to decide which reading is preferable. And when the ark was taken to the temple in Jerusalem and deposited in the inner sanctum, it was carried by priests (1 Kgs. 8: 3, 6, 10). To claim that in this instance the priests were from any tribe would be exceedingly arbitrary.

When the ark was at the hill of Kiriath-jearim, Eleazar the son of Abinadab was sanctified to guard it there (1 Sam. 7: 1). There is no evidence that this Abinadab and his son belonged to the tribe of Levi, and it seems that they did not. However, guarding the ark is not the same as carrying it on the shoulders, and when it is outside the temple it need not be guarded by priests. Priests, indeed, are not always available. Obed-edom the Gittite, at whose house the ark rested later (2 Sam. 6: 10–12), was not a Levite either.[29] When the ark was moved from Abinadab's house to that

35), and just as in contemporary conditions it was possible to bring the ark from the temple to the war-camp in an emergency (cf. 1 Sam. 4: 3–7), so too was it possible to describe the ark as being outside the temple in the camp of Israel in the desert. The perception of place and physical space turns here into a perception of time—the recognition that it is possible for the ark to be outside the space of the temple becomes a historical perception, so that the ark appears in a camp which is travelling to Canaan, in a time preceding the foundation of the temples.

[29] To be sure, the Chronicler made him a Levite, one of the gate-keepers (1 Chron. 15: 18, 24), but this is merely a retrospective combination, which cannot be taken uncritically. In just the same way the Chronicler makes Samuel a Levite (1 Chron. 6: 13, 18–23), again, out of dogmatic vindication, even though according to all that is said in the Book of Samuel this was certainly not his tribal affiliation (cf. below, pp. 307–8).

of Obed-edom it was carried on a cart, and this, again, is not the solemn, ceremonious way that priests bear it. Uzzah and his brother, the sons of Abinadab, drove the cart. This too is different from bearing the ark on the shoulders, like priests. When the oxen stumbled and Uzzah stretched out his hand and took hold of the ark, he was immediately killed. His brother was saved only because he had walked in front of the cart and did not need to touch the ark (ibid., vv. 3–7). All this is clear proof that Abinadab's family did not really belong to the priesthood, for otherwise they would have borne the ark like priests and would not have been affected by touching it. From Obed-edom's house to the city of David, however, the ark was carried in a different manner—not on a cart, but on the shoulders of men walking on foot. This time the text speaks of 'those who bore the ark' (ibid., v. 13), and though they are not identified, it can be assumed that, according to usual practice, they are taken to be priests. Here, too, it would be entirely arbitrary to claim that these bearers of the ark were not priests, or that they were priests but not as comprehended in these sources, that is, not of the tribe of Levi.

As regards the pre-Deuteronomistic sources which underlie the Former Prophets in general, one should remember that their non-technical, picturesque, and fluent narrative has little care for precise detail. In literary material of this type the narrator can blur certain aspects of the story, either because he chooses to omit them or because he does not consider them important. Thus the text of 1 Sam. 7: 1: 'And the men of Kiriath-jearim came and took up the ark of Yahweh and brought it to the house of Abinadab on the hill' certainly does not intend to explain how and with whose help the men of Kiriath-jearim carried the ark from Beth-shemesh to their city. The non-cautious reader might get the idea that the ark was taken by the townsfolk themselves, without the assistance of priests. However, it is extremely doubtful whether this is what the narrator really intended to imply.

13

As for David's sons and Ira the Jairite, of whom it is explicitly stated that they acted as priests (2 Sam. 8: 18; 20: 26), even though they were not of the tribe of Levi, all we can do is surmise that they acted as sacrificial priests, and that their task was to deal with the King's numerous offerings on the high-places and solitary altars—not necessarily in the temple. It is worth noting that David's ark-bearers were Zadok and Abiathar, the legitimate priests (ibid. 15: 24–9; 1 Kgs. 2: 26), and in the lists their names precede those of David's sons and of Ira (2 Sam. 8: 17; 20: 25). The same may be said of Zabud the son of Nathan, the 'priest and the King's friend', who is mentioned after Zadok in the list of high officials (1 Kgs. 4: 5). His function may have been simply to serve as 'the King's friend'.[30] If he served as a priest, he may have been employed for the many sacrifices at the high-places (cf. 1 Kgs. 3: 4), all the more so since the list in which he is mentioned precedes the building of the temple in Jerusalem. If, however, these instances were indeed deviations from the norm, they were probably restricted and did not become a widespread custom. Clear evidence of this is the fact that, as we have already seen, even J and E do not permit someone from outside the tribe of Levi to intrude into the circle of priesthood.

14

The general conclusion emerging from our discussion is, then, that the families who officiated in the early Israelite temples considered themselves to be of the tribe of Levi. This was the accepted norm and even Zadok's family which was granted priestly office in the temple of Jerusalem could not diverge from the rule. Had there been something out of the ordinary in that 'faithful priest' who, along with his house, deserved to 'walk before the anointed of the Lord for ever' (1 Sam. 2: 35), we might well have expected to find a different kind of response in the sources.

How did it come about that from remote times the privilege of priesthood in the houses of God was allotted to the Levitical families? We can only guess at an answer. It is reasonable to suppose that the tribe of Levi—from which Moses, the first messenger of Yahwism, came—was the first to be seized by the new faith and was active in spreading the message among the tribes. It is a fact that within the framework of Yahwism this tribe is already regarded in all the sources as dedicated to the

[30] On the title *rē'eh hammelek̲* see 2 Sam. 15: 37; 16: 16 (also 15: 32 according to LXX). On the nature of the title and its possible Egyptian parallel, see R. de Vaux, 'Titres et fonctionnaires égyptiens à la cour de David et de Salomon', *RB* 48 (1939), 403–5; A. van Selms, 'The Origin of the Title "The King's Friend" ', *JNES* 16 (1957), 118–32.

priesthood since Moses' time. Hence, according to biblical tradition, and probably also according to historical reality, no secular tribe of Levi actually existed except in the stage which preceded the emergence of the Mosaic faith. This limitation pushes us into a prehistory of which no real traces are left. The only seeming piece of evidence of a secular tribe of Levi is the story of the war in Shechem, related in Gen. 34 and referred to in Jacob's blessing (Gen. 49: 5–7). However, this story deals with Simeon and Levi in person, the sons of Jacob, not with the tribes, and it is extremely doubtful whether the story has any real historical nucleus.[31] True, Jacob's blessing of Simeon and Levi ends with a reference to the dispersion of these tribes within Israel, referring to it as a curse (ibid., v. 7); and it was indeed the fate of the Simeonites to be scattered among the tribe of Judah (Josh. 19: 1–9; cf. Judg. 1: 3), just as the Levites were scattered over all Israel. It is therefore not impossible that the dispersion of the tribe of Levi, which never gained an inheritance of its own, preceded its attachment to the priesthood and was linked to other historical circumstances. In any case, the fact that this tribe remained without an inheritance could only strengthen its connection with cult activities and make it dependent upon them.

15

Besides the occasional instances which emerge in connection with David and Solomon some other divergences from the norm may have occurred in the northern temples. It is told of Jeroboam the son of Nebat that he 'appointed priests from among all the people, who were not of the sons of Levi' (1 Kgs. 12: 31; 13: 33). Though this statement betrays an ideologically orientated author, it nevertheless testifies to a concrete reality. The two verses which mention those priests clearly state that they served Jeroboam as priests for the high-places only, and it can be contended that the high-places do not actually fall under the category of houses of God.[32] We must, however, think at least of the possibility that in the Deuteronomistic terminology the terms *bāmôt*, 'high-places' and especially *bêt bāmôt*, 'house of high-places' may include provincial temples, apart from the chosen place, just as the phrase *bêt bāmôt* is also used as a negative designation for heathen temples (2 Kgs.

[31] Cf. my discussion in 'Shechem Studies', *Zion* 38 (1973), 24–8, where the qualities of this story as a *nouvelle* are pointed out.

[32] This was the gist of my argument previously (*EM* v. 18).

17: 29, 32).[33] If that is the case, then there is evidence here of an illegitimate priesthood in northern temples—yet most probably not in all of them.[34]

Another hint of this kind may perhaps be found in the expression *hakkōhanîm halewiyyim*, 'the Levitical priests' which is characteristic of D. 'The Levitical priests' might express opposition to non-Levitical priests and allude to the existence of a priesthood which is considered unauthorized. If this is what the expression implies, it also seems to be aimed at phenomena which had a hold on the Northern Kingdom, and this could be taken as one of the traces of the northern elements incorporated in D.[35] Another allusion is to be found in the case of Micayehu's provincial temple in the hill-country of Ephraim, where, as the story has it, one of the sons of the master of the house officiated as priest at first (Judg. 17: 5). However, none of these deviations could possibly affect the general rule, and it was certainly the prevailing norm that found expression in all the Pentateuchal sources, even the earliest of them, including E, the source which even more than D reveals traces of northern origin.

[33] Cf. above, p. 25.

[34] The statement in 2 Chron. 11: 13–15 that after the split between Judah and Israel the priests and the Levites left the Northern Kingdom and came to Judah and Jerusalem, is only a *midrash* on 1 Kgs. 12: 31; 13: 33 (cf. W. Rudolph's commentary ad loc.). One cannot infer from this that all the members of the tribe of Levi there really deserted the Northern Kingdom.

[35] The northern elements of Deuteronomy have been dealt with, in various ways, by C. F. Burney, *The Book of Judges* (London, 1918), p. xlvi; A. C. Welch, *The Code of Deuteronomy—A New Theory of its Origin* (London, 1924); Alt, *KS*, ii. 250–75 (their historical conclusions are not pertinent to our discussion). See also K. Galling 'Das Königsgesetz im Deuteronomium', *ThLZ* 76 (1951), 133–8; G. von Rad, *Studies in Deuteronomy* (London, 1953), p. 68; W. O. E. Oesterley and Th. H. Robinson, *An Introduction to the Books of the OT* (London, 1953), pp. 50, 57; H. H. Rowley, *From Moses to Qumran* (London, 1963), p. 197; and most recently R. E. Clements, 'Deuteronomy and the Jerusalem Cult Tradition', *VT* 15 (1965), 300–1, 309–12; E. W. Nicholson, *Deuteronomy and Tradition* (Oxford, 1967), pp. 38, 58–78. Cf., however, below, p. 92.

V

THE AARONITES AND THE REST OF THE LEVITICAL TRIBE

I

THOUGH all the Pentateuchal sources agree as to the principle that the priesthood is confined to the tribe of Levi, they are nevertheless at variance on other important aspects implied in this principle. These can be epitomized in two questions. Firstly, what part of the tribe of Levi actually held priestly office—was it in only those families who could claim descent from Aaron, or must the extent of the group be defined differently? Secondly, was it impossible for all those Levites outside the priestly group to graduate to priestly functions and could they merely expect a status subordinate to the priests (as P assumes)—or were the gates to the priesthood open to them too, and in order to enter all they had to do was to come to one of the temples (as J, E, and D assume)?

We shall now try to answer these two questions. First, let us deal with the extent of the priestly group.

THE AARONIC GROUP—ITS RANGE AND POSITION

2

Against the background of the tabernacle and the camp, as they moved from Egypt to Canaan, only a few priests appear in P's account: Aaron and his four sons—Nadab and Abihu, who were consumed by fire before the Lord (Lev. 10: 1–2), and Eleazar and Ithamar, the two younger, who remained and continued to serve as priests (Num. 3: 4 *et al.*). If we add the sons of the third generation, who presumably might officiate during Aaron's lifetime—one of these, Phinehas the son of Eleazar, is mentioned by name (Exod. 6: 25; Num. 25: 7–13 *et al.*)—the number of priests may increase a little, but is still very small. Yet, in the list of the priestly and Levitical cities P allocates thirteen cities to the sons of Aaron: nine in the territory of Judah and Simeon and four in that of Benjamin (Josh. 21: 9–12). These would contain a considerable number of people, in fact a sizable part of the tribe as a whole, for all the remaining Kohathites are given but ten cities (ibid., vv. 20–6) and all the Levitical families apart from the Aaronites but thirty-five cities (ibid., vv. 20–40). There should be no doubt that this list reflects a certain historical reality which existed some time before P came into being (and the traits of which will be described further, in the next chapter). The priestly writers had to imagine the priests officiating in the idealized tabernacle as a single, tiny family, because tradition postulated that during the wandering from Egypt to Canaan it was Aaron, the father of the priests, who had officiated, that there had been only one temple in existence and that the priests around Aaron could only have been his sons and grandsons. Though the writers of P demanded the centralization of the cult (and described centralization as one tabernacle moving along with the camp from Sinai to Canaan), they did not intend to deprive the priests of their rights—neither did they deny that all the Aaronites possessed the priesthood, nor did they try to confine it to just a section of them. According to their own admission, then, this group was at that time spread over thirteen cities (cf. Map 2).

These thirteen cities are all the cities assigned by P to the Levites of the territories of Judah (with Simeon) and Benjamin. Outside these areas not a single city is allocated to the Aaronites. Furthermore, the Aaronites and the non-priestly Levites do not even have one city in common. This means that the dividing line between the Aaronites and the rest of the tribe of Levi is taken by P to be the line which separates the southern from the northern tribes. All the Levites scattered over the territories of Judah and Benjamin are held to be true, faultless priests—all the Levites scattered among the northern tribes are merely Levites, without either the right to the priesthood or the possibility of attaining it.[1]

[1] In P's genealogical lists of the tribe of Levi we find the Libnite and Hebronite families (Exod. 6: 17–18; Num. 3: 18–19, 21, 27; 26: 58), who are named after Hebron and Libnah, priestly cities in Judah. We also find the Korahite family there, as well as Korah himself, the leader of the rebels against Moses and Aaron (Exod. 6: 21, 24; Num. 16: 1, 5 *et al.*; 26: 11, 58), where Korah may well be an Edomite name (Gen. 36: 5, 14, 16, 18), perhaps even the name of a Judean family (1 Chron. 2: 43). On this point see: J. Wellhausen, *Die Composition des Hexateuchs*[4] (Berlin, 1963), p. 182; also commentaries on Numbers, and K. Möhlenbrink, 'Die levitischen Überlieferungen des AT', *ZAW* 52 (1934), 193–7. If these details are significant and not mere coincidences, they allude at best to the *original* provenances of these families. Appellations such as these always indicate the city of origin, not the city in which a person now resides. And it is obvious that in P at least these families are already outside the Aaronic group and are not of the priesthood.

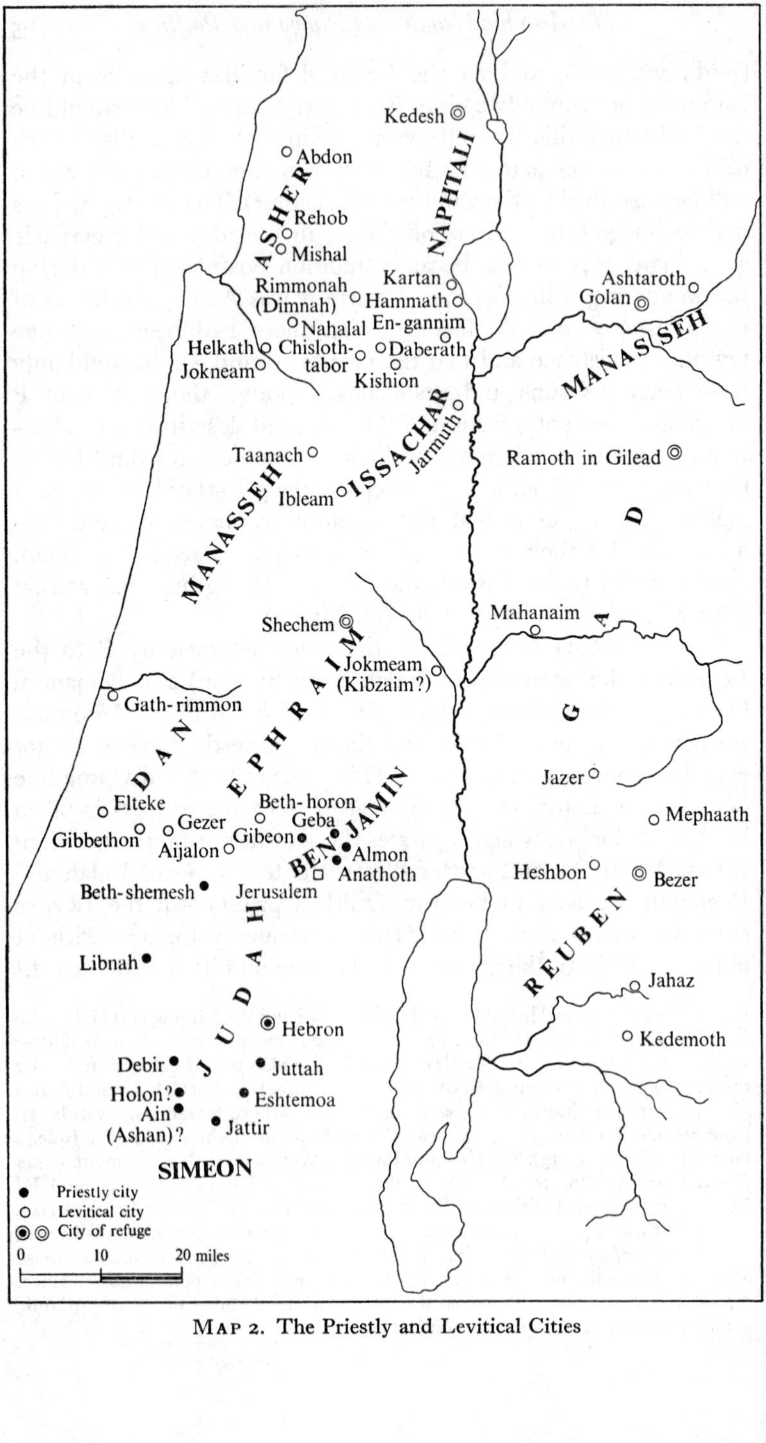

MAP 2. The Priestly and Levitical Cities

Needless to say, this interpretation is 'southern' in its viewpoint, for with the absolute separation between the two sections of the tribe of Levi, it gives an obvious preference to the members of the tribe living in the south. The northern Levites are allowed, at most, to reach the status of attendants to the priests.

3

Now despite the strict and dogmatic character of the priestly conception it is not impossible that it had some basis in reality. In the previous chapter we noted that the evidence which has come down to us concerning the tribal identity of the priestly families which were officiating in temples is sparse and fragmentary; yet, we can add, not one piece of this evidence contradicts the assumption that, in practice, sovereignty over the priesthood was really allotted to the priests of Judah and Benjamin.

Eli's family, which officiated at the houses of God at Shiloh and Nob and whose sons were among the ark-bearers, had a field in Anathoth (1 Kgs. 2: 26), whereas according to P Anathoth was one of the priestly cities (Josh. 21: 18).[2] The descent of Eli's family from Aaron seems to be indicated in the story itself when it speaks of the Lord's revelation to Eli's father's house and the latter's being chosen 'out of all the tribes of Israel' (1 Sam. 2: 27–8). This does not refer to the choice of a tribe, but to the more restricted choice of a father's house, *bêt 'āḇ*, i.e. a family circle, which was elevated above all the tribes. This is, no doubt, how the outsider would express in his narrative, non-technical manner how the priestly clan was chosen from all the other tribes, without even mentioning either the name of Aaron or the fact that he belonged to the tribe of Levi. Scholars have also observed that we find the name Phinehas in the families both of Aaron and Eli, and the name of Hophni, which equally bears an Egyptian flavour, in that of Eli. What is more, even according to P itself, the descendants of Aaron officiated at Shiloh, for it was there that the tabernacle was finally set up (Josh. 18: 1–10; 19: 51; 21: 1–3; 22: 9–12).[3]

[2] It is therefore most probable that Jeremiah, who was one of the priests at Anathoth (Jer. 1: 1), and whose family owned lands there (Jer. 32: 7–12; cf. 37: 12), was a descendant of the House of Eli. He is the only one of the prophets to mention Shiloh (Jer. 7: 12, 14; 26: 6, 9)—the place where his ancestors served as priests.

[3] Cf. below, pp. 198–9.

Similarly, it has been already stated that there is no reason to doubt that Zadok belonged to the tribe of Levi. Here one should add that, in a way, it is unlikely that this priest could turn up in David's retinue from the northern sections of Israel. It seems much more plausible that he originated from the Levites of Judah, and it is not impossible that he had come with David from Hebron, David's former capital city (2 Sam. 2: 4; 5: 1–3), which, according to P, was also a priestly city (Josh. 21: 11, 13).[4]

Again, in 1 Sam. 6: 15 it is remarked that there were Levites in Beth-shemesh who, in their capacity as priests, took the ark down from the cart and placed it on the big stone. Yet, in P's account Beth-shemesh too is listed as one of the priestly cities of Judah (Josh. 21: 16). Furthermore, the young Levite who according to the story became the father of the priests at the temple in Dan, came from Judah. Only his origin was from Bethlehem, which is not counted among the priestly cities. One should not be surprised, therefore, when one finds the text stating of the young man that when he was in Bethlehem he 'sojourned there', *gār šām* (Judg. 17: 7), that is to say, he was a *gēr*, 'sojourner' in a city where there were no local Levites. When he left Bethlehem he also sought 'to sojourn where he could find a place', לגור באשר ימצא (ibid., vv. 8–9), i.e. to live as a *gēr* wherever he happened to chance. Nevertheless, one can sense even in this story that Judah was held to be the place of origin for 'first quality' Levites. Here, so to speak, was the breeding ground for priests particularly suited for their task, so much so that even the priests of the distant Dan temple traced their descent to a Levitical priest who had come from Judah.

Moreover, in Chapter IV it has been sufficiently demonstrated that the authors of J and E, and indeed of D, are acquainted with Aaron's name and are well aware of his priesthood. Hence, according to their view, too, Aaron's family must be the family (or if preferred, one of the families) of the tribe of Levi where the prerogative of priesthood is realized. However, the non-priestly sources have not preserved any information as to whither Aaron's family was scattered, while P gives precise and detailed

[4] Albright (*ARI*, 110), in his own way, similarly expressed the view that there is no adequate reason why Zadok should not have been considered an Aaronite. Cf. also, most recently, F. M. Cross, *Canaanite Myth and Hebrew Epic* (Cambridge, Mass., 1973), pp. 207–15, who postulates, for still other reasons, that Zadok was an Aaronite.

information on this matter. One must not ignore what is clearly stated and make deductions from what is obscure. The explicit ought to complement the unexpressed, so that we are certainly entitled to hold that in this matter there is no real difference between the assumptions of the Pentateuchal sources. That is to say, even J, E, and D would have acknowledged that Aaron's descendants were mainly represented by the Levites who dwelt among the southern tribes (cf. Chapter IV, sect. 7).

4

However, the fundamental disagreement still remains, namely, that unlike P neither J and E nor D deny any Levite, even if he is not able to boast of an Aaronic pedigree, the right to become a priest whenever he wishes. What, then, is the actual difference between them? Since the non-priestly sources, too, would concede that the priesthood is already being practised among Aaron's descendants, it simply stands to reason that, in this respect, their real point is to side with the Levites who are not considered to be descendants of Aaron. J, E, and D claim that the 'other' Levites too have the right to officiate in the priesthood. Their view is that no fore-ordained ruling exists which states that the non-Aaronite Levites should be perpetuated in a less-than-priestly status, destined to serve at the most as second-rate quasi-cultic attendants.

Indeed, this seems to be the case, for the tension between the Aaronites and the rest of the tribe of Levi is clearly evident even in P itself, where, after the characteristic priestly manner, it takes the form of a cultic legend. P is able to relate that as early as the desert period Korah and his company complained to Moses and Aaron and asked that the priesthood be given to them too. But in the test of the incense, which was conducted in the presence of the entire congregation, the chosen of Yahweh were clearly identified: Korah and his band were consumed by fire (Num. 16: 1–22, 23–35 [fragmentarily]). Korah was a descendant of Kohath (ibid., v. 1) and according to P's own view—as shown in the list of Levitical cities—those of Kohath's descendants who did not belong to Aaron's group were living in the Northern Kingdom, among the tribes of Ephraim, Dan, and in the western half of Manasseh (Josh. 21: 20–6). P furthermore recounts that after the downfall of Korah and his company there was an additional test, which culminated in Aaron's rod sprouting—alone of all the rods of the tribes' princes—and this proved not only that Levi was sanctified and thus set apart from the other tribes, but that in the priesthood Aaron was the sole representative of this tribe (Num. 17: 16–24).[5] In complete contrast to this, J and E are able to relate that Moses ordained 'all the sons of Levi' to the priesthood (Exod. 32: 25–9) and they describe the entire tribe of Levi as a tribe of priests (Deut. 10: 8–9; 33: 8–10).[6] It is therefore indubitable that these sources are not prepared to admit that the priesthood is the prerogative of Aaron's family alone. At the same time, they do not deny Aaron's right to the priesthood and have no intention whatsoever of depriving him of it.

Thus, as regards the prerogative of priesthood Aaron's family enjoys a position of greater weight and prestige than all the rest of the tribe of Levi. From P who demands that the priesthood be restricted to this family alone, to J and E (and D) who demand the extension of the priesthood in theory and practice to the entire tribe of Levi, the priestly character of the Aaronic clan remains unchallenged. It appears that the most ancient and authentic embodiment of priesthood was believed to exist among the Levites of Judah and Benjamin and no one cast any doubt on their sovereignty over this role. The only argument concerned the Levites of the northern tribes.

5

Both J and E certainly acknowledge the right of Aaron's family to the priesthood, but only in E do we notice the propensity to find fault with Aaron, and here too it takes the form of a cultic legend. This tendency is expressed in the story of the golden calf (Exod. 32) which, in my judgement, belongs to E, except for a J fragment inserted into it (ibid., vv. 25–9).

Scholars have put considerable effort into determining the concrete, historical circumstances which form the background to this

[5] In P's story of Korah is to be found also the motif of the rebellion of the people against Yahweh and his representatives, Moses and Aaron—a motif which recurs in all the sources (cf. on this matter my remarks in *Tarbiz* 40 (1971), 120–1). I do not believe that it is possible to distinguish two priestly strands in this story as a whole, though a certain amount of verbosity and ellipsis is of course evident here.

[6] Cf. above, pp. 66–8.

story, but it cannot be denied that there are northern elements in it, for the very appearance of a calf as a central cult symbol directs us towards the temples of Bethel and Dan. The significant points of contact between this story and the description of the setting-up of the calves by Jeroboam have also been recognized. In both instances the ceremony commences with the proclamation: 'These are [Behold] your gods, O Israel, who brought you up out of the land of Egypt' (Exod. 32: 4; 1 Kgs. 12: 28), and both Aaron and Jeroboam had sons called Nadab and Abihu-Abijah (cf. 1 Kgs. 14: 1, 20). One might add that in both cases the two sons died before their time, though Aaron's sons were killed simultaneously and in their father's lifetime (Lev. 10: 1–2), whereas Jeroboam's sons met death separately and in different ways, and only one of them died in his father's lifetime (1 Kgs. 14: 12, 17; 15: 27–8). The northern background to E's story of the golden calf accords well with several of the characteristic features of this source in general, whose northern elements were noticed by scholars long ago.[7] Inasmuch as together with its northern background this story reveals a decidedly negative attitude to the cult of the calves, it seems to express the view of pious circles devoted to Yahwism who were not pleased with the custom which characterized the cultic centres of their own country. Though this custom acquired permanence in the king's temples and was not abolished until the fall of Samaria, it transpires that there were circles in that kingdom who thought differently, whose views were closer to those ingrained among the southern tribes. A number of indications discernible in E tend to attest that these were mainly prophetic circles.

Now the story of the golden calf intends to condemn Aaron, who according to explicit descriptions in P was considered the father of that part of the tribe of Levi which dwelt within the boundaries of Judah and Benjamin. The story does not in itself demand Aaron's removal from the priesthood, but it does not refrain from discrediting his figure. Here too one can observe the contrast between the outlooks of E and P and sense how northern E is in his viewpoint. For not only will E not recognize any categorical differentiation between the two parts of the tribe of Levi (and here J is in agreement), but he is prepared to transfer

[7] See, e.g., O. Procksch, *Das nordhebräische Sagenbuch—Die Elohimquelle* (Leipzig, 1906), pp. 175–84.

the blame for the intolerable cult, which found a home in the northern temples, on to the father of the southern Levites himself. Such a transfer could not have occurred in southern circles, where no calf cult existed; and it is very doubtful whether someone there would have intended to stain the local priesthood in this way, certainly not by a cultic deed perpetrated far away (at Bethel and Dan). But northern circles may well have harboured a less than cordial attitude towards the Levites of Judah and Benjamin, which was also incorporated in D. It may be, however, that E's (and D's) criticism of Aaron was simply directed towards the priestly families of Bethel and Dan, as both these families were considered southern, that is, Aaronic, in origin (the southern provenance of the priests of Dan is indeed explicitly pointed out in the Bible; cf. above, sect. 3). In D, the attitude towards Aaron might also be added to the traces of northern elements discernible in the source as a whole, which have already been pointed out by scholars in other connections.[8] To my mind, all this is connected with the simple fact that E alone (without J) was lying before the writers of D (and in a somewhat fuller form than as it exists in the canonized Pentateuch), and it was from E that the writers of D absorbed a good deal[9]—including the view that the right of priesthood was reserved to the whole tribe of Levi equally, and the narrative of the golden calf itself (Deut. 9: 12–28) together with censure of Aaron in this context (ibid., v. 20).

THE NON-PRIESTLY LEVITES IN PRE-EXILIC TIMES

6

Somewhat more difficult is the problem of those Levites who did not attain priesthood. Were they subordinate to the Aaronites and did they act as a kind of intermediaries between the priests and the laity, as P describes them, or were they able to become priests in the full sense, as the other Pentateuchal sources assume?

[8] Cf. above, p. 83, n. 35.

[9] The literary and ideological affinities between E and D are fully acknowledged in Pentateuchal criticism. My contention goes a step further, in that I consider only E to be the father-source of D in the sense that the authors of the latter were unequivocally dependent on the former. For the present one may consult my observations in תקופות ומוסדות במקרא (Tel-Aviv, 1972), pp. י—א׳, 37–8; see also below, pp. 262, 334, 346.

The answer to this question certainly differed according to places and circumstances. It is extremely doubtful whether Levites who lived in the provinces and for whom no function was to be found in temples differed greatly from their neighbours, except in their class and economic position, which does not appear to have been accompanied by any particular prosperity. In any case, under these circumstances their 'sanctity' could find no expression, while subordination to Aaron's descendants, even according to P, was meaningless outside the confines of a temple. Certainly nothing was detracted from the priesthood of those Levites who managed to attain ministration in northern temples (in accordance with all the sources except P and including E and D with their northern elements) and in their case, too, one cannot talk of subordination to Aaron's sons, who actually were to be found among the southern tribes only. The problem of subordination becomes significant, then, only when it is applied to Levites from the northern tribes who found themselves at the temples of Judah and Benjamin, which, in any event, were few in number and where Aaron's descendants had the main claim to the priesthood. To be more precise: in actual fact, the problem really only exists with regard to those Levites from the northern tribes who found themselves at the temple in Jerusalem, since (as will be shown in Chapter X) P's tabernacle is an idealized retrojection of that temple, and the concrete place of P's growth, as a literary product, was that same temple. Thus, the problem of Levitical status, as specifically conceived by P, centres upon the Jerusalem temple, and it is here that we must find the solution to it.

At first sight, there is no evidence of the existence of a Levitical class as an intermediary between the priests and the common people, except for P's own descriptions (and Ezekiel's demands) on this point. The only type of temple functionaries mentioned by all the other Pentateuchal sources and by the Former and Latter Prophets are priests. In the First Temple, particularly towards the end of its existence, we find a certain gradation in the functions of the priesthood, but they all are referred to as priests: in addition to 'the high priest', *hakkōhēn haggādôl* (2 Kgs. 12: 11; 22: 4, 8 *et al.*), also called 'the chief priest', *kōhēn hār'ōš* (ibid. 25: 18; Jer. 52: 24; cf. 2 Chron. 19: 11; 24: 6, 11 *et al.*), sometimes just 'the priest', *hakkōhēn* (2 Kgs. 11: 9–18; 12: 3, 8, 10; 16: 10–16 *et al.*), we find there 'priests of the second order', *kōh^anê mišneh* (2 Kgs. 23: 4; 25: 18), just 'priests' (2 Kgs. 12: 5–9; 19: 2; Jer. 29: 25 *et al.*), and 'priests that keep the threshold', *šômᵉrê hassap̱* (2 Kgs. 12: 10; 22: 4; 23: 4 *et al.*). Also the *pᵉqîdîm*, 'officers', appointed in Jehoiada's time to preserve order in the temple courts (2 Kgs. 11: 18; Jer. 29: 26), were priests (cf. Jer. 20: 1–3; and below).

Moreover, Ezekiel explicitly demands that all the non-Jerusalemite priests be turned into Levites (Ezek. 44: 10–14), reserving the priesthood to Zadok's descendants alone (ibid., vv. 15–16).[10] This means that at least in his time no Levitical class existed and Ezekiel had to create it out of the provincial priesthood. On one occasion, he applies the term 'priests' to both groups: the descendants of Zadok are called 'the priests who keep the guard of the altar', while those not descended from Zadok, who are destined to become Levites, are called 'the priests who keep the guard of the house' (ibid. 40: 45–6). Thus, Ezekiel can create Levites only by down-grading real priests. Apart from P (and Ezekiel's code) there is no mention of a categorical division into a priesthood and a Levitical rank except in the Books of Ezra and Nehemiah (Ezra 2: 36–42; 3: 8; 8: 15, 33 *et al.*) and Chronicles (1 Chron. 5: 27—6: 66; 9: 2, 10–34 *et al.*). However, these are already stamped with the imprint of the Pentateuch, which in Ezra's time was compiled with the priestly sections included in it.

At the same time, I cannot concur with the prevailing notion that in this respect (or in any other respect) P is really rooted in post-exilic conditions. This is not only for the reason already stated, that the concept of Aaronites cannot be comprehended as an extension of the sons of Zadok.[11] It has already been emphasized that the lack of a basic correlation between P and the reality of the post-exilic period is actually spread throughout the whole of P's material.[12] At this point, special attention should be paid to the fact that (as will be shown below, sect. 14) P assumes that there are several times as many Levites as there are priests, whereas in the post-exilic times the Levites were relatively few in number. And yet, while it is hardly admissible to push P's date of composition from the closing stages of the First Temple period to as late as post-exilic times, the arguments against the existence of Levites in pre-exilic times—'Levites' as defined by P—are never-

[10] Cf. above, p. 59.

[11] See above, pp. 75–6.

[12] Cf. above, pp. 3–5.

theless indecisive and there is no need to leave these arguments without an answer.

7

Silence on the part of all the non-priestly sources need not necessarily be taken to mean that there were no Levites at the temple of Jerusalem. Those sources are not familiar enough with the mysteries of the temple and with the world of priesthood as such. They can view priestly organizational arrangements and secrets of ritual as from a distance only. Details are consequently omitted and dimensions blurred. This may merely indicate a lack of adequate knowledge on the part of outsiders. It is not impossible that when these sources speak of 'priests' they are including what P calls Levites—that is to say, men descended from the tribe of Levi and officiating at the temple, who are nevertheless denied right of access to the inner circle of cultic holiness. The other sources did not come to mention the specific status of the Levites, but P's authors might have been in a position to know that a descendant of the tribe of Levi hailing from the north would remain a mere Levite and would not be permitted to penetrate to real priestly functions. We lack positive and direct evidence as to the exact time during the existence of the First Temple in Jerusalem when these were the prevailing circumstances. However, there are good reasons for believing that this was the situation during the relatively latter stages of the temple's existence, particularly around the time of the destruction of the Northern Kingdom, which is about the time of Hezekiah's reign in Jerusalem (cf. Chapter VII, sect. 7).

In the absence of Levites Ezekiel was obliged to demand the demotion of former priests to the rank of Levites, but we must not forget that he lived at the end of the First Temple period, at a time of decline. The historical situation which served as a background to his visionary temple programme is that which came into being after Jehoiachin's deportation, which goes a long way towards a correct comprehension of his code. Jehoiachin's exile involved the removal of many thousands of the city's population, the bulk of the social elite of the Kingdom of Judah (2 Kgs. 24: 14–16), including many of the temple priests. One of these was Ezekiel himself, the son of Buzi (Ezek. 1: 2–3).[13] Thus, the temple

[13] An additional reference to the exile of priests with Jehoiachin can be found in Jer. 29: 1. Yet another allusion is the fact that after this exile there remained

lost many of its priests and this may have affected the lower ranks in particular, amounting almost to a complete removal of those whom P would have described as Levites. Consequently, Ezekiel had to fill their posts with priests who were not descendants of Zadok, since he denied 'aliens, uncircumcised in heart and flesh' access to the temple (44: 6–8).

One of the duties with which Ezekiel charges the Levites is to be 'servants of the temple'; in this he agrees totally with P.[14] Now interestingly enough, in this context the prophet describes the Levites as those who '*mᵉšārᵉtîm pᵉquddôt* [RSV: have oversight] at the gates of the temple, and serve in the temple' (Ezek. 44: 11). The term *pᵉquddôt* suggests the *pᵉqîdîm*, 'officers' first appointed by Jehoiada the priest in the days of King Jehoash, and whose duty it was to watch over, and keep order in, the temple courts and gates. Jehoiada was the first to appoint '*pᵉquddôt* over the house of the Lord' (2 Kgs. 11: 18) and later they recur in the Book of Jeremiah. The cells, *tā'îm* mentioned as set into Ezekiel's temple gates, six in each gate (Ezek. 40: 7–12, 21, 24, 29, 33, 36), are apparently intended to serve as posting stations for these same Levitical teams of *pᵉqîdîm*. This being one of their tasks, Ezekiel's Levites therefore hold the same position as the First Temple priests of the category of *pᵉqîdîm*. This enables us to infer that no priestly scribe of the originators of Ezekiel's school would have refrained, just as Ezekiel did not, from applying the name Levites to these low-ranking priests as they existed at the time.

On closer scrutiny we may even come to recognize that after Jehoiachin's exile those priest-*pᵉqîdîm*, who are perhaps one of the earlier forms of 'Levites' really disappeared from the temple courts. In Jehoiakim's days mention is made of one of them, Pashhur the son of Immer 'who was *pāqîd nāgîd* in the house of the Lord', that is, one of the supervisors over the *pᵉqîdîm*, who thought it his duty to beat Jeremiah and for twenty-four hours kept him 'in the stocks that were in the Upper Benjamin Gate, in the house of the Lord' (Jer. 20: 1–2). But after Jehoiachin's exile

in Jerusalem the chief priest, but one priest 'of the second order' and three 'keepers of the threshold' (2 Kgs. 25: 18; Jer. 52: 24), while formerly there had been several 'priests of the second order' (2 Kgs. 23: 4) and, seemingly, a larger number of 'the keepers of the threshold' (cf. 2 Kgs. 12: 10; 22: 4).

[14] Cf. above, p. 61.

Shemaiah the Nehelamite writes from Babylon to Zephaniah the son of Maaseiah, 'the priest of the second order' who remained to witness the destruction of Jerusalem (2 Kgs. 25: 18; Jer. 52: 24; cf. ibid. 21: 1; 37: 3), and reproaches him for allowing Jeremiah to utter his prophecies without putting the prophet 'in the stocks and in the collar' (Jer. 29: 25–7). Thus it seems that, at any rate, Zephaniah does not act as a *pāqîd* in the house of God and in this respect differs from Pashhur, the chief *pāqîd*.[15] If this does not in itself indicate the decrease or the disappearance of the priest-*p^eqîdîm* from the temple courts, let us simply reiterate the fact that the priests were deported along with Jehoiachin and that consequently the temple in Jerusalem was deprived of many of its priests. Under such circumstances it is quite possible that the low-ranking priesthood, which in the internal, professional terminology of the priestly school would have been called Levites, faded away. Consequently, Ezekiel had to demand that their places be taken by other priests.

8

On the face of it, one could perhaps supply positive, and virtually concrete evidence, and that from the pre-Deuteronomistic sources of the Former Prophets themselves, for the existence in the

[15] The language of the text addressed to Zephaniah is far from smooth: 'The Lord has made you priest instead of Jehoiada the priest, that there should be officers, *p^eqîdîm* in the house of the Lord for every man that is mad and makes himself a prophet' (Jer. 29: 26). The LXX read: 'To be an officer, *pāqîd* in the house of the Lord', which is preferable, but the passage is still difficult since Zephaniah and even Jehoiada were not *p^eqîdîm*, though they were priests. On the other hand, Irijah the son of Shelemiah, son of Hananiah, who seized Jeremiah at the Benjamin Gate (Jer. 37: 13–14), was not of the priests, though he is called *ba'al p^eqîdût* (RSV: 'a sentry'; NEB: 'officer of the guard'). The Benjamin Gate, which was in the outer city-wall (cf. Jer. 38: 7, 10; Zach. 14: 10) should not be confused with the *Upper* Benjamin Gate which was in the wall of the temple court and contained the stocks (Jer. 20: 2). It seems that on this side the wall of the temple court and the wall of the city ran parallel, and from the wall of the temple court northward the mount began to slope, the two gates facing each other, so that the higher of them was called the Upper Benjamin Gate. At the Upper Benjamin Gate *pāqîd* of the priesthood deals with Jeremiah, while at the (outer) Benjamin Gate Jeremiah is taken by a secular *pāqîd*, who suspects him of intending to join the Chaldeans and brings him to the princes (Jer. 37: 13–14). It goes without saying that the term *pāqîd* also had a secular, civilian use, outside the temple (Gen. 41: 34; Judg. 9: 28; 2 Kgs. 25: 19 *et al.*), as did the terms *p^equddāh* (Isa. 60: 17) and *p^equddôt* (Ezek. 9: 1). In Jer. 52: 11 *bêt happ^equddôt* is used as a name for Zedekiah's prison in Babylon. For the various connotations of the root *pqd*, in verbal and nominal forms, the dictionaries may be consulted.

Jerusalem temple of low-ranking 'priests', that is, Levites in P's parlance. This seems to be expressed in the prophecy of doom on Eli and his house (1 Sam. 2: 27–36), which contains a number of threats some of which portray a reduced and impoverished quasi-priesthood.

As the narrative has it, the man of God announced to Eli: 'Behold, the days come, when I will cut off your arm, and the arm of your father's house' (1 Sam. 2: 31), that is to say, it had been decreed that this family should be deprived of its rank and diminished in stature. Further on he tells Eli: 'Yet I will not cut off any man of you from my altar, to make your eyes [read with LXX: his eyes] to fail, and your heart [his heart] to grieve . . .' (ibid., v. 33), implying that though Eli's descendants will be deprived of their priesthood, they will nevertheless be cleaving to the altar in distress.[16] As the circumstances suggest, the view that the prophecy concerning Eli is aimed at the period following Abiathar's deposition appears more plausible than the view that the prophecy is meant to apply to Abiathar himself.[17] Abiathar did not become subordinate to Zadok and the situation described in this prophecy does not fit him.[18] Apparently this was the position of Abiathar's descendants who, although their father had been dismissed from the priesthood, retained a certain connection with the temple and continued to seek their livelihood there. This also agrees

[16] Incidentally, it therefore transpires that the passage in 1 Kgs. 2: 26–7 concerning Abiathar who was 'expelled from being priest to the Lord' and went to Anathoth, is not exactly a fulfilment of the prophecy made to Eli in the passage of 1 Sam. 2: 27–36, since that prophecy did not imply that the family would be removed from the altar altogether. In fact, literary analysis tends to show, on entirely different grounds, that there is no unity of authorship between the first chapters of the Book of Samuel (1 Sam. 1–8, which is a continuous literary piece, even though it contains stories relating to different periods) and of the Book of Kings (1 Kgs. 1–2, which is the continuation of 2 Sam. 9–20). These are products of different sources. But the Deuteronomistic redactor was able to link up the two passages by the remark: 'That the word of Yahweh might be fulfilled, which he had spoken concerning the house of Eli in Shiloh' (1 Kgs. 2: 27).

[17] H. W. Hertzberg is among those holding the first view (*I & II Samuel* (OTL, 1964), pp. 38–9; in an allusion). S. R. Driver held the second view (*Notes on . . . the Books of Samuel*² (Oxford, 1913), p. 11).

[18] Even more far-fetched is Wellhausen's opinion (*PGI*, 120) that the prophecy to Eli in 1 Sam. 2: 27–36 reflects the time following Josiah's reform. This prophecy, contrary to Wellhausen, does not contain any traces of the Deuteronomistic style, and is certainly old. However, it may be noted that Wellhausen did correctly perceive that the position attributed in this prophecy to the house of Eli for the future is that of a kind of 'Levitical' status (except that according to him, the Levitical status came into being only after Josiah's reform).

with the end of the prophecy: 'And it shall come to pass, that every one who is left in your house shall come and bow down to him . . . and shall say: Put me, I pray you, in one of the priests' offices, that I may eat a morsel of bread' (1 Sam. 2: 36). It was to such people that writers of the priestly school could apply the term 'Levites'.

But then, Eli and his house were not from the north. On the contrary, they belonged to the authentic, priestly group of the tribe of Levi and, as we have seen, were able to boast of their descent from Aaron. It transpires that the prophecy on Eli and his house falls into a chronological framework earlier than that which characterizes P. Many changes have certainly taken place in the Jerusalem temple during the centuries of its existence, only weak echoes of which have made their way to the outside world. At a certain period, later than that which is reflected in the prophecy on Eli and his house, and not necessarily during one of the earliest stages in the history of the temple, it may have happened that 'priests' from the north, descendants of the tribe of Levi, began to come to the Jerusalem temple where they could find places only on the fringes of the cult (cf. Chapter VII, sect 7). It is this state of affairs which was perpetuated in P's system.

THE JERUSALEMITE PRIESTHOOD AND THE HOUSE OF AARON

9

In the eighteenth year of his reign King Josiah carried out a cultic reform, which bore the marks of being influenced by D's ideology and totally eradicated the high-places (2 Kgs. 22: 3—23: 24). However, the upheavals connected with this deed could not extend beyond their doctrinal boundaries. It was not within their power to turn priests of high-places into Levites, nor to deprive legitimate priests of their fundamental privilege to officiate in the temple. Thus, despite this reform's unshrinking attitude towards the high-places it has hardly anything to do with the formation of the post-exilic priestly and Levitical classes.

It is said of Josiah that in the course of his reform 'he brought all the priests out of the cities of Judah, and defiled the high-places where the priests had burned [grain-]offerings,[19] from Geba to Beer-sheba' (2 Kgs. 23: 8). After their removal the priests were not allowed to 'come up to the altar of the Lord in Jerusalem' (ibid., v. 9); the second half of the same verse: 'But they ate unleavened bread among their brethren', is somewhat ambiguous and scholars and exegetes have made various conjectures.[20] Yet, in its first half, the meaning of which is perfectly clear, they saw a contradiction to D's view, which explicitly permits every Levite to come from the provinces to the temple and to graduate to priesthood (Deut. 18: 6–7).[21] Some scholars even tried to base their arguments on this detail, claiming that it was one of the proofs against any historical connection between Deuteronomy and Josiah's reform.[22] In actual fact, this detail does not really contradict D's view. Furthermore, even if we were prepared to admit that from the practical point of view Josiah's reform did not correspond in all its details to D's theory, this would still not be enough to invalidate the substantial connection between D and that reform.

It is explicitly stated in 2 Kgs. 23: 8–9 that the priests who were brought to Jerusalem from the cities of Judah and were not allowed to ascend the altar, had only been *kōhanê bāmôt*, 'priests of high-places'. Since the *bāmôt* are but large (solitary) altars and by no means come into the category of temples, it is very doubtful whether these priests really traced their descent to the tribe of Levi. This detail, therefore, does not contradict D, for not only D, but all the normative schools would find it quite impossible to consider 'priests of high-places', who were actually non-Levite, as fit for the priesthood in the Jerusalem temple.

At the same time, it cannot be denied that Josiah's reform was inevitably involved also in the abolition of all the houses of God

[19] For the exact meaning of the verb *qṭr* in the *pi'ēl* conjugation cf. below, pp. 233–4.

[20] Some retain the word מצות and relate it to the eating of the Passover sacrifice mentioned in the continuation of the chapter (R. Kittel and others), or to that which is left over from the grain-offering, which according to Lev. 6: 9–10 must be eaten unleavened (A. Ehrlich). Many have accepted the reading of A. Kuenen, מניות, 'shares', even though it is quite questionable.

[21] Cf. above, pp. 61–3.

[22] See especially G. Hölscher, 'Komposition und Ursprung des Deuteronomiums', *ZAW* 40 (1923), 200–3; idem, 'Das Buch der Könige etc.', *'Ευχαριστήριον Gunkel* (Göttingen, 1923), pp. 209–11. (For schools of thought dating Deuteronomy at the post-exilic period see E. W. Nicholson, *Deuteronomy and Tradition* (Oxford, 1967), pp. 1, 4, 6.)

outside Jerusalem. Yet, in Josiah's time their number was minimal. The two Judean temples outside Jerusalem of which indications are to be found, those of Hebron and Bethlehem,[23] may already have gone into decline by the time of the early days of the monarchy. The temples in the north Israelite territories which were annexed to Josiah's kingdom, appear to have been largely devastated after the fall of Samaria. The few temples outside Jerusalem which had perhaps survived to Josiah's time were surely destroyed along with the high-places and their few priests brought to Jerusalem with the priests of the high-places. It may be, however, that priests of the provincial temples, unlike the 'priests of high-places', were not precluded from joining the temple priesthood. Priests who had remained in the priestly cities in Judah and Benjamin but did not officiate at the provincial temples would certainly not be taken to Jerusalem, for there could be no reason to uproot them. An example of a priestly family which remained in one of those cities and had no connection with the temple in Jerusalem nor, at that time, with any other temple, is provided in the case of Jeremiah who was of the priests living in Anathoth (Jer. 1: 1). He left Anathoth for Jerusalem driven by prophetic impulses; his departure had nothing to do with the reform. In fact, Jeremiah moved to Jerusalem a few years before the reform, whereas his relatives were still in Anathoth after it (cf. ibid. 11: 21–3; 12: 6; 32: 6–12). Hence, it really is impossible to prove that the legitimate priesthood scattered in the cities of Judah was harmed by Josiah's reform in a way which contradicts the conceptions of D (or of the other Pentateuchal sources) concerning the priesthood.

One can certainly concede that, as a result of Josiah's reform, the priests of Jerusalem were in a stronger position. Though the reform could not annul the ancient prerogative of Judah's priestly families to officiate in the cult, from the moment the temple in Jerusalem became the only one, the stature of its priesthood may well have risen. This found expression at least in Ezekiel's code (cf. below). But the relative rise in importance of the Jerusalem priesthood has nothing to do with D's own viewpoint and cannot be explained as a preparatory stage in the formation of the post-exilic priesthood. It was merely a side-effect of the reform's character and of the decisive way in which it was carried out. It

[23] Cf. above, p. 34.

could not determine the real fate of the priesthood and reshape its organizational principles.

10

After the destruction of Jerusalem Ezekiel made two demands: the priesthood must be restricted to the sons of Zadok; and priests not descended from Zadok must be reduced to the rank of Levites. The prevailing theory in biblical research, which takes Ezekiel to be a kind of herald announcing the appearance of P, does not believe that these demands were, for the prophet's part, only doctrinaire expectations. They are considered to be the first stage in the consolidation of P's view of the priesthood of the Aaronites and the sub-priestly Levitical rank of the rest of the tribe.[24] The truth of the matter is, however, that the historical sequence is the other way round, and on these points, as well as on others, Ezekiel's visionary code can only be explained as an epigonic growth of P.

It has already been pointed out that the concept of the 'sons of Aaron' cannot be explained as a development and expansion of the 'sons of Zadok'. But there is no difficulty in explaining the concept 'sons of Zadok' as an attempt to restrict drastically the Aaronite priesthood. Whoever wants to limit the priesthood to the sons of Zadok may be aware that the southern Levites (i.e., the Aaronites) have prior claim to the priesthood, only he intends to re-evaluate this claim and to apply it exclusively to Zadok's descendants. If that is the case, then he may well be conscious of the old principles of the school, but be trying to set them in narrower limits. Alternatively, the concept 'sons of Aaron' may have become somewhat blurred in him, but he still holds to the school's doctrine and as an epigone creates for himself a substitute-concept in the form of the 'sons of Zadok'. The attempt to put Zadok's descendants in the place of those of Aaron is indeed very reasonable in the light of the circumstances following Josiah's reform, when every place in the priesthood was actually filled by the Jerusalemite priests. However, after the canonization of the Pentateuch the term 'sons of Aaron' became a *de rigeur* epithet for any sort of legitimate priesthood. Ben Sira's reference to the

[24] Cf. Chapter IV, sects. 9 (pp. 72–3) and 10 (pp. 75–6).

sons of Zadok (Sir. 51: 29) is merely rhetorical, being a kind of echo of the text in Ezekiel.

Ezekiel's other demand, to reduce the priests not descended from Zadok to the rank of Levites cannot apply to the priests of the high-places. As has already been stated, priests of high-places were not really considered members of the tribe of Levi and it is impossible to understand how Ezekiel (or D before him) could invent a genealogy in order to make them Levites. Where did Ezekiel get his Levites from? For an answer we must carefully investigate what his code has to say on this matter.

THE LEVITES OF EZEKIEL'S CODE AND IN POST-EXILIC TIMES

II

There are four distinctive marks by which the Levites referred to in Ezekiel's code can be characterized.

(*a*) First of all, they are Levites. Since that is what the code calls them (Ezek. 44: 10; 45: 5; 48: 11–13) it follows that the utmost limits which can be implied in this term are those of the remnants of families who were formerly entitled to officiate in the priesthood. These were either scattered over the Kingdom of Judah (and were regarded as descendants of Aaron) or may also have included some remnants of the legitimate priestly families from the north who were not Aaronites, yet belonged to the tribe of Levi.

(*b*) As we shall see right away, the Levites with whom Ezekiel is concerned had already officiated in the priesthood, and against the background of his idealized temple he does not refrain from attaching to them the attribute 'priests' (Ezek. 40: 45). This means that, in point of fact, the prophet does not have in view *all* the remnants of the families who had the prerogative of priesthood, but only a part of them—that part in which the prerogative had already apparently materialized and which had already held priestly office.

(*c*) According to Ezekiel's assumption, the Levites are few in number and certainly do not exceed the sum of Zadok's descendants, the legitimate priests. In the temple programme he allocates two chambers in the inner court—one to the Levites, one to the sons of Zadok (Ezek. 40: 45–6). In the holy district he assigns two equal strips, each one twenty-five thousand cubits long and ten thousand cubits broad, one for the priests and one for the Levites (ibid. 45: 3–5; 48: 9–13). These two strips are very modest in size when compared with the tribal territories, which indicates that the number of priests and of Levites is nowhere near that of a tribe.

(*d*) Where had the Levites already officiated as priests? In an illegitimate cult which Ezekiel calls serving 'before the idols'. In his words: the Levites went far from Yahweh, 'when Israel went astray . . . from me after their idols' (Ezek. 44: 10). They officiated to Israel 'before their idols, and became a stumbling-block of iniquity to the house of Israel', wherefore they were decreed to 'bear their shame, and their abominations which they had committed' and to leave the priesthood (ibid., vv. 12–13; cf. 48: 11). Some scholars claim that these 'idols', *gillûlîm* as they are termed in the text, are simply an attribute for high-places.[25] Yet, nowhere do we find this word being applied to high-places, and it quite definitely does not mean this in Ezekiel's code either.

12

The word *gillûlîm* occurs once in the Holiness Code (Lev. 26: 30), once in D (Deut. 29: 16), and in all the other instances it is employed only in the Deuteronomistic style and in the Book of Ezekiel. Its principal meaning is really statues, idols (as most EVV render it) and this is clearly confirmed in most of the verses where it is found.[26] In Deut. 29: 16 it indicates Egyptian images, of 'wood and stone, of silver and gold', and it is placed next to *šiqqûṣîm*, 'detestable things' (cf. 2 Kgs. 23: 24; Ezek. 20: 7–8; 37: 23). In Lev. 26: 30 the text mentions 'the carcasses of your idols', *pigrê gillûlêḵem*, the reference being to images, not to structures. In 2 Kgs. 21: 21 the *gillûlîm* are worshipped by prostrating oneself before them, which is an additional indication of their nature. In Jer. 50: 2 they are applied to the Babylonian idols and

[25] See the commentaries of R. Kraetzschmar (GHK, 1900), J. Herrmann (KAT, 1924), G. A. Cooke (ICC, 1936), A. Bertholet and K. Galling (HAT, 1936), G. Fohrer and K. Galling (HAT, 1955), and others, ad loc. But W. Zimmerli (*Ezechiel* (BK, 1969), ii. 1126–7, 1132–3) does not interpret it in this manner. Cf. below.

[26] Cf. the Dictionaries of Gesenius–Buhl, Brown–Driver–Briggs, and Koehler–Baumgartner[3], s.v. גלולים; also Zimmerli, op. cit., i. 149–50; and H. D. Preuss, *ThWAT*, ii, cols. 1–5.

are mentioned in parallelism with *ʿaṣabbîm*, images, as well as with Bel and Merodach, the Babylonian gods. Ezekiel relates how he saw in one of the temple chambers 'all forms of creeping things and beasts, detestation (*šeqeṣ*), and all the idols of the house of Israel (*weḵol gillûlê bêt yiśrāʾēl*), portrayed upon the wall round about' (Ezek. 8: 10), where, again, it is clear that the reference is to images, which in this case are carved into the wall. In speaking of Egypt's *gillûlîm* he associates them with *ʾelîlîm*, false gods (ibid. 30: 13).

That the *gillûlîm* are not high-places can be further proved by the passage about Asa, which states that he removed 'all the *gillûlîm* that his fathers had made', but 'the high-places were not taken away' (1 Kgs. 15: 12, 14). Further proof is the fact that the *gillûlîm* are mentioned next to high-places, pillars, Asherim, *ḥammānîm* and other cult objects as items in their own right (Lev. 26: 30; 2 Kgs. 17: 10–12; Ezek. 6: 3–6). It is also attested to by the verbs and expressions which go with the word *gillûlîm*: to serve them (2 Kgs. 17: 12; Ezek. 20: 39), to take them into one's heart (Ezek. 14: 3–4, 7), one's heart going after them (ibid. 20: 16), one's eyes being after them (ibid., v. 24), to slaughter one's children to them (ibid. 23: 39), to lift up one's eyes to them (ibid. 33: 25 *et al.*). All these expressions are quite unsuitable when applied to high-places, but fitting for objects such as cast or graven images, or divinities, that is, strange gods. Indeed, the word *gillûlîm* is also employed as an attribute of strange gods, or strange images—of Egypt (Deut. 29: 15–16; Ezek. 20: 7–8; 30: 13), the Amorites (1 Kgs. 21: 26; cf. 2 Kgs. 21: 11), Babylon (Jer. 50: 2), Assyria (Ezek. 23: 7), and just gods and images of other nations (ibid., v. 30)—because the cult among the ancient Near Eastern peoples surrounding Israel was mostly iconographic and in Israel's normative views strange gods and statues were normally considered the same. The reference to strange gods which is frequently implied by the word *gillûlîm* also finds expression in the images of harlotry with the *gillûlîm* (Ezek. 16: 36; 23: 30), adultery with *gillûlîm* (ibid., v. 37), the contamination with which the people of Israel defile themselves by means of the *gillûlîm* (Ezek. 20: 18, 31; 22: 3–4; 23: 7, 30; 36: 18 *et al.*), as well as expressions such as: to go after the *gillûlîm* (1 Kgs. 21: 26), to separate oneself from God through one's *gillûlîm* (Ezek. 14: 5, 7), to turn away from one's *gillûlîm* (ibid., v. 6).

Now the text of Ezekiel's code speaks of the Levites who officiated to Israel 'before their *gillûlîm*' (Ezek. 44: 12) and about Israel 'that went astray from me after their *gillûlîm*' (ibid., v. 10). These expressions, with the prepositions 'before', *lipnê* and 'after', *'aḥ^{a}rê* quite clearly show that the reference is not to high-places. All the more so when all the other passages confirm decisively enough that we are here concerned not with high-places, but with cultic digression towards strange gods and images.

13

When did that cultic digression take place? There is no doubt that the shadow of Manasseh's period hovers over this accusation, just as the impressions of Manasseh's activities are discernible throughout Ezekiel's prophecy as a whole.[27] To be sure, Manasseh rebuilt the high-places, but he also introduced iconographic, alien cults into Jerusalem, into the temple court, and even right into the temple sanctums (2 Kgs. 21: 2–11).[28] All Manasseh's innovations were swept away during Josiah's reform (ibid. 23: 4–7, 10–12). However, they recur like a dreadful recollection in the Book of Jeremiah (7: 30–4; 15: 4; 19: 4–13; 32: 34–5), in Ezekiel (chaps. 8, 16, 20, 23), and in the Deuteronomistic historiography, which considers them to be *the* reason for the fall of Jerusalem (2 Kgs. 21: 10–15; 23: 26; 24: 3–4).[29] At the same time, it is hard to find any real indication that Manasseh's cult spread outside Jerusalem.

[27] I find that the Norwegian scholar N. Messel (*Ezechielfragen* (Oslo, 1945), pp. 133–6) has already stressed that the text in Ezekiel's code does not in any way refer to the service of the Levites at high-places, but to their officiation before images in Jerusalem. But this scholar was led to the extreme view that the Book of Ezekiel was composed only after Nehemiah, and that there were signs of it having been further edited in the period before Alexander (ibid., pp. 21–5). Messel was thus led to the odd notion that the idolatrous cult came into existence nowhere else but within the Second Temple, after Nehemiah's time, and that its practitioners were representatives of the syncretistic population that remained in Palestine (ibid., pp. 26–30).

[28] Cf. below, pp. 278–80.

[29] With regard to the impressions of Manasseh's activities on the prophecies of Jeremiah and Ezekiel, and the significance of these impressions, see Kaufmann, *THH* iii. 382–91, 447–50, 499–502, 538–9. Some of the verses in the Book of Jeremiah mentioning the occurrences of Manasseh's time are certainly Deuteronomistic. Yet there is no doubt that Jeremiah himself also referred to them, particularly in the prophecies from before the reform (cf. Jer. 2: 23; 8: 1–2; 13: 25–6; 17: 1–4). The impressions of Manasseh's activities in Ezekiel's prophecies served Torrey and Smith as starting points for their odd opinions on the time and character of this Book; see C. C. Torrey, *Pseudo-Ezekiel and the Original Prophecy* (New Haven, 1930; reprinted New York, 1970), pp. 45–57 (and in

From what Ezekiel's code has to say about the Levites, we cannot but deduce that it was a section of the Jerusalem priests—those who were not counted with the main (Zadokite) priesthood of the temple and had come from the provincial priestly families of Judah, or from the priestly families in the north—who were employed in the iconographic cults introduced by Manasseh. At first sight one would have thought it better to assume that Josiah's reform was connected with a change in Jerusalem's priestly houses, that is, that originally, some time after Solomon, the house of Zadok left the priesthood, to return to it in Josiah's time.[30] However, this argument is shattered by the definite statement in Ezekiel's code that the sons of Zadok, unlike the Levites, did not go astray, but 'kept the guard of my holiness, *miqdāšî*, when the people of Israel went astray from me' (Ezek. 44: 15; 48: 11). Thus, according to Ezekiel himself, Zadok's descendants were never cut off from the temple priesthood and during Manasseh's period of deviation they were the faithful guardians of the legitimate cult. Did the Jerusalem priesthood split into two sections in Manasseh's time—worship of Yahweh on the one hand, the alien cult on the other—the line of division running between the sons of Zadok and the other priests who had found their place in Jerusalem? This is not altogether impossible; at any event, this is the picture which emerges from the prophet's descriptions. However, one must take into consideration the ideological character of Ezekiel's code, as well as this prophet's tendentious polemics and his inclination to straighten out the historical perspective, to describe it in extremes—either black or white. It is therefore possible that the historical reality was not precisely as portrayed by the prophet. Yet, it is practically inconceivable that Ezekiel's Levites were ever linked to the high-places, either in the prophet's complaints or in the historical reality itself.

M. Greenberg's introduction, pp. xiv–xx); J. Smith, *The Book of the Prophet Ezekiel* (London, 1931). Other scholars tried to explain these facts by supposing that after Josiah's death his reform was abolished. In fact it is most unlikely (cf. below, pp. 135–40).

30 This is the supposition of J. M. Grintz, 'Aspects of the History of the High Priesthood', *Zion* 23–4 (1958–9), 124–30, 134–5 (Hebrew). Similar to this is the opinion of H. J. Katzenstein, 'Some Remarks on the List of the Chief Priests', *JBL* 81 (1962), 379–82. They sought to base their arguments primarily on the genealogical lists in Chronicles—a rather weak basis for decision in this matter.

14

As long as P existed independently, either as a creative school or as a literary product preserved by the quills of copyists and compilers,[31] the specific institution of the Levitical class could only have been known within the temple confines. Outsiders would not notice it, as the Levites did not stand out from the rest of the priests. In Ezra's time, however, when the priestly writings became an integral part of the Law and an attempt was made to fulfil everything that had been 'found written' (Neh. 8: 14), the existence of the Levites became public knowledge, one of the fundamental rules of the Torah. But by this time the Levites were few in number.

According to the list of inhabitants of the province of Judah who returned from exile, there were 4,289 priests (Ezra 2: 36–9; Neh. 7: 39–42), and only 74 Levites; the Levites together with the singers and the gate-keepers numbered 341 according to Ezra 2: 40–2, 360 according to Neh. 7: 43–5. When a small group of Levites joined Ezra so that the trek would not be short of temple officials he regarded it as a good omen, 'the good hand of our God upon us' (Ezra 8: 15–19). According to Jerusalem's population census, one version of which is given in Neh. 11: 3–24, there were close on 1,200 priests in the city, while the number of Levites was only 284 with 172 gate-keepers.[32] Naturally enough, against the background of David's time the Chronicler was able to speak of 38,000 Levites, from thirty years old and upwards, 4,000 of these being gate-keepers and 4,000 singers (1 Chron. 23: 3–5); but for the post-exilic period he had genealogical lists at his disposal and these would not let him ignore the fact that the Levites were few.

[31] For the transition from the first, creative stage to the second (when, in my opinion, the priestly school stagnated) cf. below, p. 147.

[32] Another version of the main part of this list (Neh. 11: 3–19) appears in 1 Chron. 9: 2–17; both versions are faulty and were apparently copied from a common source. According to the Chronicler's version there were 1,760 priests in Jerusalem, whereas the number of only 212 gate-keepers is given (ibid., v. 22). One must wonder whether in the context of Chronicles this list is mainly designed to describe the strength of the population of Second Temple times. Some signs would point to the possibility that the Chronicler actually seeks to use the list to go back, by means of the family trees contained in it, to the time of David. Yet it is incontestable that the list has its basis in the historical reality of Second Temple times.

Further proof of the paucity of the Levites in the post-exilic period is the way in which the law of the tithe was operated in those times. According to P's own conception, as is expressly stated in the Pentateuch, the tithe which derives from corn and fruit is meant for the Levites, who, for their part, set aside 'a tithe of the tithe' for the priests (Num. 18: 21–32). However, in the practice of post-exilic times the priests began to take the major portion of the tithe for themselves. This is clearly attested in the Apocrypha (Jubilees 13: 25–6; Judith 11: 13), the latter Second Temple sources,[33] and the talmudic literature.[34] The talmudic sages plainly admitted that in their time the tithe was not operating in complete accordance with the biblical injunction, for the Torah ordered it to be given to the Levites 'but we are wont to give it to the priests'.[35] They believed that giving the tithe to the priests was one of Ezra's amendments by which he punished the Levites for failing to come to Jerusalem in his time.[36] The operation of the tithe, as well as the paucity of Levites during the Second Temple period, constitute only a part of the obvious indications of the lack of primary correlation between P and the actual circumstances prevailing in that period.

15

Where did the Second Temple Levites come from? Were we to say that they had their origins in the priesthood of the high-places, then, in addition to the genealogical oddity of the matter, it would be hard to explain why, compared with the priests (who are taken to be descendants of the Sons of Zadok only), they are so few. The high-places, which had been scattered over the whole country 'from Geba to Beer-sheba' (2 Kgs. 23: 8), and according to Ezekiel were found 'in every square' and 'at the head of every way' (Ezek. 16: 24–5), must have demanded a priestly manpower

[33] Josephus, *Antiquities* xiv. 10. 6; xx. 8. 8 *et al.*; *De Josepho* xii, xv; Philo, *De Virtutibus* 95; cf. *Leges* i. 152.

[34] Bab. Tal. Kethuboth, 26*a*; Ḥullin, 131*b*; Jer. Tal. Maᶜaser Sheni v, 5, 9; Soṭah ix, 11 *et al.*

[35] ואנן קא יהבינן לכוהנים (Bab. Tal. Soṭah, 47*b*).

[36] Bab. Tal. Jebamoth, 86*b*. Concerning this problem as a whole cf. my remarks s.v. מעשר, *EM*, v. 209, where (cols. 206–8) I also pointed out, following Kaufmann (*THH*, i. 152–9), that according to P itself the tithe was considered a votive offering, but in the practice of the Second Temple times it became an annual obligation. See also *EM*, iv. 43–4; and below, p. 116, n. 8.

no smaller than that of the Jerusalem temple. It would be much more to the point to look for the solution in the tradition enshrined in P's conceptions, which in its main essence also underlies the other Pentateuchal sources.

We have seen that according to this tradition, which found quite clear expression in the list of Levitical cities, all the priestly families in Judah traced their origin to Aaron—and according to P those families alone were fit for the priesthood. Now the course of history was such that after the disappearance of the Kingdom of Samaria the Kingdom of Judah alone remained as the sole vehicle of Israelite history, and the Return from Babylonia was likely to affect mainly the offspring of the southern group of the tribe of Levi, that group which had been attached to Judah generations ago. From this group, which according to biblical tradition (the tradition which underlies J, E, and D and is explicit in P) was called after Aaron, the post-exilic priesthood descended. This means that not only the Jerusalem priests were the ancestors of the post-exilic priesthood, but all the priestly families who had been scattered throughout the Kingdom of Judah—not only the 'house of Zadok', but the entire 'house of Aaron'. Undoubtedly, after the Return to Palestine, and especially after the canonization of the Pentateuch, the fundamental right of all these to officiate in the priesthood was recognized, since, in principle, this right had never been abrogated. The large extent of the Second Temple priesthood can also clearly testify that they were not only the descendants of the Jerusalem priesthood, but that for many of them a priestly ancestry in the provincial parts of Judah was found. The formula 'sons of Zadok', as a restrictive, narrowing, concept, meaning to exclude all those who are not sons of Zadok (even when they are descendants of Aaron and able to prove it from their genealogy) does not exist but in Ezekiel's thought. There is no indication that in the post-exilic reality this formula was an active force.

Consequently, the only men who could be considered Levites were those who could prove their descent from 'priestly' families of the Northern Kingdom. All those families were not included in the Aaronic clan, and according to P they were excluded from priesthood. Indeed, it stands to reason that some northern offshoots of the tribe of Levi found their way into the community of Judean exiles. Some of these found themselves in Jerusalem even in pre-exilic times and later went into exile with Jehoiachin's deportation (above, sect. 7). Others attached themselves to the Judean community in some other way and at some other time.[37] In the post-exilic period such people could have been but few in number. The destruction of Samaria more than one hundred and twenty years before Jehoiachin's deportation and the split in the historical fate of the two kingdoms did not allow more than a trickle of Levites from the Northern Kingdom to mingle with the Judean community.

[37] Cf. below, pp. 147–8.

VI

THE DISTRIBUTION OF THE LEVITICAL TRIBE

I

ALL the biblical evidence agrees that the Levites were an indigent tribe, deprived of an inheritance of their own and scattered throughout the land of Israel. But only in P do we find a precise specification of the cities where this tribe was supposed to be found, with an explicit treatment of their legal status, whether actual or only wishful, in those cities. This matter is dealt with in three passages in the priestly work. In Lev. 25: 32–4 the legal privileges of the Levites in their cities are mentioned in connection with the jubilee legislation.[1] In Num. 35: 1–8 the people of Israel are ordered to give the Levites forty-eight cities, including the six cities of refuge. It is also explained there how to measure the *migrāšîm* (RSV: 'pasture lands'; NEB: 'common land') which are to be added on to these cities. Josh. 21: 1–40 describes how the people of Israel implemented this directive and allocated forty-eight cities to the tribe of Levi, and how the priests and the three Levitical clans apportioned the cities between them by lot, and a full register of the cities is appended. A slightly different version of this register with a few omissions is given by the Chronicler (1 Chron. 6: 39–66). Brief references to these cities are made in Josh. 14: 4 and again by the Chronicler (1 Chron. 13: 2; 2 Chron. 11: 14; 31: 15, 19).

THE CRITICAL VIEWS

2

Wellhausen assumed that the account of the Levitical cities was an entirely fictional utopian scheme which never had any historical basis. Following K. H. Graf, he pointed to the artificial character

[1] Lev. 25: 32–4 is a part of secondary (priestly) accretions to a pericope which substantially belongs to H; cf. commentaries.

of the measurements of the 'pasture lands' and emphasized that the register included various cities which, until the time of the early monarchy, were in the hands of the Canaanites (e.g. Shechem, Gezer, Taanach); 'some perhaps may even have so continued permanently'. Even those cities conquered by the Israelites did not become Levitical, as this account claims. Moreover, P assumes, and all the other biblical evidence is actually in accord here, that the priests and Levites have no inheritance in the land of Israel (Num. 18: 20, 23–4). Yet this basic assumption seems to contradict the claim that the Levites were given forty-eight cities. The account of the Levitical cities should consequently be attributed to a later stratum of P. Like all the other parts of P, this fiction of Levitical cities is, according to Wellhausen, post-exilic, based on the one hand on the vague memory that many cities of the country were originally cultic centres, and on the other on the development of Ezekiel's visionary programme concerning the holy district (Ezek. 45: 1–5; 48: 8–22).[2]

Those scholars who took issue with Wellhausen, both in his time and subsequently, maintained that this account contained actual historical data. Indeed, various allusions outside P confirm that priests or Levites resided in some of these cities (cf. Chapter V, in sect. 3). These scholars therefore sought to date the account as pre-exilic, or even argued for the beginning of the Israelite monarchy. Proof was adduced by a process of historical elimination: it is reasonable to assume that the list of cities is not later than the United Monarchy, since it embraces the whole of Israel and still recognizes the tribal boundaries, whereas Solomon redivided the land into administrative regions. On the other hand, it no longer recognizes the existence of Canaanite cities and already omits Shiloh and Nob, which were presumably already in ruins in Saul's time. Other proofs of this type were also advanced.[3]

[2] Wellhausen, *PGI*, 153–8. So in most of the studies and commentaries sharing this view (even Wellhausen's specific argumentation recurs in them).

[3] For the views of Wellhausen's contemporaries see S. Ohlenburg, *Die biblischen Asyle in talmudischem Gewande* (München, 1895), pp. 19 ff.; D. Hoffmann, *Die wichtigsten Instanzen gegen die Graf-Wellhausensche Hypothese*, i (Berlin, 1904), pp. 148–51; B. D. Eerdmans, *Alttestamentliche Studien*, iv (Giessen, 1912), pp. 132–3. See also W. W. Baudissin, *Die Geschichte des Alttestamentlichen Priesterthums* (Leipzig, 1889), pp. 45–6, 103. The opposing views became much more noticeable after Wellhausen. See M. Löhr, *Das Asylwesen im AT* (Halle–Saale, 1930), p. 34; S. Klein, ערי הכהנים והלויים וערי מקלט, *Journal of the Jewish Palestine Exploration Society*, ed. N. Slousch

One must admit that such eliminative proofs are rather susceptible to different interpretations. For instance, Gezer contained a Canaanite population during the whole of the Davidic period (1 Kgs. 9: 16). Moreover, according to these scholars it is left unexplained why such cultic centres as Bethel and Dan, whose sanctity lingered on until their destruction long after the foundation of the monarchy, were nevertheless omitted from the list of Levitical cities. To these may be added other cultic centres, such as Gilgal, Bethlehem, Beer-sheba (usually considered to have been a cultic centre, which in a sense it was), and Mizpah, all of which are missing from this list. Above all, the approach adopted by these scholars seems to have been rather one-sided. It is of little avail to try over-hastily to fix the date even before defining the specific character of the material concerned. The whole problem involved in the nature of P and its unusual concepts should be fully taken into account.

3

Strictures of the type mentioned above against those taking issue with Wellhausen were vented by Kaufmann, who reaffirmed that this account was utopian, but shifted its date to an entirely different period. He put to Wellhausen the additional argument that the list of cities did not include Jerusalem. It is inconceivable, according to Kaufmann, that Jerusalem should be missing from any programme of priestly and Levitical cities later than David, and most certainly in post-exilic times. This programme 'could therefore have been put into words only at the beginning of the period of the Conquest, before the shrines and high-places were established in the settlements of Israel'. The priests and Levites 'neither could nor would have obtained territory in accordance with the programme. They settled wherever there were shrines'. It is therefore a Utopia of the greatest possible antiquity.[4]

(Jerusalem, 1935), pp. 81–94; Albright, *ARI*, 121–5; idem, 'The List of Levitic Cities', *Louis Ginzberg Jubilee Volume* (New York, 1945), pp. 49–73.

[4] Y. Kaufmann, *The Biblical Account of the Conquest of Palestine* (Jerusalem, 1953), pp. 40–6; cf. *THH*, ii. 382–4; and his Hebrew commentary on Joshua (Jerusalem, 1959), pp. 270–82. Close to this is M. H. Segal, מסורת ובקרת (Jerusalem, 1957), p. 104.

Alt, again, took this account to be a historical one, for he was not at all inclined to admit the possibility of a utopian formulation of geographical material. He dwelt not only on the cities mentioned in this list but also on the fact that it omits many, so that there emerges a picture of blocks of territory distant from each other without any geographical continuity. Alt maintained that these territorial lacunae could be explained by Josiah's reform, for this destroyed the high-places and ejected all the priests from the cities of Judah, 'from Geba to Beer-sheba' (2 Kgs. 23: 8).[5] This approach was shared by Noth, though for his own reasons he preferred to link this account with the territorial conditions of the early post-exilic period.[6]

A suggestion made by Mazar has a certain flavour of its own. Relying upon an examination of topographical and historical evidence in Chronicles and Kings, he dates the list of Levitical cities in the reign of Solomon. In his opinion, the list comprises the fortified cities in which the Levites settled at the command and in the service of the king, and is chiefly based on an official document—perhaps the archives of the Jerusalem priesthood.[7]

Thus, explanations of this account hover between two basic approaches—a historical–realistic and a utopian. The historical–realistic approach dates it somewhere in the period of the United Monarchy or after Josiah. The utopian approach places it at the end or at the very beginning of biblical history, even before the Conquest. I would argue that the true character of this account accords with neither of these categories. In the first place, however, let us examine a number of the prior assumptions made by those who have concerned themselves with this subject. Clarification of these is vital if the account is to be properly understood.

[5] Alt, *KS*, ii. 294–301. Moreover, Alt suggests that there is an inner connection between the blocs of Levitical cities in Judah and the Judean fortress cities listed in 2 Chron. 11: 5–10. The Chronicler attributes the fortifying of these cities to Rehoboam, but Alt is inclined to believe that this list, too, reflects the activities of Josiah (ibid. 310–15).

[6] M. Noth, *Das Buch Josua*² (HAT, 1953), pp. 127, 131–2. Noth resorted to the argument that the passage in Num. 35: 1–8 was secondary and had been composed on the basis of Josh. 20–1. On this point too he relied on Alt (*KS*, ii. 295, n. 9). The fact that these sections actually belong to P (denied by Alt and Noth with regard to Josh. 21) will be touched upon below, pp. 129–30.

[7] B. Mazar, 'The Cities of the Priests and the Levites', *SVT* 7 (1960), pp. 193–204; idem, *EM* iv. 481–5. This view is also shared by Z. Kallai, נחלות שבטי ישראל (Jerusalem, 1967), pp. 379–89.

THE DISTINGUISHING FEATURES OF THE LEVITICAL CITIES

4

Scholars take it for granted that the gift of the cities to the Levites contradicts the fact that in all the sources the Levites are described as impoverished and landless. In actual fact this account, far from contradicting that description, only confirms and complements it. For these forty-eight cities are granted to the Levites unaccompanied by any landed property. They therefore cannot serve as a 'substitute' for agricultural land, or as a source of income and wealth.

In order to prove that the city on its own could not have served its residents as a source of livelihood we need only look at the law of the jubilee. The jubilee law states that fields of ancestral possession, *'ᵃḥuzzāh* (i.e. the agricultural lands) that had been sold, must be redeemed before the advent of the jubilee year. In any event, the jubilee automatically removes them from the purchasers and restores them to the original owners (Lev. 25: 28–9, 31). But walled cities do not come under the category of *'ᵃḥuzzāh* for this purpose. A house in a walled city can be redeemed only within one year of purchase; failing that, it remains permanently in the hands of the purchaser (vv. 29–30). That is to say, it is not found necessary for the jubilee law to protect rights of tenure over ancestral property in the cities. The reason for this is simple: a person's livelihood is not lost if he is deprived of a house that he owns in the city. For the city houses serve no economic function in that tribal-agricultural society that is depicted in the Pentateuchal laws (in all of them, including in those of P). Wealth chiefly comes from agriculture, whereas the city is only a place to live. There is as yet hardly any real commerce, industry, or trade in the city, and no other real sources of income. And it certainly did not occur to people in those days to earn profit through renting houses; a man lived in his own house or was likely to lose it.

Lacking any land of their own, the Levites had to live in cities of some sort. This is what actually emerges from the priestly account. According to P the Levites are supported by tithes, which in his system are classed as votive offerings (Num. 18: 21–32).[8] At

[8] The text speaks here of a vow offering, not of an annual obligation. The tithe dealt with in this text is of agricultural produce alone. It is the same tithe mentioned in Lev. 27: 30–1, where it is stated that it is redeemable by payment of

the same time, P 'settles' the Levites in forty-eight cities—but he does not assume that they have any land-holdings outside the walls. Outside the walls the Levites merely have *migrāšîm* of fixed dimensions, and these are not to be confused with the agricultural lands that encircle the city. The *migrāšîm* are designed for keeping livestock (Num. 35: 3; Josh. 14: 4; 21: 2), but not for agricultural cultivation and crops. This distinction is even more obvious in Ezekiel: *migraš hā'îr* is the term applied by him to a thin strip of two hundred and fifty cubits skirting the built-up area (Ezek. 48: 15–17), whereas *'ᵃḥuzzat hā'îr* is an extensive area cultivated by the residents of the city and from which they derive their livelihood (45: 6; 48: 18). What is apt to mislead in this matter is the fact that there are also registers of cities in the Book of Joshua for most of the other tribes. The difference, however, is that in the case of the other tribes the city lists are meant to indicate whole *territories*, whereas the list of the Levitical cities refers merely to a series of walled cities, separate from the lands surrounding them. It is no accident that, with respect to all the other tribes, the text punctiliously adds to the word 'cities' the word *wᵉḥaṣrêhen*, 'and their villages' (Josh. 15: 32–62; 16: 9; 18: 24, 28; 19: 6–8, 15–16 *et al.*). Whereas in the Levitical city list the text adds to every city the term *ûmiḡrāšehā*, 'and its pasture lands'. For the *ḥᵃṣērîm*, 'villages' or 'hamlets', 'are reckoned with the fields of the country' (Lev. 25: 31).

Indeed, there is no doubt that the lands of the Levitical cities had, according to P's own assumption, to remain in the possession of those tribes within whose borders they were located. In one case the text explicitly refers to such a situation, because of the importance of the personage in whose domain the landholding of that city lay: Hebron 'with its *migrāšîm* round about it' was granted to the descendants of Aaron, 'but the fields of the city and its *ḥᵃṣērîm* they gave to Caleb the son of Jephunneh as his possession' (Josh. 21: 10–12).[9] Here, P does not attempt to solve an

the principal and a fifth part. Incidentally, the tithe of cattle mentioned in Lev. 27: 32–4, which is not redeemable, is actually also a vow (or a free-will offering). The same applies to the tithes mentioned in Gen. 14: 20; 28: 20–2; and Amos 4: 4–5. The tithe as an annual obligation exists only in D's code (Deut. 14: 22–9; 26: 12). Perhaps it was the latter which influenced in this respect the ('first') tithe of the Second Temple times, when it was conceived as an annual obligation (Neh. 10: 38–9; 13: 5). Cf. my discussion of this subject s.v. מעשר, *EM* v. 206–8 (and above, p. 109).

[9] Another reason for the explicit exposition made in the case of Hebron: The city was conferred on Caleb not through lot, as, according to P, were all the tribal

apparent contradiction, as some scholars were quick to conclude, but rather accidentally explains the situation actually existing, according to P, in all the Levitical cities.

At least within the confines of these forty-eight cities P seeks to strengthen the Levites' status. Since, even in his view, the Levites are landless, they are to all intents and purposes socially and economically weak and could easily be forced out of the city houses. On this account, the houses of the Levitical cities are turned into an *'ᵃḥuzzāh*, an ancestral inheritance, in P, as far as the jubilee is concerned. The houses of the Levites are granted the privilege of 'a perpetual right of redemption', *gᵉ'ullat 'ôlām*. Thus no property of theirs in the city can be permanently alienated from them, 'for the houses of the cities of the Levites are their possession, *'ᵃḥuzzātām*, among the people of Israel', whilst 'the fields of the pasture land, *śᵉdēh migrāš*, belonging to their cities' cannot be sold at all, 'for that is their perpetual *'ᵃhuzzāh*' (Lev. 25: 32–4).[10] It is obvious that these special privileges granted by P to the Levites in their cities do not spring from economic strength. Had they in practice enjoyed such stability, they would not have stood in need of legal dispensations, and that in a city which apparently belongs to them. In actual fact, the law of the Levitical

inheritances to the west of the Jordan (cf. above, p. 41), but on the basis of the oath made by Moses (Josh. 14: 6–14; Judg. 1: 20) and 'according to the commandment of Yahweh to Joshua' (Josh. 15: 13), that is, by prophetic instruction. This instruction overrode the lot and violated its procedure. In this respect Hebron was, according to P, an extraordinary case among all the cities inherited in the promised land. The only parallel is Timnath-serah, which was also conferred on Joshua 'by the commandment of Yahweh' (Josh. 19: 49–50), and possibly Gibeath-Phinehas in Mount Ephraim too (24: 33). It is on account of this that the text emphasizes that, though Hebron was 'given' to the priests, it remained in the possession of Caleb, since the fields of the city and its *ḥᵃṣērîm* had already been granted to him.

10 The explanation of this passage is difficult, though its general drift is clear. 'A perpetual right of redemption' (v. 32) may mean until the jubilee, as it is hardly conceivable that this law ignores the jubilee. 'A perpetual right of redemption' is the converse of 'within a whole year after sale' mentioned with regard to an ordinary walled city (v. 29). This implies that the law applying to a Levite's house in his city is nearly the same as that applying to an Israelite's ancestral (agricultural) land. Particularly difficult is v. 33: ואשר יגאל מן הלוים, 'and if a man redeem of the Levites . . .', where all moderns read: ואשר לא יגאל מן הלוים, 'and if a man does *not* redeem of the Levites', following the Vulgate. Traditional Jewish exegetes from Rashi to Hoffmann wrestled with its meaning and suggested various explanations after their own manner. A reasonable explanation may possibly still be given to the (correct) reading found in the MT as well as in all the ancient versions (except the Vulgate).

cities is intended to protect them from final dispossession, to safeguard their insecure existence in their cities, living as they do on votive offerings. This law serves to underline their economic and social weakness.

5

Scholars take it for granted that the forty-eight cities were chosen by P as Levitical cities because they had originally been cultic centres. At all events, all admit that a Levitical city and a shrine city are two sides of the same coin or, at least, are closely related. Those who date the list by means of historical elimination wish, for instance, to support their argument with the fact that the important temple cities of Shiloh and Nob are not included in the list. From another angle this connection is expressed in the type of argument that important temple cities, amongst them Jerusalem, had *not yet* been included in the list of Levitical cities, leading to the conclusion that this list constitutes, as it were, an ancient Utopia.

In actual fact, such a connection has no place either in P's own thought or in actual history. The Levitical cities and the temple cities are two quite separate categories. To confuse the two means to put our problem incorrectly and hopelessly to complicate it. The authors of P never so much as considered that the Levitical cities, as such, must necessarily centre upon temples. These cities were merely 'to dwell in' (Num. 35: 2; Josh. 14: 4; 21: 2) designed for residence of the Levites, with the adjoining *migrāšîm* for keeping of their cattle and livestock.[11] The Levites in these cities are endowed by P with all-important legal privileges. From this point of view they are justified in being called 'the cities of their possession' (Lev. 25: 32), since they constitute the inheritance which the Levites receive and are to bequeath to their descendants. But there is no doubt that according to P's own assumption, the temple where some members of this tribe (that is, the ones able to boast of Aaronic descent) have the right to perform cultic functions, is located elsewhere.

As it happens, an example of this situation (of a priestly family living in one city and officiating in another) has come to us from a non-priestly source. We have already seen that Abiathar

[11] In 1 Chron. 13: 2 they are called *'ārê migrāšîm*, but in the talmudic phraseology (Bab. Tal. Soṭah, 48*b*; and Rashi, ad loc.) *'ārê migrāš* with the *nomen regens* in the singular.

possessed a field in Anathoth, though he officiated at Nob and Jerusalem.[12] The field had presumably come down to him from his ancestors, since it is inconceivable that Solomon would have granted him the field when dismissing him from the priesthood, especially since he tells him quite simply: 'Go to Anathoth, to your own field' (1 Kgs. 2: 26). Hundreds of years later there appears among the priests of Anathoth the prophet Jeremiah[13] whose family similarly holds fields in that same city. Moreover, Jeremiah redeems the field of his kinsman, Hanamel the son of Shallum (Jer. 32: 6–25), apparently also a priest. Scholars have already noted that Anathoth is included in our list of priestly cities (Josh. 21: 18); but it seems that the significance of this fact has not been fully appreciated. Anathoth was not just a city where priests were found, but—what is more—the place or *residence* of that family of priests which at the same time was said to have officiated at Shiloh. Here we are confronted by that very phenomenon of mutually exclusive priest cities and temple cities, and this time, not as mirrored by P. The landholding of these priests in Anathoth is termed in the narratives 'field', *śādeh*. Perhaps if priestly terminology, which is more punctilious, had been used, it would have been called *śᵉdēh migrāš* (cf. Lev. 25: 34) and not *śᵉdēh ʿîr* (cf. Josh. 21: 12). At any rate, it would seem that this landholding was rather small and meagre, the real support of the family being the cultic officiation (said to have been performed at the temple at Shiloh). After the decline of Shiloh, a part of this family officiates at Nob. But Shiloh and Nob were not, according to P's own conceptions, priestly cities. Priests, of course, officiated in their temples, but they had neither any sort of tenure over the *migrāšîm* of these cities nor legal privileges there with respect to the jubilee year (either in theory or in practice).[14] Thus, the absence of Shiloh

[12] Cf. above, pp. 87, 98.

[13] Cf. above, p. 87, n. 2.

[14] Nob is admittedly called *ʿîr hakkōhᵃnîm*, 'the city of the priests' (1 Sam. 22: 19). This attribute may certainly be used in the narrative because of the relatively large number of priests who officiated there: 'eighty-five persons who wore the linen ephod' (v. 18). However, it is in P itself that this term, *ʿîr hakkōhᵃnîm*, is not found at all. Even from Amos' words to Amaziah the priest of Bethel: 'and your land shall be parcelled out by line' (Amos 7: 17) no conclusion can be drawn regarding this point. They may simply be threatening words. Otherwise it is possible that the priest Amaziah's lands were not at Bethel but in one of those *ʿārê migrāšîm*. If he, nevertheless, owned land at Bethel, it was evidently for agricultural cultivation and not what is called by P *migrāš*. In this case the land must have been a royal gift. The king was accustomed to confer lands on his nobles (cf. 1 Sam. 8: 14–15; 22: 7; Ezek. 45: 8; 46: 17–18), and he

and Nob, and similarly the other temple cities, from our list tells nothing at all about the *date* of the list but is simply an indication of the *character* of those cities that did not belong to the category of priestly and Levitical cities of residence.

There were some cities regarded by P as priestly or Levitical, which also possessed houses of God. These were quite few (cf. below). Such cities exemplify a purely accidental combination of two characteristics in one place. It would be inaccurate to draw any conclusions from these hybrid phenomena regarding the basic character of the cities of Levites.

6

Another combination of varying characteristics in one city might occur if it serves as a city of Levites and of refuge at one and the same time. All the six cities of refuge are Levitical cities too (Num. 35: 6). This combination may not be accidental. It is not impossible that, being regarded as Levitical cities, these six were chosen as extra-territorial domains with respect to the tribes. Furthermore, it is not impossible that the 'priestly' character of these cities served to strengthen their function as asylums and to act as a brake on the passions of the blood-avenger. To be sure, any altar might also have offered asylum to the persecuted (Exod. 21: 14; 1 Kgs. 1: 50–1; 2: 28–9). But the truth is that these two forms of asylum existed at the same time, parallel to each other, and the privilege of asylum was surely attached to the cities of refuge in their own right and applied to the whole of the built-up area within the walls, without having anything to do with 'shrines' or altars which might have been also found in these cities.[15]

would not distribute *migrāšîm* but proper cultivable lands. Again, this case has no bearing at all on those priestly cities of which P speaks.

[15] Of the six cities of refuge only one, Hebron, is attested as having been a temple city (above, p. 34). The first allusion to cities of refuge is in an insertion into an ancient set of laws, succinct (and casuistic) in form (Exod. 21: 12–17), where it says: 'But if he did not act with intent . . . I will assign you a place to which he may flee' (v. 13). Many moderns, following Wellhausen (*PGI*, 156), assume that vv. 13–14, which expand and modify the murderer's penalty of death mentioned in v. 12, speak of asylum by an altar, as these verses still know nothing of cities of refuge. However, the characteristic, quasi-technical expressions *lō' ṣādāh*, *'ašer yānûs šāmmāh*, which emerge both in v. 13 and in the P and D sections dealing with the cities of refuge (cf. Num. 35: 11, 15, 20, 22, 25–6; Deut. 19: 3–4; Josh. 20: 3, 6, 9), as well as additional considerations, give good reason for believing that only a city of refuge is meant in this verse. In

At the same time it should be clear that the priestly legislation does not extend the privilege of asylum to all the Levitical cities. The talmudic law assumed that the Levitical cities provided such asylum,[16] but there is no trace of this in P itself, nor in the actual conditions of the biblical period.[17] If we wish to clarify the historical basis and actual character of the Levitical cities, we must leave out the subject of asylum, which is of a different order. Except for the six special cities, there is no proof that the right of asylum was attached to the whole built-up area of any city, either in the demands of the law or in actual historical practice.

BETWEEN UTOPIA AND HISTORICAL REALITY

7

It seems to me that the account of the Levitical cities is in its nature too distinctive and intricate to be fitted into either of the ready-made categories of Utopia or historical records. In fact, simply because it does contain both historical and utopian elements it cannot be understood in terms of the one to the exclusion of the other. Let us now consider these two elements and note how they intermingle in this account.

fact, asylum by an altar was rated as more powerful than asylum in a city of refuge, and the two verses describe two cases of ascending order: he who kills somebody inadvertently can find a place (that is, a city of refuge) to flee to, *but* (the *wāw copulativum* in *w*ᵉ*ḵî* introduces a new contrast; cf. Gesenius–Kautzsch–Cowley, *Grammar*, § 154*a*) if a man wilfully attacks another and kills him treacherously, you shall take him *even* (as JB, NEB) from my altar to be put to death. In the Greek world, too, these two forms of asylum coexisted with each other; see, e.g., Tacitus, *Ann.* iii. 60–3. Cf. also my remarks in *Zion* 38 (1973), 28–30.

16 הללו קולטות בין לדעת בין שלא לדעת, הללו לדעת קולטות, שלא לדעת אינן קולטות 'These (i.e. the six cities of refuge) afford asylum with or without cognizance (without the refugee being aware of his safety there), whilst these (the other forty-two cities) afford asylum knowingly but not without cognizance' (Bab. Tal. Makkot, 10*a*; cf. 13*a*).

17 Klein (art. cit., 88–91) sought to deduce from Hos. 5: 1 ('For you have been a snare at Mizpah, and a net spread upon Tabor') that the prophet alludes to the fact that these two cities—Mizpah (according to Klein to be identified with Mizpeh Gilead and with Ramoth in Gilead) and Tabor (mentioned as a Levitical city in 1 Chron. 6: 52)—served as cities of refuge. Now the question still remains whether the Mizpah mentioned there can be really identified with the city of refuge, Ramoth in Gilead. In any case, it is impossible to prove that Hosea—and even P itself—regarded Tabor as a city of refuge.

On the one hand, it is impossible not to acknowledge the existence of utopian elements here (mainly already pointed out by Wellhausen and his school), and nothing is gained by ignoring them. To sum them up briefly they would be as follows:

(*a*) The measurements given for the *migrāšîm* of the city, an exact square of two thousand cubits (Num. 35: 4–5). It would seem that the area of the city itself was supposed to be a square.[18]

(*b*) Moreover, these dimensions are the same for all forty-eight cities. It has been said that such precise and general measurements can only be made in the steppes of southern Russia or the western States of America, not in hilly and rugged Palestine.[19] Yet, this tendency to give exact measurements to objects and areas, sometimes schematic to the point of abstraction, is peculiar to the biblical priestly school in general.

(*c*) To a large extent, even the jubilee legislation, which is inextricably linked with the notion of Levitical cities, is utopian. The actual existence of the jubilee depends, for instance, on an over-all fixed counting of years. Even if such an era existed in Israel in biblical times, it is at the very least unlikely that it was familiar to the people at large. It could only have been a kind of priestly 'esoteric' practice.[20]

[18] The elucidation of the text is difficult, since there is no doubt that Num. 35: 5 implies a square of two thousand cubits; yet a thousand cubits 'from the wall of the city outward' (v. 4) do not make such a square feasible, unless the area of the city itself is nil. Various solutions have been propounded that resort to complicated geometrical figures or emendations of the text which are far too bold. See G. B. Gray, *Numbers* (ICC, 1912), pp. 467–9. It should be noted (as Gray has done there) that in biblical terminology *qîr* refers to the wall of a house or an altar (Exod. 30: 3 *et al.*) and in one other instance, to the fence of a vineyard (Num. 22: 25). In Ps. 62: 4 *qîr* and *gādēr*, 'fence' are mentioned together. But it never occurs in the meaning of city wall, *ḥômāh* in biblical Hebrew (no objection can be raised from Josh. 2: 15, where a construct form, *qîr haḥômāh* is used). Thus we may assume that the term *qîr hāʿîr* means not the city wall but the built-up area. Accordingly, the thousand cubits extend from the centre of the city and are measured *miqqîr hāʿîr* and *wāḥûṣāh*, that is, partly in the built-up area, partly outside the city. The whole city is thus included in the square of two thousand cubits, the city itself not necessarily being square. An additional conjecture of mine is mentioned in *Tarbiẓ* 27 (1958), 430–1, n. 15. Yet another attempt was made by M. Greenberg, 'Idealism and Practicality in Num. 35: 4–5 and Ezek. 48', *JAOS* 88 (1968), 61–3. In contrast to Greenberg (ibid., 60, n. 6) I would say that to take the combination *miqqîr hāʿîr* as an ellipsis of *miqqîr ḥômat hāʿîr* is merely possible, and certainly not essential or inevitable.

[19] This statement was made by K. H. Graf, who is referred to by Wellhausen, *PGI*, 153–4.

[20] The only historical nucleus of the jubilee legislation was the custom of proclaiming *d^erôr*, 'liberty, release' once in a few years. This is indicated in

(*d*) To depict these cities as the exclusive preserve of the Levites is quite abstract and unhistorical. According to P, hardly anyone who was not a Levite was given a house within such a city and this applied even to members of the tribe within whose boundaries the city lay, since possession of property in the city by a non-Levite was purely temporary. This point adds weight to the previous one. For even if it is assumed that the law of the jubilee was valid in biblical times, it is still questionable whether the specific privileges applicable to the houses of the Levitical cities were in force, and whether they were in force in these forty-eight particular cities.

(*e*) To a certain extent, the very distinction made between priests and Levites as portrayed by P, a distinction which is inseparable from the concept of the Levitical cities, is somewhat unrealistic. To be sure, this distinction has a historical basis, as we have tried to demonstrate in the preceding chapter. However, to describe it as applying to the entire tribe of Levi, even to its northern clans, with an absolute disregard of the other point of view, that typified by the non-priestly sources, is rather a bold telescoping of the actual perspective.[21]

extra-Pentateuchal passages (Isa. 61: 1; Jer. 34: 8, 15, 17; Ezek. 46: 17) and was undoubtedly similar to *andurâram šakânum*, 'instituting freedom, release', which the Mesopotamian kings used to announce from time to time (and which, for that matter, was related to *mešâram šakânum*, 'instituting equity, justice'). By this they would declare the exemption of citizens from levies, payment of taxes, forced labour, and also from slavery. See G. R. Driver and J. C. Miles, *The Babylonian Laws*, i (Oxford, 1952), pp. 224–5; ii (Oxford, 1955), p. 207; *CAD*, Vol. 1. ii, pp. 116–17; F. R. Kraus, *Ein Edikt des Königs Ammi-Ṣaduqa von Babylon* (Leiden, 1958), pp. 194 ff.; J. J. Finkelstein, 'Ammiṣaduqa's Edikt and the Babylonian "Law-Codes" ', *JCS* 15 (1961), 91–104; idem, 'Some New Misharum Material and its Implications', *Studies in Honor of Benno Landsberger* = *Assyriological Studies* 16 (1965), 233–46; F. R. Kraus, 'Ein Edikt des Königs Samsu-Iluna von Babylon', ibid., 225–31. It seems that H (in the first layer of Lev. 25) already sought to turn this custom into a regularly recurring matter, once in a period of fifty years, while P (in the priestly accretions to Lev. 25) applied to the same fixed year the obligation to return sold lands to their owners.

[21] Albright (*ARI*, 125 ff.) sought to prove the existence of the Levites (as understood by P) in the Davidic period from the argument that the practice of music in the Israelite temples was very ancient and can be traced to Canaanite origins. But this proof does not seem adequate. This music, i.e. the psalmody, was certainly ancient, but during the First Temple period it certainly was not restricted to any *sacral* class. Even if we assume that this liturgy was professional, it does not follow that it was entrusted to the Levites. *P's* Levites are not singers. It was only in the post-exilic period that professional temple music became the prerogative of the Levites and at the same time further functions were entrusted to them. Cf. on this point Kaufmann, *The Biblical Account of the Conquest of Palestine*, 42–3.

8

On the other hand, the account of the Levitical cities contains features so obviously realistic that we cannot dismiss it as pure fiction. In a number of ways this account contradicts the assumptions of P itself, and by the same token it dovetails with historical realities. In particular the realistic features clearly emerge from a comparison with Ezekiel's programme regarding 'the holy district' (Ezek. 45: 1–5; 48: 8–14), which, in contrast to P's account, has no foundation in any historic reality. It is precisely this comparison that may indicate that P's account of the Levitical cities cannot be regarded as having been influenced by Ezekiel's code or as having 'evolved' from it.[22] An affinity no doubt exists between the two, just as there are all-important common aspects shared by P as a whole and Ezek. 40–8, to the extent that they are really included in the framework of one school. But chronologically speaking, with respect to the Levitical cities (as with other particulars) P comes first.

These, then, are the realistic elements of our account:

(*a*) Had it been an outright fiction, P would undoubtedly have concentrated all the Levites in one central place; in fact, he would have had to concentrate them round a certain temple. This is what he does in his utopian representation of the camp (Num. 1: 50–3; 2: 17; 3: 23–38). Ezekiel does likewise, allocating a special strip in his holy district to the Levites (Ezek. 45: 5; 48: 13, 22). According to P's account, however, the Levitical tribe is dispersed throughout the entire territory of Israel. In this P agrees with the assumption of all the other sources and is also faithful to historical reality.

(*b*) Furthermore, we have already stated that the forty-eight cities in which P disperses the Levites were, in most cases, not temple cities. From the point of view of historical authenticity, this fact is most instructive. In P's schematic camp, the Levites surround the tabernacle. The strip of land which Ezekiel allots them also adjoins the temple. There is no doubt that had the account of the forty-eight cities been pure fiction, P would have

[22] When it is admitted that, in this regard, P is 'more realistic' than Ezekiel, one cannot persist further in postulating that P comes after Ezekiel and argue that P tended to be 'more traditional' than his apparent predecessor; cf. P. R. Ackroyd, *Exile and Restoration* (London, 1968), p. 100 (who actually tends to put P somewhat before Ezekiel, though not earlier than the Babylonian Exile).

settled the Levites around the temple.[23] If he had not allotted a single area near the legitimate temple to the Levites, he would at least have granted them cities possessing temples where they had officiated previously (as Wellhausen was apt to assume). But the fact is that his forty-eight cities have nothing to do with temple cities, either in the pre-Josianic period or in any other period in the history of Israel. Even the thirteen cities in the territories of Judah and Benjamin which were granted to the Aaronites (Josh. 21: 4, 9–10) did not for the most part possess temples. In actual fact, they include just one temple city—Hebron. These difficulties are not likely to be solved by claiming the account is a concoction of geographical phrases, but only by assuming that at a certain period in Israelite history these forty-eight cities actually had a Levitical population. As we have stated, the Levitical families only resided in these cities; they did not officiate in them.

(*c*) Even if we admit that P was capable of dispersing the Levites into forty-eight cities far removed from each other—had our account been a fictional creation, P would at least have located these cities within the ideal boundaries of the land of promise (Num. 34: 1–12). In fact, Ezekiel does confine the Levitical strip, with the entire holy district and all the tribal territories, within these ideal boundaries (Ezek. 47: 13–20). The idea, based on politico-territorial conditions of remote times, of the antiquated boundaries of the province of Canaan, came to Ezekiel in the form it took in the priestly school. These boundaries, believed to have been prescribed for the tribes of Israel by an ancient divine promise, did not include trans-Jordan but stretched to the north as far as Lebo Hamath.[24] The Levitical cities, however, are dispersed on both sides of the Jordan, over all those areas where the Israelite

[23] In the same way, had P been indifferent to the centralization of the cult and had he been inclined to permit a multiplicity of temples, as was argued by D. Hoffmann (*Die wichtigsten Instanzen gegen die Graf-Wellhausensche Hypothese*, i. 79–82) and in a slightly different way also by Kaufmann (*THH* i. 113–18, 126–38), he would undoubtedly have settled the Levites around temples.

[24] This concept of the ideal land of Israel is dealt with by Kaufmann, *THH* i. 190–3; ii. 377–81; *The Biblical Account of the Conquest of Palestine*, 46–61; and, in a slightly different way, also by B. Mazar, 'Lebo Hamath and the Northern Boundary of Canaan', *BIES* 12 (1946), 93–5, 99 (Hebrew). All the Pentateuchal sources conceive of the promised land in its ideal extent only. P, in his usual manner, gives it exact boundaries on the four sides (Num. 34: 1–12), and these same boundaries are described in Ezek. 47: 13–20 with the aid of slightly different geographical indications and in a somewhat obscure phraseology. Cf. on this subject also my comments in *VT* 17 (1967), 282–3; and above, pp. 39–41.

tribes actually settled. In this respect, too, a most pronounced historical element is evident.

9

(*d*) According to P the social and economic position of the priests does not necessarily have to be similar to that of the Levites. The priests partake of the holy offerings and are abundantly endowed with gifts. The Levites, on the other hand, are granted the tithe votive offerings alone (Num. 18: 21–32).[25] Had the account of Levitical cities been essentially utopian and had P been consistent with his own visualization, this difference would have had practical repercussions in this account. There was neither rhyme nor reason in placing the priests, in this respect, under the same conditions as the Levites.

It may be observed that in Ezekiel's Utopia the priests really are different from the Levites in this respect. Admittedly, in his programme both receive the same strips of land, each being 25,000 cubits long and 10,000 cubits broad; but there is still a certain difference concerning the status of the two. The prophet explicitly states that the priests have no possessions in Israel (Ezek. 44: 28). Accordingly, nowhere does he term the priests' strip *'ᵃḥuzzāh*, 'possession'. This strip is 'a portion set apart from the holy portion of the land, a most holy place' (48: 12). In his view, it serves merely for residential purposes and is not cultivated. The priests shall have there only 'a place for their houses' (45: 4), while their livelihood shall be provided from the temple that stands in their strip. It is otherwise with the Levitical strip which is conferred on them 'for a possession' (45: 5) and is explicitly termed *'ᵃḥuzzat halᵉwiyyîm*, 'the possession of the Levites' (48: 22). Ezekiel undoubtedly assumes that the Levites will be able to gain a livelihood from the land of this strip, just as the produce of *'ᵃḥuzzat hā'îr*, 'the possession of the city' (45: 6–7), is destined to sustain the inhabitants of his utopian city (48: 18). Only the land 'of possession' granted by him to the Levites is limited when compared with that of any other tribe, and it is holier than others because of its proximity to the temple and inclusion in the holy

[25] It must again be pointed out that in P, as well as in all non-Deuteronomic sources, the tithe is taken to be a votive offering—not an annual obligation; cf. above, n. 8.

district.[26] The tithe is not mentioned in Ezekiel's code—this may perhaps be accidental, or may simply reflect the eclectic and fragmentary character of his code.

But in P's account of the forty-eight cities there is no distinction between priests and Levites; the same legal status and the same social and economic position characterize all the cities. The difference between the Levitical and priestly cities is merely expressed in the genealogical descent of the families in residence. This fact can only be explained if we assume that in this respect the account of the cities reflects historical reality. Historically speaking, all the families of the tribe shared the same degree of sanctity, even if traditions current among them argued for the superiority of the descendants of Aaron (the representatives of the tribe's southern section). Their living conditions in all their scattered cities were certainly equal (with the exception of those who actually graduated to priesthood). In this respect, too, P's account of the Levitical cities is thus based on quite reliable foundations.

(*e*) Lastly, the numerical proportion of priests to Levites is very instructive. Against the background of the camp there appears in P a tiny group of priests, totalling over three generations hardly a dozen, and this at a time when the males over thirty years old of the tribe of Levi exceed 8,500 (Num. 4: 46–8), the Kohathites alone numbering over 2,700 (vv. 34–7), and the total male population of the tribe from one month upward is about 22,000 (Num. 3: 39; cf. 26: 62). No doubt these statistics contain much imaginative padding. But even if we examine the *genealogical* accounts alone, we still find that the number of priests in the sum total of the tribe of Levi would have been insignificant.[27] Had P been

[26] The prohibition on the sale of lands, mentioned in Ezek. 48: 14, refers to the strips of land of both the priests and the Levites. Many commentators, ancient and modern, understood this correctly (most recently W. Zimmerli, *Ezechiel* (BK, 1969), ad loc.; in contrast, e.g., to G. A. Cooke, *Ezekiel* (ICC, 1936), p. 534, who understood the prohibition to apply to the Levitical strip only). If we accept the LXX reading of the previous verse (48: 13: 'The whole length . . . and breadth twenty thousand', the area of both strips together being here summed up), the first explanation becomes the only possibility. The practical status of these two strips is similar to that of the *migrāšîm* of the Levitical cities, which likewise cannot be sold (Lev. 25: 34), but for an entirely different reason: 'for it is holy to Yahweh'.

[27] In the third generation after Levi, we find there are already eight heads of families: Amram, Izhar, Hebron, and Uzziel, the sons of Kohath; Libni and Shimei, the sons of Gershon; Mahli and Mushi, the sons of Merari (Exod. 6: 17–19; Num. 3: 18–20). In the fourth generation after Levi, that is, Aaron's generation, there could easily be twenty heads of families.

consistent in his imaginary construction, he could not have allotted more than two or three cities to the Aaronites. In this account, however, the number of priestly cities is thirteen, while only ten cities are allotted to the remaining Kohathites and thirty-five to the remaining Levites (Josh. 21: 4–7).

This can only be explained on the assumption that in the account of the cities P was bound to a certain historical reality. He could embellish this reality with various utopian features, but he did not see himself free to ignore it altogether. Indeed, the numerical proportion of priests to Levites in this account (13 to 35) is much more reasonable than in the camp scheme. A single small family could not have claimed for itself the prerogative of priesthood in the face of the demands of a whole tribe. And we are not here discussing the actual holding of the priestly office, but merely the claim to it. Even the claim of a single tiny family would have been quickly and easily erased from the memory of succeeding generations. But it is otherwise when the family is scattered throughout thirteen cities within the boundaries of two tribes like Judah and Benjamin.

CONCLUSIONS

10

We may infer, then, that the account of the Levitical cities basically reflects a particular historical situation, overlaid, however, by utopian features. Remove the latter, and a bedrock of reality stands revealed, which can be unreservedly accepted as the description of a geographical situation at a particular moment in Israelite history. This can be done, or course, only if the work is carried out with extra special care and if the actual separation of the fictional from the real is accurate. This rule applies with equal validity to the lists of the tribal boundaries and their cities (Josh. 14–19) which likewise belong in the main to P[28] (except for fragments

[28] Most probably to P, not to D. All scholars engaged in literary criticism, from J. Wellhausen to G. von Rad, W. Rudolph, O. Eissfeldt, and S. Mowinckel, have admitted that these geographical accounts belong to P. Alt's school alone has asserted that they are part of a Deuteronomistic composition, in spite of the clearly priestly traits found in them. M. Noth (*Überlieferungsgeschichtliche Studien*, Schriften der Königsberger Gelehrten Gesellschaft, Geisteswissenschaftliche Klasse, 18 (1943), pp. 82–9) went so far as to state that the whole Book of Joshua belongs to the Deuteronomistic work that ends with 2 Kings,

whose character recalls JE, being in the nature of quotations which P integrates into his accounts; e.g., Josh. 14: 6–15; 15: 14–19, 63; 16: 10; 17: 11–18). The utopian accretions in these lists are, however, fewer than in the account of the Levitical cities, for they are presented to us in virtually their 'primary' state. The account of the Levitical cities is loaded with heavier utopian embellishments. But this fact need not mislead us into thinking that it is divorced from historical reality.

We can even say that the realistic elements determine the importance of these accounts, not only as geographical-historical documents, but as all-important keys to the study of P itself; and that, because the utopian and unreal line adopted by P is broken here—to a certain degree (in the list of Levitical cities), or almost totally (in the lists of tribal inheritances). Most of P's material is distinguished, as we know, for the extremely schematic form it takes, to the extent that it is often the despair of the scholar searching for points of contact with reality. But in these accounts a basis of reality peeps through the literary material. Admittedly, even this descent into the realm of the actual does not always free the material from utopian accretions. Nevertheless, an obvious change is evident. For it goes without saying that the meandering tribal boundaries and the cities of the Levites dispersed all over the land of Israel cannot constitute a continuation equivalent to those neatly arranged symmetrical tribal camps and that single camp of Levites centred around the tabernacle.

Accordingly, the geographical-historical reality underlying the account of the Levitical cities may be summarized as follows: at the time when this account was formulated these cities actually contained Levitical inhabitants; their population was mixed, the Levitical families forming only a part.[29] In P's utopian reflection these cities turned into an exclusive reservation for this tribe, but in terms of historical actuality it is difficult to imagine that the Levitical element really was dominant in them. At the very least, members of those tribes in whose territories these cities were located resided in them side by side with Levites. At a somewhat

and that with the exception of a few random verses neither priestly portions nor priestly redaction can be found within it. Thus, in the first edition of his commentary to Joshua (HAT, 1938), p. 14, Noth still assumed that Josh. 21 belonged to P. In the second edition (HAT, 1953), p. 10, which appeared after the *Studien*, he attributes this chapter to the supposed Deuteronomistic work.

[29] Cf. on this point Albright, *ARI*, 123; also D. Hoffmann, op. cit., p. 151.

earlier time, a number of them might even have contained groups of non-Israelites, slaves or freemen, survivors of the previous population. The chronological framework within which this reality was committed to writing and became a literary document was hinted at in the preceding chapter and will be discussed further in the following one.

VII

THE CENTRALIZATIONS OF THE CULT

I

An occasional onlooker is liable to pay insufficient attention to the fact that not one but two cult reforms took place in the Kingdom of Judah—namely, in the days of Hezekiah and of Josiah. About a hundred years separate the two reforms, but they were nevertheless both based on the same idea—the abolition of all cultic institutions outside Jerusalem and the restriction of cultic activity to the Jerusalem temple alone. The reform carried out by Josiah was more decisive than its predecessor. Even so Hezekiah's is of special interest just because it came first. It is worth trying to delineate its ideological motives.

On the strength of the cult reforms Hezekiah and Josiah merited the superlative esteem of the Deuteronomistic historiography. Both of them were compared with King David in righteousness and of them alone was it said that no such king ruled before or after (2 Kgs. 18: 3, 5; 22: 2; 23: 25). However, the actual accounts of the reforms are quoted from earlier sources of different scope. Hezekiah's reform is referred to only in two verses, one of which is mentioned incidentally in a prophetic narrative devoted to a different matter (2 Kgs. 18: 4, 22).[1] Josiah's reform is described in

[1] Verse 22 is within the section 2 Kgs. 18: 13—20: 19, which, with certain changes, also appears in Isa. 36–9 (thus the verse occurs in Isa. 36: 7 too). The section concerns the deliverance of Jerusalem from Senacherib's seige, wondrous acts performed by Isaiah, and prophecies he gave. 2 Kgs. 18: 4 is cast in the Deuteronomistic style, but the facts related in it are taken from an earlier source. In this verse, the limpness of the remark: 'for until those days the people of Israel had brought grain-offerings (*m^eqaṭṭ^erîm*; cf. below, pp. 233–4) to it' is particularly recognizable. The remark was put in in order to add an explanatory detail about the bronze serpent, and this resulted in the splitting of the main sentence: 'And he [Hezekiah] broke in pieces the bronze serpent that Moses had made . . . and [Moses] called it Nehushtan'. Cf. J. Gray, *I & II Kings* (OTL, 1964), ad loc. (where the annalistic character of this verse is noted and other textual suggestions are mentioned). The Chronicler greatly expanded the story of this

detail in two chapters (ibid. 22: 3—23: 24), and though here too an element of prophetic miracle is evident (ibid. 23: 15–18; cf. 1 Kgs. 13: 1–32) it is on the whole a chronographic, realistic account of the type found at the end of the Books of Kings and examples of which are also embedded in the Book of Jeremiah (Jer. 39: 1–10; 40: 7—41: 18; chap. 52). Yet, a number of Deuteronomistic amplifications have been introduced into this account.[2]

THE DISTINGUISHING FEATURES OF THE TWO REFORMS

2

We are told that in addition to removing the high-places and their appurtenances, King Hezekiah broke in pieces the bronze serpent (2 Kgs. 18: 4) which had formerly been considered a

reform and gave it obvious priestly overtones (2 Chron. 29–31), but did not mention the smashing of the bronze serpent. According to him the reform began in the first year of Hezekiah's reign, in the first month (ibid. 29: 3) and continued for about two months. Its main stages were as follows. The temple is purified of 'all the uncleanliness' that had collected in it during previous generations (ibid., vv. 4–19). After the purification, burnt- and sin-offerings are made (ibid., vv. 20–4). The Levites sing hymns to the Lord and play musical instruments (ibid., vv. 25–30). The congregation bring thanksgiving offerings (ibid., vv. 31–6). All Israel celebrate the Passover and the Feast of Unleavened Bread in the second month (chap. 30), because they did not finish the purification in the first month (cf. ibid. 30: 17) and, furthermore, the people were far away and could not manage to gather in Jerusalem; this is in an exact accordance with P's law (Num. 9: 1–14). Only afterwards do all Israel go forth to break down the high-places (2 Chron. 31: 1). Hezekiah sets up the divisions of the priests and the Levites and organizes the tithes and other sacral contributions (ibid., vv. 2–21).

[2] They are as follows: the main part of Huldah's speech (2 Kgs. 22: 15–19); the expansions on the stories of the making of the covenant (ibid. 23: 3: 'and to keep his commandments and his testimonies and his statutes . . . that are written in this book') and of the celebration of the Passover (ibid., vv. 22–4); and a few more phrases that crept into the language of the section. All the rest of the section is a literary source. It should not be divided into a description of the discovery of the book and historical 'annals'—the whole is one account (connected with 1 Kgs. 13). Although the account was composed after the reform, it is not to be identified with the Deuteronomistic strand (as was correctly noted by Wellhausen, *PGI*, 278, note). A. Jepsen (*Die Quellen des Königsbuches*[2] (Halle, 1956), p. 27), however, following Th. Östreicher, tried to discern in the body of this account a merging of different sources. See also Gray's commentary ad loc.; M. Weinfeld, *Encyc. Judaica*, x (Jerusalem, 1971), cols. 290–1; and most recently H. Hollenstein, *VT* 27 (1977), 321–36.

legitimate symbol in the worship of Yahweh (Num. 21: 4–9).[3] The detailed account of Josiah's reform also shows that the destruction of the high-places was not the king's sole reforming act.

The account of Josiah's reform itself consists of several links. According to the sequence of events portrayed, it appears that after the book of the law was found in the temple (2 Kgs. 22: 3–20) the king and the people made a covenant before the Lord to fulfil the precepts written in that book (ibid. 23: 1–3). Immediately after the covenant ceremony the reform began and to all appearances spread outwards. In the first place the temple was cleansed of all the pagan cult vessels used there in the days of Manasseh and Amon (ibid., vv. 4–7). Afterwards all the cult sites and cult objects in the city of Jerusalem and in Judah, were destroyed, irrespective of whether they were considered illegitimate appurtenances in the service of Yahweh or devoted entirely to alien gods—the Topheth, the sun chariot, high-places and Asherim for Yahweh and for alien gods (ibid., vv. 8–14).[4] Then it was the turn of all the high-places in the cities of Samaria, where the altar at Bethel merited special attention in the account, because of the prophetic miracle connected with it (ibid., vv. 15–20). When the

[3] A few scholars have doubted the very existence of Hezekiah's reform, since there is no reference to it in Isaiah's prophecies. They argued that it is a mere retroflex of Josiah's reform and all that actually happened at that time was the smashing of the bronze serpent. Thus already Wellhausen, *PGI*, 25; followed by B. Stade, *Geschichte des Volkes Israel*, i (Berlin, 1887), p. 607; G. Hölscher, *Die Profeten* (Leipzig, 1914), pp. 165, 261; H. Schmidt, *Die grossen Propheten* (SAT ii. 2, 1923), p. 9; and others. All this is, however, quite unlikely, as others have already pointed out.

[4] In the passage 2 Kgs. 23: 4–7 it is mentioned (v. 5) that the *k^{e}mārîm*, illicit priests 'whom the kings of Judah had ordained to make grain-offerings (reading *l^{e}qaṭṭēr*, as most scholars have correctly done, following Lucian and the Peshitta, for MT *way^{e}qaṭṭēr*; for the meaning of *qiṭṭēr* cf. below, pp. 233–4) in the high-places in the cities of Judah and round about Jerusalem' were deposed, even though this passage as a whole describes the purification of the temple. It seems that the *k^{e}mārîm* were referred to here incidentally after the mention of the pagan vessels in the temple. On the other hand, in the following passage (vv. 8–14) there are mentioned in v. 12 'the altars which Manasseh had made in the two courts of the house of the Lord', this being referred to incidentally after 'the altars on the roof of the upper chamber of Ahaz', although these verses as a whole describe the destruction of the cult places in the city and in the provinces, not in the temple court. The horses and the sun chariot ('chariot' in the singular, as in LXX) were kept somewhere outside the temple, but the custom was for them to be brought into the temple (v. 11). The upper chamber of Ahaz was in the court of the king's palace (cf. 2 Kgs. 20: 4–11). Upon this upper chamber the 'kings of Judah', i.e. Manasseh and Amon, made altars (ibid. 23: 12), apparently to the sun and moon and the host of heaven (cf. v. 5).

purge was over a Passover sacrifice was made as prescribed in the book found in the temple (ibid., vv. 21–3). Finally, in a kind of short appendage, we read that the mediums and the wizards, the teraphim, the *gillûlîm*, 'idols' and all the *šiqqûṣîm*, 'abominations' were also destroyed (ibid., v. 24).[5]

These facts clearly demonstrate that even though the descriptions differ greatly in scope and we only have passing allusions to Hezekiah's reform, it is impossible to avoid the conclusion that the two reforms differed from each other in character and in profundity. In this respect there is no need to build on details mentioned in only one of the two descriptions, such as the smashing of the bronze serpent by Hezekiah or the destruction of the pagan cult by Josiah. One can certainly claim that such actions could have formed part of either reform. Josiah would no doubt have broken the bronze serpent had Hezekiah not preceded him, and the latter would doubtless have swept away all pagan cults had he been preceded by a king like Manasseh, who indulged in such a cult and established it in the temple and in the city.[6] Even though the

[5] Like that of Hezekiah, Josiah's reform underwent a change in the Chronicler's description (2 Chron. 34: 3—35: 19). Its commencement was moved back to the twelfth year of Josiah's reign (while Josiah's seeking the God of David his father was pushed back as far as the eighth year of his reign), and the destruction of the high-places was made to precede the discovery of the book itself (ibid. 34: 3–7). Only afterwards is the story of the discovery of the book and the making of the covenant brought in (ibid. 34: 8–32), and here it is based on 2 Kgs. 22: 3—23: 3 (whereas 2 Chron. 34: 33 is a hasty, cursory summary of the account in 2 Kgs. 23: 4–20). The account of the celebration of the Passover, mentioned in the continuation of the passage in the Book of Kings, was greatly expanded and embellished with clear priestly overtones (2 Chron. 35: 1–19). Some claim that the description in Chronicles does not result entirely from synthesis, but contains certain kernels of truth. However, even if we assume that this is indeed so, these kernels will by no means contradict the inherent authenticity of the description in the Book of Kings and will not change it in any essential. They would merely add something to it (if they really have anything to add). There is therefore sufficient reason to be confident that this contains nothing that might weaken our arguments. See also below, note 7.

[6] I can find no justification for H. H. Rowley's opinion (*Men of God* (London, 1963), pp. 127–9), which others also share, that Hezekiah's reform must have involved the removal of Assyrian cult, just because it is supposed that Ahaz took up such a cult. Our sources do not allude to any worship of Assyrian gods by Ahaz (even 2 Chron. 28: 23 relates only that he sacrificed to the gods of Damascus), and the incident of the altar built according to the plan of an altar in Damascus (2 Kgs. 16: 10–16), frequently mentioned by these scholars (and first propounded by Th. Östreicher, *Das deuteronomische Grundgesetz* (Gütersloh, 1923), p. 38), is hardly relevant to the question. An altar in Damascus is not necessarily Assyrian; it is more reasonable to suppose, as certain scholars actually did, that it was Syro-Aramaean. Were we to assume that Assyrian architecture had

mediums and the wizards are not mentioned in the reference to Hezekiah's reform it can be said that he, in fact, abolished them too, but then they were restored by Manasseh (2 Kgs. 21: 6). To all appearances, such abolitions took place in the days of earlier kings as well, whenever they were caught up with zeal for the authentic character of Yahweh's religion; thus we are told that King Saul had already acted in this manner (1 Sam. 28: 3, 7–20).

However, disregarding details such as these, which are mentioned in either of the two reforms, there are still items mentioned in one reform which could not have been included in the other. These are evidence of a difference in the intrinsic nature of the two reforms.

3

These are the items which differentiate the reform of Hezekiah from that of Josiah.

(*a*) Only in the case of Josiah's reform was a covenant first made with Yahweh by the king and the people, in the temple court, 'before the Lord'. In saying that this did not happen in the case of Hezekiah I am not arguing *ex silentio*. In Josiah's time the making of the covenant was the direct outcome of the abolition of the pagan cult which had been installed in the temple by Manasseh (2 Kgs. 21: 1–9), and the ceremony was one of the expressions of repentance and of renewed attachment to the national religion. Throughout the history of the Kingdom of Judah the only other covenant of this kind was made in the days of King Jehoash and Jehoiada the priest, when it marked the destruction of the Baal cult in Jerusalem (ibid. 11: 17–18). However, Josiah's covenant was based on the book found in the temple and was related to a public commitment to abide by the words written in that book (ibid. 23: 1–3). In this respect, it does not resemble even the covenant made by Jehoash and Jehoiada.

(*b*) According to the account of Josiah's reform, the book which

some influence there (or that it was Aramaean in form) this still does not prove anything. The influence of Phoenician architecture was already present in Solomon's temple (with regard to Ahaz's altar, which was destined for sacrifices only to Yahweh, cf. below, p. 194, n. 9). J. W. McKay, *Religion in Judah under the Assyrians* (London, 1973) is, in the main, certainly convincing when he contends that during its subjugation to Assyria Judah was under no obligation to introduce the cult of Assyrian gods, and that the reform of Hezekiah, and possibly even that of Josiah, were much more acts of religious zeal than of political rebellion.

formed the basis of the covenant was then found for the first time, having hitherto been entirely unknown. It falls into the hands of the court as a sensational surprise. On hearing the contents of the book the king rends his garments and is seized by consternation (2 Kgs. 22: 11–13). It appears that this book was indeed Deuteronomy, or its main part, and the recognition of this point forms one of the cornerstones of modern biblical research.[7] That it was Deuteronomy is evidenced by the fact that after Josiah's covenant the Book of Deuteronomy comes to the fore, making its presence felt in the literary activity and in the communal life of Israel, and this presence was not to disappear even after Deuteronomy had merged into the Pentateuch. This fits in perfectly with the didactic character of Deuteronomy, with its homiletic tone, and its declared demand that it be learned by the king and by every single Israelite and that its contents be present in their minds at every hour of the day (Deut. 6: 6–9; 11: 18–20; 17: 18–20). Another question is the exact time of D's composition, which may have preceded that event somewhat. At any rate, it is clear that legal material and literary elements of greater antiquity were absorbed into this book.

It is extremely doubtful, however, whether it was this book that also formed the basis of Hezekiah's reform—and that, not

[7] It was first investigated critically by W. M. L. de Wette in his *Dissertatio critico-exegetica qua Deuteronomium a prioribus Pentateuchi libris diversum*, etc., which appeared in 1805; reprinted in *Opuscula* (Berlin, 1833). The following year de Wette developed this thesis in *Beiträge zur Einleitung in das AT*, i (Halle, 1806). Henceforth this recognition was not shaken, and in spite of attempts to criticize it, it has maintained itself and in fact been further refined. For a succinct survey of this matter see O. Eissfeldt, *Einleitung in das AT*[3] (Tübingen, 1964), pp. 226–9. For a list of the early authorities, from Jerome to Lessing, who foreshadowed de Wette in the awareness that Deuteronomy was the book found in the days of Josiah, see also R. Smend, *W. M. L. de Wettes Arbeit am Alten und am Neuen Testament* (Basel, 1958), p. 36. According to the Chronicler the book found in Josiah's time could only have been the complete Pentateuch, and his accounts actually reflect this assumption (see 2 Chron. 34: 14–15 and commentaries). However, this discovery could not have brought a new book into the world, for according to the Chronicler's viewpoint the whole Pentateuch was known in Israel from the earliest times and even King David acted in accordance with it (cf. 1 Chron. 6: 34; 15: 15; 16: 40 *et al.*). For this reason the Chronicler found it necessary to reverse the order and put the destruction of the high-places (2 Chron. 34: 3–7) before the discovery of the book in Josiah's time. In this manner he makes the destruction of the high-places into a consequence of the piety of the king, who even in his youth 'began to seek the God of David his father'. Thus, in the Chronicler's opinion the discovery of the book leads only to a covenant-making ceremony and to a certain extent to the celebration of the Passover sacrifice too—acts which, at all events, are befitting a God-fearing king.

necessarily because there is no reference to the discovery of a book in Hezekiah's reform, but because it is not in the nature of a work like Deuteronomy to be destined to concealment. The appeal to the public and the effort to influence the people's outlook are its inherent qualities: they account for, and justify the very existence of this work. At the same time, D's militant, zealous character and his insistence on religious and national devotion indeed look as though they arose as the natural consequences of the pressure of Manasseh's period. In any event, it must be pointed out that if this book already existed in Hezekiah's time, it is hard to understand why it was considered so new at the time of Josiah. And if this same book had already succeeded in bringing about an earlier reform some hundred years before Josiah, one wonders why the account saw fit to depict its discovery as of a completely unknown work, the like of which had never been known until that time.

(*c*) The high-places which Hezekiah removed were rebuilt by Manasseh (2 Kgs. 21: 3), but after their destruction by Josiah they were never restored. The reason for this is that Josiah was not content with pulling down the high-places. He also took trouble to defile them, and in such a manner that ruled out any possible purification in the future. To be sure, according to the priestly law, which is quite strict in its approach, even defilement through corpses is not considered absolute and leaves a possibility of purification (Num. 19: 11–21; 31: 19–24). Josiah used human bones, but he burnt them on the high-places so that the ashes penetrated into the ruins and, consequently, the defilement was irreversible.

The burning of bones is mentioned explicitly in connection with the altar in Bethel and all the high-places in the cities of Samaria (1 Kgs. 13: 2, 32; 2 Kgs. 23: 16–20). There can be no doubt that this system is assumed to have been also employed to defile the high-places in Judah and the neighbourhood of Jerusalem, as well as to defile the Topheth in the Valley of ben Hinnom (ibid., vv. 8, 10).[8] The bones were mainly taken from graves in the vicinity

[8] It is said that after Josiah destroyed the high-places, the pillars, and the Asherim that Solomon set up near Jerusalem to the foreign gods, he filled the places where they had stood with human bones (2 Kgs. 23: 13–14). Apparently the style is elliptical here, and the implication is that he did to those bones what he did in other places. The statement in 2 Kgs. 23: 20: 'And he sacrificed, *wayyizbaḥ* all the priests of the high-places who were there, upon the altars' is explained by its parallel: 'and he burned the bones of men upon them', i.e.

of the high-places—it was mostly priests of the high-places who were buried there, generation after generation, though other corpses, too, were occasionally interred there (1 Kgs. 13: 30–31; 2 Kgs. 23: 17–18). The practice of taking bones out of graves was a custom of the Assyrian period, introduced into Josiah's circle, and its echo is heard in one of Jeremiah's early prophecies (Jer. 8: 1–2).[9] But there was something frightful, out of the ordinary about the application of this custom to the high-places in order to defile them by means of burning the bones to ashes. It is this dreadful feature that inflamed the imagination in the tale about the bones of the man of God from Judah and the prophet from Samaria who found their resting-place in a common grave. In any case, this practice served to demonstrate how extreme and uncompromising was Josiah's reform in its attitude to high-places and how much further it went than the earlier reform.

(*d*) The pronounced extremism of Josiah's reform was also demonstrated by his transferring all the priests from the high-places in Judah to Jerusalem (2 Kgs. 23: 8–9). Hezekiah did not do this, and again we draw no inference from silence. By uprooting the priests from the high-places the reformers sought to obtain an additional guarantee that the cult would not be renewed in those places. It is, therefore, no mere accident that it was only the reformers of Josiah's time, those who did not shrink from burning bones of corpses on the high-places, who removed their priests. The reformers of Hezekiah's time, who in the words of 2 Kgs. 18: 4, 22 only 'removed' the high-places (the verb *hēsîr* being used in the text), but did not defile them, certainly did not go so far as to transfer the priests to Jerusalem. Of the priests in the cities of Samaria nothing is said in Josiah's reform either, possibly

Josiah sacrificed the priests of the high-places by means of burning human bones, the bones of the priests of the high-places, on those altars. The two sentences are also interconnected and explain each other in 1 Kgs. 13: 2, and they are in fact one of the links connecting the two parts of the account (1 Kgs. 12: 31—13:32 as against 2 Kgs. 22: 3—23: 24). It is unthinkable that Josiah made human sacrifices (and that the biblical narrative praised him for it, even if the men sacrificed were unlawful priests), though some exegetes erroneously assumed so.

[9] It may be that the burning of the bones of the king of Edom into lime, as Amos accuses the king of Moab of doing (Amos 2: 1), was also connected with the practice, common in the Assyrian period, of removing the bones of the dead from the graves (in that case, too, in order to burn them). On the historical background to the contents of this strophe one may consult the comments in my book תקופות ומוסדות במקרא (Tel-Aviv, 1972), pp. 314–15.

because the latter was not actually prepared to remove those priests—perhaps the danger of the cult being renewed at the high-places in Samaria was already less likely than in Judah.

(*e*) The absence of the Passover sacrifice from Hezekiah's reform is not accidental either. The Passover sacrifice at the end of Josiah's reform was made according to the specifications given in the book of the covenant—the book that had just been found in the temple (2 Kgs. 23: 21). Since Hezekiah's reform did not include a ceremony of covenant, nor is a book which served as a basis for making a covenant mentioned, one cannot be surprised that not even a Passover sacrifice was performed there. When the Deuteronomist finds it necessary to remark that no such Passover had ever been observed in either the days of the Judges or in those of the kings of Judah and Israel, but only in the eighteenth year of King Josiah (ibid., vv. 22–3), we can well believe him. The Passover which formed the festive conclusion to Josiah's reform could be taken as a positive cultic expression of the correctness of the doctrine of the reform, and as a symbol of the renewal of the temple cult. It is a well-known phenomenon that the erection of a new temple tends to reach its culmination in the sacrifice or the celebration of the feast which fall closest to the date of the completion of the temple. Thus, Solomon celebrates the Feast of Booths after the completion of the temple (1 Kgs. 8: 65–6). The Passover sacrifice is made and the Feast of Unleavened Bread is celebrated after the consecration of the Second Temple (Ezra 6: 19–22). In like manner, the priestly legend has it that after the Exodus the Passover was celebrated 'according to all its statutes and all its ordinances' when the tabernacle had been put up (Num. 9: 1–5; cf. Exod. 40: 2, 17).

THE IDEOLOGICAL BACKGROUND OF HEZEKIAH'S REFORM

4

Scholars believe that the reforms of Hezekiah and Josiah were in the main based on the same ideology and that the historical place of D is somewhere between these two reforms, or that the first reform constituted a kind of signal and harbinger for the approaching appearance of D.[10] The points mentioned above, however, lead

[10] See, for example, the typical statement by Eissfeldt: '. . . it may be considered comparatively unimportant whether the book is regarded as having been

me to believe that although these reforms were both based on a common idea, namely, the categorical affirmation of the centralization of the cult, they nevertheless differed from each other in their concrete manifestations and ideological patterns. Josiah's reform was more aggressive and uncompromising than its predecessor and achieved decisive results. Since only this reform was based on D and was bound up with its ideology, I am inclined to conclude that Hezekiah's reform took shape in a different manner and was sustained by another ideology.

I am prepared to suppose that the ideological conception which formed the basis of Hezekiah's reform was that which found its literary expression in P. This is indicated by the fact that apart from D we find no other source but P in the Pentateuch (and in the whole of the Old Testament), which is based on the idea of cult centralization and which does not explicitly belong to the post-exilic period. We must, however, not forget that the account of Hezekiah's reform is not given to us by the authors of P. Indeed, within the framework of P it is practically impossible to arrive at an account of this event because P's story is bound by certain chronological limitations and is completely detached from contemporary occurrences. The priestly writers begin with the creation of the world and end with the conquest of the land. Their last utterances are recognizable in a few notes inserted into the description of Solomon's consecration of the temple (1 Kgs., beginning of chap. 8).[11] This story thus comes to its end at a time

composed only in Josiah's time, shortly before it was discovered, or half a century or a century earlier [*sic!*], in the time of Manasseh or Hezekiah' (op. cit., p. 227). Similar statements are to be found in, for example, Kaufmann (*THH*, i. 86, 109; ii. 266, 270–1). A number of scholars (E. Sellin, C. Steuernagel, E. König, G. A. Smith *et al.*) went so far as to claim that D itself constituted the foundation of Hezekiah's reform. Rowley sensed the forced nature of such a conjecture, and suggested that D was composed at the beginning of Manasseh's reign and then forgotten until it was discovered in Josiah's time (H. H. Rowley, 'The Prophet Jeremiah and the Book of Deuteronomy', *Studies in OT Prophecy Presented to Th. H. Robinson* (Edinburgh, 1950), pp. 159–67 = *From Moses to Qumran* (London, 1963), pp. 190–8; cf. *Worship in Ancient Israel* (London, 1967), pp. 96–7, 106–7). But see the arguments above.

[11] The priestly expansions discernible here (according to the MT reading) are as follows: 'and all the heads of the tribes . . . before King Solomon' in v. 1; 'which is the seventh month' as an explanatory note to the month of Ethanim in v. 2; 'and the tent of meeting and all the holy vessels etc.' to the end of v. 4 (the suggestion made by V. W. Rabe, *JNES* 25 (1966), 133 about a part of this verse is entirely inadmissible); 'to the holy of holies' as an explanatory note to *d^e^bîr habbayit*, 'the inner sanctuary' in v. 6. See also commentaries. 'The priests

which is a distant past for the priestly writers. What is included in its scope is an idealized, utopian tale of events which reflects the views and aspirations of the priestly writers, but does not evolve into a chronographic account of their own period (as it does in the case of the other sources). Furthermore, the account of Hezekiah's reform, delivered to us in two verses, is incidental and scanty in the extreme. It contents itself with merely an abrupt reference to the actual event. However, since even so it accords with P's outlook and conceptions, let us not reject out of hand the possibility that there is some connection between the latter and the event itself. If only a slightly more substantial description of the event had come down to us, either from the priestly school or from the angle of other writers, we might have been in a better position to perceive the ideological connection between that reform and the concepts of P.

5

Moreover, strange as it may seem, P, as a literary and theological document, is well-suited to be the basis for a cultic reform of Hezekiah's type, one which lacks the specific features of vehemence and extremism which marked Josiah's reform, as outlined above.

(*a–b*) A reform which based itself on P's doctrines could not possibly be accompanied by the making of a covenant between Yahweh and the congregation of Israel, nor is P designed to serve as 'the book' of such a covenant. The term 'book of covenant', *sēper b^e^rît* is itself foreign to P. As we know, even the tables and the ark are called *'ēdût*, testimony and *'^a^rôn hā'ēdût*, ark of the testimony, in P, without the term *b^e^rît*, covenant being employed (Exod. 16: 34; 25: 16, 21–2 *et al.*). Even when speaking of the revelation at Sinai P does not say that a 'covenant' was made between Yahweh and Israel, but that Yahweh gave them an *'ēdût*, testimony, that the Israelites made a tabernacle that God might dwell amongst them, that God uttered various laws, *tôrôt*

and the Levites' are mentioned only in v. 4, while in the main part of the narrative the priests alone bear the ark (cf. above, pp. 78–80). Minor priestly expansions are also discernible at the beginning of chap. 6 of 1 Kgs. In several chapters of the Books of Kings, especially those containing descriptions of the temple (1 Kgs. 6; 2 Kgs. 12: 7–17; 16: 10–18), a relatively intimate knowledge of the arrangements of the temple and its form is recognizable, more than is indicated in those sources in general, and there are even several terms in these chapters which recall the language of P. Nevertheless, these sections are non-priestly in their literary identity and should by no means be ascribed to P as such.

to Moses and Aaron from between the wings of the cherubim, and that the Israelites were charged with commandments.[12]

The reason for the absence in P of a covenant ceremony between Yahweh and Israel is perfectly plain—for by its very nature P is not intended to be made public. P itself is designed to serve as a book for priests alone. What is written in its scrolls is in the nature of a *tôrāh* in the priestly sense of this term. When such a *tôrāh* has implications for the wider public, the priest would be consulted and he who seeks counsel would surely be given proper instruction. If that *tôrāh* deals with matters which are solely the concern of priesthood, it would remain an esoteric in-group teaching. It any event, it is held to be priestly property and its proper place is consequently within their circle.[13] True, in Ezra's time circumstances caused this priestly, semi-esoteric *tôrāh* to be handed over to the general public, after it had been joined to D and served as material for compiling the canonical Pentateuch. But as long as P existed as an independent literary work, it remained

[12] Instead of *sēper habbᵉrît*, which is not to be found in P, the expression characteristic of the priestly style is *'ôt bᵉrît*, sign of a 'covenant', which is used with reference to the rainbow in the clouds in the covenant of Noah (Gen. 9: 13–17), the circumcision in the covenant of Abraham (Gen. 17: 10–14), and the Sabbath in the Sinai pericope (Exod. 31: 13–17). In the priestly thought, this expression therefore serves to impart to the Sinai revelation, the significance of 'covenant'. P also tells about 'a "covenant" of perpetual priesthood' granted to Phinehas (Num. 25: 13), and employs the epithet *bᵉrît melaḥ*, '"covenant" of salt' with regard to sacrifices (Num. 18: 19; cf. Lev. 2: 13; also Ezek. 43: 24) whose regulations were given to Israel at Sinai. I therefore would not say that P tends to eliminate, or to depreciate the covenant of Sinai in favour of that of Abraham (W. Zimmerli, *Gottes Offenbarung, Gesammelte Aufsätze* (München, 1963), pp. 213–16; R. Clements, *Abraham and David* (London, 1967), pp. 74–7; P. R. Ackroyd, *Exile and Restoration* (London, 1968), p. 95), but rather that P comprehends the association of Yahweh with Israel at Sinai in his own terminology. In his style, the characteristic combination is *hēqîm bᵉrît*, to fulfil a 'covenant', and the term *bᵉrît* actually approaches the meaning 'promise', 'obligation' (i.e., which, in this case, was given to Abraham and was realized at Sinai); it hardly means 'covenant' in the proper sense. Yet, the connection between the covenants of Abraham and Sinai (or Horeb) exists in the non-priestly sources as well. On the meanings of the term *bᵉrît* in the Old Testament see also the entries ברית by E. Kutsch, *Theologisches Handwörterbuch zum AT*, i (Zürich, 1971), cols. 339–51; M. Weinfeld, *ThWAT*, i, cols. 783–98; and J. Barr's valuable observations in *Beiträge zur Alttestamentlichen Theologie, Festschrift f. W. Zimmerli* (Göttingen, 1977), pp. 23–38.

[13] Thus, according to P, the *tôrāh* is kept in scrolls, and is transmitted from the priests to the people orally. But when D speaks of the *tôrāh*, he is referring to a book only (Deut. 29: 20; 30: 10; 31: 9 *et al.*) and this is supposed to be known to the whole people (Deut. 1: 5; 4: 8, 44; 31: 11 *et al.*) and studied by every Israelite; cf. above, sect. 3(*b*).

sectarian and professional in character. During the preceding period, in pre-exilic times, a reform which could be said to result from P's ideology would only mean that under certain circumstances the influence of the priestly school increased to the degree that it was given the opportunity to modify cult practices and abolish cult institutions in accordance with its doctrines. Such a reform would not have found expression in public ceremony and would certainly not have brought the priestly *tôrāh* scrolls into the public domain.

(*c–d*) Paradoxical though it may sound, I think also that it is entirely to be expected that a priestly reform would content itself with removing the high-places and would not go so far as to obliterate them completely by defiling them with human bones and removing their priests to Jerusalem.

For generations scholars have emphasized P's extremism, its dogmatic character, legalistic inflexibility, cultic formalism, and stringency (and since biblical studies have been based on the principle of historical and dialectic evolution, they go on to claim that in this respect P attests to a later stage than that of D).[14] There is no point in denying that P is rigorous in its cultic inclination and in its dogmatic and formalistic outlook (though this does not necessarily substantiate the prevailing opinion as to its date of composition, or the claim that it is a development of D). One has to attempt to determine, however, the nature of this priestly extremism—is it only theoretical or is it also practical? It is possible for an ideology to be exceedingly extreme in its speculative contemplation, and yet, when applied to the sphere of reality, it contents itself with obtaining its aims, loses all its vitality, and allows its vigour to evaporate. Irreconcilable dogmatism does not necessarily lead to extreme aggressiveness in the concrete—on the contrary, theoretical radicalism is quite likely to hide the feeling of restraint the ideologist sometimes feels when faced with reality.

As regards the attitude to the high-places, scholars continuously assure us that while D demands their destruction and the centralization of the cult in a chosen place, P takes this centralization 'for granted' and moves it back to the revelation at Sinai.[15] I, for one,

[14] Cf. above, p. 6.

[15] The first to point this out as proof of the dating of P was K. H. Graf (*Die geschichtlichen Bücher des AT* (Leipzig, 1866), pp. 51–66). In his wake A. Kuenen (*Historisch-kritische Einleitung in die Bücher des AT*, i. 1 (Leipzig, 1887), pp. 203–14, 251 ff.) and especially Wellhausen (*PGI*, 17–52) availed themselves of this argument.

am prepared to say that the fact that P takes cult centralization for granted does not necessarily imply a practical militancy, but just a theoretical outlook which is radical in its suppositions alone. After all, one cannot deny that while D explicitly and outspokenly demands that Israel utterly destroy all the cult places except for the chosen place (Deut. 7: 5; 12: 2–3), P makes no such explicit demand.[16] Instead, it paints a picture of ideal conditions, which address, as it were, the priestly writers from a distance in space and time and by means of which they intend to give expression to what they consider to be the legitimate norm in all aspects of cult and of life. This is not so much evidence of the vigour of uncompromising fighters, prepared to attack and refashion prevailing circumstances; rather is it evidence of the dream of utopians, whose main strength lies in their very aspiration to a different reality (it is a good general rule that historically and chronologically utopians appear before the practical revolutionaries). P's utopian image contains no reference to high-places, not because by that time the centralization of the cult was actually taken for granted, but for the opposite reason that high-places still existed and centralization was mere aspiration on the part of the priestly school. During Hezekiah's reign this school found an outlet for its aspiration and the high-places were removed. However, reformers of P's type could consider this a sufficient realization of their desire, without proceeding to defile the high-places and uproot their priests.

(*e*) One might still add that a celebration of the Passover is no more fitting a conclusion to a reform stamped with the views of P than it is to one based on D. P too, as we know, adheres to the idea of cult centralization, and its system presupposes that the Passover sacrifice must be made in the court of its only temple.[17] As has been mentioned, in its depiction of the ideal camp P does not refrain from telling of the celebration of the Passover after the completion of the tabernacle (Num. 9: 1–5). Nevertheless, neither the transfer of the Passover to the precincts of the single temple nor the very idea of the centralization of the cult assume in P that declared, antagonistic attitude to the current state of affairs that

[16] Num. 33: 52 originates from H, which approaches D in spirit and, to a certain degree, even in language. The words *maśkiyyôt* ('figured stones') and *bāmôt* that appear in this verse do not occur in P (but they do appear in Lev. 26: 1, 30). See also commentaries (and above, p. 20, n. 11).

[17] Cf. below, pp. 347–8.

we find in D: 'You may not offer the Passover sacrifice within any of your towns . . . but at the place which Yaweh your God will choose to make his name dwell in it, there you shall offer the Passover sacrifice etc.' (Deut. 16: 5–7). On this subject, too, P's tone is not aggressive towards the present, and the form of the Passover sacrifice which it enjoins is employed not as a war slogan against existing usage, but as a model of perfection which is part of a utopian image. The absence of this sacrifice from Hezekiah's reform may thus be by no means accidental.

THE TIME-SPAN OF THE PRIESTLY SCHOOL

6

It is here assumed, then, that Hezekiah's reform was based on the priestly ideology. This does not imply, however, that we can date P exactly to the period of Hezekiah's reign. We cannot possibly consider that the Pentateuchal sources are the literary products of the labours of individual writers, each one of them managing to encompass the enormous material stretching from Genesis to the end of Joshua (in fact even further, well into the Former Prophets and down to the Books of Kings). In each case we are actually dealing with the output of a school, each possessing its own institution for training scribes and the whole of its work having distinctive characteristics and bearing an individual literary stamp. In each case, the question is not when was a given source composed, that is, committed to writing by a specific author, but how long and during what period did the school exist—that is, when was the literary circle, or the succession of writers, which built up the source, in existence and active.[18] The literary milieus of J and E, sources imbued with extraordinary narrative skill, made their appearance in the beginning of the monarchy and continued in existence till later times (which is why they contain early as well as relatively later literary crystallizations). D burst

[18] Long ago scholars considered the possibility that despite the stamp of unity impressed on each of the sources, they nevertheless all constitute collective, non-individual, works; see, e.g., G. F. Moore, *Judges* (ICC, 1895), pp. xxvi–xxvii, xxxiii (note); C. F. Burney, *The Book of Judges*[2] (London, 1920), p. xl; J. Skinner, *Genesis*[2] (ICC, 1930), pp. xlvi–xlviii (and the references there). My interpretation takes a somewhat different form. It should be added that I do not refer here to stages of oral transmission that preceded the literary crystallization of the sources, but to the literary crystallization itself, which in my opinion occurred within the time-span of the activity of a school of scribes.

upon the scene in Josiah's time, and immediately became a pattern for the Deuteronomistic school (which continued until the time of Ezra). P's school was in existence against the background of Hezekiah's reform, but this does not mean that its entire life-span was restricted to that period. It was apparently already in existence during the reign of Ahaz, as certain signs serve to indicate. In Hezekiah's days the ideological aspirations of this school achieved a realization, at least as far as the centralization of the cult was concerned. And it seems that during Manasseh's rule it was dealt a serious, almost fatal blow.

P's comparatively brief halcyon period may explain its considerable uniformity, its solid structure, and its well defined scope, which is entirely confined within the framework of a utopian story, without the slightest intention of being drawn into its own time. Even so it transpires that, after Manasseh's time, this school did not vanish altogether, and some artery fed by it still continued to run. There must have been compilers and copyists who preserved this literary heritage (otherwise it would certainly have been doomed to oblivion). That is what enabled the special epigonic growth, which is revealed in Ezekiel's visionary code, to blossom out at the end of the artery which derived ultimately from P's school. Ezekiel's code is a small-scale transcript of P and at the same time a flat contradiction of P (in many tangible particulars).[19] Needless to say, this code had already been exposed to the influence of D, just as D's influence is clearly discernible in all Ezekiel's prophecies. The employment of phrases such as 'the priests the sons of Levi', 'the Levitical priests' in this code (Ezek. 40: 46; 43: 19; 44: 15) constitutes but one of the indications of this influence.

7

The comparatively short period of P's flourishing ran parallel to the period of the Northern Kingdom's decline. Now it appears that at that time priests from the north found their way to Jerusalem, although in accordance with P's doctrine they did not gain admittance to the cultic sanctity and were destined, as we described in Chapter V, to remain in a sub-priestly rank. The right to the priesthood was reserved for those families scattered among the southern tribes who prided themselves on their Aaronic descent.

[19] On the nature of Ezekiel's code as an epigonic extension of the priestly school, cf. my observations in *Tarbiẓ* 44 (1975), 30–53.

This right was valid enough to keep all those not descended from Aaron out of the priesthood, but could not prevent tension and counter-claims by the rejected 'Levites', who according to the custom in any other temple—especially those of the north—had never had their path to the priesthood barred (in accordance with the view of the non-priestly sources). This contrast found expression in P's cultic legend in the story of the attempt at rebellion by Korah and his company and the sprouting of Aaron's rod.[20] Even though in Hezekiah's time all cult places outside Jerusalem were removed, the old right of all the Aaronites to the priesthood did not lapse (just as, similarly, it remained in the wake of Josiah's reform, which was still more firm and decisive in character). The priestly legend contented itself with depicting all the Aaronites as officiating in the single, model temple of the desert period.

As described in Chapter V, the distinction between the Aaronites and the rest of the tribe of Levi was perpetuated in P's doctrine and was given concrete form in the image of the tabernacle surrounded by the camp, but in reality the line of division ran differently, namely, as given by P in the list of the priestly and Levitical cities (Josh. 21: 1–40). Now the geographical and historical foundations of this list, like those of the lists describing the tribal boundaries in Joshua, not to mention the boundaries of the land of Canaan in Num. 34: 1–12 (for the northern and southern limits cf. Num. 13: 21; Josh. 15: 1–4), may well precede the times of Ahaz and Hezekiah, just as early traditions and even earlier literary materials may have been absorbed by all the sources. It seems difficult, however, to date the literary crystallization of any of these lists, in the form as found in P, to the period of the United Monarchy.[21] The form and the formulation of these lists are those of P, and anyone wishing to determine when they were set down as literary products cannot remove them too far from the period which marks P as a whole.

[20] See above, pp. 89–90.

[21] As it has been pointed out in Chapter VI, certain scholars relate the list of the Levitical cities to that period and some of them seem to have shaken off the problem of the literary identity of this list. Others date the list to the time following Josiah, but seek to remove it from P (pp. 113, 115, 129–30).

VIII

THE PRIESTLY IMAGE OF THE TABERNACLE

I

THE tabernacle, the imaginary temple described as having been with the Israelite tribes before their settlement in Canaan is the central phenomenon of the priestly Utopia. According to P, Yahweh himself showed Moses its form with all its paraphernalia on Mount Sinai (Exod. 25: 9, 40; 26: 30; 27: 8). Its erection was the Israelites' first act after Moses' descent from the mountain. The whole of the work was superintended by Bezalel the son of Uri whom the Lord had specifically 'called by name' for this task and who was assisted by Oholiab the son of Ahisamach. Both were filled with 'the spirit of God' and endowed with the ability and skill to perform all the necessary kinds of artistic craftsmanship and to teach others to do the same (ibid. 35: 30–5). So enthusiastic were the Israelites that they continued to offer materials for use in constructing the tabernacle even after Bezalel and his aides had begun their work. So large was their offering that Moses was forced to proclaim throughout the camp that no more offerings were to be brought (Exod. 36: 3–6). At the same time, the priestly writers themselves find the subject so fascinating that not only do they describe the tabernacle in two lengthy parallel sections (Exod. chaps. 25–30, 35–9) but they are also prompted to recapitulate the list of its appurtenances time and again (Exod. 30: 26–30; 31: 7–11; 35: 11–19; 39: 33–41; 40: 2–15, 18–33). Their tendency to indulge in technicalities and stereotyped repetitions has here reached its furthest limits. There is no doubt that it was intensified in this case by the importance and appeal of the subject.

Let us first outline the form of this tabernacle, since it is indispensable to our subsequent observations. In spite of P's minute and repetitious descriptions, some architectural details are puzzling. Various matters are not stated explicitly, but are either left to be taken as obvious or have to be inferred by deductive reasoning. We are faced with a unique combination of long-winded description on the one hand and total omission of various particulars on the other. Nevertheless, the general character of the structure is quite clear.[1] As we shall see, the tabernacle's form is an amazingly fitting expression of its institutional essence and perfectly correlates with the cultic acts said to have been performed in it.

THE FORM

2

Basically, the tabernacle is made of planks, *qᵉrāšîm*, in rows on three sides—north, west, and south. The *qᵉrāšîm* are conceived as heavy wooden beams and 'covered wagons' harnessed to oxen

[1] Exegesis of the form of the tabernacle begins with Philo, *De Vita Mosis*, ii. 71–148; Josephus, *Antiquities*, iii. 6–7; and the talmudic sages. An ancient collection of talmudic material on this theme is the בריתא דמלאכת המשכן (hereafter referred to as Baraytha) printed in various editions, the latest that of A. Jellinek, בית המדרש, iii (Leipzig, 1856; second printing, Jerusalem, 1938), 144–54; H. Flesch (Hamburg, 1899); and M. Ish-Shalon–Friedmann (Vienna, 1908; photographic reprint, Jerusalem, 1967). An English translation of the Baraytha is to be found in J. Barclay's volume *The Talmud* (London, 1878), pp. 334–58. Out of the vast literature written on the theme down the ages, in addition to the ancient and modern commentaries on the text of Exodus itself, attention should be paid to the following Hebrew treatises: Joseph Shalit Richetti, חכמת המשכן (Mantua, 1676); Immanuel Ḥay Ricchi, מעשה חושב (Venice, 1716, and later editions); A. Z. Deglin, מקדש אהרן, 3rd printing (Vilna, 1896, Russian and German translations are extant); Moshe Qaṭan, בית ישראל (Vilna, 1908), pp. 1–12. The most important works in the European languages, written chiefly in the nineteenth century, including those of the architects K. Schick, *Die Stiftschütte, der Tempel in Jerusalem* etc. (Berlin, 1896) and J. Fergusson, *The Temples of the Jews* (London, 1878), pp. 18–25, are indicated in the bibliographies at the end of the articles 'Tabernacle' by A. R. S. Kennedy, *DB* iv. 668; and I. Benzinger, *EB* iv. 4874–5. Later monographs on the form of the tabernacle seem to be of little importance. Of those suffice it to mention the following: E. M. Epstein, *The Construction of the Tabernacle* (Chicago, 1911); J. Strong, *The Tabernacle of Israel in the Desert* (Grand Rapids, Michigan, 1952; lithographic reproduction of a previous printing). Both contain bibliographical surveys of the subjects. See also G. Henton Davies, s.v. 'Tabernacle', *IDB* iv. 498–506; and most recently also B. S. Childs, *Exodus* (OTL, 1974), pp. 547–50. On the form of the priestly garments see: J. Gabriel, *Untersuchungen über das alttestamentliche Hohepriestertum* (Wien, 1938), pp. 25–118. Other works, though more recent in date, mostly lack a critical approach. A few publications on specific aspects are mentioned in the footnotes later on. Since the technical problems involved in the form of the tabernacle are rather complicated, we shall content ourselves with mentioning only the solutions that appear the most plausible.

are needed to carry them (Num. 7: 8).[2] The planks are set in place side by side, close together, joined by bars suspended along the width of the walls, each one of them being inserted with the aid of two tenons, *yādôt*, into two sockets, *'ªdānîm*.[3] The height of the tabernacle, identical with the length of a plank, is ten cubits; the length of the tabernacle is thirty cubits, and its breadth ten cubits (Exod. 26: 15–30; 36: 20–34).[4] On the eastern side, the entrance to the tabernacle, there are no planks.

Over these three walls are spread the lower curtains (the tabernacle curtains). Each of these measures 28×4 cubits and there are ten in all. They are joined lengthwise in two sets, five to each set; the two sets are joined together by loops and clasps. Accordingly, the combined area of the two sets is 28×40 cubits (Exod. 26: 1–6; 36: 8–13). The way in which these curtains are placed on the planks is not described, but it seems likely that each curtain is supposed to be stretched lengthwise over the breadth of the tabernacle. The line joining the two sets is probably twenty cubits from the door—that is, ten cubits from the western wall—and thus comes over the partition between the outer and inner sanctums (see Exod. 26: 33). Accordingly, for most of their area the walls are also covered by these curtains.

[2] Kennedy, op. cit., pp. 659–61, seems to have been the first to express the interesting view that the *qᵉrāšîm* may be thin wooden frames rather than heavy beams. His argument was based mainly on their weight. Many scholars and commentators have been attracted to this view which found its way into EVV. But the fact that the *qᵉrāšîm* are said to have been transported on 'covered wagons' is in itself sufficient to invalidate this argument. Even if we accept the view of Rabbi Judah that the *qᵉrāšîm* were 'at the bottom the thickness of a cubit, and at the top tapering to the thickness of a finger' (Bab. Tal. Shabbath, 98*b*), we must still admit that they were heavy, though oxen could still move them. On the other hand, if they had been thin, solid boards (so U. Cassuto, *A Commentary on the Book of Exodus* [Jerusalem, 1967], 357; cf. Josephus, *Antiquities* iii. 6. 3) the text would certainly have called them *lûḥôt*, as with the outer altar (Exod. 27: 8). The word *qrš* is found in the Ugaritic texts, always within the phrase: *qrš mlk 'b šnm* (*UT*, 49. i. 7–8; 51. iv. 24; 129. 5 *et al.*), where its meaning is 'room', 'abode' (not 'plank' or 'beam').

[3] For technical details on the way the tenons are held in the sockets, see Baraytha, chap. i; Bab. Tal. Shabbath, 98*b*; Rashi, on Exod. 26: 17.

[4] The last two measurements may be deduced from the text. On the southern as well as the northern sides stand twenty planks, the width of each being a cubit and a half. Six planks stand on the western side, making up nine cubits with the addition of two planks 'for corners of the tabernacle at the rear', which are apparently somewhat narrower (or, alternatively, part of their width is taken up by the thickness of the adjoining walls; see Rashi on Exod. 26: 23). The thickness of the planks is not mentioned in the text—perhaps because this measurement is included in the breadth and length of the tabernacle itself.

Above these curtains are placed the outer curtains (the tent curtains). There are eleven of them in sets of six and five, the measurements of each being 30×4 cubits (Exod. 26: 7–13; 36: 14–18).[5] It seems likely that the extremities of the curtains—both those of the tabernacle and the tent—are secured by pegs, evidently with the help of cords. This is the proper function of the tabernacle's pegs and cords mentioned, almost incidentally, in various places (Exod. 27: 19; 35: 18; 38: 20, 31; Num. 3: 26, 37; 4: 26 *et al.*). A covering of tanned rams' skins and skins of *t^eḥāšîm*[6] is placed over the tent curtains (Exod. 26: 14; 36: 19).

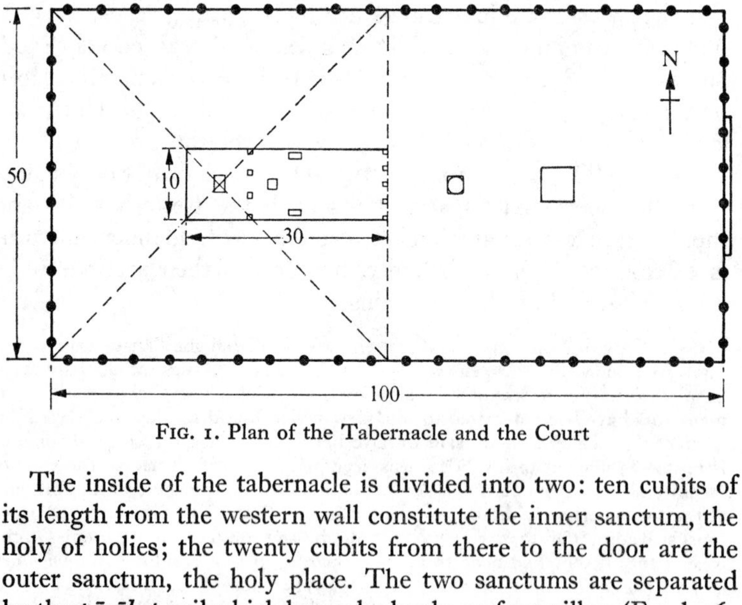

FIG. 1. Plan of the Tabernacle and the Court

The inside of the tabernacle is divided into two: ten cubits of its length from the western wall constitute the inner sanctum, the holy of holies; the twenty cubits from there to the door are the outer sanctum, the holy place. The two sanctums are separated by the *pārōḵet*-veil which hangs by hooks on four pillars (Exod. 26: 31–3; 36: 35–6). In the holy of holies which is shaped like a cube

[5] The lower curtains are not long enough to cover the whole height of the northern and southern walls, so that the bottom cubit at least remains uncovered (the same is true of the western wall). But the outer curtains overhang them by one cubit both on the northern and southern sides, whilst the eleventh outer curtain (four cubits wide) allows for the creation of a curve over the entrance and the covering of the whole western wall. See Exod. 26: 9, 12–13; Josephus, *Antiquities* iii. 6. 4; Philo, *De Vita Mosis* ii. 85–6; Rashi on Exod. 26: 5. Probably, the loops and clasps of the two sets of outer curtains do not join at the same place as do the lower curtains, but slightly to the east of them.

[6] KJV: badgers; RV: seals; RSV: goats; AT: porpoises (similarly, NEB); NJPS: dolphins. Cf. below, p. 162, n. 28.

(length, breadth, and height all ten cubits) are placed the ark (Exod. 25: 10–16; 37: 1–5) and the ark-cover, *kappōret* (Exod. 25: 17–22; 37: 6–9). The ark is shaped like a chest open at the top, while the *kappōret* fits over it exactly as a covering (an ordinary ark, or chest, would certainly have had a much simpler covering). The ark and the *kappōret* are considered to be two fundamentally distinct objects, although they are joined together.[7] At the end of the *kappōret* are two cherubim: their wings outspread and their faces downwards inclined, as if not daring to look at what is above them. Above their wings is the place where God meets and speaks with Moses.

Three articles of furniture stand in the outer sanctum in front of the *pārōḵet*-veil. By the northern wall (Exod. 40: 22) stands the table (25: 23–30; 37: 10–16) and opposite it, by the southern wall (40: 24)—the lampstand (25: 31–40; 37: 17–24).[8] The altar of incense (30: 1–10; 37: 25–8) stands between these two, opposite the ark.[9] Just as the *pārōḵet*-veil shuts off the inner sanctum, so an outer veil hangs across the entrance to the tabernacle, 'a screen for the entrance of the tent', which shuts off the outer sanctum. The pillars of the latter are five in number (26: 36–7; 36: 37–8).

3

The court is marked by hangings stretched over pillars (or posts), *'ammudîm* (Exod. 27: 9–19; 38: 9–20). Unlike the planks, each one of which is inserted into two sockets, the pillars, whether of the tabernacle veils or of the court, are each inserted into one socket. This indicates that the planks are thought to be heavier and larger

[7] The fact that they are distinct from each other may be demonstrated by various observations. Cf. below, pp. 248–51.

[8] The measurements of the lampstand are not mentioned in the text. The Rabbis gave it exact specifications, fixing its over-all height at eighteen handbreadths, which is about three cubits. See Bab. Tal. Menaḥoth, 28*b*; Rashi on Exod. 25: 35; Maimonides, הלכות בית הבחירה , iii. 10. See also Baraytha, chap. x. The lampstand's design, consisting of three pairs of branches with a central axis, seems to be based on the stylized tree of the ancient Near Eastern art. For this point cf. G. Widengren, *The King and the Tree of Life in Ancient Near Eastern Religion* (Uppsala, 1951), pp. 64–7; E. R. Goodenough, *Jewish Symbols in the Graeco-Roman Period* iv (New York, 1954), pp. 71–7; and most recently Carol L. Meyers, *The Tabernacle Menorah* (Missoula, Montana, 1976), pp. 98–122.

[9] Cf. Rashi on Exod. 30: 6.

than the pillars. The pillars of the court are five cubits in height[10] and they stand five cubits apart. Since twenty pillars are said to be posted on each side of the court, north and south, its length must be one hundred cubits. In width it is fifty cubits, ten pillars being

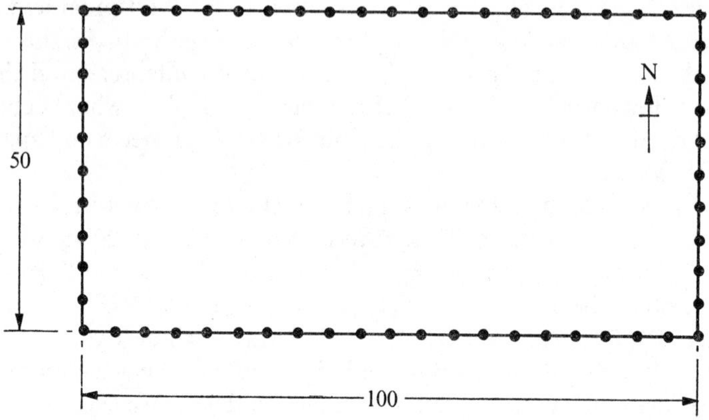

FIG. 2. An Alternative Arrangement of the Court Pillars

posted on its western side. On the eastern side the hangings are stretched on both flanks of the gate, fifteen cubits (and three pillars) to each flank. Over the gate itself hangs a screen of twenty cubits on four pillars.[11] It seems that the court hangings, like the

[10] Since the pillars are apparently all considered to be of the same height, the pillars inside the tabernacle should also be five cubits high. Consequently, the *pārōḵet* and the outer veils of the tabernacle would not reach the height of the tabernacle's roof. But the space above would be covered from the outside, over the outer veil, by the extra curtain remaining from the outer curtains of the tent (Exod. 26: 9). Cf. above, p. 152, n. 5.

[11] The number of pillars on each side of the court creates a minor geometrical puzzle. If we assume, as indeed emerges from the text, that the space between each pillar is five cubits, and, moreover, that the pillars start from the corners, the number of pillars across the length of the court will be found to be 21 (or 19, without reckoning the corner pillars) and across its width 11 (or 9). See fig. 2. On the other hand, if we say that there should be exactly 20 pillars across the length of the court and exactly 10 to the width, every corner being counted twice (the total number of pillars on all four sides thus being 56), we shall find that the space between each pillar is not five cubits. Furthermore, the distances between the pillars of the court lengthwise will be less than those across its width (100:19 as against 50:9). This point has puzzled many commentators. The solution would lie, in my opinion, in the system suggested in the Baraytha, chap. v. It explains that the pillars stand in the *middle* of each imaginary space of five cubits (100:20), and that there are no pillars at all at the corners. This emerges from

curtains of the tabernacle and tent, are also fastened to pegs by cords. The pegs and cords of the court like those of the tabernacle are mentioned in a number of places (Exod. 27: 19; 35: 18; 38: 20, 31; 39: 40[12] *et al.*; cf. above, sect. 2). On the other hand, the screen to the court, like the *pārōḵet*-veil and the outer veil of the tabernacle, certainly hangs loosely and whoever enters lifts up its extremities.

It is not stated exactly where, within the court, the tabernacle stands. But it may be presumed that the pillars of the outer veil of the tabernacle stand on a line dissecting the court widthwise, the tabernacle extending into the fifty cubits of the western section. There remains, therefore, a space of twenty cubits between the western wall of the tabernacle and the west side of the court. It would seem that the same gap is maintained between the northern and southern sides of the court and the corresponding walls of the tabernacle: fifty cubits, the width of the court minus ten, the width of the tabernacle, with forty left over; the latter is then divided into two equal parts—twenty cubits on each side of the tabernacle.[13]

In the fifty-cubit square section in front of the tabernacle stands

the Baraytha's statement that the hanging was rolled on the pillar כמין קלע של ספינה, 'like the sail of a ship': נמצא הקלע יוצא מן העמוד שתי אמות ומחצה מצד זה ושתי אמות ומחצה מצד זה, וכן לעמוד השני; הא למדת, שבין עמוד לעמוד חמש אמות 'It follows that the hanging extended from the pillar two cubits and-a-half on one side, and two cubits and-a-half on the other side; and so with the second pillar. This teaches that between each pillar there were five cubits'. In other words, the 'internal' distances between the pillars add up to five cubits, though the distance from the last pillar of each side of the enclosure to the end of that same side is only two and a half cubits (see fig. 1). The most recent editors of the Baraytha (H. Flesch, p. 63; M. Ish-Shalom, pp. 35–6) evidently did not notice that there is here a distinctive system. I found it explained properly by Ricchi, מעשה חושב v. 5–6.

[12] The word *mêtārāyw*, 'its cords', in this verse (though the pronominal suffix is masculine) refers to *heḥāṣēr*, 'the court' (mostly a feminine noun), not to *hammāsāḵ*, 'the screen' (a masculine noun). The change in gender of the same noun in the same verse is not unusual. Cf., e.g., Exod. 35: 17 and Ibn-Ezra ad loc.

[13] Cf. Philo, *De Vita Mosis* ii. 91–2; Bab. Tal. Erubin, 23*b*; Baraytha, v; Rashi and Rashbam on Exod. 27: 11, 18. Some continue this thesis, and assume that the site of the outer altar would be the exact centre of the eastern square, with the *kappōret* and ark opposite in the centre of the western square. See H. Holzinger, *Exodus* (KHC, 1900), p. 133; Kennedy, *DB* iv. 657. The Baraytha (ibid.), however, maintains that 'from the tabernacle to the altar there were ten cubits' only.

the outer altar (Exod. 27: 1–8; 38: 1–8).[14] Between this and the tabernacle, we find the laver, filled with water for the priests to wash their hands and feet (30: 17–21; 38: 8).

4

Most of the articles of furniture listed are alike in that they have rings in which poles, *baddîm*, may be inserted so that they can be carried on the shoulders. The lampstand is carried on a 'carrying bar', *môṭ* (Num. 4: 10). The *kappōret* is not carried separately but always coupled with the ark. There are no details in MT of how the laver is to be carried, but from its shape ('hammered work' like the lampstand; cf. below, sect. 7) a *môṭ* would be indicated. This is stated explicitly in the LXX and Samaritan Versions of Num. 4: 14.

The ark is distinguished from the rest of the movable articles of furniture in that its poles always remain in the rings, 'they shall never be removed from it' (Exod. 25: 15), even during encampment.[15] On the other hand, the poles of the table and of the altars are only put in place for transportation, and the same applies to the lampstand's carrying bar (Num. 4: 8, 10, 11, 14).[16]

5

In addition to the appurtenances already listed, the text mentions *kēlîm*, implying minor utensils attached to the major pieces of furniture (they are termed as *kᵉlê šārēt*, 'utensils of officiation' in Num. 4: 12; 2 Chron. 24: 14; cf. Num. 3: 31). Thus we find that frequent allusion is made to 'the table and its utensils', 'the lampstand and its utensils' and the like. The table utensils are bowls, ladles, jugs, and jars (Exod. 25: 29; 31: 8; 35: 13; 37: 16; 39: 36 *et al.*). The lampstand utensils are tongs and also *maḥtôt*,[17] lamps, and the

[14] The altar of incense, the fire on which is small and not continuously alight, has a 'roof' (see Exod. 30: 3 and the remarks of Rashi and Obadiah Sforno), whereas no 'roof' is mentioned in the case of the outer altar. Thus it would basically consist of four walls filled with earth and gravel on which the fire is kindled. This could possibly be a reason for its being called *nᵉḇûḇ lûḥôt*, 'hollow with boards' (Exod. 27: 8), i.e. a framework of four sides without a roof or bottom.

[15] So it was in Solomon's temple too (1 Kgs. 8: 8); cf. below, p. 190.

[16] The words *wᵉśāmû baddāyw*, 'they shall put in its poles', referring to the ark (ibid., v. 6) apparently crept in here under the influence of subsequent verses, in which they recur verbatim. Cf. commentaries.

[17] KJV, AT: snuffdishes; RSV, JB: trays; NJPS, NEB: firepans.

rest of the oil utensils (25: 37–9; 37: 23–4 *et al.*; Num. 4: 9–10). The utensils of the outer altar are: pails, scrapers, basins, forks, and again *maḥtôt*[18] (Exod. 27: 3; 38: 3; 40: 10 *et al.*; Num. 4: 14). The utensils of the altar of incense are not mentioned specifically. It is interesting to note that while travelling they are put on to a special carrying bar (Num. 4: 12),[19] unlike the utensils belonging to the table, lampstand, and outer altar, which are packed with them. No utensils are attached to the ark and the *kappōret* since they require none. Sometimes all the utensils of service are lumped together under the phrase *kᵉlê haqqōdeš*, 'the utensils of holiness' (Num. 3: 31; 4: 15) since they are held to be as holy as the major articles of furniture themselves.

We find that the text makes mention of yet more *kēlîm* of the tabernacle and enclosure (Exod. 27: 19; 31: 7; 39: 40; Num. 3: 36; 4: 26, 32) which are needed only for the maintenance of the latter. These include hooks, clasps, pegs, and perhaps cords as well.

6

Three categories of appurtenances are thus integrated in the tabernacle: furniture (all that is inside the tabernacle and in the court); fabrics (all the curtains, the veils, the hangings and the court screen); beams (the planks, the pillars of the tabernacle, and of the court). On journeys the Kohathites carry the furniture (Num. 4: 1–20), the Gershonites the fabrics (ibid., vv. 21–8), the Merarites the beams (ibid., vv. 29–33). However, the furniture is treated with greater deference than the other articles. It is carried from place to place as it is, whereas the fabrics and beams

[18] EVV mostly: firepans. Later on we render *maḥtôt* as 'censers', for it is clear that these utensils were used for burning incense (Lev. 10: 1; Num. 16: 6 *et al.*), though in Ezek. 8: 11 another term, *miqṭeret*, is employed for an implement used for the same purpose. Cf. below, p. 238.

[19] From the context it is clear that the utensils of the altar of incense are meant here (as Rashi explains), though it is not actually specified to which appurtenance they belong. This mode of blurring the exact identity of a subject by means of vague terminology left to be understood by the reader is a characteristic of P's style. Frequently, however, we are able to pinpoint the character of the subject by means of analogy or by examining the context (cf., for instance, Lev. 4: 2; 5: 17; Num. 5: 6; 15: 23). The roof of the altar of incense, one cubit square, is apparently too tiny to hold all its utensils. In Exod. 30: 27–8, on the other hand, no mention is made of the utensils of the altar of incense, though utensils of the table, lampstand, and outer altar are referred to—perhaps because in comparison with the latter the former are fewer in number. Cf. Ibn-Ezra's commentary ad loc.

are dismantled and folded for travelling. The furniture is carried on the shoulders by means of poles, whereas the fabrics and beams are loaded on to 'covered wagons' pulled by oxen (Num. 7: 7–8). On journeys the furniture is covered with cloths of blue and purple, and on top of these further coverings of *taḥaš* skins are placed, but no cloths nor coverings are mentioned in connection with the fabrics and beams. 'Pure gold' is mentioned in connection with the furniture, whereas just 'gold' without any additional epithet is used to describe the tabernacle's planks and pillars (see below, sect. 9). The furniture is indeed the essential constituent in the cult and cultic sanctity, whereas all the other objects merely serve as protective and separating accessories.

However, an order of importance and a clear and meticulous gradation of holiness may easily be discerned even within each of the three categories of appurtenances. There are many aspects of this scale. Further on I shall discuss just how far it is reflected in the actual workmanship of the various vessels and the material out of which they are made.

THE MATERIAL GRADATION

7

The most important pieces of furniture are the *kappōret* and the ark on which it rests. According to the peculiar priestly doctrine which cannot conceive of the ark being outside the tabernacle, these two articles are not seen by the priests the whole year round, not even, in fact, by the high priest (as will be shown in Chapter IX). The poles are not even removed from the ark when it is placed in position inside (cf. above, sect. 4). The ark and the *kappōret* alone are covered for travelling, first of all with the *pārōḵet*-veil itself (Num. 4: 5). The ark is also differentiated from the other articles of furniture in that a cloth of 'pure blue', *kᵉlîl tᵉḵēlet*, is placed over it during journeys (ibid., v. 6), whereas the epithet 'pure' is lacking from the cloth of blue in the case of the other vessels.[20]

[20] The clothing of the ark is different in yet another way, in that the pure-blue wool cloth is put on top of the skin of *taḥaš*, whilst in the other furniture, the *taḥaš* skin goes on top of the blue cloth. This detail has already been noted, e.g., by F. Delitzsch, in his introduction to S. I. Curtiss' *The Levitical Priests* (Edinburgh–Leipzig, 1877), p. xvi. We could, however, assume, as Ibn-Ezra does in

After these two we descend to the furniture of the outer sanctum, all of which shares the same degree of sanctity.[21] Most of them are made of acacia wood and overlaid with gold. Only the *kappōret* and the lampstand, together, apparently, with the various minor utensils, are made of single pieces of hammered gold. But this difference seems to be dictated by mere technical considerations. The ancients knew how to put a metal overlay on surfaces that were easily beaten out: but in order to achieve delicate carvings and embellishments, such as those on the lampstand and cherubim, they had to use the metal alone and mould it into the shape required.[22] The value of an article was evidently determined mainly by its outer appearance. From this point of view it did not particularly matter whether it was hammered work or overlay.

The articles in the court, unlike the inner furniture, are of copper (or bronze), that is, overlaid with copper (the outer altar), or constructed of hammered-out copper pieces (the laver, apparently, its stand, the utensils of the outer altar, and some other items). For travelling a cloth of purple, considered slightly coarser and cheaper than blue (cf. below, sect. 8) is spread over the bronze altar (Num. 4: 13).

The laver and its stand are said to be made not from copper offered when the tabernacle was being erected, but from the mirrors of the women 'who served, *ṣāḇᵉ'û*, at the entrance of the tent of meeting' (Exod. 38: 8).[23] Indeed, these two are considered to be the least important vessels, since they are not intended for ritual purposes. The fact that the priests washed in them is regarded only as a preliminary to an act of cult, not as an actual part of cultic ceremonial itself.

his comment on Num. 4: 6, that the wording of the verse is not precise and that, in fact, the ark was covered in exactly the same way as the other vessels.

[21] The table is remarkable here in that during journeys it is covered by two cloths, one of blue and the other of crimson, and the utensils are placed between them (Num. 4: 7–8), whereas the other articles of furniture have a covering of blue cloth only. But this difference seems to be the result of practical necessity only, since the utensils of the table are greater in number than those of the lampstand and altar of incense.

[22] The cherubim in Solomon's temple were not made of hammered work but were simply overlaid with gold (1 Kgs. 6: 23–9). However, since they were enormous in size, this method was much easier. The lampstands were certainly made of hammered work even there.

[23] This tallies with the fact that in Exod. 38: 29–31, where we find a list of all the appurtenances made of the copper of the offering, the laver and its stand are not mentioned. Cf. Cassuto, *Exodus*, p. 467.

8

If we are to distinguish between the various grades of fabric, we must remember, first, that the text specifies three techniques of weaving in descending order: *ḥôšēḇ* workmanship (Exod. 26: 1 *et al.*), *rôqēm* workmanship (ibid., v. 36 *et al.*), and *'ôrēg* workmanship (39: 22 *et al.*). Second, that three dyed wools are mentioned as being used in weaving: blue, purple, and crimson. There can be no doubt that the text lists these varieties in order of importance. Blue is accordingly regarded as the most expensive, purple slightly less so, crimson less still. In addition, reference is made to goats' hair (25: 4 *et al.*) which is undyed and possesses only its natural colour. As against the four kinds of wool, the text mentions the *šēš*, which is not wool but linen, apparently of fine quality.[24]

Now the workmanships of *ḥôšēḇ* and *rôqēm* are mentioned only in connection with a mixture of all kinds of dyed wool and of linen. It serves as a deliberate feature of those appurtenances, since according to Old Testament tradition the appearance of a heterogenous mixture is taken as a hallmark of holiness. It is precisely for this reason that such a mixture, described as *kil'ayim* in the Old Testament, was forbidden in all its possible forms in everyday life (Lev. 19: 19; Deut. 22: 9, 11).[25] At the same time, it was assumed as a matter of course within the closed circle of priests. From the sacral–cultic point of view, the fabrics made of *kil'ayim*-mixture are thus superior to those made of one kind of wool or linen. It is difficult to determine the difference between the works of *ḥôšēḇ* and *rôqēm*. In any event, the former is more elaborate than, and superior to, the latter. In the context of

[24] This fabric was probably imported from Egypt. Cf. Gen. 41: 42; Ezek. 27: 7 and the commentaries. The *šēš* used in the tabernacle is qualified in the text as *mošzār* (rendered by EVV as twined, twisted). For *šēš* as the early equivalent of *bûṣ*, which is typical of post-exilic usage, see A. Hurvitz, *HThR* 60 (1967), 117–21.

[25] Note the reason appended to the prohibition: 'lest the crop you have sown become holy'. The verb *tiqdaš* used here means neither 'be defiled' (KJV) nor 'be forfeited to the sanctuary' (RV, RSV; similarly, NEB), but that the crop will acquire the quality of holiness through the act of mixing different species. NJPS conveys the meaning of the verb by referring to its practical implication: lest the crop 'may not be used'; whereas AT and JB render it more directly: lest the produce 'become taboo', 'become consecrated'. A mixture of wool and linen is also called *ša'aṭnēz* (loc. cit.), a non-Semitic word—perhaps, as some have suggested, of Egyptian origin.

ḥôšēḇ workmanship cherubim usually occur. It seems likely, therefore, that the distinguishing feature of this workmanship is that it contains figures, whereas *rôqēm* workmanship involves a mixture of colours and varieties, but has no figures.[26] On the other hand, *'ôrēg* workmanship is applied only to fabrics made of but one kind of material, whether dyed wool or linen. Accordingly, the ephod's robe is of *'ôrēg* workmanship and woven solely from blue wool (Exod. 28: 31–2; 39: 22). The priestly tunics are of *'ôrēg* workmanship and made solely of linen (39: 27). The *'ôrēg* work thus contains neither a multiplicity of colours nor figures.

Pre-eminent among the fabrics is, then, the *parōḵet*-veil. This is made of a wool-linen mixture according to *ḥôšēḇ* workmanship and is patterned with figures of cherubim (Exod. 26: 31; 36: 35). On journeys it serves as a covering for the *kappōret* and the ark (Num. 4: 5) and thus it is the only fabric carried by the Kohathites. In cultic ceremonies this veil sometimes serves as a kind of projection and 'shadow' of the *kappōret* behind it (Lev. 4: 6, 17).

Next come the tabernacle curtains. At first sight it would seem that they are of the same mixture as the *pārōḵet*-veil woven with figures of cherubim according to the *ḥôšēḇ* workmanship (Exod. 26: 1; 36: 8). Nevertheless, neither in composition nor in outward

[26] The talmudic sages described *ḥôšēḇ* workmanship as a combination of threads interwoven in such a way that different figures emerge on the two sides of the fabric, whereas in *rôqēm* workmanship, taken to be needlework, one figure only emerges, either just on one side, or on both sides of the fabric. Cf. Baraytha, chap. iv; Bab. Tal. Yoma, 72*b*; Jer. Tal. Sheqalim viii. 2 *et al.*; and Rashi on Exod. 26: 1, 36. Essentially this interpretation has been accepted by English scholars and is reflected in EVV. I find, however, that German scholars put forward a much more plausible exposition. Generally they consider *rôqēm* workmanship to be not needlework but rather a multi-coloured weave, a *Buntweberei*, in contrast to *ḥôšēḇ* workmanship, which is a *Bildweberei*, i.e. a weave which represents figures or designs. Cf. A. R. S. Kennedy, s.v. 'Weaving', *EB* iv. 5289; and the commentaries on Exodus. Indeed, the only thing we can learn from biblical allusions outside P is that the *riqmāh* fabric was multicoloured (Judg. 5: 30; cf. Ezek. 17: 3) or that it is at least mentioned alongside blue or purple or linen (ibid. 16: 13; 27: 7, 16, 24)—but there is no evidence in any part of the Bible of this fabric including figures or designs. The meanings attached to this root in cognate languages offer no decisive evidence. Needlework was apparently forbidden, according to P, in the manufacture of the tabernacle fabrics for the same reason that a tear in Aaron's robe was to be avoided (Exod. 28: 32; 39: 23; cf. Josephus, *Antiquities* iii. 6. 4), that is, out of considerations of respect. A quite detailed discussion of the difference between *ḥôšēḇ* and *rôqēm* workmanships can already be found in K. Ch. W. F. Bähr, *Symbolik des mosaischen Cultus*, i (Heidelberg, 1837), pp. 266–9. He decided in favour of the rabbinic explanation, which in its turn is the basis of the LXX and was accepted by the early Christian exegetes.

appearance are they actually identical to the *pārōḵet*. For it may be noted that, when the constituents of the *pārōḵet* are mentioned, blue yarn is mentioned first and linen last, while the converse is true of the tabernacle curtains: linen is mentioned first and only then the three kinds of wool. This order of words which punctiliously recurs in the two parallel descriptions obviously refers to the way in which this wool-linen mixture is to be made, that is, what proportions of the different materials are to be woven together. The *pārōḵet* is to be made up, in the main, of the varieties of wool with the linen added to the blend only at the end. The reverse is true of the lower curtains.[27] It may be said that just as the *pārōḵet*-veil, the most important of the fabrics, corresponds in its level of sanctity to the articles of furniture in the inner sanctum, so the tabernacle curtains may be taken as corresponding to the furniture of the outer sanctum. They are, in essence, the fabrics associated with this sanctum, though part of them is spread over the holy of holies.

Another step down is formed by the outer veil of the tabernacle and the court's screen (Exod. 26: 36; 27: 16; 36: 37; 38: 18). These too are of a mixed weave, the first ingredient mentioned this time being the blue wool, not the linen. However, their weave is of the *rôqēm* workmanship with no figures of cherubim.

Next come the tent curtains which are made of undyed goats' hair only (26: 7; 36: 14). The text does not specify what material should be used to make their loops, but it seems likely that dyed material is not intended. In the case of the lower curtains, the loops are of blue wool (26: 4; 36: 11). The clasps of the tent's curtains are not gold, as are those of the lower curtains (26: 6; 36: 13), but of copper (26: 11; 36: 18). Similarly, the hangings of the court are made not of mixed stuff, but of linen only (27: 9; 38: 9). A covering of tanned rams' skins and skins of *tᵉḥāšîm* is placed on the upper curtains (26: 14; 36: 19).[28] We cannot deter-

[27] See also below, sects. 12, 13, in connection with the ephod and Aaron's girdle.

[28] The ram's skins have to be tanned, whereas the skins of *tᵉḥāšîm* evidently have their natural colour. What the *taḥaš* is, it is difficult to determine. For etymological parallels see dictionaries; also F. M. Cross, 'The Tabernacle', *BA* 10 (1947), 62 n. 22. The late zoologist, I. Aharoni, in his article אילה ותחש, *Tarbiẓ* 8 (1937), 319–30, endeavoured to identify it with *Monodon monoceros*, a one-horned animal of the *Cetacea* family, with its habitat between the seventieth and eightieth northern latitudes in the Red Sea. N. H. Tur-Sinai, גמר מצווה וקשייו, *EI* 4 (1956), 215–16, however, tried to interpret *taḥaš* as an archaic

mine which of these three ranks lowest in value: goats' hair, *šēš*-linen, or skins of rams and *t^eḥāšîm*.[29]

9

At the top among the beams are the pillars of the *pārōḵet*-veil (Exod. 26: 32; 36: 36), and the tabernacle's planks (26: 15–29; 36: 20–34). These, together with the bars joining the planks, are overlaid with gold. The hooks of the *pārōḵet*'s pillars, however, and the rings of the bars are made of solid, seemingly beaten, pieces of gold ('hooks of gold', 'make their rings of gold'—no mention is made of overlay as it is in the case of the other accessories). Again, the hooks and rings are made of single pieces for technical reasons alone (cf. sect. 7). The sockets of both these pillars and the planks are silver. Next come the pillars of the outer veil. These too are overlaid with gold, their hooks similarly being of gold, but their sockets are copper (Exod. 26: 37; 36: 38).

It should be pointed out that the text sometimes refers to *zāhāḇ ṭāhôr*, 'pure gold' and sometimes just to *zāhāḇ*, 'gold' without the qualification, but the former phrase is strictly applied only to the inner furniture (see Exod. 25: 11, 17, 24, 31, 36, 38–9; 30: 3; also in the parallel description in chap. 37). As a rule, the phrase 'pure gold' occurs in all these contexts at the beginning of the description of the particular piece of furniture. The priestly writer presumably thereby indicates that all the gold used in that object is pure, thus precluding the need to repeat the epithet 'pure' each time gold is referred to again. Note also the attributes *hamm^enôrāh haṭṭ^ehôrāh*, 'the pure lampstand' (31: 8; 39: 37; Lev. 24: 4) and *haššulḥān haṭṭāhôr*, 'the pure table' (ibid., v. 6). In contrast to this, the phrase 'pure gold' does not occur at all in connection with the tabernacle's planks and pillars. In this respect

form of *tayiš*, he-goat, on the assumption that the enunciation of the guttural *ḥ* was slurred into a *y* sound.

[29] Each one of them serves a different purpose. Ezekiel mentions both the *šēš* and *taḥaš* as examples of expensive products in relation to what common people were used to (Ezek. 16: 10). From him we infer that the first was used for wrapping up a head-dress (in this meaning the verb *ḥbš* is used there), while with the second sandals were prepared. Similarly the linen is used for hangings in the tabernacle (and the priests use it for clothes), while the skins, being more hard-wearing, are placed on the roof, to act as a covering to the part most exposed to the elements.

they are regarded as slightly inferior to the inner articles of furniture.[30]

We are not told what kind of wood the pillars of the court are made of (Exod. 27: 10–18; 38: 10–19), but only acacia wood was included in the offering (25: 5; 35: 24). We are not told whether they are overlaid, but it would appear that they are not. Only their hooks and bands are made of silver, their sockets, however, being of copper (bronze) like those of the pillars of the outer veil.

10

Basic to the above-mentioned technical and material gradations is the premiss that the more important the object, the more expensive and magnificent it has to be. Such a rule is ingrained in many cultures remote from each other—the higher an item is on the scale of sanctity, the greater man's efforts to embellish it. At the same time, two further principles are manifest in these gradations.

The first is that of the eastern axis. All the entrances to the tabernacle face east. Moreover, the line traversing the inner sanctum eastward is superior to all the rest of the corners of the compass. The inner curtains are somewhat similar to the *pārōḵet*-veil. Nevertheless, the latter is superior to them, as we have seen, both in quality and holiness. The outer veil of the tabernacle ('the screen of the tent') made of a wool-linen mixture, is more elaborate and important than 'the tent curtains'. Similarly, the screen of the court, made of that wool-linen mixture, is more elaborate and important than the court's hangings. It should be emphasized that this superiority does not apply to the whole eastern side, but only to that axis which enters the inner sanctum from the east, that is, only to the screens of the entrances which face the ark and the cherubim. An antiquated symbolism is evidently embodied in

[30] Similarly, the epithet 'pure', *ṭāhôr*, is used in the context of making the incense of 'spices' (Exod. 30: 35; 37: 29). It can likewise be seen how meticulous the text is in applying the epithet 'pure' *zāḵ*, *zakkāh*, to the oil for the lighting (Exod. 27: 20; Lev. 24: 2), and the frankincense mixed in the incense of 'spices' (Exod. 30: 34) or put on the shewbread (Lev. 24: 7), all of which are used inside the tabernacle. No such stipulation is made in connection with materials used in the court (cf. below, pp. 208–10). Note further the stipulation for 'complete blue' in the ark's cloth (above, sect. 7) as well as in the ephod's robe (sect. 12), and the application of 'pure gold' to the overgarments of the high priest (below, sect. 12).

this principle.[31] It seems to hark back, like the concept of the sacredness of wool-linen mixture, to pre-biblical patterns, but was retained in biblical times out of adherence to convention.

The second principle is that of concentric circles. In the focal point we find the *kappōret* with its cherubim, the holiness and the value of an object progressively diminishing with its distance therefrom. The pillars of the court are less elaborate than the tabernacle planks and pillars. Those of the outer veil are less elaborate than those of the *pārōḵet*-veil. Both the hangings of the court and the outer curtains are less elaborate than the lower curtains of the tabernacle. The court's screen and the tabernacle's outer veil are less elaborate than the *pārōḵet*-veil. And it goes without saying that the outer furniture is less elaborate than that inside.

Two, or rather three, concentric circles may easily be discerned: the inside of the tabernacle, itself divided into two, on the one hand, and the court, on the other. The inside is made of gold, overlaid or solid;[32] if a fabric is involved, it is a wool-linen mixture, of the elaborate *ḥôšēḇ* workmanship, adorned with cherubim. The outside is made, for the most part, of copper (or bronze), overlaid or solid;[33] if a fabric is involved, it is woven of one kind of material (undyed wool or linen), or indeed of wool-linen mixture, but of the simple *rôqēm* workmanship without cherubim. These two circles are not merely a matter of externals. They demarcate two gradated spheres, each of which contains its own set of ritual acts and symbols, as will be shown in Chapter XI.

THE PRIESTLY VESTMENTS

II

To the tabernacle with its three categories of appurtenances, a detailed description of the special priestly vestments is appended (Exod. chap. 28; 39: 1–31). In the last resort, these are considered

31 The plan of the temple at Jerusalem was based on this principle; cf. below, p. 190. Some parallel material from Egypt and Babylon is cited by F. I. Hollis, 'The Sun-cult and the Temple at Jerusalem', *Myth and Ritual*, ed. S. H. Hooke (London, 1933), pp. 87–110.

32 The silver sockets of the tabernacle's planks are evidently sunk in the ground.

33 The tabernacle's pegs are made of copper (see above, sect. 3 and the references there) just like the pegs of the enclosure (above, sect. 4). However, in function and location they belong to the court, though the tabernacle's lower curtains are bound to some of them from the outside by cords.

to be a fourth category of tabernacle appurtenances, with the difference that they need not be carried by any of the Levitical clans. They are made in much the same way as the fabrics except that in some of them gold and precious stones are added to the wool-linen mixture. In all, eight garments are listed, four of which are used by the high priest alone, the other four both by him and by the ordinary priests.[34] The ritual function for which each garment is designed will be dealt with in Chapter XI. Here the discussion will be limited to the technical-material aspect, in which two grades can de detected, and we shall see that they conform to the technical and material gradation of the tabernacle as a whole.

12

(*a*) The most distinctive of the garments exclusive to the high priest is the ephod (Exod. 28: 6–12; 39: 2–7). Despite the detailed description given in the text, many essential aspects of its form are still obscure. It may be conjectured, however, that it is a sort of apron encircling the body from the loins downward. The apron is kept in position by means of the *kᵉtēp̄ôt*, 'shoulder-pieces' and also by the fact that on its upper part, that part called the '*ḥēšeb̄*[35] of the ephod' it is girdled to the loins (see Exod. 29: 5; Lev. 8: 7). It may be that this apron could be fastened and unfastened at the back, since the text refers to its *maḥberet*[36] (Exod. 28: 27; 39: 20). This *maḥberet*, which from the context seems to be at the back of the wearer,[37] should be regarded as something akin to the *maḥberet* (also *ḥôb̄eret*) mentioned in connection with the lower and outer curtains of the tabernacle (26: 4–5, 10; 36: 11–12, 17), that is, two ends of parallel curtains—in this case, of one rounded piece of cloth—that can be joined or knit to each other.[38] If that

[34] The fact that the priestly vestments were eight in number was noted by the talmudic sages (Mishnah Yoma vii. 5). Shoes are not included, which serves to indicate that the priests officiated barefoot. Actually this was essential if they were to stay in a holy place. Cf. Exod. 3: 5; Josh. 5: 15; and the Rabbis' remark in Shemot Rabbah, end of section ii.

[35] KJV: curious (AT: skilfully made) girdle; RV: cunningly woven (RSV: skilfully woven, NJPS: decorated) band; NEB: waist-band.

[36] KJV: coupling; RSV: joining; NJPS, NEB: seam.

[37] *lᵉʿummat maḥbartô* (ibid.) would be 'opposite to [rather than close to, or at] the joining'.

[38] Note that when referring to the fastening of the ephod (not just to the shoulder pieces!) the text uses the verb *wᵉḥubbār*, 'and it (i.e. the ephod) will be joined' (Exod. 28: 7), 'and it was joined' (39: 4), which is cognate to *maḥberet*. This is a further indication that the fastening is to be made along that 'seam'.

is the case, we may assume that when the priest wishes to remove the apron from his waist, he need not lift it over his head or let it down to his feet, but can untie the 'joining' at his back and take off the ephod frontwards. The rounded shape of this garment is apparently preserved even when it is not being worn, for it is quite heavy, as will immediately be seen.

The ephod is made of the sacred mixture—all kinds of wool with linen, *ḥôšēḇ* workmanship, and hence it seems to be similar to the *pārōḵet*-veil or the lower curtains. Nevertheless, it differs from the latter in some important details. First, no mention is made of cherubim, though the fabric is of *ḥôšēḇ* workmanship. There are presumably then no cherubim, but simply designs of a general nature woven into the material.[39] Secondly, the fabric contains gold, as well as woollen and linen thread. What is more, gold becomes the predominant ingredient, outstripping in quantity all the other materials woven into this fabric. This is indicated, above all, by the fact that in the list of materials used in the ephod gold is mentioned first and only then blue, purple, crimson stuff, and linen. The punctilious order in which the materials are listed betokens a sliding scale of preference, just as in the case of the *pārōḵet*-veil and lower curtains (cf. above, sect. 8). Furthermore, when the text wishes to explain how the gold was combined with the threads of wool and linen, it notes that gold sheets were 'beaten out and cut into cords to work into the blue and into the purple and into the crimson stuff and into the fine twined linen' (Exod. 39: 3). The repetition of the preposition 'into', *bᵉtôḵ*,[40] seems to indicate that the gold cords are not assumed to be worked into a ready-made fabric, but woven together with every individual thread of wool or linen from the very beginning, the ephod thus being prepared from these partly golden threads. Therefore, neither hammered-out work nor gold overlay is involved here, nor even golden embroidery. And yet the gold becomes the main element in this garment, producing its dominant colour and constituting the principal part of its weight.[41] In essence it can therefore be regarded

[39] Perhaps these designs do not cover the whole of the ephod but are confined to its upper part, girdled around the thighs. This would account for the name of that part of the ephod—*ḥēšeḇ*, cognate with the workmanship of *ḥôšēḇ*.

[40] Not reflected in the AT, NJPS, JB, NEB Versions.

[41] The talmudic sages concluded that each thread in the ephod was indeed entwined with gold, but they further assumed (a point which has no basis in the text itself) that every single thread was of wool-linen mixture. In a midrashic strain they went so far as to say that every thread of each material, whether it was

as a golden ephod and, as I have tried to demonstrate elsewhere,[42] is the very same ephod as that referred to in non-priestly sources.

(*b*) On the ephod, or strictly speaking, on the shoulder-pieces of the ephod, above the 'waist-band', the high priest wears the breastpiece, *ḥōšen* (Exod. 28: 15–30; 39: 8–21). It is a cross between a square plate and a hollow pouch. It is made in exactly the same way as the ephod—gold is combined with a mixed fabric of wool and linen, of *ḥôšēḇ* workmanship. Twelve precious stones are fixed to it. In contrast to the two *lapis lazuli* (or the cornelians, the onyx stones) on the shoulder pieces of the ephod (28: 9–11; 39: 6–7), these twelve do not protrude from their background but are sunk into the body of the breastpiece; hence their name *'aḇnê millû'îm* (25: 7), stones for setting.[43] On each one of them the name of just a single tribe is engraved, whereas six names are engraved on each of the ephod stones. This would indicate that they are thought to be smaller than those two. The breastpiece is attached to the ephod by means of three pairs of rings, two chains, and two frames, all of them gold, as well as by means of a lace of blue.

(*c*) Under the ephod the high priest wears the ephod's robe (Exod. 28: 31–5; 39: 22–6) which is made according to *'ôrēg* workmanship, of woollen thread alone, of 'complete blue' (cf. above, sect. 7). Its ritual accessories are the golden bells attached

wool or linen, was multiplied by six: כל המינין חוטן כפול ששה. In this way they propounded a very complicated method by which the ephod was prepared: one gold thread to six of blue wool, one gold thread to six of purple wool, and the same with the crimson wool and linen—and all these four intertwined again as one thread. In all, each thread is thus formed by twisting 28 threads together, 4 of these being of gold, i.e., a seventh of the whole weave. Cf. Bab. Tal. Yoma, 71*b*–72*a*; Baraytha, chap. iv; Maimonides, הלכות כלי המקדש iv. 5. According to my explanation, the fabric as a whole, rather than each single thread, was a wool-linen mixture, and the proportion of gold actually amounted to about half of the fabric. The inclusion of gold cords in a woven fabric should not surprise us. Something akin to this is possibly referred to in Ps. 45: 10 (cf. LXX: ἐν ἱματισμῷ διαχρύσῳ) and v. 14; S. of S. 3: 10. Examples of this sort of workmanship containing a large proportion of gold or silver threads in the weave are known at least from the Hellenistic period; cf. Kennedy, *EB* iv. 5289, and the references there.

[42] 'The Form of the Ephod in the Biblical Sources', *Tarbiẓ* 24 (1955), 380–91 (Hebrew). In the non-priestly ephod, too, there is an allusion to purple and precious stones (of necklaces), as well as to gold (Judg. 8: 24–7).

[43] The word 'other' (before 'stones ready for setting') ought to be omitted from the NJPS and NEB Versions of this verse. The two halves of this verse correspond to each other: the *lapis lazuli* (cornelians, onyx stones) are destined for the ephod—that is, for its shoulder-pieces—while the 'stones for setting' are for the breastpiece only.

to the skirts. Between each bell a pomegranate is suspended, made of a mixture of dyed wool and linen.[44]

(*d*) Another article of apparel restricted to the high priest is the golden diadem, *ṣîṣ*, also *nēzer* (Exod. 28: 36–38; 39: 30–1). Like the two stones of the ephod and the twelve of the breast-piece, it bears 'seal engravings', but whereas the stones are engraved with the names of the tribes of Israel, the diadem bears the tetragrammaton, or rather the words 'Holy to Yahweh'.[45]

It is worth mentioning that the gold which is woven into the high priest's garments is also mostly pure (cf. above, sect. 9). 'Pure gold', *zāhāḇ ṭāhôr*, is explicitly referred to in connection with the chains joining the breastpiece to the ephod (Exod. 28: 14, 22; 39: 15), with the bells (39: 25), with the diadem (28: 36; 39: 30) and according to LXX Version in connection with the frames to which the chains are attached (28: 13). The mention of 'pure gold' in these cases alone, may simply be the result of brevity. It may also be prompted by the fact that the purity of the gold can only be evident when it is cast or at least used in a considerable concentration—not when it is cut into fine cords and woven in a fabric. Anyhow, the high priest's garments are equivalent in this respect to the inner furniture, not to the planks and pillars.

13

These are the garments which, essentially, are common to both the high and the ordinary priests. All of them are made of *šēš*-linen except for the high priest's girdle.

(*a*) The *kᵉtōnet*, tunic, is of *'ôrēg* workmanship (Exod. 39: 27). In the case of Aaron it is 'chequered' (Exod. 28: 4), but this

[44] In MT the words *wᵉšēš mošzār*, 'and fine twined linen', in Exod. 28: 33, are omitted; in 39: 24 the word *mošzār* alone occurs. There is no doubt that in both places the LXX and Samaritan Versions are correct in supplying the missing words. There is no allusion in the text to the number of bells and pomegranates. The Rabbis and Church Fathers made this the subject of fanciful expositions. See the references in E. Nestlé, 'Die Zahl der Granatapfel und Glockchen am Klied des Hohenpriesters', *ZAW* 15 (1905), 205–6; idem, 'Zu den Glocken am Gewand des Hohenpriesters', ibid. 32 (1912), 74.

[45] The Rabbis assumed that the diadem was engraved with the two words *qōdeš lᵉ Yahweh* (Bal. Tal. Shabbath, 63*b et al.*). But according to the Hellenistic sources it was only the tetragrammaton which was inscribed. Cf. Josephus, *Antiquities* iii. 7. 4; idem, *Wars* v. 5. 7; Aristeas, 98; Philo, *De Vita Mosis* ii. 114, 132.

ornamentation is absent from the tunic of the ordinary priests (28: 39, in contrast to v. 40).[46]

(*b*) The *'abnēṭ*, girdle, is girded round the loins over the tunic. Aaron's is of *rôqēm* workmanship, whereas girdles without qualification are mentioned in connection with the ordinary priests (Exod. 28: 39–40). What this *rôqēm* workmanship consists of in the case of Aaron's girdle is indicated in the parallel description (39: 29)—a mixture whose primary basis is linen, with the various dyed wools added in the last place. This shows that in composition Aaron's girdle is similar to the tabernacle's lower curtains, which are primarily of linen too, but in finish and execution (*rôqēm*, not *ḥôšēḇ*, workmanship) it equals the outer veil and the screen of the enclosure.[47] Indeed, its place is at the end of a series of fabrics, all of which are a wool-linen mixture, but demonstrate certain variations: the *pārōḵet*-veil is of *ḥôšēḇ* workmanship and the blue stuff comes first; the tabernacle's lower curtains are likewise of *ḥôšēḇ* workmanship but there the linen comes first; in the outer veil and enclosure screen, the blue stuff comes first but they are of *rôqēm* workmanship; Aaron's girdle, by contrast, is also of *rôqēm* workmanship but linen is its primary basis.

(*c*) The head covering for Aaron is a *miṣnep̄et*, turban, for the ordinary priests *migbā'ôt* or *pa'ᵃrê migbā'ôt*, that is, caps (Exod. 28: 39–40; 39: 28). The *pᵉ'ēr*, cap, is also taken to be a sign of 'dignity and adornment', as the text has it, and the common people certainly did not wear it in their everyday life (cf. Isa. 3: 20; 61: 3, 10; Ezek. 24: 17). But the *miṣnep̄et* is of greater superiority. The *pᵉ'ēr* is mentioned in connection with a bridegroom who adorns himself (Isa. 61: 10), while the *miṣnep̄et* is linked with the king, being synonymous with *'ᵃṭārāh*, crown (Ezek. 21: 31; cf. Isa. 62: 3).

(*d*) Linen breeches 'to cover their nakedness' are worn by all the priests (Exod. 28: 42; 39: 28). Breeches were not the usual attire in those times (see Exod. 20: 26). The priests alone required them for reasons of modesty, lest they expose themselves (cf. Ezek. 44: 18).

[46] This detail was noted by Ibn-Ezra in his commentary on Exod. 28: 37; cf. also on v. 41.

[47] Note the use of number in Exod. 39: 27–9: the tunics and the linen breeches are mentioned in the plural, since both Aaron and his sons wore them; on the other hand, the turban and the girdle (or sash), are referred to in the singular (AT and NJPS make it sashes, apparently taking *'abnēṭ* to be a collective plural here). The reason is that just as there was only one turban and that belonged to Aaron exclusively, so the girdle mentioned here is unique and belongs to Aaron.

14

The four garments reserved exclusively for the high priest are not a substitute for the last four, but are additional to them. At the same time, there is an all-important difference in quality between the four undergarments common to all the priests and Aaron's four overgarments. The former are made entirely of linen material, like the court hangings, with the exception of Aaron's girdle which is woven of linen-wool mixture. However, even this girdle is of the 'simplest' mixture, since linen is its basis and it is made according to *rôqēm* workmanship. It is thus even lower down the scale than the outer veil and the enclosure screen (above, sect. 13, *b*). The overgarments, by contrast, are made of gold (the bells and diadem) or linen-wool mixture (the pomegranates) or a combination of gold cords and a fabric of linen-wool mixture of *ḥôšēḇ* workmanship (the ephod and breastpiece)[48]—all correspond to the tabernacle's inner appurtenances. While the undergarments common to all the priests are equivalent in material and workmanship to the court, the overgarments may be equated with the tabernacle itself. This correlation is not merely a matter of externals. The technical–material equivalence is meant as a concrete expression of an identity of inwardness and function, since the two gradated categories of vestments merge into the two gradated spheres of ritual, as will be shown in Chapter XI.

15

When the text speaks of the high priest's vestments it does not make the distinction we made between his over- and undergarments. All Aaron's eight garments are lumped together as one single whole and along with them are listed the four garments of his sons. There is a reason for this classification too, since, as we have noted, with the exception of the breeches Aaron's linen undergarments differ somewhat and are more elaborate than those

[48] It seems to be assumed that even the pomegranates attached to the hem of the ephod's robe (cf. sect. 12), are intended to be of *ḥôšēḇ* workmanship, but in practice it would be impossible to discern this. It was apparently only possible to distinguish between *ḥôšēḇ* and *rôqēm* workmanships on large areas of fabric—not on small, rounded pomegranates. The way in which the pomegranates were made is therefore not even referred to. On the function of the blue wool from which the ephod's robe is made, see below, pp. 180–1.

of the ordinary priests: a 'chequered' tunic instead of an ordinary one, a girdle of wool-linen mixture instead of an ordinary one, a turban instead of a cap.

Three phrases are used to denote the groups of priestly garments: 'the garments of *śᵉrād*[49] for officiating in the holy place',[50] 'the holy garments of Aaron the priest', 'the garments of his sons for priestly service'. The most puzzling is the first of these. The relevant root שרד does not occur elsewhere in biblical Hebrew and it is difficult to find its parallel in other Semitic languages.[51]

If we wish, first of all, to determine what is implied by the name

[49] KJV: of service (after the LXX, see further), so also NJPS (for other reasons); RV: finely wrought, similarly JB: sumptuous; AT: woven; NEB: stitched.

[50] In this clause the word *baqqōdeš*, 'in the holy place' denotes not necessarily the outer sanctum, as may appear at first sight, but any area where the priests officiate—even the outer altar. In P's usage the word *haqqōdeš* does not serve as a definitive technical term. Thus, in the description of the Day of Atonement service it indicates nothing else than the inner sanctum (Lev. 16: 2–3, 16, 20, 23); and the same is true of Lev. 10: 4; Ezek. 41: 21, 23. In Lev. 10: 17 it implies a part of the court (more precisely: that part of the court which is the priests' sphere, i.e. the 'holy place' inside the court; cf. below, pp. 184–5). In Num. 28: 7 it describes the outer altar. Similarly, in P's terminology *haqqōdeš* may indicate all the articles of furniture, the sacred burden of the Kohathites (Num. 3: 28; 4: 15, 20; in 3: 38 the selfsame articles are termed *miqdāš*, on which cf. above, pp. 14–15). Even those sacred materials used by the priests when officiating inside the tabernacle and in the court, namely, the oil for the light, the incense of spices, the daily grain-offering, and the anointing oil are called *qōdeš* (Num. 3: 32; cf. 4: 16 and below, p. 182, n. 17). Likewise, the phrase *qōdeš qodāšîm*, 'holy of holies', usually applied to the inner sanctum, is not a definitive term in P's own vocabulary (as it is in mishnaic Hebrew). Thus it may also mean the outer altar (Exod. 29: 37; 40: 10), that portion of the grain-offering consumed by male priests (Lev. 2: 3, 10), the altar of gold (Exod. 30: 10), its incense (ibid., v. 36), the tabernacle and all its paraphernalia (ibid., v. 29), and other similar objects. Even the *ḥērem*, a strictly devoted thing—a concept which has nothing to do with the circle of contagious holiness (on this cf. below, pp. 176–7)—is called *qōdeš qodāšîm* (Lev. 27: 28), in that it may not be redeemed. The same is true of the *qōdeš qodāšîm* mentioned in Ezek. 43: 12; 45: 3; 48: 12.

[51] The Rabbis assumed these to be the garments of the high priest, thus considering them to be simply another appellation for the 'holy garments of Aaron the priest'. See Bab. Tal. Yoma, 72*b*; Naḥmanides in his commentary to Exod. 31: 10. The LXX who rendered it: *στολαὶ λειτουργικαί* sought to provide an explanation for a difficult word, or perhaps read בגדי השרת, 'the garments of officiation' (as is also found in a number of Samaritan manuscripts)—but as a reading it certainly cannot be correct. Jewish medieval commentators (Rashi, Rashbam, Ibn-Ezra) maintained that these were the blue and purple cloths destined to cover the furniture on journeys (Num. 4: 7–14; see p. 180). The forced character of these explanations is obvious. Moderns have sought to connect this word with the Aramaic סרדא, plaiting (a hint of this is already discernible in the words of Rashi and Rashbam), but this explanation is difficult too.

bigdê haśśerād, we can do no more than say that it covers all the priestly vestments, those of Aaron and those of his sons. In other words, 'the holy garments of Aaron' and 'the garments of his sons' are two categories included in it. This connection suits admirably all the passages where these related phrases occur in consecutive order (Exod. 35: 19; 39: 1,[52] 41). In only one place do we have a conjunctive *waw* in the middle: 'And the garments of *śerād and* the holy garments, etc.' (31: 10). But one will not be far from the truth if one asserts that in this single case the *waw* has crept in incidentally, especially as that passage is replete with *waws* prefixed to the accusative particle *'et*. Regarding the etymology of *śerād*, it is conceivably an ancient Semitic noun, which must have been associated in some way with ritual officiation.[53] For it is one of the basic premises of P that vestments specially designed for the purpose must be worn in order to perform ritual acts. The antiquated attribute *śerād* is applied, then, to all these vestments taken together.

The 'holy garments' are the garments of Aaron the priest, as is explicitly stated in the text (loc. cit.; and 28: 3–4; 29: 29; 40: 13). They comprise not only the four overgarments of gold and wool-linen mixture, but also Aaron's four undergarments. 'The garments of his sons' are the four linen garments of the ordinary priests. Aaron's garments are more important than the latter and are intended for a higher ritual purpose. It may, therefore, be said that the epithet 'holy' does not actually separate them from the other priestly garments, which are also considered holy. It indicates only their *superior* sanctity.

16

There are still four other vestments which Aaron wears once a year in order to enter the inner sanctum. They constitute a third

[52] There is no doubt that the word והשש slipped out of this verse (possibly because of its graphic similarity to the preceding word השני), since we hardly find any priestly garment that is without this linen material. It is therefore impossible to assume, as did some Jewish medieval commentators (cf. the previous note), that the garments of *śerād* were made of the dyed wool only.

[53] No conclusive parallel has yet been found. K. Galling, *Exodus* (HAT, 1939), p. 151 tried to connect it with the Akkadian *serdu* the meaning of which is, in effect, 'cords', 'straps', and has hardly any connection with our *śerād*. M. Held maintains that a cognate verb occurs in Ugaritic writings (*UT*, Krt, 77) in the sense of ritual officiation. See his article 'An Obscure Biblical Word and its Ugaritic Parallel', *EI* 3 (1954), 102–3 (Hebrew).

category of priestly attire: in form they resemble the four undergarments (breeches, tunic, girdle, and turban), except that they are made of *bad*, that is, plain linen, not the fine *šēš* (Lev. 16: 4).[54] The talmudic sages maintained that these were white in colour,[55] which may well be the truth. Corresponding to these four, we find plain linen garments, which an ordinary priest wears when ascending to the outer altar to remove the ashes (ibid. 6: 3). It stands to reason that these, too, include approximately the same four garments, that is, breeches (which are actually referred to in the text), tunic, girdle, and cap.

The four plain linen vestments reflect a holiness transcending that of gold and wool-linen mixture, and the text finds it necessary to emphasize that 'they are holy garments' (Lev. 16: 4). Linen garments were regarded as specially holy in the Egyptian priesthood. Angels of the heavenly entourage are described in the Old Testament as clothed in linen (Ezek. 9: 2–3, 11; 10: 2; Dan. 10: 5; 12: 6–7). No wonder, therefore, that according to P the linen garments became a prerequisite of entry into the two focal points of the cultic holiness of the tabernacle and court: the inner sanctum and altar. These garments serve to indicate a kind of dialectical elevation into that sphere which is beyond even the material, contagious holiness characterizing the tabernacle and its accessories, as will be shown in the following chapter.

[54] In the first group of undergarments (above, sect. 13) only the breeches are made of *bad* (Exod. 28: 42). The words *šēš mošzār* in Exod. 39: 28 seem to be duplicated from the following (ibid., v. 29).

[55] Mishnah Yoma iii. 6.

IX

GRADES OF SANCTITY IN THE TABERNACLE

I

THE articles of the tabernacle furniture and their immediate vicinity are regarded in P as taboo to all non-priests. Thus the tabernacle and most of the court become an enclosed domain, inaccessible to the common people. At the same time, there is a gradation in the taboo of the ritual circles. It is least strong when applied to the court and becomes progressively more powerful as one proceeds inside the tabernacle, until the area which is taboo even for the priests themselves is reached. This gradation finds clear expression in the existence in P's system of a number of prohibitions, in ascending order, which serve to protect the holiness of the tabernacle and its paraphernalia. Nowhere do the priestly writers themselves, in spite of their tendency to indulge in details and repetitions, explain the nature of these prohibitions in an orderly manner. They are referred to incidentally, when describing other matters, or are suggested indirectly as if they did not require explicit mention. However, there is no difficulty in providing an outline of these prohibitions, since the whole priestly regime is based upon them.

The prohibitions are three in number: they deal with touch, sight, and approach. The validity of each of them varies with the ritual circles, and, moreover, it does not apply equally to all sections which P distinguishes within the community of Israel—i.e. Priests, Levites, ordinary Israelites.

THE PROHIBITIONS OF TOUCH AND SIGHT

2

A non-priest may not touch any piece of furniture, no matter how insignificant, in the tabernacle. This prohibition creates a drastic and clear-cut distinction between the sphere of cult and the rest of the world, and acts as a protective barrier round the most extreme degree of holiness. For all the pieces of furniture are endowed with a contagious holiness, that is, that can be transmitted from one object to another.

The concept of contagious holiness in the Old Testament is by no means restricted to P,[1] but the particular emphasis given to it here is indeed one of the distinguishing characteristics of this source. It is conceived of as being virtually tangible, a physical entity, the existence and activity of which can be sensorially perceived. Any person or object coming into contact with the altar (Exod. 29: 37) or any of the articles of the tabernacle furniture (30: 29) becomes 'holy', that is, contracts holiness and, like the tabernacle appurtenances themselves, becomes consecrated. At the opposite extreme there is a tangible, contagious defilement. But contagious holiness has one advantage over the latter: it cannot be removed from a person or object. It is possible to purify one who has contracted uncleanness since this substance may be thrust out of the community and into the desert.[2] Contagious holiness, by contrast, actually exists at the very centre of the camp, in the tabernacle, and we are told of no activity or rite which can deprive a person or object of it. Complete avoidance of all contact with this holiness is an absolute necessity, for anyone who contracts it is liable to meet immediate death at the hands of heaven. Indeed, the Kohathites are explicitly warned not to touch the furniture lest they die (Num. 4: 15). An object that has contracted holiness must be treated in exactly the same way as the tabernacle furniture and all steps should be taken to prevent it affecting other objects. The censers belonging to Korah and his company which had come into contact with the altar became holy like the altar itself and henceforth their holiness could not be removed. They were hammered out into 'sheets as plating for the altar' (ibid. 17: 3). Thus they were a reminder of sin and calamity, but their removal from the area of the tabernacle was unthinkable.

Only one group of people is permitted, by the grace of God, to

[1] It is also found in the non-priestly sources, except that there it is applied to the ark alone (1 Sam. 6: 19–20; 2 Sam. 6: 6–9), that is, to one of the very few items which, according to the non-priestly conception, may be taken out of the temple (the only other item of this kind seems to be the ephod; cf. above, p. 35).

[2] The purificatory rites of the temple on the Day of Atonement (Lev. 16) and of one suffering corpse defilement by the ashes of the red heifer (Num. 19) are based upon this notion.

come into contact with most of the tabernacle's appurtenances—these are the priests. When the censers of Korah's company had to be beaten into sheets for plating the outer altar, it was Eleazar the son of Aaron who performed this, certainly with the assistance of other priests, not of Levites (ibid. 17: 2–5). And when the furniture has to be covered with blue and purple cloths, it is the priests who do it and only afterwards are the Kohathites allowed to come and lift up the burden (ibid. 4: 5–15). And it goes without saying that only the priests are allowed to perform an act of ritual in the vicinity of the furniture.

An indication of the contagious holiness ascribed to the tabernacle furniture is the fact that this furniture is anointed with the holy oil (Exod. 30: 22–9; 40: 9–11; Lev. 8: 10–11; Num. 7: 1; for the outer altar alone: Exod. 29: 36; Num. 7: 10 *et al.*).[3] But Araon and his sons are also anointed with this oil (Exod. 28: 41; 30: 30; 40: 13–15; Lev. 7: 36). The anointing endows the priests and their vestments with the same holiness as that of the tabernacle. Henceforth the priests are in no danger when they come into contact with the furniture, not because they are immune to the lethal impact of contagious holiness but just because they have contracted it, as it were, from the very outset. Both they and their vestments together with the furniture have entered one common circle of sanctity. This serves to indicate that a non-priest must not come into contact even with the priests—that is, whilst they are anointed with the holy oil or are officiating near the tabernacle furniture. Indeed, it is explicitly stated in connection with the priests as a whole, and, for emphasizing the point, also mentioned with reference to the high priest alone, that during the period of their ordination they are not allowed to leave the entrance to the tent of meeting (Lev. 8: 33) or to go out of the *miqdāš*, that is, the sacred area of the tabernacle (ibid. 21: 10–12).[4]

[3] From this list of appurtenances the *kappōret* is missing. This may just be a scribal oversight. However, the opposite may be true too—namely, that the anointing begins with the ark and is applied downwards to the other items, whereas the *kappōret* is of even greater holiness than that which is symbolized in the anointing oil (cf. sect. 16 in Chapter VIII).

[4] The latter verses speak only of when the high priest is in his days of ordination; cf. Ibn-Ezra ad loc. (for the significance of *miqdāš* in this context cf. above, p. 15). Similarly, it is stated in Ezekiel's code that when the priests 'go out into the outer court, to the people' they must put off the priestly vestments, leave them in the holy chambers, and put on 'other garments' (Ezek. 42: 14; 44: 19). These 'other garments' are virtually secular clothes; and they are referred to

3

A non-priest may not even look at any of the articles of furniture within the tabernacle. In this respect, the inner furniture is distinguished from the outer: it is concealed behind curtains, removed from visual as well as physical contact. The Kohathites are explicitly told not to look at the furniture while it is being covered up lest they die (Num. 4: 18–20). This warning can obviously apply only to the inner articles. This state of affairs, furthermore, takes it for granted that no-one but a priest is allowed to set foot inside the tabernacle. Indeed, post-exilic evidence does not entertain such a possibility with regard to the temple.[5] The talmudic sages, too, observed that only the priests are allowed access to the temple, adding, however, that 'in the absence of priests, Levites may enter; in the absence of Levites, Israelites may enter', etc.[6] P's own view is much more rigid (and, as we shall see, more fatalistic, too): it categorically forbids non-priests to look at the inner furniture even when it is removed from the tabernacle.

There is at least one article which even priests may not look at—the *kappōret*. The *pārōḵet*-veil conceals it from them and makes around it, as well as around the ark, a mysterious hiding-place. The high priest alone may enter there, and that only on the Day of Atonement, performing for this purpose a special rite and even changing his garments (Lev. 16: 4). In actual fact, even he does not see anything on that day: he is exhorted to put the incense on the glowing coals on the censer so that the cloud may screen the *kappōret*, in this way saving him from death (ibid., vv. 12–13).[7] In the process, of course, the ark too becomes hidden from him.

thus in Lev. 6: 4. It follows that during their period of ordination the priests were actually forbidden to wear 'other garments'.

[5] See Nehemiah's exclamation: 'And what man such as I could go into the temple (*hêḵāl*) and live? I will not go in' (Neh. 6: 11). Also the story told of King Uzziah (2 Chron. 26: 16–21). Several passages in Chronicles might at first sight give the impression that the Levites were allowed to enter the temple (2 Chron. 23: 6; 29: 5, 15), but a closer examination clearly shows that only the court is implied. In 2 Chron. 29: 16 it is stated explicitly that only the priests entered inside the temple while the Levites received from them the load which was flung out into the court.

[6] See Bab. Tal. Erubin, 105*a*; Maimonides, הלכות בית הבחירה vii. 23.

[7] The claim, made by some scholars that the expressions used in Lev. 21: 23 and Num. 18: 7 mean that ordinary priests were primarily allowed to enter the inner sanctum, is incongruous. On this point see below, p. 206, n. 1. Regarding Num. 18: 7 see also further, sect. 5.

4

Some of the contagious holiness is apparently attached, in P's system, also to the planks, inner fabrics, and pillars during encampment.

The close proximity of these to the inner furniture gives rise to the possibility, at least, that contagious holiness will spread to them. Indeed, the anointing with the holy oil is also performed on 'the tabernacle' (Exod. 30: 26;[8] 40: 9; Lev. 8: 10; Num. 7: 1), that is, on 'the tabernacle curtains',[9] its planks, and inner pillars. Similarly, in the Day of Atonement rite, the high priest sprinkles the blood of the sin-offerings over the whole inside of the tabernacle (Lev. 16: 16–17, 20).[10] What is more, the constitution and the material components of these appurtenances (gold, wool-linen mixture, *ḥôšēḇ* workmanship, and embellishments of cherubim)—which are closely akin to those of the inner furniture and the *pārōḵet*-veil—suggest that these all enjoy the same level of sanctity. It, therefore, seems that essentially, these appurtenances too should not be seen or touched. In any event, the outer curtains actually hide them from the world without. The outer veil, which is slightly less sacred than the inner curtains, is evidently only forbidden to be touched.[11]

However, these sacral niceties can be adhered to only during encampment. Practical considerations nullify them when the tabernacle is being dismantled or moved. On travelling, nothing more than a minor degree of holiness can be attributed to these appurtenances. Contagious holiness is bound, in these circumstances, to the furniture (and the *pārōḵet*-veil) alone.

[8] 'Tent of meeting' mentioned here is simply another way of referring to the tabernacle, since in P these two terms are interchangeable. The 'tent of meeting' is not to be confused, of course, with the outer curtains which are frequently called 'the tent curtains' (sects. 2, 8 in the preceding chapter).

[9] Not on 'the tent curtains', which are the outer ones. The anointing is to be performed inside only.

[10] In these verses too 'tent of meeting' is merely an alternative term for 'tabernacle' (cf. n. 8; and below, pp. 271–3).

[11] As we have seen, the outer veil is in the same grade as the outer altar: in form (wool-linen mixture of *rôqēm* workmanship) it is typical of the court and a parallel to it is found in Aaron's girdle (sects. 8, 13 in Chapter VIII). But the pillars of this veil that are overlaid with gold are hidden from outside, though their sockets are of bronze like the appurtenances of the court. Regarding the court's screen which is likewise made of wool-linen mixture of *rôqēm* workmanship, see below, sect. 6.

In fact, during encampment, the outer curtains should mark the limit of contagious holiness. These curtains are made of undyed goats' hair, and no taboo is attached to them as such. According to P's specific system, the wool, which is not mixed with linen, serves as an intervening material between contagious holiness and the 'profane' world. To prove this, we simply have to compare the outer curtains of the tabernacle with the cloths put on the pieces of furniture for travelling. The latter too are of wool and differ from the outer curtains only in being dyed blue or purple (Num. 4: 7–14). On these cloths too, just as on the outer curtains of the tabernacle (Exod. 26: 14; 36: 19), 'a covering of skin of *taḥaš*' (Num. 4: 7–14) is placed.[12] The goats' hair curtains do not form part of the tabernacle proper. They act, as the text points out, only 'for a tent over the tabernacle' (Exod. 26: 7; 36: 14). The blue and purple cloths too are of the nature of small 'tents' over the separate objects. During encampment, the larger curtained tent envelops the whole of the tabernacle. On journeys its place is taken by the blue 'tents' each separately containing one of the inner articles of furniture, while the outer altar is encased in a 'tent' of purple (to protect against touch only). In this way is the tabernacle taboo maintained during encampment, and the furniture taboo alone on journeys.

It should be added that the ephod robe too, which is of blue wool with no admixture of linen, forms a 'barrier' between the ephod with its breastpiece, both of which belong to the inner circle of the tabernacle, and the undergarments, which belong to the court.[13] Perhaps this is connected with the further fact that anointing with holy oil is frequently attributed to the high priest alone (Lev. 6: 13; 16: 32; Num. 35: 25). Similarly, it is said that the high priest's special garments should be for him 'to be anointed in them' (Exod. 29: 29; cf. Lev. 21: 10), and it is mainly he who is designated by the title 'the anointed priest' (Lev. 4: 3, 5, 16; 6: 15), though in one place the regular priests too are dubbed as 'the anointed priests' (Num. 3: 3). Yet, the anointing of the high priest is more elaborate than that of the priests as a whole (contrast Exod. 29: 7;

[12] In the case of the blue and purple cloths, 'a skin of *taḥaš*' in the singular is mentioned, whereas the plural 'skins of *t*^e^*ḥāšîm*' is employed with reference to the outer curtains. This is because the latter are much bigger. Added to these are the tanned rams' skins (see sect. 8 in Chapter VIII).

[13] Cf. sects. 12, 14 in Chapter VIII.

Lev. 8: 12 with Exod. 29: 21; Lev. 8: 30). This tallies with the fact that the rites which are performed within the tabernacle are the exclusive prerogative of the high priest, and it is only when he is officiating there that he wears the garments of gold and wool-linen mixture, as will be demonstrated in Chapter XI.

THE PROHIBITION OF APPROACH AND THE COURT AREA

5

Non-Levites may not approach the furniture of the tabernacle and the outer altar. The Levites are explicitly permitted to come near the sacred furniture and this is a special act of grace distinguishing them, in this matter, from ordinary Israelites (Num. 8: 19; 16: 9–10; 18: 22–3). By virtue of this they are charged with 'the work, *ʿabôdāh*, of the tent of meeting', that is, its dismantling, transportation, and reassembling at a new site (Num. 1: 48–54; 4: 3–15; 18: 6). But this privilege of access is available to them only whilst the sacred furniture is covered. When its cloths are removed during encampment, the Levites are explicitly forbidden to come near (Num. 18: 3). Thus no taboo is attached to the wool coverings themselves, since the Levites touch them and absorb none of the contagious holiness. However, it is inconceivable that the Israelites should touch even the wool coverings for this would involve a violation of the prohibition of approach, which to them is absolute.

The second function assigned to the Levites in P is also based on their privilege of access to the covered holy furniture: it is their task 'to keep guard around' (to be *šômᵉrê mišmeret*)[14] the tabernacle and its appurtenances, that is, they must ensure that no one else approaches them. This is essentially a passive function, involving merely their presence in the vicinity of the sacred paraphernalia. In contrast to 'the work of the tent of meeting' which devolves on every Levite between the ages of thirty and fifty years (Num. 4: 3, 23 *et al.*)[15] the 'guarding' devolves upon every male member

[14] EVV mostly: keep the charge of; NJPS: perform the duties of.

[15] According to another account of P the age limits are twenty-five and fifty (Num. 8: 24–5). Still others are presupposed by the Chronicler in this context (1 Chron. 23: 24–7; 2 Chron. 31: 17; Ezra 3: 8). See also 1 Chron. 23: 3 and the reference in E. L. Curtis, *Chronicles* (ICC, 1910), pp. 266–7.

of the tribe from a month upwards (ibid. 3: 14–39) and also from fifty years upwards (ibid. 8: 25–6). On journeys each one of the three Levitical clans 'guards' those objects with whose carrying it has been entrusted (Num. 3: 25–6, 31, 36–7). In camp, all the Levites 'guard' the tabernacle as a whole (ibid. 1: 50–3; 3: 7–8; 18: 3–5). Indeed, the fact that the Levites camp around the tabernacle is seen as a sort of 'guarding'.[16] Similarly, the priests keep 'guard' of the holy furniture by camping at the gate to the court (ibid. 3: 38).[17] In this way access to the sacred objects is barred to all who are not permitted to draw near, that is to say, even to the Levites themselves during encampment. The warning recurring

[16] On the 'work' and the 'guarding' performed by the Levites and the non-cultic character of these tasks, see also J. Milgrom, *Studies in Levitical Terminology*, i (Berkeley, 1970), pp. 8–15, 60–6, 72–6. It should be pointed out, however (despite Milgrom, pp. 15, 16, 21–2, 27 *et al.*), that it is inconceivable that, according to P's assumption, the Levitical guards were armed with weapons. One need only remember that the guarding is carried out by Levites of one month and upwards, and it is unimaginable that babes would be armed. The execution of a transgressor definitely need not be carried out on the spot, still less would it be done within the tabernacle's court. Rather, he would first be taken out of the camp, and then he would be stoned. Athaliah was actually treated after this manner when they killed her outside the temple confines (2 Kgs. 11: 15–16).

[17] In the account of the census of Levitical clans (Num. 3: 14–39) the stages of encampment and journeying are pictured indiscriminately. Whenever the text specifies the families included in a particular Levitical clan and gives the total number of their males, it adds where they encamp and what the object of their 'guard' is. However, this guarding can take place only in the context of a journey, for it is only then that any meaning can be attached to the specific charge of each of the three Levitical clans. In camp the Gershonites cannot 'keep guard' over the fabrics, nor the Merarites over the beams nor the Kohathites over the furniture. One cannot seriously accept the opinion of, e.g., H. Holzinger, *Numeri* (KHC, 1903), p. 13, that this section assumes that 'die Leviten jedenfalls im Heiligtum aus- und eingehen'. But when the text informs us at the end, in v. 38, of the place and guarding of the priests, it is only thinking of the periods in camp. Note the difference in wording: 'The families of the Gershonites shall encamp behind the tabernacle, to the west . . . and the object of the guard (*ûmišmeret*) of the Gershonites etc.' (ibid., vv. 23–5). The same stereotyped phraseology is applied to the Kohathites and Merarites (ibid., vv. 29–31, 35–6). With regard to the priests, however, the text assumes a different tone: 'But those who are to encamp (*wᵉhaḥônîm*, the *waw* being adversative) before the tabernacle on the east . . . are Moses and Aaron and his sons, keeping the guard (*šômᵉrîm*) of the holy furniture (*hammiqdāš*) etc.', the verbs being all in the participle (ibid., v. 38). For this priestly guard, unlike that of the Levites, is imagined against the background of the camp only. When on the move the priests transport and guard, under Eleazar's leadership, the holy items—*haqqōdeš* (ibid. 3: 32), which in this case means the oil for lighting, the incense of spices, the grain-offering of *tamîd*, and the oil of anointing (ibid. 4: 16); cf. above, p. 172, n. 50.

in this context is: 'And if *zār*, an outsider, comes near, he shall be put to death' (Num. 1: 51; 3: 10, 38; 18: 7). According to P's usage, *zār* implies nothing more than a non-priest; cf. the explicit statement: ''*îš zār*, an outside person, who is not of the descendants of Aaron' (Num. 17: 5). Also Exod. 29: 33; 30: 33; Lev. 22: 10–12; Num. 18: 4.[18] It was not for nothing that the Israelites, in their anxiety, complained to Moses after the plague which followed Korah's uprising saying: 'Lo, we perish! We are lost, we are all lost! Everyone who comes near, who comes near to the Lord's tabernacle, shall die. Are we doomed to perish?' (Num. 17: 27–8). In response to this a new section (ibid. 18: 1–7) is introduced, which is just an expanded repeat of statements already made (ibid. 3: 5–10) and in which the role of the Levites as keepers of guard around the tabernacle and as a barrier between the priesthood and the people is again emphasized.

In this last section the priests are also admonished to 'guard' their own priesthood, תשמרו את כהנתכם, 'for all that concerns the altar and that is behind the *pārōḵet*', לכל דבר המזבח ולמבית לפרכת (Num. 18: 7). What is actually meant by these words is not that the priests have to 'attend to' their priesthood (RSV), nor even that they should 'perform their priestly duties' (NJPS), or 'fulfil the duties of their priestly office' (NEB), but rather that they remember certain taboos which appertain to their own circle, to wit, that they must not ascend the altar unless clad in the special linen vestments (Lev. 6: 3)[19] and must not enter behind the *pārōḵet*-veil. Only the priests, of course, can ensure that these prohibitions are respected. This too is how we must understand

[18] In the same way, *'ēš zārāh*, 'strange fire' (Lev. 10: 1; Num. 3: 4; 26: 61) is fire that does not belong to the outer altar, and *qᵉṭōret zārāh*, 'strange incense' (Exod. 30: 9) is incense which does not belong to the altar of gold (cf. below, pp. 243–4). In P's style, the term *zār* is employed for circumscribing the closed circle of priests and priestly contagious holiness. For the significance of *zār* cf. L. A. Snijders, *The meaning of* זר *in the OT* (Leyden, 1935), pp. 124–45. Despite Snijders (p. 138) and Milgrom (op. cit., p. 5) it should be emphasized that in the Book of Numbers, too, the term *zār* denotes anyone who is not a priest, not just someone who is not a Levite. It is the Levitical guard which prevents any non-priest from approaching the tabernacle. The suggestions made here by NEB and JB are quite satisfactory, when they render *'îš zār* as 'unqualified person' (NEB), 'layman', 'lay person' (JB); *'ēš zārāh* as 'illicit fire' (NEB), 'unlawful fire' (JB); and *qᵉṭōret zārāh* as 'unauthorized incense' (NEB), 'profane incense' (JB)—except that, in this case, the same Hebrew adjective is represented by different English words.

[19] Cf. sect. 16 in Chapter VIII.

the abbreviated wording in the parallel section, if we accept the MT reading there: ושמרו את כהנתם, 'And they shall guard their priesthood' (Num. 3: 10)—Aaron and his sons shall guard, i.e. make sure they observe the prohibitions of, their priesthood 'for all that concerns the altar and that is behind the *pārōḵet*'. In LXX these last words also occur in the actual text of Num. 3: 10.

6

Just as the prohibition of entry into the tabernacle is a natural consequence of that of looking at the inner furniture (above, sect. 3), so a prohibition of entry to the court is apt to result from a prohibition of approach. Indeed, such a prohibition is latent in P's system, but it never achieved the form of an explicit 'don't'.

A number of unequivocal phenomena do, of course, argue against the factual existence of any such prohibition: after, for instance, Nadab and Abihu met their death in the court, the Levites drew near to them and bore them outside the camp (Lev. 10: 4–5). Similarly, we find that the place where a layman brings his sacrifices and lays his hands upon them is *petaḥ 'ōhel môʿēd*, 'at the entrance to the tent of meeting' (Lev. 1: 3–4; 3: 2, 8 *et al.*). The phrase *petaḥ 'ōhel môʿēd* in itself is rather vague and undefined and one still has to infer its exact location. Yet, at any rate, it cannot be outside the court.

The court actually includes two different areas: one of a minor degree of holiness and one of a stricter, contagious holiness. It stands to reason that the first is located between the gate and the altar; it is this area that is mostly referred to by the phrase 'at the entrance to the tent of meeting'. There is the place where laymen slaughter peace-offerings (Lev. 3: 2, 8,13) and wave the breasts given to the priests as their portion (ibid. 7: 29–30), in addition to laying hands on sacrifices. In general, any 'wave offering before the Lord' is waved here (cf. ibid. 14: 11–12, 23–4; Num. 5: 16–25; 6: 10–20; 8: 9–13). Furthermore, the people may cook their peace-offerings here (ibid. 6: 18) and, in certain cases, even assemble here (Lev. 8: 3–4; Num. 10: 3; 16: 19 *et al.*). The second area is evidently located between the altar and the tabernacle as well as in close proximity to the altar, and is denominated *māqôm qādôš*, 'a holy place'. There, on the northern side of the altar, the burnt-offerings, and sin- and guilt-offerings are slaughtered (Lev. 1: 11; 6: 18; 7: 2 *et al.*). In that area the male priests partake of the sin-, guilt-, and grain-offerings (ibid. 6: 9,[20] 19; 7: 6; 10: 12–13, 17–18; 24: 9; Num. 18: 10), and there a garment sprinkled with any blood of a sin-offering is washed (Lev. 6: 20).[21] In that area, 'beside the altar', the priest puts the ashes before carrying them out of the camp (ibid., v. 3). There should therefore be no doubt that this second area is out of bounds to both Israelites and Levites.[22] But P does not prohibit the Israelites from entering the court as far as a certain distance from the altar.

These undoubted facts notwithstanding, it seems that P's system betrays an implicit tendency towards regarding the whole court as the exclusive domain of the priests. A number of points bear this out:

(*a*) The court is not one of those things which cannot be dispensed with, and it is certainly difficult to assume that in P's unique ideology it serves simply as 'architectural' ornamentation. Since we have already come across the prohibition of approaching the tabernacle and altar, as well as the concept of 'holy place', it seems even more likely that there is a connection between the latter and the very existence of the partition of hangings. This partition may reflect, then, the desire to mark out the minimum distance in all directions, any contraction of which would constitute a violation of the prohibition of approaching the holy objects.

(*b*) As has been stated, the 'guarding' of the tabernacle is performed by the encampment itself of the Levites and priests around the court. Now, while the Levites encamp beyond the partition of hangings, the priests encamp and keep 'guard' in front of the court's gate (sect. 5). This fact too is indicative of P's innate desire to regard the whole of the area within this gate as the priests' exclusive preserve.

(*c*) The court's screen is exactly of the same weave as the outer veil of the tabernacle—a mixture of dyed wool with linen and of

[20] In this verse the text reads: במקום קדוש בחצר אהל מועד, 'in a holy place, in the court of the tent of meeting' (cf. also v. 19), but this should not be understood as in apposition, to mean that the whole court is regarded as 'a holy place'. Rather it is a further localization: the holy place is somewhere inside the court. Study and analogy should tell us where it is. Cf. Lev. 10: 12–13.

[21] On the association of the sin-, guilt-, and grain-offerings, according to the priestly school, with the circle of contagious holiness and the special reason for it, see for the present my remarks in *EM* iv. 40; v. 26–7.

[22] The area 'between the vestibule and the altar' is also qualified in Joel 2: 17 as an exclusively priestly domain.

rôqēm workmanship.[23] In view of P's strict principles it is unlikely that this would be a mere accident. As has been emphasized, the material and the workmanship of each article indicates its place on the sliding scale of sanctity and prohibitions. This fact may, therefore, be regarded as another expression of P's inherent tendency: just as the outer veil of the tabernacle shuts off the area forbidden to non-priests, so does the court's screen. These two domains then differ only in that the former is subject to a taboo of sight, the latter only to one of contact and approach.[24]

(*d*) Still another pointer is the designation 'the court of the priests' which the Chronicler applies to the inner court of the Solomonic temple (2 Chron. 4: 9). This designation is not used by the Chronicler accidentally, as it is his actual intention to conceive of the temple's inner court as reserved for priests. For in addition to this designation the Chronicler finds it necessary to remark that when Solomon uttered his prayer 'in the presence of all the assembly of Israel' he did it from a bronze 'laver', *kiyyôr*, which had been set, as if it were, 'in the *ʿᵃzārāh*', that is, in the outer, great precinct (ibid. 6: 13). It is a moot point whether in the Second Temple the inner court was really the exclusive preserve of the priests.[25] But the notion itself has no ground in any biblical text or source other than P. In the Chronicler's conception it could emanate only from the priestly sections, which at that time were already a part of the canonized Torah. Hence it appears that P is indeed liable to give rise to such a notion.

If the aforementioned tendency never developed in P to the point of non-priests being explicitly forbidden access to the court, a major stumbling block was on the one hand perhaps the objec-

[23] See sect. 8 in Chapter VIII.

[24] My considerations in this regard were not properly presented by Milgrom, nor do his counter-arguments hit the mark (op. cit., pp. 54–5; also *JAOS* 90 (1970), 207–8). It should not be forgotten that I definitely admit that P allows Israelites and Levites to go beyond the court's gate. Yet, it is my contention that a tendency inheres in P to regard the whole court as an area of priestly, contagious holiness. See also further on.

[25] In the Herodian temple it was only ends of flagstones protruding from the pavement which separated the court of Israel from that of the priests (Middoth ii. 5–6), and, at any rate, the Israelites were allowed to enter the court of the priests, where they laid hands on, and slaughtered the sacrifices, or waved the sacrificial portions (Kelim i. 8). In times of pilgrim-feasts the people extended as far as behind the western wall of the temple (Bab. Tal. Yoma, 21*a*). However, at the early, pre-Hellenistic stages of the Second Temple period the practice might perhaps have been different.

tive necessity of moving the tabernacle from place to place (cf. above, sect. 4). On the other hand, there was at work here the actual need for a special area of the holiness of minor degree, on whose existence as well the proper maintenance of cult depends. Only in Ezekiel's visionary programme, whose temple is encircled by two courts, did this tendency fully materialize: the outer court became a sphere of minor holiness (Ezek. 44: 3, 11–14; 46: 21–4); the inner court, however, including the altar within it, was reserved for the contagious, priestly holiness (ibid. 42: 13–14; 44: 17–19; 46: 1–3, 19–20).[26]

THE LETHAL AURA SURROUNDING THE HOLINESS

7

For a fuller comprehension of the exact nature of the three aforementioned prohibitions it should be added that their violation is not conditioned by deliberateness or inadvertence on the part of the doer. This is one of the outstanding characteristics of the nature of holiness in general (as well as of its opposite extreme, defilement)—that the influence ascribed to inner intentions is strictly limited. The reaction of these two entities is impersonal, 'blind', and as a rule it is only the act itself that is noteworthy.

At any rate, these three prohibitions are so strict that any violation of them is bound, according to P, to have immediate and fatal consequences. Besides the formularized warning which recurs in four passages and states that a stranger, *zār*, should not come near lest he be put to death (above, sect. 5), all the other warnings which appear in this context speak of an unnatural death only. Warnings of this kind emerge in connection with the high priest (Exod. 28: 35; Lev. 16: 2, 13) and the priests as a whole (Exod. 28: 43; 30: 20–1; Lev. 10: 6–7, 9; 22: 9), the Kohathites (Num. 4: 15, 19–20) and the Levites as a whole (ibid. 18: 3), even with the Israelites (ibid. 1: 53; 8: 19; 17: 25; 18: 5, 22), though for the latter such warnings are of only limited significance, since the Israelites are

[26] Interestingly enough, though in Ezekiel's code the Levites are left without any function in the inner court, they are nevertheless not removed from there but are given a special chamber opposite the one which is for the priests, the sons of Zadok, 'the keepers of the guard of the altar' (Ezek. 40: 44–6). It seems that Ezekiel was in no position to free himself of the school's evident tenets. What had been explicitly granted to the Levites in P itself could not be forbidden them in a code which is only an epigonic growth of the school.

supposedly barred by the Levites from access to the priestly circle. When the priestly writers come to illustrate these warnings in narrative form, they leave no doubt that these are not judicial death penalties. Fire going forth from Yahweh devours Nadab and Abihu (Lev. 10: 2) as it does the company of Korah (Num. 16: 35). A plague which suddenly breaks out kills thousands of people at a stroke (ibid. 17: 11–14).[27] Some of the warnings are indeed accompanied by an explicit mention of *negep̱*, plague, or *qeṣep̱*, 'wrath' (ibid. 1: 53; 8: 19; 18: 5), which makes it still clearer what kind of death is implied here.

The nature of the 'wrath' is such that it spreads far away from its focal point and is liable to strike those who have not violated any prohibition, and may even affect the whole people. Moses warns the priests that if they perform mourning rites when the anointing oil is upon them, they will die and 'he [Yahweh] will be wrathful, *yiqṣōp̱*, upon all the congregation' (Lev. 10: 6). Likewise, the text finds it necessary to warn the priests that if the Levites come near to the holy vessels when these are exposed, 'both they and you will die' (Num. 18: 3). After wrath had gone forth from Yahweh it was impossible to stop it except by making Aaron stand 'between the dead and the living' with a censer of incense in his hand (ibid. 17: 11–15). The lack of discrimination between deliberateness and inadvertence is thus inherent in the fatal, demonic character of the wrath's action—in the very slaughter of crowds, where those who have not sinned either deliberately or inadvertently are also struck down. In the case of Nadab and Abihu at least it is quite obvious that they had no intention of rebelling against Yahweh. On the contrary, they only intended to pay homage to him, and their error, namely, putting 'strange fire' in their censers, was one of ignorance;[28] nevertheless, they immediately perished (Lev. 10: 1–2). After their death there is the divine announcement to the effect that it is just among those who are permitted to come near to Yahweh that he shows himself holy by fatal events, and in this way is he glorified before all the people. Aaron accepts this austere declaration in the silence of consent (ibid., v. 3).

[27] In the case of Uzziah it was a leprosy that immediately broke out upon his forehead (2 Chron. 26: 19–21). Apparently, the Chronicler, who in this respect is influenced by P, was somewhat restrained by historical events; otherwise, he would certainly have thought up a much more serious punishment for this king.

[28] Cf. above, p. 183, n. 18; and below, p. 222.

X

TEMPLE AND TABERNACLE

1

It is evident that as depicted in P the tabernacle is largely imaginary and never existed in Israel. Anyone who believes that the semi-nomadic tribes who made their way from Egypt to Canaan were capable of erecting such a magnificent edifice in their midst violates the laws of historical reality, and it is up to him to substantiate his argument. As far as we know, the most likely—if not the only—time when such a magnificent mode of building was feasible in Israel, in Old Testament times, was the short-lived heyday of Solomon's reign. However, it was not a tabernacle that was constructed then, but a cedar-roofed 'exalted house', *bêt zᵉḇûl* (1 Kgs. 8: 13). Indeed, the correspondence between P's tabernacle and Solomon's actual temple is such that the latter is undoubtedly reflected in the former.

PROJECTIONS OF THE TEMPLE

2

The correspondence between P's tabernacle and Solomon's temple is apparent, first of all, in the articles of furniture that appear in both of them: cherubim and an ark in the inner sanctum; a table (or tables),[1] a lampstand (or lampstands), and an altar of incense in the outer sanctum; a burnt-offering altar and water containers in the court. In both houses we find that all the inner

[1] According to 1 Chron. 28: 16; 2 Chron. 4: 8, 19 there were ten tables of gold in the temple. In 2 Chron. 23: 11 and 29: 18, where just one table is mentioned, the Chronicler's thought is apparently arrested by the model of the tabernacle so prominent in the Pentateuch. The only explicit evidence for one table in the temple of Solomon is the text of 1 Kgs. 7: 48, where the singular form *haššulḥān* is used. However, even this form may here be understood in the collective sense, in a way not unknown in biblical Hebrew. The opinion adopted by many modern commentators, from E. Bertheau to W. Rudolph, *Chronikbücher* (HAT, 1955), p. 209, that the ten tables mentioned in 2 Chron. 4: 8 are meant merely to serve as position bases for the lampstands, seems hardly acceptable to me.

articles of furniture are made of gold, the outer of copper or bronze (with regard to the temple see 1 Kgs. 6: 28; 7: 23–39, 48–50). In both of them we find, further, that poles are fixed on to the ark, not only when it is being removed, but also when it is resting in the inner sanctum (Exod. 25: 15; 1 Kgs. 8: 8). All the inner surfaces of Solomon's temple—walls, floors, and even doors of the inner and outer sanctums—like the planks and the inner pillars of the tabernacle, are overlaid with gold (1 Kgs. 6: 20–2, 30, 32, 35), but there is no gold in the court. Carvings of cherubim appear on the walls and doors of the inner and outer sanctums of Solomon's temple (ibid., vv. 29, 32, 35; cf. Ezek. 41: 18–20, 25) in a similar manner to the inner curtains and the *pārōḵet*-veil of the tabernacle (Exod. 26: 1, 31; 36: 8, 35).

Moreover, the plans of both Solomon's temple and the tabernacle demonstrate the principles outlined in Chapter VIII: that of the eastern axis, and that of concentric circles of declining order the further they move away from the focal point of the cherubim in the inner sanctum. The floor of the inner sanctum of the temple was apparently lined with cedar-wood, while that of the outer sanctum was lined with cypress which is inferior to cedar.[2] The doors of the inner sanctum were of olive-wood (1 Kgs. 6: 32)—the choicest variety of wood, from which the cherubim too were made (v. 23). The doors of the outer sanctum, on the other hand, were only of cypress (v. 34). The doorposts of both the inner and outer sanctums of the temple were made of olive-wood, but the doorposts of the former were framed in a pentagon, while those of the latter formed a square (vv. 31, 33; cf. Ezek. 41: 21). The square was undoubtedly simpler in form than the pentagon.[3] Needless to say, the court, with its bronze (or copper) furniture, was inferior in

[2] In the description of the *d^eḇîr*, inner sanctum, it is stated (1 Kgs. 6: 16): 'He built . . . with boards of cedar from the floor to the walls (LXX: rafters)'. But in the description of the outer sanctum the following sentence is added: 'and he covered the floor of the *bayit* with boards of cypress' (v. 15)—which is not said in the case of the *d^eḇîr*. This *bayit* mentioned in v. 15 applies only to the outer sanctum, not to the 'house' as a whole; cf. v. 17. On the use of cedar and cypress woods and gold overlay on walls of temples and palaces by the Assyrian and late-Babylonian kings, see J. A. Montgomery, *Kings* (ICC, 1951), p. 151.

[3] A 'pentagonal', *ḥ^amiššit*, doorpost may indicate a post planed on five sides, unlike the 'square', *r^eḇiʿît*, which was planed on four parallel sides. Otherwise, the *ḥ^amiššit* may signify a pentagonal doorframe, that is, with a peaked roof. Such a pentagonal doorway is pictured on a third-century B.C. coin of Byblos; cf. Montgomery, op. cit., p. 158.

status to the temple itself, with its furniture and surfaces overlaid with gold.

The correspondence between P's tabernacle and Solomon's temple is particularly in evidence in the form of the altars, so much so that it stands to reason that in these matters P's descriptions are merely a retrojection of the altars in Solomon's temple. The altar in the court of Solomon's temple was also of bronze (1 Kgs. 8: 64; 2 Kgs. 16: 14; Ezek. 9: 2) just like the altar in the court of the tabernacle. Apart from these two, there is no mention of another bronze (or copper) altar in the Old Testament. Historical circumstances would indicate that the outer altar of Solomon's temple was the only one of bronze that the Israelites were familiar with. At any rate, this was the first bronze altar made in Israel, for it seems that bronze began to be used for building and engraving in Israel only during Solomon's reign, and at that time Tyrian artisans were employed for 'any work in bronze' in the temple court (1 Kgs. 7: 13–14).[4] Even the special ornamentation of the

[4] The account of the building activities in 1 Kgs. 6–7 is divided into several sections: first comes the description of the edifices built by Solomon—the temple (6: 2–38) and the royal palaces (7: 1–12). The materials used here were: hewn and undressed stones, cedar, cypress, olive, and gold. The cedar and cypress woods were supplied by Hiram king of Tyre (5: 22–4), but the work is attributed to Solomon himself, as it seems to have been performed mainly by Israelite labourers and craftsmen. This is followed by a description of all the bronze articles sited in the temple court (7: 13–47). Making these articles, unlike previous work, is frequently and as a rule termed *m^elā'ḵāh*, as it required special skill. The text is careful to attribute this work to another Hiram, also from Tyre—a bronzesmith, the son of an Israelite widow and a Tyrian father. Solomon supplies him with the bronze (v. 46) but does not interfere with his work, and Hiram is responsible to him only in respect of the final products. This son of a Tyrian was presumably not allowed into the temple, but was allowed to work only in the court and in bronze. The Chronicler, however, attributes to him command of all skills—in silver and gold; iron, stone, and wood; purple and other dyed wools (2 Chron. 2:13). Indeed, at the end, the golden vessels placed inside the temple are listed (7: 48–50), and again their making is attributed to Solomon himself, evidently referring to Israelite craftsmen who were not so unfamiliar with working in gold. Though the section dealing with Hiram's bronze work takes on a very schematic style, closely resembling the style of P, with stereotyped paragraphs and an over-all summing up at the end, it nevertheless constitutes an integral part of the account. One can hardly accept the views of those commentators (B. Stade, R. Kittel, A. Šanda, J. A. Montgomery *et al.*) who find in these descriptions literary combinations. But it cannot be denied that the text itself has undergone certain corruptions. On the authenticity of the description in general, cf. C. Watzinger, *Denkmäler Palästinas*, i (Leipzig, 1933), p. 88. N. Glueck's discoveries in the Araba region and at Tel el-Kheleifeh might have furnished proof of Solomon's use of bronze (cf. also Albright, *ARI*, 136–7). Only the bronze mines and refineries of the Araba are now defined as pre-Israelit

altar which P mentions (Exod. 27: 4–5; 35: 16; 38: 4–5), particularly the horns (27: 2 *et al.*), make it likely that here we have a reflection of Solomon's altar. Horns as an altar decoration, also known from archaeological finds and even outside Israel, do not seem to have come into vogue in Israel until the beginning of the monarchy. In the Old Testament (with the exception of P) they are mentioned only against the background of the monarchical period (1 Kgs. 1: 50–1; 2: 28; Jer. 17: 1; Amos 3: 14; Ps. 118: 27).

Similarly, the gold altar of incense described in P is certainly a retrojection of the parallel altar in Solomon's temple (1 Kgs. 6: 20, 22; 7: 48). According to P's description, this altar too has horns, as well as a splendid ornamentation of 'moulding of gold round about' (Exod. 30: 3–4). In the latter respect it resembles the gold table (ibid. 25: 24). Moreover, it seems that the tabernacle's lampstand, described with such detail in P, is likewise based on the ten lampstands posted in Solomon's temple (1 Kgs. 7: 49), and it is not impossible that each of those ten, just like P's lampstand, consisted or seven branches (Exod. 25: 32–7). A hall of the dimensions of Solomon's outer sanctum could hardly be adequately lit by ten single lamps.[5]

3

In addition let it be noted that both the temple and the tabernacle obviously presuppose the existence of a surrounding court. At the same time, it seems that during the first half of the First Temple period only one court, the one which directly encircled the temple, was considered to be the temple court (1 Kgs. 6: 36; 7: 12;[6] 8: 64), since the outer 'greater court' actually enclosed both the temple area and the king's court and palaces (ibid. 7: 9, 12). Only afterwards did the temple come to be considered to have two courts

by B. Rothenberg; see the summing-up of his work in that region in his latest volume *Timna, Valley of the Biblical Copper Mines* (London, 1972). The Old Testament, however, testifies that Solomon's bronze was produced in the plain of the Jordan (1 Kgs. 7: 46), not in the Arabah.

[5] Cf. my discussion on this point in *EM*, s.v. מנורה, v. 17–18; in a somewhat shortened form also in *Encyc. Judaica*, vi (Jerusalem, 1971), cols. 1355–9.

[6] The phrase חצר בית יהוה הפנימית occurring in this verse is described by M. Noth, *Könige* (BK, 1968), p. 140, rightly enough, as 'a pleonastic contamination of the two expressions חצר בית יהוה and החצר הפנימית'. Cf. the reading of LXX, Luc. here, and the remarks of C. F. Burney, *Notes on the Hebrew Text of the Books of Kings* (Oxford, 1903), p. 83.

of its own, possibly as a result of some slight alteration in the arrangement of the courts. This change seems to have taken place about the time of Ahaz or of Hezekiah. In the records of the Books of Kings, no mention is made of 'the two courts of the house of the Lord' until the time of Manasseh (2 Kgs. 21: 5; 23: 12). The earliest reference to the temple 'courts', in the plural, thus implying the existence of two, occurs in Isa. 1: 12. Likewise, in the Psalms only the temple 'courts' in the plural are referred to (Ps. 65: 5; 84: 3, 11; 92: 14; 96: 8 *et al.*), reflecting a state of affairs which did not precede the last centuries of the First Temple (and persisted down to the early stages of the Second Temple). Ezekiel is already well aware of the existence of two courts around the temple (see Ezek. 8: 7, 14, 16; 9: 3; 10: 3–5). Such two courts were taken for granted in the Second Temple (Isa. 62: 9; Zech. 3: 7; Neh. 8: 16; 13: 7 *et al.*), while the Chronicler even projected them back into the times of David (1 Chron. 23: 28; 28: 12), Solomon (2 Chron. 4: 9; 6: 13), and Jehoash (ibid. 23: 5).[7]

It thus transpires that the priestly conception of the tabernacle being enclosed by just one court actually reflects conditions which were characteristic of the time prior to Manasseh (a conclusion to which we are also led by other considerations and from some other directions). Ezekiel's imaginary temple, in contrast, surrounded as it is by two courts (Ezek. 40–6) must look to a subsequent stage of the First Temple history for its interpretation.

In this context, attention should be also paid to the fact, already mentioned in Chapter II, that the *lᵉšāḵôt*, 'chambers' appeared in the Jerusalem temple courts only after the time of Hezekiah.[8] In P's tabernacle, however, there is no sign of their existence, while in Ezekiel's temple they are already taken for granted (Ezek. 40: 17, 44–6 [cf. LXX]; for other chambers, reserved exclusively for priests see 42: 1–14; 44: 19; 46: 19–20). Again, the rule that it is the temple's pre-Hezekianic stage that is reflected in P's tabernacle

[7] 'The court of the Lord's house' mentioned in Jer. 19: 14; 26: 2 as the place where the prophet addresses the people is probably the outer court, the natural setting for such scenes. It is its northern part that seems to be referred to in Jer. 36: 10 as 'the upper court' (note 'the entry of the New Gate' mentioned in the selfsame verse as well as in 26: 10 [this gate had been built by King Jotham; cf. 2 Kgs. 15: 35 and above, p. 97, n. 15]). 'The new court' mentioned by the Chronicler in connection with Jehoshaphat (2 Chron. 20: 5) is rather difficult to identify. Rudolph (*Chronikbücher*, p. 260) takes it as an application of 'post-exilic terminology'.

[8] Cf. above, p. 24 n. 20.

can be further substantiated by the fact that P mentions only a bronze altar in the court. Ahaz, however, had this altar removed northwards and replaced by one patterned upon the Damascene model (2 Kgs. 16: 10–16). In fact, Ezekiel already refers to the bronze altar as standing close to one of the northern gates of the temple court (Ezek. 9: 2; cf. 8: 5), while the large principal altar described with great detail in his visionary programme (43: 13–17) is apparently none other than the one set up by Ahaz.[9] Still other points pertinent to this principle, that the priestly tabernacle mirrors the Jerusalem temple only in the latter's pre-Hezekianic form, will be indicated in subsequent discussions (in this regard, one should pay heed especially to the implications of Chapter XV).

THE PRIESTLY TRADITION AND THE UNIQUENESS OF THE TABERNACLE

4

Inasmuch as the correspondence between the temple and the tabernacle is quite obvious, it has become an accepted truth of Old Testament scholarship that the priestly writer merely projected—presumably, in post-exilic times—an image of Solomon's temple on to the Exodus story.[10] The account can, therefore, contain no evidence whatsoever of the period preceding Jerusalem

[9] Cf. my discussion of this matter in *EM* iv, s.v. מזבח, 769, 773–5, where I chose to follow and to confirm the suggestion already made by such scholars as A. R. S. Kennedy, G. A. Barton, J. Pedersen, and others. This altar was apparently built of bricks, as in 1 Kgs. 13: 3, 5 the verb *qr'* in the *nip'al* conjugation ('to be rent', 'to be torn to pieces') is applied to it.

[10] This opinion was already held by W. Vatke and J. F. L. George, both of whom are quoted by K. Ch. W. F. Bähr, *Symbolik des mosaischen Cultus*, i (Heidelberg, 1837), pp. 117–18. See also, e.g., Th. Nöldeke, *Untersuchungen in Kritik des AT* (Kiel, 1869), pp. 120–1; Wellhausen, *PGI*, 36–7, 253; A. Kuenen, *The Religion of Israel* (London, 1874–5), i, pp. 258–9; ii, pp. 166–7; H. Gressmann, *Die Lade Jahves und das Allerheiligste des solomonischen Tempels* (Berlin, 1920), p. 45; I. Benzinger, s.v. 'Tabernacle', *EB*, iv. 4874; idem, *Hebräische Archäologie*[3] (Leipzig, 1927), p. 333; Pedersen, *ILC* i–ii. 30; iii–iv. 200, 218, 233, 245–6; A. Bentzen, *Introduction to the OT*[2], ii (Copenhagen, 1952), p. 34; the commentaries on Exodus by H. Holzinger (KHC, 1900, pp. 126, 129–30), S. R. Driver (CBSC, 1918, pp. 430–2), G. Beer and K. Galling (HAT, 1939, pp. 131, 135, 137; on their theory, in relation to layer P^B alone), M. Noth (ATD, 1959, p. 163), and many others.

and at best can but reflect a Jerusalemite (in the main, post-exilic) reality.

Nevertheless, however clear the connection is between P's tabernacle and Solomon's temple there is actually no reason to suppose that P's description is altogether a late retrojection. It also has a certain substratum of ancient and quite authentic tradition. This tradition did not attain literary crystallization until a relatively late period (to my mind, not exactly in post-exilic times), and hence later details were superimposed on it with the result that its ancient aspects were largely blurred. The later details are particularly recognizable in the descriptions of great magnificence—the gold, silver, bronze, the dyed wools—and these are, in truth, nothing more than 'a fiction'. Some of these details even give a special shape to a number of aspects which are of the very bedrock of the tradition. But for all that, they have not totally obscured the pre-Jerusalemite elements in this tradition.

5

First of all we must remember that in form the tabernacle is not an artificial projection of a solid building. It is a type of dwelling in its own right, reflecting, in its structure, nomadic or semi-nomadic conditions, and has a basis in the early stages of Israelite history, prior to the settlement in Canaan.

In fact, a tabernacle is a sort of tent, which again is characteristic of nomadic life. It differs from the orthodox tent in that tent cloths are usually stretched over comparatively thin poles,[11] whereas tabernacle hangings—so we must infer from biblical descriptions—are spread over temporary walls made of 'planks', *qᵉrāšîm*. In both of them pegs and cords are used. The tabernacle is the more stable structure of the two, and yet it is also a typical habitation of nomads. The term 'tabernacles', *miškānôt* (rendered by EVV as 'tents' or 'dwellings') is used once in connection with shepherbs (S. of S. 1: 8). The wandering 'people of Qedem' mainly lived in tents (Judg. 6: 3–5 *et al.*), but reference is also made to their being encamped in tabernacles (Ezek. 25: 4). Hence, the parallelism tent (*'ōhel*)—tabernacle (*miškān*) was stamped as a stereotyped form of style, both in biblical poetry (Num. 24: 5; Isa. 54: 2;

[11] See the Assyrian, Egyptian, and ancient Arab examples illustrated in Benzinger, *Heb. Archäologie*, 95–6; *EM*, 124–5; cf. Alt, *KS* iii. 235–9.

Jer. 30: 18; Ps. 78: 60; cf. Job. 21: 28) and in the Ugaritic texts (*UT*, 128. iii. 18–19; 2 Aqht, v. 31–3).[12] Likewise, in the Israelite camp in the wilderness mention is made of tabernacles (Num. 16: 24, 27; 24: 5; Ps. 78: 28). There, however, the tabernacle in the centre of the camp, the 'tabernacle of Yahweh' (Lev. 17: 4; Num. 16: 9; 17: 28 *et al.*), is described as being larger and more splendid than any other in the camp.[13] The frequent use, in P and in other parts of the Old Testament, of the verb *škn* to denote divine or human residence also harks back to nomadic conditions of life when at least part of the camp consisted of tabernacles, just as the verb *'hl* (Gen. 13: 12, 18; Isa. 13: 20) is applied to tent dwellers.

Thus, the form of the tabernacle, P's portable temple carried by the wandering Israelites, does not necessarily run counter to historical truth.

6

We must further bear in mind that the tabernacle in P is not conceived of as provisional, as valid only till the land is conquered. It is to remain for the generations after the occupation of Canaan too. It is this very tabernacle whose plan is imparted to Moses by Yahweh on Sinai (Exod. 25: 9, 40; 26: 30 *et al.*) that P regards as the everlasting house of God. Even Bezalel who built it was, as we noted, specifically 'called by name' by Yahweh for this task (Exod. 31: 2; 35: 30). The text assumes that this work was not carried out for temporary need; it is charged with that aura of solemnity which befits a superlatively sacred and unique event. The tabernacle is not even intended to serve as a pattern for other temples which might be erected in the course of generations. P appears to be completely unaware of any other house of God which might be built at any other time, under other conditions.

[12] Concerning this parallelism see most recently Y. Avishur, *Semitics* [Pretoria] 2 (1971–2), 19–20. The word משכנא has lately been found in the Aramaic inscriptions of Hatra (see D. R. Hillers, *BASOR* 206 (1972), 54–6). However, its meaning there appears to be merely 'abode', 'dwelling place'—not 'tabernacle', nor even 'shrine'. Such a meaning is sometimes signified by the word *miškān* (in the singular) in biblical Hebrew too, especially outside P; cf. above, p. 14, n. 3.

[13] Although the tabernacles mentioned in the Ugaritic epics are the residences of gods and thus belong to the sphere of mythology, they are nevertheless in a real sense parallel to P's 'tabernacle of Yahweh'. But this is not necessarily because in P too the tabernacle is based on a divine pattern (F. M. Cross, 'The Tabernacle', *BA* 10 (1947), 62). In reality, just the opposite was usually the case: the divine habitation was simply a heavenly image of an earthly house.

It may be said that just as P's tabernacle is unique in the physical sphere, since the cult is concentrated within it, so is it unique in the temporal sphere.[14]

7

Scholars dealing with this subject for the most part assume, either explicitly or implicitly, that P's account of the tabernacle is a kind of historical fiction. The priestly writers were aware that when the Israelite tribes left the land of Egypt they were still nomads, and hence, it is assumed, it was only natural that against such a background these writers should describe the imaginary portable shrine as a tabernacle. The fiction was invented, it is assumed, as a vehicle for the specific priestly cultic concepts and legalistic demands.

Now it cannot be denied that the picture of square camps with the tabernacle at their centre greatly facilitates P's writers in presenting their utopian views. However, one can hardly suppose that the writers themselves totally did not believe in what they related and described. Whoever attributes to them conscious literary invention of an imaginary state of affairs fails properly to grasp the character of the material before us. This priestly work, as well as other parts of the Pentateuch and even the sacral literature of the ancient Near East as a whole, in which the traditional element is prominent, all mean exactly what they say. They betray no tendency towards the deliberate creation of situations completely

[14] The enduring and 'eternal' character of the tabernacle has been acknowledged by T. E. Fretheim ('The Priestly Document—anti-temple?', *VT* 18 (1968), 313–29), except that he draws an exaggerated conclusion from it. He claims that the priestly writers opposed the building of the Second Temple because they adhered to the old tradition of a specifically portable shrine. This thesis overlooks the fact that what P considers legitimate and proper is not necessarily the tabernacle's portable form as such, but rather the existence of the very tabernacle that was set up under divine inspiration at Mount Sinai. Zeal for the historical identity of the tabernacle could hardly merge into opposition to the erection of a temple when there was none in existence. At the same time, I am prepared to admit that a degree of opposition to a temple is discernible in P's ideology. However, it is directed rather against the First Temple itself, which apparently fell short of the expectations of the priestly reformers and did not satisfy their desires, so that they had to content themselves with a Utopia drawn against the background of the desert period, as has been pointed out in Chapter VII (while their disciple, Ezekiel, had to resort to a visionary programme). On the supposed theological significance which some scholars attribute to the structure of the tabernacle claiming that by means of this P's authors indicate the impermanent character of this shrine, see my remarks in *Biblica* 50 (1969), 259–62.

'artistic' in nature. Those who committed these traditional–literary compositions to writing undoubtedly believed in the reality of the subject-matter transmitted through them.

At the basis of P's Utopia is a legend (a 'temple legend'), the absolute authenticity of which is taken for granted by its authors. The legend invests a particular house of God with a halo of extraordinary sanctity and glory, linking its construction to the covenant at Sinai. The house of God of which the legend speaks cannot be the one built by Solomon in Jerusalem. For P's tabernacle, according to its own story, was never moved to Jerusalem. Jerusalem is not even mentioned in P, while, on the other hand, the account of the foundation of Solomon's temple was not transposed to the period preceding Solomon.[15] P's legend actually speaks of a more ancient temple.

THE OBJECT OF THE TEMPLE LEGEND

8

Which temple is involved in the priestly account of the founding legend? In order to answer this question, it is sufficient to ponder over what, according to P, happened with this temple. To what extent this account mirrors historical truth is, for the moment, of no importance to us.

After the tabernacle was erected at Mount Sinai it was transported through the wilderness, brought to the conquered land of Canaan, and, after apparently making a short stay at Gilgal on Jordan (Josh. 4: 19; 5: 10) it was immediately set down at Shiloh. Here 'at Shiloh before the Lord, at the door of the tent of meeting' Joshua casts lots and determines the territories of the seven tribes on the western side of the Jordan (Josh. 18: 1–10; 19: 51). Here also the Levitical cities are allocated (21: 1–2), and from here the tribes of trans-Jordan are sent home at the end of the war (22: 9). At Shiloh the western tribes of Israel assemble to fight those of the other side of the Jordan when they learn that the latter built 'an

[15] Even the Chronicler does not place it any earlier than David, who according to his account made all the preparations for the building (1 Chron. 22–4). In one place the Chronicler hints that the site of Solomon's temple was on Mount Moriah (2 Chron. 3: 1), thus connecting it with the legend of the attempted sacrifice of Isaac (Gen. 22: 2). At any rate, even the Chronicler cannot, of course, conceive of identifying the tabernacle erected at Sinai with the Jerusalem temple.

altar other than the altar of the Lord our God that stands before his tabernacle'. Phinehas the priest is sent from Shiloh at the head of ten chiefs to try to discover why the trans-Jordanian tribes had undermined the cultic unity of the tabernacle. But when they learn that the altar by the Jordan is designed 'not for burnt-offering nor for sacrifice' they are content and dissension is avoided (22: 10–34).

There is no hint in P of the tabernacle being moved from Shiloh to any other site. In the priestly redaction of Judg. 19–21 we find 'the camp' referred to, and its site is 'at Shiloh which is in the land of Canaan' (21: 12). Phinehas the son of Eleazar son of Aaron is mentioned as well (20: 28), and that, again, in those editorial accretions to the story which frequently contradict its basic assumptions. On the other hand, 'the ark of the covenant of God', said 'in those days' to be in Bethel (20: 27), appears in the non-priestly layer of the story, and has no connection with P's tabernacle.[16] Reference to the 'tent of meeting' is made in 1 Sam. 2: 22, within an editorial note attached to the narrative, where the priestly writers are applying that epithet to the Shilonite house of God mentioned therein.[17] The Chronicler relates that in David's

[16] Note the appellative: *'ᵃrôn bᵉrît hā'ᵉlōhîm*, 'the ark of the covenant of God'. In P it is never so described, but only as *'arôn hā'ēdût*, 'the ark of testimony'. The phrase *'ômēd lᵉpānāyw*, 'stands before him' (v. 28), which here has a technical, cultic flavour (cf. Deut. 10: 8; 18: 7; 19: 17; 29: 14; Jer. 15: 1, 19; 35: 19 *et al.*; also 1 Kgs. 17: 1; 18: 15; 2 Kgs. 3: 14 *et al.*), is also very rare in P's style and is never used in such a way there. Thus it appears that the whole parenthetical clause in Judg. 20: 27_{β}–28_{α}a (to 'in those days') is a Deuteronomistic rather than a priestly expansion, or (if the mention of Phinehas the son of Eleazor son of Aaron is an indication of P) a conflation of both Deuteronomistic and priestly additions. As a matter of fact, the Deuteronomists might have been acquainted with the name of Phinehas, just as the names Aaron and Eleazar were known to the non-priestly sources in the Pentateuch (above, pp. 69–70). The Deuteronomistic editors (or the narrative itself, before them) here seem to conceive of the ark as temporarily placed outside the confines of a temple. In this respect they follow in the wake of the non-priestly sources (above, pp. 78–9).

[17] The end of the verse 1 Sam. 2: 22, reading: 'and how they lay with the women who served at the entrance to the tent of meeting', does not appear in LXX (nor in the version of 4QSam[a]), which leads modern commentators to claim that it was a later addition in allusion to Exod. 38: 8. However, since the above-mentioned sentence bears the imprints of P's style, it seems plausible that it is not just a mechanical addition to the text but a sign of priestly editorial activity, and therefore is a part of the actual text in the form it has been delivered to us. In this part of the composition of the Former Prophets, though, priestly 'redaction' exists in the form of only very slight and solitary touches. In the version of LXX and Qumran, on the other hand, that sentence may have been deleted—possibly in order to turn a blind eye to a shameful act of the priests (A. Geiger, *Urschrift und Übersetzungen der Bibel*[2] (Frankfurt a. Main, 1928),

and Solomon's reigns the tabernacle stood 'in the high-place at Gibeon' (1 Chron. 16: 39; 21: 29; 2 Chron. 1: 3–6), but this detail is only a forced attempt on the part of the later historiographer to vindicate facts known to him from the Book of Kings (cf. 1 Kgs. 3: 4); it tells us nothing of P's own assumptions.

The latest traces of priestly penmanship appear, as it has been said, at the beginning of chap. 8 of 1 Kgs.,[18] where 'the tent of meeting and all the holy vessels that were in the tent [LXX: of meeting]' are mentioned (ibid., v. 4). But the site of the tent is not indicated here. If we wish to make deductions from what is explicitly stated in other contexts of P, we must conclude that the priestly writers assumed the tabernacle to have been still at Shiloh. This single verse is a slender thread in P's chronicle by which to connect the tent of meeting at Shiloh with Jerusalem. It goes without saying that the miraculous tale of the exile of the ark to the land of the Philistines and its return to Israelite territory (1 Sam. 4–6) contains no signs of P and is irrelevant here.[19] The priestly doctrine cannot conceive of the ark being separated from the tabernacle.

Shiloh is, then, really the only place in the land of Canaan to which P's tabernacle is linked. From Sinai it is transferred to Shiloh, and there, according to P, it stays at least until the days of Phinehas the son of Eleazar. Subsequently it 'melts away'. We cannot therefore escape the conclusion that the legend related by P is that of the Shiloh temple. This legend is based on the belief which the priestly writers shared with all those who had earlier transmitted it, that the house of God at Shiloh was brought from Sinai after having been erected there on divine instruction, just as Mesopotamian temple legends, for instance, were apt to relate that their temples had been erected in accordance with instructions

p. 272), or because of the manifest tension between that sentence and the rest of the narrative.

[18] Cf. above, p. 141, n. 11.

[19] Neither is it of vital importance to us here as to when Shiloh was actually destroyed. Historically speaking, the evidence of the excavations (cf. above, pp. 27–8) as well as that of Judg. 18: 31; 1 Kgs. 11: 29; 14: 2, 4 would indicate that the city remained in existence right until the last stages of the Northern Kingdom and that in the wake of the Philistine wars it was only of the ark that Shiloh was deprived. The statements of Jer. 7: 12–15; 26: 6, 9 would attest that in the course of time the temple of Shiloh was abandoned, while the city incurred destruction only from the hands of the Assyrians. On the other hand, Judg. 21: 19; Jer. 41: 5 may testify that subsequently a tiny settlement re-emerged on the site. Cf. R. A. Pearce, *VT* 23 (1973), 105–8; and above, loc. cit.

imparted by the gods themselves.[20] On the other hand, this legend is based on the assumption, historical and actual, that the temple which stood at Shiloh was in the form of a tabernacle. Indeed, this assumption is not inaccurate, for the temple at Shiloh does appear to have been a tabernacle, in spite of what seems to be the contrary evidence of non-priestly sources.

9

The contradictory evidence appears mainly in the story at the beginning of the Book of Samuel, where the text speaks of a solid house (1 Sam. 1: 7, 24; cf. Judg. 18: 31), 'the *hêḵāl* of the Lord' (1 Sam. 3: 3) and references are also made to doors (1 Sam. 3: 15) and a doorpost (1: 9). However, this evidence is cancelled out by the explicit statement in Nathan's prophecy to the effect that since the Exodus from Egypt and until the time when the temple was built in Jerusalem Yahweh, i.e. the ark, was 'moving about *bᵉ'ōhel ûḇᵉmiškān*, in a tent and in a tabernacle' without ever demanding that a house of cedar should be built for him (2 Sam. 7 6–7).[21] These words come from a non-priestly text, and can thus be accepted as 'reliable', since nobody even claims that they have been edited from a priestly viewpoint.[22] Yet they make sense only if one assumes that the Jerusalem temple was the first solid house

[20] When Gudea the *ensi* of Lagash intended to rebuild the temple of Ningirsu, the god appeared to him in a dream, commanded him to execute it, and showed him the plan. See quotations from Cylinder A in H. Frankfort, *Kingship and the Gods* (Chicago, 1955), pp. 255–6 (for a section describing the work of construction see *ANET*, p. 269). See also the prayer of Nabonidus in the temple of Larsa: 'O Lord, Supreme God, Prince Marduk, without thee no dwelling is founded nor its plan designed' (Frankfort, op. cit., p. 268). Cf. also Esarhaddon's prayer when he decided to reconstruct the Babylonian temples which is also cited there. At a later period the Chronicler recounts a similar thing, namely, that David prepared the programme of the Jerusalem temple 'from the hand of the Lord' (1 Chron. 28: 19).

[21] The combination *'ōhel ûmiškān*, 'tent and tabernacle' is a hendiadys, implying a structure of the sort usual among nomads that can be dismantled and transported. This word-pair occurs in biblical as well as in Canaanite poetry in the separated form, broken up into its components (cf. U. Cassuto, *Tarbiẓ* 14 (1943), 7), and it may be added to the list of E. Z. Melammed, 'Break-up of Stereotype Phrases as an Artistic Device in Biblical Poetry', *Scripta Hierosolymitana*, viii (1961), 115–43.

[22] Nor do they belong to the Deuteronomistic expansions met with in this chapter. However, even if they were a part of the Deuteronomistic redaction (and not of the narrative source itself, as they really are) this would not detract from their validity as a substantiation of the priestly tradition. On this point see also my remarks in *Biblica* 50 (1969), 266.

in which the ark was installed. One is therefore obliged to concede that those elements in the story at the beginning of Samuel which describe the Shiloh shrine as a solid structure are nothing more than anachronistic touches based on conditions existing during the monarchical period (a well-known characteristic of biblical narratives). Indeed, it is not difficult to show that this story cannot have received its present shape before at least Solomon's time (see 1 Sam. 2: 10 and especially v. 35; also 3: 1: 'in those days'). In reality, however, the Shiloh shrine could have had the form of a tabernacle which had survived from the nomadic period down to the time of sedentary life in Canaan because of strict adherence to an outmoded yet venerable institution.[23] In this respect the priestly tradition appears to contain a nucleus of historical truth.[24]

10

At the same time, we must stress that what we have in P is no longer the temple legend of Shiloh in its original, direct form, but

[23] This is a well-known phenomenon of cultic practices. Cf., for instance, the use of flint knives for circumcising (Josh. 5: 2), and the avoidance of using iron tools for building an altar (Exod. 20: 25; Deut. 27: 5–6) or the temple (1 Kgs. 6: 7)—probably, vestiges of earlier ages which survived down to the Iron Age; also the use of manuscript scrolls by Jews for liturgical reading even after such scrolls became outmoded with the introduction of *codices* and the invention of print. For possibly another anachronistic point in the narrative of 1 Sam. 1–3 (and that, even later still) see above, p. 24, n. 20. Cf. also p. 27.

[24] This was perceived by the talmudic sages too, who remarked that the shrine at Shiloh was constructed 'of stones below and of curtains above'. See Bab. Tal. Zebaḥim, 112*b*, 118*a*; Jer. Tal. Megillah i, 14 (in the Gemara). Exactly the opposite view is held by most of the modern scholars. See, e.g., the comment of Eissfeldt, *KS* iii. 423: 'Wenn David nach 2 Sam. 7 den Plan erwogen hat, der Lade einen steinernen Tempel zu bauen, so hat auf diesen Plan doch gewiss die Tatsache eingewirkt, dass in Silo ein Tempel die Stätte der Lade gewesen war'. In fact, David's intention here expressly conflicted with the tabernacle tradition and it was only Solomon who brushed this tradition aside. The contradiction between the words of Nathan in 2 Sam. 7: 6–7 and the depiction of the Shiloh shrine in 1 Sam. 1–3 had already been noticed by nineteenth-century scholars. Wellhausen (*PGI*, 45–6, in the note) maintained that the words of Nathan presuppose states of war, when the ark was carried out to battlefield (though, in actual fact, the tabernacle at least has nothing to do with a battlefield). Of late this matter was touched upon by Jan Dus, 'Der Brauch der Ladewanderung im Alten Israel', *ThZ* 17 (1961), 1–3; G. W. Ahlström, 'Der Prophet Nathan und der Tempelbau', *VT* 11 (1961), 120 ff., 127 (both of whom made quite forced suggestions). On the other hand, W. Beyerlin, *Herkunft und Geschichte der ältesten Sinaitraditionen* (Tübingen, 1961), p. 137, maintains that Shiloh was primarily the site of a tent like that described in Exod. 33: 7–11 (the actual character of this will be discussed later on, in Chapter XIV) and that this was subsequently replaced by a solid building.

rather the Jerusalemite recasting of this legend. The legend here assumes a form which has its own features and colouring, a form which is wholly a production of Jerusalem. It is fashioned very much in the priestly manner, with technical minutiae and a rather wearisome style. Many details of Jerusalemite post-Solomonic circumstances have thereby been retrojected and superimposed on this legend. But for all that, none of these details can either abolish the sacral–legendary element of this material, or turn it into a totally Jerusalemite legend. We are faced with a pre-Jerusalemite temple legend now extant only in its Jerusalemite dress.

The Shiloh temple legend is transmitted in P not only in a Jerusalemite form, but also being divorced from its original subject. By the time the priestly writers cast it into its present literary shape, the temple at Shiloh no longer existed. Only under such conditions could they picture it as arrayed in extravagant splendour (which was certainly not true from the historical point of view), adorned with gold and other precious materials—all retrojections of the actual glory of Solomon's temple. It was only because it no longer existed that they could presuppose, too, that God was continually present in a cloud in the inner sanctum of this tabernacle (Lev. 16: 2; cf. Exod. 25: 22; Num. 7: 89).

There is further no doubt that just as P's authors believed in the authenticity of the temple legend which they transmitted, so the details of Jerusalemite circumstances were retrojected on the body of this legend unconsciously, without any deliberate intention on the part of these authors. They were certainly confident that the temple erected at Sinai and brought to Shiloh was of the most extravagant grandeur which they were capable of grasping and describing—and an illustration of the latter could be found in what actually existed in Solomon's temple. The case may be exemplified by those artists of the Renaissance who painted biblical figures and early Christian saints with countenances and attire typical of their own time. One cannot therefore be surprised that the authors of P paid no attention to historical accuracy—they were only striving to give the most solemn and fullest expression, in their own manner and to the best of their literary ability, to a sacrosanct tradition. After all, they were only writers, recorders of tradition which provided a framework for their Utopia; they were not critically-minded historians.

In brief, the authors of P report a temple legend severed from its actual referent, a legend which turned into a literary treatise when the temple itself was no longer in existence. The temple of Shiloh became at their hands an artistic monument, the centre of a recorded utopian system, within the atmosphere of the temple of Jerusalem.

XI

THE RITUAL COMPLEX PERFORMED INSIDE THE TEMPLE

1

TURNING now to the ritual acts performed by the priests in the Jerusalem temple let us first remark that they took place, as was usual for all temple-services in antiquity, both in the court and in the temple itself. In the court various sacrifices were offered and incense was burnt in censers (the latter will be described later on, in Chapter XII). The rites performed inside the temple, however, combined to form a unique cultic whole, distinct in itself. This chapter will be devoted to elucidating the character and symbolical significance of these rites. The most complete and most important description of this ritual is to be found in P, where it is set against the background of the tabernacle. The following discussion, therefore, will concentrate upon the evidence concerning this subject as contained in P. As the non-priestly sources were remote from the inner sphere of the temple they were not in a position to provide any significant evidence on this score.

THE CULTIC GRADATION AND THE RITUAL OF *TĀMÎD*

2

Just as the whole interior of the temple is held to be more sacred than the area of the court, so the ritual acts performed inside the temple are considered more important than those performed in the court. As we have seen, in the priestly apprehension this superiority even finds external, concrete expression in the materials from which the tabernacle and its contents are made. Furthermore, according to P's concepts, the whole area set aside for the ritual performed by the priests, including the court, is barred to the common people. Yet, the ritual acts associated with the court are done in the open, whereas no-one but a priest is allowed to set foot inside the tabernacle itself. Hence the inner part of the tabernacle (which, as has been pointed out, is just a correspondent representation of the temple), together with all the ritual acts performed in it, is hidden from public gaze. We shall see later that the altar rites are mainly performed by the ordinary priests (though, of course, the high priest may also take part in them), while those of the tabernacle are considered the sole prerogative of the high priest.

All the ritual acts, both those performed inside the tabernacle and those performed in the court, are sometimes referred to in P by the all-embracing formula: 'when they go into the tent of meeting, or when they come near the altar to minister . . .' (Exod. 28: 43; 30: 20; cf. 40: 32; in Lev. 10: 9 the phrase is undoubtedly truncated, with the second half, 'or when you come near the altar', omitted). This formula makes it clear that there are two areas of ritual activity—the tent of meeting (i.e. the tabernacle) and the altar. At the same time, let us anticipate what follows and stress that the plural forms of the verbs—'when they go', *beḇô'ām*, 'when they come', *begištām*—is no real proof that Aaron's sons, too, may enter the tabernacle and officiate there: a legal distinction of such a sort is too fine for the style of P. The subject of 'going into the tent of meeting' in these passages is not 'Aaron and his sons', but Aaron alone; and the meaning is simply: 'when Aaron goes into the tent of meeting (to minister) or when Aaron and his sons come near the altar to minister'.[1]

[1] A similar mode of expression is used elsewhere of the priest who is suffering from some physical defect: 'but he shall not go behind the veil (MT: אל הפרכת) or approach the altar' (Lev. 21: 23), where the meaning must be: if he is a high priest, he shall not go behind the *pārōḵet*-veil (and likewise not perform any other ritual act which is a typical prerogative of the high priest), and if he is an ordinary priest he shall not approach the altar. It is inconceivable that the assumption underlying this verse should be that an ordinary priest may pass through to the inner side of the *pārōḵet*-veil. Num. 18: 7 is to be understood in the same way: Aaron and his sons shall guard (i.e. be cautious not to violate the prohibitions of) their priesthood 'for all that concerns the altar' (cf. above, p. 183), and Aaron alone shall guard (his priesthood) for all that concerns 'behind the *pārōḵet*'. Some scholars have sought to prove from this verse that ordinary priests were originally permitted to enter the holy of holies. See, e.g., Marti's view, quoted by H. Holzinger, *Numeri* (KHC, 1903), pp. 72–3; R. H. Pfeiffer, *Introduction to the OT* (New York, 1948), p. 261; A. Bentzen, *Introduction to the OT*[2] (Copenhagen, 1952), ii, p. 39. However, the true meaning of the text does not support this view. On Lev. 21: 23, cf. Ibn-Ezra's commentary. Rashi

It is true that Aaron's sons are nowhere forbidden to go into the tabernacle, that is, into the outer sanctum, the space in front of the *pārōḵet*-veil. Yet, as will be seen, they are given no ritual function there.

3

A feature common to both these spheres, the court and the tabernacle, is the fact that a permanent ritual, denoted by the term *tāmîd* is performed in both of them. On the outer altar there is a daily burnt-offering of two lambs, *tāmîd* (Exod. 29: 38–42; Num. 28: 3–8), while the rites performed inside the tabernacle are all also denoted by *tāmîd*. However, here this term does not necessarily mean 'non-stopping, unceasing, continual', but rather that the ritual acts in question are to be repeated at regular intervals and at fixed times. The lamps, for example, do not burn 'continually', but only from nightfall until the morning. Similarly, the inner incense is not burnt all day long, but only at certain hours of the day. In such cases, the principal requirement is that the ritual acts should be regularly repeated.[2] This regular repetition occurs twice a day: in the morning and, according to the priestly terminology, 'at the twilight', בין הערבים. There is also a rite that recurs once a week, namely, the laying-out of the shewbread (but cf. below, sect. 9).

interprets אל הפרכת as meaning not 'behind the veil', but 'in front of the veil', the reference being to the seven sprinklings of blood on the *pārōḵet*-veil mentioned in Lev. 4: 6, 17. In this sense it seems to have been rendered by most EVV (KJV: 'unto the veil'; RSV, JB: 'near the veil'; NEB: 'up to the veil').

[2] This is the explanation given by several of the medieval commentators. See Ibn-Ezra on Exod. 27: 20; Rashi, ibid., and on Lev. 24: 2. So also the commentaries on Exodus by S. D. Luzzatto (Padua, 1872, p. 305), U. Cassuto (Jerusalem, 1967, p. 370), S. R. Driver (CBSC, 1918, p. 296). Some moderns have found a crux here. See, e.g., the commentaries on Exodus by G. Beer and K. Galling (HAT, 1939, pp. 138–9) and H. Holzinger (KHC, 1900, p. 134; Strack's opinion quoted there). But in the case of the fire of *tāmîd* which must burn on the altar all the time, the text adds: 'it shall not go out' (Lev. 6: 12–13). Similarly, the expressions *leḥem tāmîd* (2 Kgs. 25: 29; cf. 2 Sam. 9: 7–13) and *'ᵃrûḥat tāmîd* (2 Kgs. 25: 30; Jer. 52: 34), which are used of food served on the tables of kings (cf. also *mišteh tāmîd* of Prov. 15: 15), clearly do not denote an orgy of incessant eating, but refer to the daily meal that is taken regularly at a fixed hour. However, Josephus (*Antiquities*, iii. 8. 3) maintains that three of the lights on the lampstand had to burn throughout the day. Possibly this is a reflection of the Second Temple practice, derived from a secondary interpretation of the text. Cf. the remarks attributed by Josephus to Hecataeus of Abdera, *Contra Apionem* I. 22; also Mishnah Tamid iii. 9; Bab. Tal. Yoma, 33*a*.

RITES PERFORMED WITHIN THE TEMPLE

4

These are the ritual acts performed by the high priest inside the tabernacle, the movable temple of the Israelite camp:

(*a*) He offers up the incense of *sammîm* on the altar of gold (Exod. 30: 7–8). This rite is explicitly assigned to Aaron: 'And Aaron shall burn incense of *sammîm* on it . . . and when Aaron sets up the lamps . . . he shall burn it' (ibid.).[3] Since Aaron repeats this act twice a day, every morning and 'at the twilight', the incense burnt by him is also characterised here as 'regular incense', *qᵉṭōret tāmîd*. Further on it will be demonstrated that this incense differs, according to P's own conceptions, from that which is offered up in censers in the court. The difference is one of ingredients. The incense of the court is always mentioned without any additional epithet, whereas that of the tabernacle is punctiliously referred to as 'the incense of *sammîm*'. It is so called because, in addition to frankincense, it has three other ingredients, which are the *sammîm*, 'spices' (Exod. 30: 34–8)—something that is not usual in ordinary incense. Moreover, because of the special ritual character of this 'inner' incense, it is stated that the frankincense added to it must be 'pure' (ibid., v. 34)—a requirement which is not mentioned in the case of the frankincense added to the ordinary grain-offerings.

(*b*) Another act to be performed inside the tabernacle is the ritual tending of the lamps. Here again it is stated that the oil put into the lamps must be pure (Exod. 27: 20; Lev. 24: 2)—a stipulation not made concerning either the anointing oil or the oil added to grain-offerings, both of which are mainly used in the court. As the tending of the lamps is also done twice a day regularly, they too are called *nēr tāmîd*.[4] Indeed, the lamps do not burn throughout the twenty-four hours of the day, but only, as stated, 'from evening to morning'.[5]

[3] According to talmudic law, this incense might be offered by an ordinary priest (Mishnah Tamid iii; v. 2; Yoma ii. 4). Naḥmanides, in his commentary on Exod. 30: 7, was puzzled as to why the burning of the incense should have been described here as Aaron's prerogative, and tried to remove the difficulty.

[4] The noun *nēr* being used here in a collective sense, as is evident from Lev. 24: 2–4, where the singular *nēr tāmîd* and the plural *nērôt* refer to the same object.

[5] This is also implied by the non-priestly narrative in 1 Sam. 3: 3, where the passage relates that in the temple of Shiloh, during the night-time, 'the lamp of

This rite too is mentioned as Aaron's prerogative (Exod. 30: 7–8; Lev. 24: 1–4; Num. 8: 1–4; cf. Exod. 25: 37). It is associated with 'Aaron and his sons' only in Exod. 27: 21, where the word *ûḇānāyw*, 'and his sons' seems to have crept into the text. Indeed, in Lev. 24: 1–4 (a parallel passage to Exod. 27: 20–1) Aaron is mentioned alone.[6] Even without this, all the other verses referring to the lamps—and, as we shall see, also the character of the whole ritual performance inside the tabernacle—are enough to outweigh this single word (cf. below, sect. 15).[7]

(*c*) A third ritual act to be performed inside the tabernacle is the arrangement of the twelve loaves of bread, in two rows of six each,

God had not yet gone out'. Incidentally, here too the *nēr* might be used in the collective sense, i.e. an assemblage of lamps; cf. the preceding note.

[6] Many critics assume that the passage in Exod. 27: 20–1 is an editorial doublet from Lev. 24: 1–4. If we were to accept this assumption, it would serve to strengthen the argument against attributing any weight to the word *ûḇānāyw* in Exod. 27: 21. Nevertheless, I find it unacceptable, because there is a small detail which seems to have gone unnoticed: in Exod. 27: 20 the text reads, 'and you shall command the people of Israel', whereas in Lev. 24: 2 the reading is, 'command the people of Israel'. This means that in the first passage, which predates the setting-up of the tabernacle, Moses is not yet actually being ordered to take the lamp-oil, but is merely forewarned of his future duty (cf. Rashi's commentary). Only in the second passage (Lev. 24: 1–4) is it implied that the act is actually meant to be performed. It may be objected that lamp-oil had been included in the gift-offerings from which the tabernacle was constructed (Exod. 25: 6; 35: 28). But on closer examination it will be found that this single, unrepeated offering would not have provided enough lamp-oil for the prolonged use for which it was required (cf. Ibn-Ezra's remark on Exod. 27: 20). Continual, prolonged use is what the passage in Lev. 24: 1–4 refers to, and is what is announced in advance in Exod. 27: 20–1. It is therefore no editor that has duplicated the passage through mechanical copying, but rather a scribe who uses a stereotyped repetitious style. The practice of giving advance notice of what is going to happen is also found in, for example, the passage Exod. 29: 38–42, which begins with the words: 'Now this is what you shall offer upon the altar'—i.e. when it has been built and the priests have been anointed. And since the offering of the daily sacrifice on the outer altar is a conspicuous indication of an established cult, the priestly writer hurriedly introduces advance notice of it immediately after his description of the inauguration of the priests into their office. Thus this passage, too, despite its verbal similarity to Num. 28: 3–8, is not necessarily an editorial addition, but an integral part of the text. However, while conceding that the passage Exod. 27: 20–1 as a whole is in about the right place, I cannot accept the authenticity of the word *ûḇānāyw*, which, in my opinion, is an erroneous insertion.

[7] Again, according to talmudic law, the lamps might be lit by an ordinary priest (Mishnah Tamid iii; Bab. Tal. Yoma, 33*a*, and the parallel passages; Maimonides, הלכות תמידין ומוספין vi. 1–4). Naḥmanides, in his commentary on Exod. 30: 7, also expresses surprise that lighting the lamps is assigned to Aaron alone; and the same difficulty was also felt by Obadiah Sforno, in his commentary on Lev. 24: 3, where a halting attempt at explanation is made.

on the table of gold (Lev. 24: 5–9). This is done once a week, on the Sabbath, and, since it is a regularly repeated act, the loaves too are called 'regular bread', *leḥem tāmîd* (Num. 4: 7). Presumably, the text does not imply that the high priest enters the tabernacle on the Sabbath for the specific purpose of laying out the loaves, but that, when he is already there in the morning or 'at the twilight' to perform his duties with regard to the inner incense and the lamps, he stays to set out the loaves too. Again, the third person singular of the verb is used—*ya'arḵennû*, 'he shall set it in order' (Lev. 24: 8)—it being clear from analogy with parallel acts that Aaron is the subject.

In actual fact, this bread is treated as a grain-offering. As with most grain-offerings, frankincense is sprinkled on it and each week it is eaten by male priests in a holy place (Lev. 24: 9). But in two respects this grain-offering is unique. First, it is stipulated that its frankincense must be 'pure' (ibid., v. 7), like the frankincense of the inner incense, a stipulation which is absent from grain-offerings presented in the court; and secondly, no portion of this bread is burnt on the outer altar, even though it is stated (ibid., v. 9) that it is given to the priests as if it formed part of 'the offerings of the Lord [made] by fire', *'iššê Yahweh.*[8] In truth, the shewbread is unique among the grain-offerings in being an integral part, not of the sacrificial ritual of the court, but of the rites performed inside the tabernacle.

5

It has already been noted that eight priestly garments are listed in P. Four undergarments are worn by all the priests: the tunic, the girdle, the breeches, and the cap (in the case of the high priest, a turban). Four overgarments are worn by Aaron only: the robe, the ephod, the breastpiece, and the diadem. In quality, materials, and workmanship the first four are correlated with the hangings and curtains of the court, while the second four are correlated with the inner curtains of the tabernacle and the golden vessels within it. This correlation, so far from being purely fortuitous, is P's characteristic method of giving concrete expression to an identity of cultic function.

[8] For the ritual significance of the expression *'iššê Yahweh*, particularly in the priestly ideology, reference may be made, for the present, to my observations in *EM* iv. 40; v. 27.

For there is no doubt that, according to the conceptions of P, only the four undergarments are meant to be worn for officiating at the outer altar, while the four overgarments are added to the high priest's dress only for those rites that it is his duty to perform within. The implication, in other words, is that when Aaron takes part in offering sacrifices in the court, he wears the same linen vestments as the ordinary priests, and is distinguished from them only by his special girdle and turban. But when he enters the tabernacle to perform his ritual duties there, he puts on the garments of gold and linen-wool mixture which he alone may wear.

Furthermore, it is clear that the overgarments, with all their gold trappings, are too heavy and unwieldy for the high priest to be able to perform his duties at the bronze altar in them; and they are also too costly and magnificent to be worn for such tasks as splashing the blood, cutting up the carcasses of the victims, washing their entrails, and the like. Under the weight of such splendid apparel, the high priest is certainly incapable of anything more than a slow, stately walk and the performance of tasks that do not necessitate bending down, but can easily be done with the hands only. Indeed, P seems to assume that Aaron puts on these overgarments only twice a day, in the morning and evening, and that, while wearing them, he slowly walks the twenty cubits' length of the outer sanctum until he stands to attend to the incense, the lamps, and—once a week—also to the shewbread.

It may be argued that, as far as one can perhaps infer from Sir. 50: 11–15, in the post-exilic times the high priests used to adorn themselves with the overgarments even when officiating in the court. However, if this was the case, then this practice, like many others of the Second Temple period, was based only on a secondary interpretation of the canonized Law and can therefore have no bearing on the cultic conceptions embodied in P as taken by itself. A further possible argument is that it is nowhere stated that the priestly overgarments must be worn only for the rites performed inside the tabernacle. The truth, however, is that P starts from certain assumptions. Some of these, of the most fundamental importance, are nowhere 'declared' as such, but are obviously implicit in the technical descriptions contained in the text itself. Nowhere in P is it stated, as we have pointed out, that the inner curtains and the veils of the tabernacle, together with the ephod and the breastpiece, are all made of a wool-linen *kil'ayim*-mixture.

Yet, this fact is self-evident from the descriptions of these accessories given by the priestly writers. Moreover, this mixture is in itself an indication of the holiness of these accessories, as is shown by the prohibitions in Lev. 19: 19; Deut. 22: 9, 11.[9] It should likewise be understood that the correlation between the priestly overgarments and the inner ritual is clearly implied by the relevant descriptions in P, and is indeed one of the 'natural', if not avowed, axioms of the writers of this source.

In fact, it is only this correlation between the priestly overgarments and the inner ritual that can provide us with a *raison d'être* for these garments. Let us suppose for a moment that, according to P, Aaron takes part in sacrifices in the court wearing these garments of gold and mixed stuff, while, conversely, the ordinary priests are allowed to participate in the inner ritual without wearing these same garments. We should now not be able to explain the functional significance of the overgarments or how they came into existence at all. The division of the priestly vestments into two categories, one subordinate to the other, cannot be fortuitous, cannot be completely divorced from historical causation. It is usual in human affairs for every variation in dress to reflect a functional change, all the more so in the case of priestly vestments, whose functional character is quite conspicuous.

6

For an even clearer understanding of our argument, it should be noticed that the four priestly over-vestments of gold and mixed stuff are not merely garments in the usual sense of the word—even though, as has already been stated, they constitute a heavy, unwieldy weight of clothing which seriously hampers the wearer's movements. They are not a preliminary 'preparation' for the ritual, donned by the priest only so as to set about his cultic duties. In P they are also conceived as ritual appurtenances in their own right, on a par with the altar, the lampstand, and the table inside the tabernacle. In other words, the wearing of these garments inside the tabernacle becomes an act of ritual significance, in the course of which Aaron performs several genuine rites additional and complementary to the first three (above, sect. 4).

The sacral–ritualistic character of the acts performed by the

[9] Cf. above, pp. 160–1.

high priest while wearing the overgarments is further indicated by the use, in connection with each of them, of the expression 'before the Lord', *lip̱nê Yahweh* (see below). This expression is also applied, of course, to all the acts performed with the inner appurtenances of the tabernacle: the burning of the inner incense (Exod. 30: 8), the tending of the lamps (ibid. 27: 21 = Lev. 24: 3–4), and the setting-out of the 'regular bread' (ibid., v. 8). As it has already been remarked, this is the expression usually employed to denote any act of a sacral–ritualistic character within the confines of the temple, both in the style peculiar to P and in that of other biblical writings.[10]

It further goes without saying that those ritual acts performed by the high priest while wearing the overgarments are also done 'regularly', *tāmîd*, as stated in the text in almost every case; they are an integral part of the regular complex of rites, the *tāmîd*-rites, performed inside the tabernacle.

7

These are the acts performed by the high priest whilst wearing his special overgarments:

(*d*) It is of ritual significance that he carries the two onyx-stones (cornelians) on the shoulderpieces of the ephod and the twelve stones set in the breastpiece 'for a reminder before the Lord' (Exod. 28: 29; cf. ibid., v. 12). Since all these stones are engraved with the names of the tribes, they can be said to 'remind' Yahweh of the names of Israel when they are brought before him. Hence, the two stones on the ephod are actually called 'stones of reminder for the sons of Israel' (ibid. 39: 7), meaning that they remind *the Lord* of the sons of Israel. This act is said to be done 'regularly', *tāmîd* (ibid. 28: 29), where *tāmîd* is undoubtedly used in exactly the same sense as in connection with the inner incense and the lamps, i.e. every time that Aaron enters the outer sanctum to officiate there—which is twice a day, in the morning and 'at the twilight' (but not all day long)—he 'bears the names of the sons of Israel' before the Lord.

To the breastpiece Aaron occasionally attaches the Urim and Thummim, by means of which he inquires the Lord's will (Exod. 28: 30; Lev. 8: 8; Num. 27: 21). In such cases the ephod takes on a mantic significance, over and above its customary ritual use

[10] Cf. above, p. 26 (and n. 24).

which is our sole concern here. However, it is not impossible that even when Aaron inquires of the divine will by means of the Urim and Thummim, he is not supposed to enter the tabernacle at any hour of the day, but makes use of his regular morning and 'at the twilight' visits for this purpose; he merely adds the Urim and Thummim to his vestments to give him divinatory powers. Hence it is said that 'Aaron shall bear the judgment [i.e. the judgment of the Urim; cf. Num. 27: 21] of the people of Israel upon his heart before the Lord regularly', *tāmîd* (Exod. 28: 30), that is to say, at the regular times appointed for any rite of *tāmîd*. It would follow from our assumption that, according to P, the desire to know the divine will must wait for satisfaction until the proper times of the priest's entry into the temple.

(*e*) Another characteristically ritual act is the jingling of the bells on the skirts of the ephod's robe (ibid. 28: 35). The special technical term *tāmîd*, which denotes the regular repetition of a ritual act, happens to be omitted here. But we are told that 'it [the ephod's robe] shall be upon Aaron for ministering' (ibid.; cf. 39: 26), meaning when he ministers inside the tabernacle; as the verse continues more specifically: 'when he goes into the holy-place [i.e. the outer sanctum] before the Lord, and when he comes out'. However, Aaron is actually supposed to do this at the times appointed for the other inner rites too. It is at these times, when Aaron is walking in heavy and stately splendour the twenty cubits' distance up to the *pārōḵet*-veil or retracing his steps from it, that 'his sound [i.e. of the bells] shall be heard'.

(*f*) An act of ritual significance is also performed with the aid of the diadem. This object, too, is carried by Aaron on his forehead 'regularly', *tāmîd* (Exod. 28: 38), that is, not 'always' as EVV render it, but only at the times appointed for this rite, namely, in the morning and 'at the twilight'. The actual significance of this rite seems to be somewhat obscure, despite the efforts made by many commentators, both ancient and modern, to explain it.

The essence of the ritual function of the diadem is described in a single verse whose construction is to be understood as follows: 'It shall be upon Aaron's forehead, and Aaron shall take upon himself any guilt incurred in the holy offerings which the people of Israel hallow as their holy gifts; it shall regularly be upon his forehead before the Lord, that they [i.e. the gifts] may be acceptable for them' (ibid.). Thus the intention of the act performed with the diadem is, in short, to arouse divine remembrance, in much the same way as do the stones of the ephod and the breastpiece. Indeed, there are letters stamped on the diadem too, just as on the stones, with the difference that the stones are engraved with the names of the Israelite tribes and the diadem only with the two words 'Holy to the Lord', *qōdeš l^eYahweh* (Exod. 28: 36; 39: 30).[11] This is most probably a standard formula to indicate the sanctity of the offerings (see Lev. 19: 8; 27: 14, 21, and *passim*; also Josh. 6: 19; Isa. 23: 18; Jer. 2: 3 *et al.*). The stereotyped character of this formula is perhaps most evident in passages such as Ezek. 48: 14; Zech. 14: 20.[12] Be this as it may, their presence on the diadem is evidently due to the fact that the diadem serves as a symbol of all the holy gift-offerings. This also explains the difference between it and the ephod and breastpiece: the stones remind Yahweh of the tribes of Israel, whereas the diadem symbolizes in his presence 'all their holy gifts'.

To be more precise, the function of the diadem is not so much to awaken divine remembrance as to evoke divine *grace*, the idea being expressed in MT by the words *l^erāṣôn lāhem*. It is the diadem on Aaron's forehead which serves as the concrete symbol, morning and evening, of the holy gifts of Israel, that makes all their gifts 'acceptable for them' (*l^erāṣôn lāhem*), that is to say, acceptable for them to Yahweh, calling up Yahweh's *rāṣôn*. The three ritual functions performed by the high priest's overgarments are thus distinguished by the three different expressions used to describe them, to which the common characteristic formula, 'before the Lord', *lip̱nê Yahweh*, is attached in each case: the stones are 'for a reminder before the Lord' (Exod. 28: 29), the sound of the bells 'shall be heard . . . before the Lord' (ibid., v. 35), while the diadem is 'to make [them] acceptable before the Lord' (ibid., v. 38).

[11] Cf. above, p. 169.

[12] The meaning of this verse is as translated by EVV: 'On that day there shall be inscribed on the bells of the horses "Holy to the Lord" ' (RSV). This is the explanation given by Qimḥi and also by some moderns (W. Nowack, F. Horst). The whole significance of the dedication of the bells to the Lord lies in the fact that they were cast in metal, usually a precious metal. The dedication thus applied only to the ornaments worn by the horses, not to the horses themselves (as wrongly assumed by, e.g., H. G. Mitchell, *Zechariah* (ICC, 1937), p. 356). Nowhere in the Old Testament do we find horses being dedicated to the God of Israel.

THE UNITY OF THE COMPLEX OF INNER RITES

8

Taken together, the six regular rites performed inside the tabernacle (above, sects. 4, 7) are at once seen to embrace almost all the human senses, and to cater, as it were, for almost all man's possible needs. The incense provides for the sense of smell, the lamps for the sense of sight, while the loaves of bread are a symbol of the need for food. The bells attract the sense of hearing, the stones on the ephod and the breastpiece awaken the 'sense' of memory, and the diadem on the high priest's forehead evokes the 'sense' of grace (for even these last two qualities could be conceived, by the ancients, as manifestations of spiritual or 'sensorial' activity).

There are signs that, originally, there was also a drink-offering on the table to correspond to the human need for drink. This is clear from the fact that some at least of the table utensils are actually regarded as libatory vessels. Thus, the function of the jugs, *qᵉśāwôt* and the jars, *mᵉnaqqiyyôt*, both of which belong specifically to the table, is defined by the words 'with which to pour libations' (Exod. 25: 29; 37: 16); and the *qᵉśāwôt* are elsewhere specifically called 'the *qᵉśāwôt* (in a construct state, *qᵉśôt*) for drink-offering' (Num. 4: 7). It is something of a puzzle how a drink-offering could be included in the rites performed inside the temple, since the offering of libations on the incense-altar is forbidden by P (Exod. 30: 9), while the outer altar must have had its own libatory vessels.[13] The most probable explanation is that these inner liba-

[13] These were, apparently, the basins, *mizrāqôt* (Exod. 27: 3; 38: 3; Num. 4: 14) which to judge from indications in the Bible, were designed to hold flour (Num. 7: 13 ff.) and wine (Amos 6: 6; Zech. 9: 15) as well. They may also have been used to throw the blood, since the blood of the sacrifices is described as 'being thrown' against the altar, the verb *zrq* being used in the text (Exod. 24: 6, 8; 29: 16, 20 *et al.*), but some of them at least were apparently used for wine-libations. Hence it is hard to accept the opinion of several scholars (such as S. R. Driver and U. Cassuto in their commentaries on Exod. 25: 29) who argue that the jars, *mᵉnaqqiyyôt* of the inner table were used for wine-libations on the outer altar. Such a possibility never occurred to the medieval commentators. For their part, they derived the verb in the expression אשר יסך בהן in Exod. 25: 29; 37: 16 (RSV: 'with which to pour libations'; similarly other EVV) from the root *skk* = 'to cover' and understood it to mean that these vessels were used to cover the bread. However, this explanation is equally untenable. Apparently, the word *qśt* (= *qš*[?], *qś*[?]), has been found in the Ugaritic texts, in the sense of a vessel containing drink (*UT* 51. iv. 45; ʿnt, v. 41), where it appears in parallelism with *ks* = Heb. *kôs*, 'cup'. See H. L. Ginsberg, כתבי אוגרית (Jerusalem,

tory vessels were placed on the table merely to serve as a *reminder* of drink-offering. While they were presumably assigned to contain a choice libation, i.e. an offering of wine,[14] this wine was not actually poured out on any altar. It was apparently consumed by male priests in a holy place, just as were the loaves of shewbread. It may also have originally been the custom to change this wine every Sabbath, together with the loaves of shewbread, though there is no longer any reference to this in our texts.

9

The association between these ritual functions cannot have been merely accidental; rather, they must have been conceived of as interrelated and complementary parts of a single cultic phenomenon. They cannot be explained as a random hotch-potch of acts which came together for no clear reason, but must be understood as a deliberately designed and essentially homogeneous ritual complex deriving its unity from the fact that all its component rites are performed simultaneously by one and the same priest, at the same times fixed by the regularity of *tāmîd*. This unity is also evident in the typological (and, as will be seen immediately, also the symbolical) unity underlying all these acts: in each of them separately there is some stimulation of 'senses' and satisfaction of needs, and all of them together provide satisfaction for virtually all human needs.

We are therefore forced to the conclusion, fundamental to P, that there is no possibility of breaking this ritual complex up into its component parts: no single constituent act can be performed in isolation, without involving all the rest. It is, for instance, out of the question that Aaron should burn the inner incense every morning or evening without at the same time performing all the ritual acts associated with the other vessels in the tabernacle and with his wearing the high priest's special garments.

In the case of the bells, indeed, there is an explicit warning

1936), glossary, s.v. קשת; U. Cassuto, 'Il palazzo di Baal nella tavola IIAB di Ras Shamra', *Orientalia* 7 (1938), 283; idem, *The Goddess Anath* (Jerusalem, 1971), pp. 102–3.

[14] Otherwise they could only contain a libation of water, which is mentioned twice in the Old Testament (1 Sam. 7: 6; 2 Sam. 23: 16). However, this kind of libation seems too ordinary to be offered inside the temple.

against any such dissociation of functions, in the solemn injunction that their sound must be heard when Aaron enters the tabernacle and when he leaves it, 'lest he die' (Exod. 28: 35). This warning can be taken as an express insistence upon the use of the high priest's garments (together with the ritual functions involved in them) at the appointed times of *tāmîd*. At the same time, the fact that the death-penalty is only mentioned in connection with the bells should not be taken to indicate that the bells are different in this respect from all the other elements in the inner ritual complex, but rather that in keeping with P's style (which for all its tendency to formalism, is not really juristic), the reference to the death-penalty is simply brought in to round off the particular verse. This example may be considered symptomatic of P's basic belief (that the omission of any one of the details of the inner ritual complex would have fatal consequences); it should not be made the starting-point for an attempt to single out the bells as being of special significance in this respect.

One may further assume, that, just as the complex of rites performed inside the tabernacle has to be complete and all-inclusive on every occasion, so it is inconceivable that it should ever be interrupted. According to the conceptions of P, it cannot be allowed to stop even for a single day (any more than the daily sacrifice on the outer altar can), even though the community's wanderings through the desert meant that the portable temple was constantly being moved. In this respect, the term *tāmîd* has something of its second sense as well (cf. above, sect. 3), to wit, that the regular ritual acts have always, 'continually' to be performed and can never be abandoned.

10

The symbolical significance underlying this complex of inner ritual acts is simple and clear: the daily satisfaction of the 'needs' of the deity. It is these rites, performed regularly and continually, that give the tabernacle–temple its character of a dwelling-place of the deity. The ritual vessels that stand inside the temple—the table, lampstand, and incense-burner—are the furnishings of this 'residence'. With the aid of these furnishings the special priest, who, as already mentioned, is denominated 'the Lord's servant', *m^e^šārēt Yahweh* ministers to all the requirements of the master of the residence.

At best, this complex of rites can fall into two parts: those that are performed with the inner vessels of the tabernacle and those that are performed by the priest–servant's wearing his special garments. The former are meant to provide for the 'physical' needs of the deity, while the latter are merely to stimulate certain of his 'senses' and thereby to attract his gracious attention to the tribes of Israel. We may say that, if the acts performed with the three inner appurtenances are a kind of 'necessity' for the daily existence of the deity, the three associated with Aaron's special vestments are a necessity for the survival and well-being of the community in whose midst the deity dwells. At the same time, it is clear that, in terms of P's ideology, all these acts form a single cultic phenomenon.

It would, of course, be possible to add to the inner complex of rites the regular, continual (sometimes also additional) sacrifices made on the outer altar: this daily portion of the flesh of cattle and sheep, the 'God's food', *leḥem 'elōhîm* (Num. 28: 2; cf. Lev. 3: 11; 21: 21–2), would fittingly complement the bread and drink offered inside. Nevertheless, the animal sacrifices seem to constitute a set of ritual acts essentially different from that performed inside the tabernacle. And this is not merely because the two sets are performed in different spheres, and are consequently of different degrees of importance and sanctity (cf. above, sect. 2). In fact, the outer altar has its 'own' varied grain-offerings and wine-libations that are presented on it, corresponding to the bread (and drink) offered inside. Moreover, it has already been mentioned that, down to the time of Hezekiah or Josiah, animal sacrifices and grain-offerings could be made on altars scattered up and down the country which were not part of the enclosure of any temple, and at which ordinary Israelites could officiate without the mediation of priests.[15] This implies that these two sets of ritual were not essentially derived from a common origin. The 'outside' was attached, so to speak, to the house of God, and the regular and continual repetition common to both these ritual complexes simply marked them with the same stamp. It may be conceded, as has been stated, that in Old Testament times there was hardly a temple without an

[15] Cf. above, pp. 15–16, 64–5, 132–5 (P himself does not, of course, admit the legitimacy of altars of this kind).

outside altar adjoining it (possibly in its court),[16] but not all outside altars necessarily adjoined temples.

II

At this point we are in a position to comprehend the function of the ark-cover, *kappōret* (with the cherubim attached to it) and the ark in the inner sanctum.

In a later chapter we shall sum up the evidence which proves that these two objects, when placed in position amongst the other temple appurtenances, serve as symbolical representations of throne and footstool. Thus, if the ritual complex within the outer sanctum symbolizes the satisfaction of the deity's 'needs', the inner sanctum is the place where the actual presence of the deity is symbolized. This is clearly indicated by the cloud which, in P's fancy, is perpetually suspended between the wings of the cherubim (Lev. 16: 2); by the explicit statement that Yahweh 'meets' Moses and addresses him from between the wings of the cherubim (Exod. 25: 22; Num. 7: 89); and by all the images in the Old Testament (and the ancient Near East) connected with the holy of holies. That is why this room is curtained off from the rest of the tabernacle by the *pārōḵet*-veil, and—when the movable temple takes the form of a permanent building—by a fixed dividing wall.

Consequently, the interior of the temple is also divided into two rooms, the inner one of which is, as we know, possessed of greater holiness: if none but a priest is allowed to set foot in the outer sanctum, not even the high priest can pass behind the *pārōḵet*-veil (except once a year, on the Day of Atonement).[17] At the same time, these two spheres are interdependent, neither of them having any significance without the other. The rites performed in the outer sanctum are directed towards the divine cloud in the inner sanctum and derive all their content from this latter space which

[16] Any large and aesthetically proportioned house could have, and probably had, a court attached to it. Apart from the many passages in the Old Testament where this fact is explicitly stated, it is also evident from the parallelism of 'house', *bayit* with 'court', *ḥāṣēr*, which is common both in biblical and Ugaritic poetry. Incidentally, in the Old Testament this parallelism occurs only in those passages dealing with the temple at Jerusalem (Zech. 3: 7; Ps. 65: 5; 84: 11; 92: 14 *et al.*); similarly, in the Ugaritic texts it occurs only in references to 'the house' of Baal or of some other god (*UT*, 51. iv. 50–1; iv–v. 62–3, 90–1; 129, 19–20; 'nt, v. 46–7; Krt, 132–3, 203–5 *et al.*). Where it occurs in the incantation text from Arslan Tash, however, there is no connection with a temple (Donner–Röllig, *KAI*, Text 27, 5–8).

[17] Cf. above, p. 178.

though of superior holiness, is entirely 'passive' as regards the performance of ritual acts. There the deity sits on his throne, hidden from mortal gaze, while here in the outer sanctum he is attended to every morning and 'at the twilight'. Hence, despite the partition erected between them, these two rooms are indivisible parts of a single structure. This is in contrast to the outer altar which, as already mentioned, could stand on its own, unconnected with temple and court.

THE PRE-BIBLICAL ORIGINS

12

Since the foregoing is a greatly simplified description of the symbolic significance of the inner ritual complex, it must now be stressed that all these acts were certainly not understood by the priestly writers literally.

There is no doubt that the priestly writers, like all the authors of biblical literature, did not envisage their God in such a form as to be in daily need of food, incense, and light. Even the pagan religions of the ancient Near East had long since ceased to conceive of the deity in such crudely anthropomorphic terms. As found in the ancient religion of Israel, this ritual complex was undoubtedly a heritage from a pre-biblical conception of the world. It has been already pointed out that, in all the religions of the ancient Near East, the temple was held to be essentially the dwelling-place of the divinity, in just the same way as any king, and indeed any man, had his own abode. This explains, as we said, the figurative expressions used of the temple in the Old Testament—'the house of Yahweh', 'the house of God', 'the tent of Yahweh', and the like,[18] while in P it is called 'the tabernacle of Yahweh' (Lev. 17: 4; Num. 16: 9; 17: 28 *et al.*), that is, the tabernacle in which, figuratively speaking, the deity dwells.

It is equally certain that every religion of the ancient Near East had a complex of daily rites which were performed inside the temple in order to provide for the deity's needs and to sustain, as it were, his very being. There were, of course, local variations in the form actually taken by this inner ritual. In Egypt, in a series

[18] See above, pp. 13–14, 17–18, 196.

of ritual acts, the image of the god was first cleansed, beautified, and robed, and then food and drink were offered to it.[19] The appointments of a Babylonian temple were many and various, and the ritual performed in it was also distinguished by the lavishness and variety of food and drink offerings.[20] The Hittites apparently had their own special form of daily inner rite,[21] while still another type seems to have been customary in Canaan.[22]

[19] This series of rites is depicted on reliefs in the temple of Seti I at Abydos, and described in the Berlin Papyrus No. 3055, written in the time of the Twenty-Second Dynasty for the temple of Amon-Re at Thebes. Scholars have supplemented these two mutually complementary pieces of evidence with further material from other sources; there is also the analogy with the rites for the dead. A short excerpt from the Berlin Papyrus is given by John A. Wilson, *ANET*, pp. 325–6. The whole subject is treated in detail by A. Moret, *Le rituel du culte divin journalier en Égypte d'après les papyrus de Berlin et les textes du temple de Séti I à Abydos* (Paris, 1902); and also by A. M. Blackman, *Journal of the Manchester Egyptian and Oriental Society*, 1918–19, pp. 51 ff.; idem, s.v. 'Worship (Egyptian)', *ERE* xii. 777–9; A. Erman and H. Ranke, *Aegypten* (Tübingen, 1923), pp. 312–16. A brief description of the essential points is to be found in J. Černy's little volume *Ancient Egyptian Religion* (London, 1952), pp. 101–3; and in S. Sauneron's *The Priests of Ancient Egypt* (New York–London, 1960), pp. 83–90. A series of similar ceremonial rites was performed daily in Egypt on the reigning monarch himself, and also on the body of a dead king (which was sometimes represented by a statue). On the daily rites in honour of the dead King Amenhotep I, see *Hieratic Papyri in the British Museum, Third Series: Chester Beatty Gift*, ed. Alan H. Gardiner (London, 1935), pp. 78 ff., 101 ff. The threefold parallelism of the ceremonial rites performed alike for the gods, the living, and the dead was derived from the basic Egyptian belief which held that these were three parallel manifestations of a single being, a being which in each of its incarnations had the same physical needs, the same habits, and the same appetites.

[20] Some idea of the Babylonian form of the continual ritual may be obtained from a tablet from Uruk, which records the quantities of food to be set before Anu and other gods that had temples in that city at the four meals served them daily. The tablet is all that has survived of a much fuller Akkadian text (which apparently contained many ritual details about the cults of Anu and other gods). It was written in the Seleucid era, but its contents are derived from earlier sources. The text was recently translated by A. Sachs, *ANET*, pp. 343 ff.; and there is a general discussion of it by C. J. Gadd, *Myth and Ritual*, ed. S. H. Hooke (London, 1933), pp. 41–4. Mentioned on the recto of the tablet are drinks (beer of various kinds, wine, and milk), loaves of bread (which were changed for every meal), and fruit (two kinds of dates, figs, and also apparently raisins), all of which seem to have been presented inside the temples. On the verso of the tablet there is a list of sacrifices of animals and birds, pigs, and also some birds' eggs—all of which, apparently, were offered in the precincts.

[21] On this see A. Goetze, *Kleinasien*² (München, 1957), pp. 162–3. The daily 'meal' served inside consisted of loaves of bread and libations (of wine and beer) but the quantities apparently varied from temple to temple: in a central shrine lavish portions were no doubt offered, while in provincial sanctuaries a symbolical helping was considered sufficient—a single pinch of flour and a single cup

[*Footnotes 21 and 22 continued on following page*]

Now, when comparing P's inner ritual with any one of these other rituals, we must first of all judge it, as has been already stated, as a single phenomenon. Thus, the distinguishing feature of the ritual in P is not, for example, that the jingling of bells fulfils a ritually significant function: a similar act was common in many cults all over the world.[23] What is peculiar to P is the com-

of beer (loc. cit.). It is, incidentally, interesting to note that, just as ordained by P (cf. above, sect. 4(*c*)), when these loaves had performed their ritual function they were eaten by male priests in a 'holy place', in this case inside the temple. The priests' wives, children, and servants were forbidden even to cross the threshold. Moreover, here we are explicitly told that just as the male priests ate the loaves, so they also drank the drink offerings (see A. Goetze, *ANET*, p. 208, sect. 6). In his daily prayer, in addition to the loaves and the drink-offerings, the king mentions cedar essence (ibid., p. 396, ll. 11–14).

[22] The form of this can only be inferred from the Ugaritic texts. A full list of the appurtenances of El's house is given in tablet 51. i. 31–44, which no doubt reflects the component parts of a typical earthly temple. Of the appurtenances mentioned there, those the significance of which is not in doubt are three in number: a special seat, *kḥt*, a footstool, *hdm*, and a table, *ṯlḥn*. In addition, there are three others the significance of which is disputed: *kt*, *nʿl*, *ṣʿ*. The various interpretations given of this passage up to 1943 are listed by W. F. Albright, 'The furniture of El in Canaanite Mythology', *BASOR* 91 (1943), 39–44. For later discussion see T. H. Gaster and W. F. Albright, ibid. 93 (1944), 20–5; H. L. Ginsberg, *ANET*, pp. 131–2; G. R. Driver, *Canaanite Myths and Legends* (Edinburgh, 1956), pp. 92–3. It may have been customary for the Canaanites to have two or even more tables in some of their temples. This is suggested by the occurrence of the form *ṯlḥnm* as well (ʿnt, ii. 30) which is dual, and also of *ṯlḥnt* (51. iv. 36) which is the plural. It was usual to place on the table bread and libatory vessels, the latter of two kinds: *ks* = Heb. *kôs* (often in the combination *ks ḫrṣ* = a goblet of gold) and *krpn*. These two vessels frequently appear in parallelism in poetical language, closely associated with the parallelism *yn—dm ʿṣm* = wine—blood of vines (51. iii. 43–4; vi. 58–9; 67. iv. 15–18; cf. ʿnt, i. 10–16 *et al.*). From this we can deduce that the usual drink-offering was of wine. The words *ks* and *krpn* appear in parallelism with *ṯlḥn* (51. iii. 14–16; iv. 35–8; cf. Ps. 23: 5); and we also find the parallelism *lḥm lḥm—šty yn* = eat bread—drink wine (52. 6, 71–2; 62. 42–4; 67. i. 24–5; cf. Prov. 4: 17; 9: 5; also Gen. 14: 18). These linguistic combinations are all derived from the routine arrangements in a temple (and to some extent, in a royal palace too).

[23] But, apparently, is not yet known in the cults of the ancient Near East. Innumerable examples of the ritual use of bells are given by J. G. Frazer, *Folklore in the OT*, iii (London, 1919), pp. 446–80. In explaining the significance of the bells' sound, Frazer agrees with Wellhausen and other biblical scholars in regarding it as an exorcistic–apotropaic act, i.e. as designed to drive away evil spirits from inside the sanctuary (ibid., p. 447). In actual fact, however, the idea of demonic powers taking a hold inside the tabernacle is entirely foreign to P's ideology, and the bells' sound there is intended 'to minister' to the deity, not to drive away evil. Moreover, this sound must be understood as part of a much larger ritual complex which has not been noticed by scholars. Frazer concludes his remarks on the subject (ibid., p. 480) with an alternative explanation, viz., that the sound was not meant to drive away the demonic powers, but 'to attract

bination of this act with several others to form a single organic whole. The same is true of all the other rites performed inside the tabernacle. What makes them unique is not their performance as such, but their fusion into a single whole with a symbolical and ideological unity. It is thus hardly surprising that archaeology is as yet unable to bring to light precise and direct pre-Israelite analogies for the particular synthesis of inner rites as portrayed in P. It seems likely, though, that this cultic institution actually found its way into Israel by means of a Canaanite heritage, developing in the course of time its distinctive colouring and embellishments.

13

However, even if we confine our observation of this institution solely to the description given by the priestly writers and do not refer to non-Israelite analogies, we shall still be forced to admit that the signs of its pagan, pre-Israelite origin are clearly recognizable, while, at the same time, in P it has become a mere fossilized shell, a routine rite the original inner content of which had long ceased to have any meaning for those who perform it. This institution is only one of the many to have been absorbed into the Yahwistic religion. For this religion, like all religions throughout history, did not create all its practices out of nothing, but adapted to its purposes many existing forms and conventions which it imbued with a new spiritual meaning. Exactly the same may be said of the outer sacrificial rites, which also go back to pre-biblical culture (as do such observances as circumcision, the Sabbath, the New Moon, and the Passover), so that the inner ritual should not be considered any more 'pagan' in character than that performed outside.

It cannot be supposed that the priestly writers took over such an institution from the popular religion of the pre-exilic times and then adapted it to their own 'needs'. A ritual pattern of this kind cannot originate with the common people, but of necessity is an 'esoteric' prerogative of the priestly family, and is, in fact, performed only by one of the priests. As has been said, this ritual takes place in the *arcana* of the house of God, unseen by the people as a whole. The people may know of its existence, but in practice

the attention' of the godhead—an explanation which, as Frazer himself admits, fits many of the examples given by him, and is the only one that is correct in the case with which we are concerned. For the widespread religious use of bells, cf. also Addison J. Wheeler, s.v. 'Gongs and Bells', *ERE* vi. 313–16.

it is no concern of theirs. Indeed, it can easily be demonstrated that the inner ritual is, so to speak, beyond the ken of the non-priestly sources. Not that it is completely unknown to them; on the contrary, some details have indeed managed to slip out of the mysteries of the temple and catch the attention of the non-priestly writers (see 1 Sam. 2: 28; 3: 3; 21: 1–7), but their acquaintance with this cultic institution is nevertheless 'external' in character. And it would be only reasonable to admit that the ritual complex as performed within the priestly tabernacle is merely a representation of the actual ritual which was habitually practised within the Solomonic temple. It should be also pointed out that in a post-exilic, or post-Ezekielian (or even just post-Deuteronomic) work, as P is usually taken to be, one would not normally expect to find evidence or recollection of an indoor cultic institution of this sort, certainly not in the concrete form we find described in the priestly scrolls. All the more so when there is, indeed, no evidence at all in Ezekiel for the existence of the ark, the inner appurtenances of the temple, or even the high priesthood itself.

FURTHER COROLLARIES

14

There are incidental references in the works of several scholars to the fact that P's tabernacle symbolizes the habitation of the deity, but in most cases their arguments seem to be based on isolated features of this structure.[24] Particular prominence is given for this purpose to the ark, in so far as it is understood to be the symbolical representation of a throne. Or again, much is made of such allusions as the use of the expression 'before the Lord' in ritual matters, or the verses indicating that the Lord dwells permanently in the midst of Israel (Exod. 25: 8; 29: 45; Num. 5: 3; 16: 3).

In fact, as will be shown in Chapter XIII, the symbol of the

[24] See, e.g., I. Benzinger, s.v. 'Tabernacle', *EB* iv. 4870; M. Dibelius, *Die Lade Jahves* (Göttingen, 1906), p. 71; Driver, *Exodus*, pp. 260, 267; particularly G. von Rad, *Die Priesterschrift im Hexateuch* (Berlin, 1934), pp. 182 ff.; idem, *Gesammelte Studien zum AT* (München, 1958), pp. 109–12. Also E. L. Ehrlich, *Kultsymbolik im AT und im nachbiblischen Judentum* (Stuttgart, 1959), p. 23; and most recently, e.g., W. Brueggemann, s.v. 'Presence of God', *IDB*, Supp. Volume, 681.

deity's perpetual presence is not exactly the ark, but rather the cherubim above it. However, what really gives P's tabernacle the character of a divine 'dwelling' is neither the cherubim nor the ark as such, but the combination of this throne and footstool with a table, a lampstand, and an incense-burner; and furthermore the fact that, when the high priest paces solemnly towards the deity, he is accompanied by a jingle of bells and is carrying 'seal-engravings' stamped on stones and diadem to evoke divine remembrance and grace. All these separate symbols are simply different facets of a larger, all-inclusive symbolism, and, taken all together, it is they that endow the tabernacle with the character of a habitation. The planks and the curtains then form the necessary depository for the articles of furniture contained in the two chambers. P's conception of the temple as the dwelling-place of the deity is thus not hidden behind a veil of allusions—it is plainly visible as the foundation on which the whole structure is based. And yet, for all that, there is, in fact, no such conception in P. For, as has already been remarked, all the daily rites performed by Aaron are no longer possessed of their original significance for the priestly writers. To them they are simply a traditional form of cult, a conventional cloak, not the direct expression of a mythic idea.

15

The fact that all the rites performed inside the tabernacle are interdependent parts of a single organic whole deserves to be emphasized again. Apart from anything else, it further strengthens the contention that this whole sphere of ritual activity is the sole prerogative of the high priest.

We have already noted the following points:

(*a*) The existence of Aaron's special garments can only be explained by their ritual–functional distinctiveness. Since the ordinary priests officiate in the court wearing the four usual vestments of linen, Aaron's additional garments must symbolize, first and foremost, some change in his functional status (above, sect. 5).

(*b*) This change could be expressed only in the acts performed by Aaron inside the tabernacle; for in workmanship and material, the four overgarments correspond to the inner curtains and fittings. Moreover, the weight and magnificence of the four overgarments, which make them unsuitable for the ritual functions performed at the outer altar, are in keeping with the nature of the inner service (above, sect. 5).

(*c*) Furthermore, we have seen (above, sect. 9) that Aaron is forbidden to forgo wearing the bells, and consequently any one of his overgarments, when ministering inside the tabernacle; thus, the ordinary priests are in practice not able to minister there.

(*d*) It has been further shown (above, sect. 4) that, even in passages referring to the rites performed beside the three inner appurtenances, only Aaron is mentioned by name—apart from one verse to which we shall return immediately.

However, this whole argument need not necessarily be based on the assumption that the overgarments (as it has been maintained) have an independent status as ritual 'accessories'. Even if we regard them simply as garments, we shall still be forced to the conclusion that the performance of the inner ritual is held to be the sole prerogative of the priest who wears them, viz., the high priest. Now that we have established the ritual significance of these garments (above, sects. 6–7) and their integral connection with the inner appurtenances as parts of one and the same symbolism (above, sects. 8–10), this conclusion becomes all the more cogent. It is true that talmudic law permitted an ordinary priest to officiate inside the temple[25] and that this is the opinion held by all the Jewish medieval commentators and likewise by all moderns. But the only warrant for the traditional Jewish and modern scholarly viewpoint on this question is a single Hebrew word, *ûḇānāyw*, in a single verse (Exod. 27: 21). Moreover, this one word is itself of doubtful authenticity (as it has been pointed out, it is missing in the parallel verse, Lev. 24: 3) and cannot therefore be regarded as decisive. Even judging solely by the wording of the relevant passages, one would still be entitled to assume that the inner rites had to be performed by Aaron and by Aaron alone; all the more so when Aaron's exclusive prerogative in these rites provides the only satisfactory explanation on general grounds.

16

The fact that all the inner rites combine to form a single phenomenon can also be used as an argument against the excision of Exod. 30: 1–10 from the main narrative of P.

[25] Cf. above, pp. 208–9, nn. 3, 7. Concerning the shewbread see Mishnah Menaḥoth xi. 7.

This passage (which is repeated with slight variations in Exod. 37: 25–9) is the only place in the two parallel descriptions of the tabernacle where the incense-altar is mentioned. Many scholars believe it belongs to a secondary layer of P, or that it is an isolated insertion.[26] This proposed excision is, in part, the result of a failure to distinguish between the two different kinds of incense. In the following chapter it will be demonstrated that according to the conceptions of the priestly writers themselves, the incense burnt on the inner altar was of a special kind, quite distinct from the ordinary incense offered up in censers in the court. Here I would only state that, by this operation, scholars (all unknowingly, of course) strip the inner ritual complex of one of its principal components. The existence of the incense, as a luxury article used daily, which in antiquity it was customary to 'savour' (and which was always found in the homes of the rich) is clearly implied here by the tabernacle's significance as a 'dwelling-place'. So much so that even if the priestly writers had made no mention of the incense, one would still be entitled to conjecture that it had been accidentally omitted from the complex of inner rites. All the more reason for not doubting the authenticity of the passage in which it is actually mentioned and explicitly included in this complex.

The contention that the passage in question (Exod. 30: 1–10) is not in its proper place, while of course correct in itself is extremely weak as a starting point for a literary analysis. No doubt the literary form in which P has come down to us does not satisfy the requirements of classical taste; its various sections are marred by frequent repetition, by a discursive style, and by an excess of detail in one place and complete silence (even on apparently important matters) in another.[27] But such phenomena, though to us

[26] The first to suggest this seems to have been Wellhausen, *PGI*, 64–6; idem, *Die Composition des Hexateuchs*[4] (Berlin, 1963), pp. 137–9. He has been followed by almost all the modern commentators on Exodus. In addition to the commentaries see, e.g., S. R. Driver, *Introduction to the Literature of the OT*[9] (Edinburgh, 1913), pp. 37–8; G. F. Moore, s.v. 'Incense', *EB* ii. 2166–7; and many others. Von Rad (*Die Priesterschrift im Hexateuch*, pp. 61, 75–7, 183) considers Exod. 30: 1–10 to be a later addition bearing no relation to either P^A or P^B. This view has been accepted by Beer and Galling, *Exodus*, pp. 128–9.

[27] These phenomena also characterize, for example, the descriptions of the lampstand, to which four widely scattered passages are devoted, each dealing with a different aspect of the subject. One of them (Exod. 25: 31–40) is devoted to a description of the lampstand's form. Two others, which are really two variant versions of the same passage (Exod. 27: 20–1; Lev. 24: 1–4), deal with the preparations of the lamp-oil, and we have already noted (above, p. 209, n. 6) that

they seem indications of slovenliness, cannot be taken as an argument for splitting up the sources into different strata. One may explain the misplacement of the passage in question by assuming that the copyists or the editors themselves were not sufficiently careful about inserting it where it belonged, and that this was the natural result of an editorial method which gave rise to loose joints and rough edges. It is a good general rule that, while a fairly systematic and strict sense of order may be found in P's doctrinal system and ritual regulations, it is sometimes lacking in its literary exposition and still more so in the arrangement of its sections.[28] Thus, on stylistic evidence alone, one would still have to maintain that the passage in question belongs, as its contents show, to the complex of the tabernacle; all the more so when this conclusion is confirmed by the whole nature of the ritual performed within the temple.

there is a reason for this repetition. A fourth passage (Num. 8: 1–4) contains the instruction that 'the seven lamps shall give light in front of the lampstand'. This passage seems to be set in an unsuitable context (within a tiny collection of miscellanea), and has tacked on to it a repeated description of the lampstand. Yet, the specific task of tending and refilling the lamps was not thought worthy of a passage to itself. This task is either merely implied in the four passages above, or is taken as understood and squeezed into a parenthesis. It is also incidentally referred to in the ordinances about the offering of the incense of 'spices' (Exod. 30: 7–8). Apparently, these phenomena have also something to do with the fact that each of the Pentateuchal sources is itself a collecive work (on which cf. above, pp. 146–7).

[28] Scholars have hardly done themselves credit by connecting our problem with the fact that in LXX the passage about the incense-altar has been omitted from the second description of the tabernacle (Exod. 37: 25–8). The LXX Version of the sections dealing with the tabernacle (from which several other passages are missing) has hardly anything to do with the literary question of Pentateuchal sources. On this point cf. D. W. Gooding, *The Account of the Tabernacle* (Cambridge, 1959), pp. 31–2, 66 ff.

XII

INCENSE OF THE COURT AND OF THE TEMPLE INTERIOR

I

THE spices were, for the most part, the products of distant lands—Southern Nubia and Arabia—but for centuries they had been brought along the caravan routes to the centres of civilization in the Fertile Crescent and even to the Mediterranean countries.[1] The use of spices, or of a mixture of their fine powder (which is the 'incense' proper, the *q*ᵉ*ṭōret* as it is termed in the Old Testament), was a regular feature in all rites in antiquity. In the cultic practices of ancient Israel we find that spices were used in three ways.

The first of these took the form of adding the spice, in its powder form, as a supplement to the sacrifice, namely, the grain-offering. In this case, the spice was usually part of the *'azkārāh*, the 'memorial portion' (or the 'token') of the grain-offering, and as such was burnt up on the altar. The spice generally employed in grain-offerings was *l*ᵉ*ḇônāh*, frankincense (Lev. 2: 1, 15; 6: 8 *et al.*). There are no examples of spices being added to animal or bird sacrifices, but it is not impossible that at times the priests may have seen to it that some spices were scattered on the altar in order to catch fire and mingle with the smoke of the offerings and thus ameliorate the stench of the burning flesh. This would explain the frequent use of the verb *qṭr* in the *hip̄'îl* conjugation, to indicate the burning of the fat and the sacrificial portions, a usage which is especially characteristic of P's style.[2] It may also be that the 'pleasing odour', *rê*ᵃ*ḥ nîḥô*ᵃ*ḥ*, which in biblical descriptions accompanies the burning of the sacrifices and which God is accustomed to savour, is a further indication that the smoke was not merely

[1] See M. Löhr, *Das Räucheropfer im AT* (Halle–Saale, 1927), pp. 155–8, 160–3; R. Le Baron Bowen Jr., 'Ancient Trade Routes in South Arabia', *Archaeological Discoveries in South Arabia* (Baltimore, 1958), pp. 35–6, 40, 42; G. W. Van Beek, 'Frankincense and Myrrh', *BA* 23 (1960), 86, 91–2.

[2] Occasionally, also found in non-priestly sources (e.g. 1 Sam. 2: 15–16; 2 Kgs. 16: 15). On the use of this verb in the *hip̄'îl* and in the *pi'ēl* see below, sect. 3.

that of burnt flesh, but was sometimes blended with a more fragrant odour of spices.[3]

More significant for the present discussion are the two other cultic uses of the spices, in both of which the spices take the form of sacrifices in their own right, and only one of which is relevant to the ritual complex performed inside the temple.

THE CENSER INCENSE AND THE ANTIQUITY OF ITS CULTIC USE

2

In several Old Testament passages where both spices and grain-offerings are mentioned, it is difficult to determine whether a separate spice-offering is meant, or whether the spices are merely regarded as a supplement to the grain-offering (Isa. 43: 23–4; Jer. 6: 20; 17: 26; 41: 5; also Neh. 13: 5, 9). There are, however, other passages especially in P and the Book of Ezekiel, that is, in the writings of the representatives of the priestly school, where the existence of a separate spice-offering is clearly recognized. In every one of these passages the noun *qᵉṭōret*, 'incense' is used, indicating the mixed powder of ground spices which gives off a fragrance when burnt.

A separate incense-offering is mentioned by Ezekiel in his vision of the seventy elders in the temple, led by Jaazaniah the son of Shaphan (Ezek. 8: 10–11). The prophet denounces them for the idolatrous intention of their deed, for its being performed before 'every form of creeping things, and loathsome beasts, and all the idols of the house of Israel', portrayed upon the wall around them. But the act of offering incense as such is not regarded by him as unfit for legitimate ritual. In two other references, seemingly to a separate incense-offering, Ezekiel again denounces this offering because it was made to idols, but at the same time he calls it 'mine incense', thereby implying that the incense itself was actually fit to be offered to the God of Israel (16: 18; 23: 41).

[3] Hence even the burning of those grain-offerings which contained no frankincense, namely, the one which served as a substitute for a sin-offering (Lev. 5: 12) and the one offered by an unfaithful wife (Num. 5: 26), might nonetheless be expressed by the verb *qṭr* in *hip'îl*. An animal sacrifice is apparently also meant by the 'incense (*qᵉṭōret*) of rams' mentioned in Ps. 66: 15. Some scholars were baffled by this use of the verb *qṭr* in connection with sacrificial portions of animal offerings. Of late, cf. also O. Keel's remark in 'Kanaanäische Sühneriten auf Ägyptischen Tempelreliefs', *VT* 25 (1975), 434.

In P there are several unmistakable references to a separate incense-offering. Nadab and Abihu intended to make an offering of incense in their censers (Lev. 10: 1–3). They were punished because they offered it to Yahweh in 'strange fire', that is, fire other than that which was kept burning on the altar for the daily sacrifice.[4] Nadab and Abihu apparently took their fire from somewhere outside the altar-area and placed it in their censers, as it is stated: 'each took his censer and put fire in it'. One may contrast with this the order given to Aaron by Moses in Num. 17: 11: 'Take your censer, and put fire therein from off the altar'; cf. also Lev. 16: 12. In retrospect, too, the only crime ascribed to Nadab and Abihu is the use of strange fire (Num. 3: 4; 26: 61). In their offering of incense as such the priestly writers find nothing illegitimate.

A similar case is that of Korah's two hundred and fifty followers, who met their end because they sought to usurp the functions of the priesthood—not because they offered up incense in censers (Num. 16: 16–18). Here, too, the offering in itself is completely acceptable as a genuine ritual act; indeed, it is precisely because the act is ritually legitimate that it can be used to test whether Korah and his company are fit to officiate as priests. After all, Aaron too offers up incense in his censer, but is not harmed. It is worth noting, incidentally, that the fire used by Korah's company was also taken from outside the altar-area and was, therefore, unfit to continue in ritual use as may be inferred from the com-

[4] Cf. Ibn-Ezra's explanation ad loc. P assumes that the fire that came forth from before the Lord on the eighth day of the consecration ceremony (Lev. 9: 24) continued to burn on the altar and was carried by the Israelites until they reached Canaan. Indeed, in none of the ritual acts mentioned by P is fire brought from outside the altar. The wording of Lev. 1: 7 ('and the sons of Aaron the priest shall put fire on the altar') seems to lack juridical coherence, or its meaning should be something like this: the priests are to fan the continual fire on the altar higher so that it would consume the individual burnt-offering which in this case is an entire bull. At any rate, elsewhere it is explicitly stated that the fire on the altar must never be allowed to go out, even at night (Lev. 6: 2, 5–6). The talmudic sages expounded Lev. 1: 7 to mean that 'it is a positive duty to bring some ordinary fire (to the altar)', מצוה להביא מן ההדיוט (Bab. Tal. Yoma, 21*b*, 53*a* and parallel passages). However, it is hard to reconcile this interpretation with the plain meaning of the text. The incident of Nadab and Abihu, in which the central point is the heresy involved in bringing fire to the altar from outside, was correctly explained by, e.g., W. W. von Baudissin, *Geschichte des alttestamentlichen Priesterthums* (Leipzig, 1889), p. 22; see also R. Gradwohl, 'Das "fremde Feuer" von Nadab und Abihu', *ZAW* 75 (1963), 289–91.

mand given to Eleazar in Num. 17: 2: 'and scatter the fire far and wide'. Only the sin of Korah and his followers in using this fire was overshadowed by their yet more heinous sin of attempting to usurp the priestly function.

Another separate incense-offering made by Aaron is that by the aid of which he stops the plague (Num. 17: 12–13). Again, at the consecration of the tabernacle, each of the twelve princes brings a spoonful of incense (Num. 7), which must have been intended for separate incense-offerings, not as a supplement to the memorial-portions of grain-offerings. This is clear from the fact that in the last case *lᵉḇônāh* is always mentioned and not *qᵉṭōret*, as at the consecration of the tabernacle.

3

Separate incense-offerings of this kind are also meant in the two non-priestly passages in which the noun *qᵉṭōret*, or *qᵉṭôrāh* is specifically used: Deut. 33: 10: 'they shall put incense in thy nostrils'; and 1 Sam. 2: 28: 'And I chose him out of all the tribes of Israel to be my priest . . . to burn incense'.

The verb *qṭr* is, of course, common in biblical passages which do not bear the stylistic stamp of P, but when used in the *pi'ēl* conjugation it nowhere refers to an offering of incense. In P this verb is only used in the *hip̄'îl* conjugation, whether referring to the sacrificial portions of an animal offering, or to a grain-offering and incense. In the non-priestly sources, on the other hand, the verb, though found occasionally in the *hip̄'îl*, is employed mainly in the *pi'ēl*. Now the *pi'ēl* of *qṭr* is never used of incense (as rendered by most EVV),[5] but only of the grain-offering which, according to the conception of the non-priestly sources, should be consumed by fire in its entirety.[6] It is true that the *pi'ēl* of this verb usually has no object, but from the contexts in which it appears its meaning can be confidently established as nothing but 'to offer (or to burn)

[5] The sole exception now seems to be NEB, where this verb is generally translated as 'to burn sacrifices', occasionally (e.g. in 2 Kgs. 12: 4) 'make smoke offerings'; cf., however, in this same version, Isa. 65: 3; Hab. 1: 16 note.

[6] P and Ezekiel's code suppose that the grain-offering is to be eaten by the male priests in a 'holy place' after its memorial-portion has been burnt on the altar. But all the other biblical works (excluding books, such as Chronicles, which are influenced by P), assume that the grain-offering is burnt on the altar in its entirety. On this point see, for the present, my observations in *EM* v. 26–7.

grain-offering'. Hence the frequent parallelism of the verbs *zbḥ–qṭr*, both in the *pi'ēl* (1 Kgs. 22: 44; 2 Kgs. 12: 4; 14: 4 *et al.*; Hos. 4: 13; 11: 2; Hab. 1: 16; cf. Isa. 65: 3), the first indicating an animal offering and the second a cereal offering. In Jeremiah we find *qaṭṭēr* in parallelism with *hassēḵ nᵉsāḵîm*, 'to pour drink-offerings' (Jer. 19: 13; 32: 29; 44: 17–19, 25) where the meaning is undoubtedly exactly the same as that of *minḥāh wānesek̲* ('grain-offering and drink-offering') in Joel 1: 9, 13; 2: 14 and in Isa. 57: 6. From the passages in Jeremiah we can learn what it was, at least on some occasions, that was offered in this way: the substance in question was dough kneaded into *kawwānîm*, 'sacrificial cakes', or 'crescent cakes' (Jer. 7: 18, 44: 19; here too the grain-offering of the *kawwānîm* is paralleled by *nesek̲*). Moreover, there is one passage where the *pi'ēl* of *qṭr* does take an object: 'and offer (*wᵉqaṭṭēr*) a thank-offering of that which is leavened' (Amos 4: 5), i.e. the grain-offering accompanying the thanksgiving sacrifice which, according to non-priestly custom, would probably have taken the form of leavened bread and might even have been offered up on the altar (in contrast to the priestly laws of Lev. 2: 11; 6: 10; 7: 12).[7]

It is not difficult to understand why the bringing of a grain-offering is on these occasions expressed by means of *qṭr* in the *pi'ēl*. The reason, evidently, is that the grain-offering too was sometimes made in the form of a powder (this time of flour), and moreover had some spice (frankincense) added to it. Hence it could easily come to be associated with the powder which contained nothing but spices, i.e. the *qᵉṭōret*. This also explains why, in Isa. 1: 13 and Ps. 141: 2, the word *qᵉṭōret* (again, not as EVV render it) is apparently used simply to mean a grain-offering, *minḥāh*, the word which actually appears in the parallel member of each verse.[8] In Jer. 44: 21 the same grain-offering is called *qiṭṭēr* (but in most EVV: 'incense'; NEB 'sacrifices').[9]

[7] Consequently, even where this verb has no object its meaning would be the same. Thus, in 2 Kgs. 18: 4 it is related that the people of Israel were *mᵉqaṭṭᵉrîm* to the bronze serpent, which should be rendered as just 'burned grain-offerings' (not 'incense'). Indeed, offerings of pure spices would surely be too expensive for the common people, as even animal offerings were.

[8] The term *minḥāh* in the sense of grain-offering may well be found even in non-priestly texts which preceded the canonization of the Pentateuch (Judg. 13: 19, 23; 1 Sam. 3: 14; Amos 5: 22, 25; Jer. 14: 12 *et al.*).

[9] At the same time it must be admitted that the verb *qṭr* in the *pi'ēl* is employed, in the Deuteronomistic language and elsewhere, only of cultic acts which are

The ingredients of the separate incense-offering must remain uncertain,[10] since neither P nor Ezekiel, which contain the principal references to it, specifies its composition. If recourse is had to the evidence of such verses as Isa. 43: 23–4; Jer. 6: 20; 17: 26; 41: 5 (cf. above, sect. 2)—evidence which, for various reasons, is doubtfully admissible in this context—we would be able to assume that the *qᵉṭōret* powder too consisted mainly of *lᵉḇônāh*, frankincense, but sometimes contained 'sweet cane', *qāneh haṭṭôḇ*, as well (Jer. 6: 20; cf. Isa. 43: 24). 'Sweet cane' is perhaps identical with the 'aromatic cane', *qᵉnēh bōśem*, which was one of the ingredients of the anointing oil (Exod. 30: 23), but none of the other spices mentioned in the preparation of the latter has anything to do with the *qᵉṭōret*. There are, of course, several other kinds of spices known in the Old Testament which have no cultic applications whatsoever.

4

For a long time the theory prevailed that, for most of the First Temple period, the use of incense was a characteristically idolatrous form of worship which did not find its way into the ancient Israelite cult until the seventh century B.C. Most of the classical prophets make no mention of it, while P, which is well acquainted with incense-offerings, was thought to reflect a later stage of cultic development here too. Although reference to such verses as Deut. 33: 10; 1 Sam. 2: 28 could have actually disproved this assumption, it nevertheless became virtually axiomatic.[11] Subsequently, however, it was contested by scholars using mainly archaeological evidence.

Among the archaeological finds of Syria and Palestine there are specimens of objects designed for burning incense. Most of these are high, rounded stands, variously shaped and ornamented, to

considered illegitimate by these authors, such as the worship of Baal, the queen of heaven, the bronze serpent, offerings at the high-places, and the like (the employment of *zbḥ* in the *piʿēl* is reminiscent of the same).

10 For the incense of *sammîm* see below, sects. 7–8.

11 Its propounder was Wellhausen (*PGI*, 63–4), followed by B. Baentsch, *Exodus* (GHK, 1903), pp. 259–60; I. Benzinger, *Hebräische Archäologie*³ (Leipzig, 1927), p. 365, and many others. Cf. the opinions cited by Löhr, *Räucheropfer*, pp. 164–5. All these scholars naturally concluded that the incense-altar mentioned in Solomon's temple (1 Kgs. 6: 20; 7: 48) was simply a later addition.

which the term *thymiateria* has been sometimes applied. Since the *thymiateria* were rarely found in Israelite strata, they could prove only the antiquity of the ritual use of incense in general (a point which hardly required proof), not the antiquity of its use in the Israelite cult.

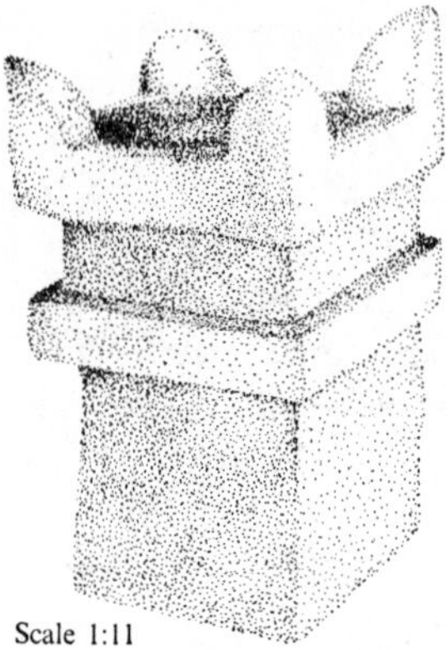

FIG. 3. An Incense Altar from Megiddo (Sketch)

More important for our purpose are those objects which have the form of an actual altar, viz., a rectangular stand topped by a flat surface, something like a small table in all, on which there are four horns. Quite a few incense-altars of this type dating from the beginning of the Iron Age—all, of course, made of stone or terra-cotta—have been discovered inside and outside Palestine. Scholars deduced that as these altars were too small for animal sacrifice but were apparently suitable for an incense offering, they were of the same type as the golden altar of P and of Solomon's temple; thus they sought to prove that incense was in ritual use in Israel throughout the First Temple period. To be sure, there was a basic difference that rendered this deduction difficult, if not implausible. For the incense-altars so far discovered were mostly portable, or even a kind of domestic altar, while the biblical altar of gold was a permanent fixture inside the temple.[12] This difference, however, was quite casually disregarded and for some time the archaeological case against the above-mentioned theory appeared to

[12] This difference had already been rightly observed by S. A. Cook (see next note).

reinforce the arguments of literary criticism.[13] But subsequently, as a result of the decipherment of an inscription on one such altar at Palmyra, many scholars concluded that all those incense-altars were related to, or actually served as bases for, what in biblical terms was called *ḥammānîm*. Since *ḥammānîm* are denounced in the Old Testament as a specifically idolatrous form of worship, the original question came once more to the fore: when did incense become a part of the Israelite cult? At any rate, there remained nothing in the archaeological data to impugn the theory that the use of incense was not introduced to the Israelite cult until a relatively late stage. If the data have not confirmed the theory, they have not disproved it either.[14]

The truth of the matter is that archaeological evidence will remain somewhat irrelevant to the question of the place of incense in the Israelite cult (as distinct from its secular use in everyday life) until actual remains of Israelite temples eventually come to light.[15] For the Old Testament itself assumes that the customary and proper place for the ritual use of incense is the temple alone. If anyone wishes to prove the antiquity of this use, but does not

[13] See H. M. Wiener, *The Altars of the OT* (Leipzig, 1927), pp. 23–31; S. A. Cook, *The Religion of Ancient Palestine in the Light of Archaeology* (London, 1930), p. 62. For the incense-altars at Megiddo, see especially H. G. May and R. M. Engberg, *Material Remains of the Megiddo Cult* (Chicago, 1935), pp. 12–13, Plate XII; C. C. McCown, 'Hebrew High Places and Cult Remains', *JBL* 69 (1950), 210, 218–19. The argument for the relative antiquity of the use of incense in the Israelite cult did not only stem from archaeological data, but was also based on literary analysis. See, for instance, B. D. Eerdmans, *Alttestamentliche Studien*, iv (Giessen, 1912), pp. 28–30; Löhr, op. cit., pp. 165, 172–88, where the literary argumentation predominates.

[14] This point was especially emphasized by W. F. Albright. See his unsigned review of Wiener's book, *JPOS* 9 (1929), 52–3; idem, *The Archaeology of Palestine and the Bible* (New York, 1932), pp. 108 ff.; idem, *From the Stone Age to Christianity* (Baltimore, 1940), p. 237; idem, *ARI*, 72, p. 216, n. 58; G. E. W(right), ' "Sun Image" or "Altar of Incense" ', *BA* 1 (1938), 9–10; K. Galling, *Biblisches Reallexikon* (Tübingen, 1937), cols. 19–20. The identification of the incense-altars with the *ḥammānîm*, on the basis of the inscription from Palmyra, was first suggested by H. Ingholt, 'Le sens du mot Hamman', *Mélanges syriens offerts à R. Dussaud*, ii (Paris, 1939), p. 795. For further views on the exact nature of *ḥammānîm*, see: K. Elliger, 'Chammanim—Masseben?' *ZAW* 57 (1939), 256–65 (with the view of J. Lindblom quoted there); R. Amiran, 'Note on the "Double bowl" found in an EB tomb at Tel Aviv', *BIES* 17 (1953), 148–9 (Hebrew); J. Leibovitch, 'Le Griffon dans le moyen-orient antique', *'Atiqot*, i (Jerusalem, 1955), 82–5; A. Dupont-Sommer, *Mélanges Isidor Lévy* (Bruxelles, 1955), pp. 149–52; H. Beinart, *EM* iii. 183–5, K. Galling, *IDB* ii. 699–700.

[15] No incense-altar of the above-mentioned type was found in the supposed temple of Arad (on which cf. above, pp. 37–8).

consider the traditions recorded by P as ancient enough for his purpose, he can safely take his stand on such evidence as Deut. 33: 10; 1 Sam. 2: 28.

5

In this second ritual use of spices here under consideration, there was no need at all for the incense to be placed on the altar. It was burnt in a long-handled censer, *maḥtāh* (Lev. 10: 1; Num. 16: 6 *et al.*), or in an upright censer, *miqṭeret* (Ezek. 8: 11). These implements, which were held in the hand, were more than mere receptacles for the incense-powder: it was in them that the actual burning took place. It was from the censer that the 'smoke of the cloud of incense' rose and it was in the censer that the incense attained the sanctity of an offering. Thus it may be called 'the censer incense', since the censer was, so to speak, its 'altar'.

There is, in fact, no example of this particular incense being placed on an altar. In the incidents involving Korah and his company, and Nadab and Abihu the sons of Aaron, nowhere is it stated that the incense was transferred from the censers to the altar. We are told only that, after the destruction of Korah and his followers, Eleazar was commanded to beat the censers out into 'hammered plates as a covering for the altar' (Num. 17: 3). This was done, of course, after incense had been offered in the censers and Eleazar was given the command because the censers of Korah's company had become 'holy', i.e. impregnated with contagious holiness by their contact with the fire that 'came forth from the Lord'. For the ordeal Korah and his followers took their own censers, which, the priestly writer assumes, had never been part of the sanctified vessels appertaining to the tabernacle (see Num. 16: 6: 'Do this—take you censers, Korah and all his company'; cf. vv. 17–18). Then, after all this large number of censers had in fact become sanctified, the only possible way of disposing of them was to add them to the bronze plating of the outer altar. The censers of Nadab and Abihu, on the other hand, had been holy from the beginning like all the appurtenances of the tabernacle, and thus presented no problem in this respect.

Again, there is no warrant for thinking that even the incense mentioned in Deut. 33: 10; 1 Sam. 2: 28 was placed on the altar. The expression 'to burn incense' used in the latter verse is not subordinated to what goes before it. The verse is simply listing side by side three typical priestly functions: 'to go up to my altar, to burn incense, to wear an ephod before me'. The priests ascend the altar not to offer incense, but to perform various rites—mainly those connected with the burning of the sacrificial portions—that require no explicit mentioning. The burning of incense is a separate rite which can be assumed to have been performed in censers. These two priestly functions are similarly mentioned side by side in Deut. 33: 10, where the putting of incense in the Lord's 'nostrils' is parallel to the sacrificing of a whole burnt offering on the altar. (The third typical function, the wearing of the ephod, is also referred to in that passage: two verses earlier there is mention of the Thummim and Urim which are carried on the ephod.)[16]

However, the fact that this incense was burnt in censers must not be taken to imply that it could be offered anywhere. True, when plague broke out among the people, Aaron took such a censer into the camp (Num. 17: 11–12). But this was nevertheless an exceptional occurrence. So far as we can tell from the biblical evidence, incense was usually burnt within the temple's precincts. Nadab and Abihu, as well as Korah and his followers, offer up their incense in the court (Lev. 10: 1–2; Num. 16: 7 ff.). Similarly, the 'chambers of imagery' (Ezek. 8: 12), in which Jaazaniah and his company offer up their incense, are built into the wall of the inner court of the temple. According to the priestly view, it is forbidden that 'any stranger, who is not of the descendants of Aaron, draw near to burn incense before the Lord' (Num. 17: 5). This clearly implies that for P the offering of incense is specifically the exclusive prerogative of the priests—of all the priests, not only of the high priest. It is no mere coincidence that the two non-priestly passages which explicitly mention the offering of incense (Deut. 33: 10; 1 Sam. 2: 28) are also concerned with characteristically priestly rites, which were undoubtedly part of the temple phenomena.

6

The custom of offering incense in censers apparently goes back to Egyptian practices, in which the use of the altar for this purpose

[16] It can also be assumed that the incense mentioned in these passages is the one described below (sects. 7–8), which appertains to the interior of the temple. Even so, however, the altar referred to in these texts is not the one upon which the incense is placed. For the altar of gold is not the one of which it can be said that priests 'go up' to it.

was completely unknown. This manner of worship would seem to have spread from Egypt to Canaan well before the Israelites arrived there. In the Egyptian cult the burning of incense in a long-handled or upright censer could often have an apotropaic significance: the worshippers sought thereby to ward off the demonic powers of impurity and to this end they used to carry the

FIG. 4. An Upright Censer in a Siege of Ashkelon by Ramesses II

censers in processions and on other solemn occasions. The use of incense is also found even in connection with cities under siege. Egyptian drawings from the New Kingdom which depict sieges in Canaan and Syria usually contain figures of men standing on the wall with their arms outstretched, apparently in prayer. At the head of these figures, right at the end of the wall, we often find another man holding an upright censer in which incense is burning. Such a man can be distinguished, for example, in the pictures of Seti I's siege of the Canaanite city of Yanoam, of Ramesses II's sieges of the Hittite fortress at Deper and of Ashkelon, of Ramesses III's siege of a Hittite city in Syria,[17] and in several others. If in these pictures the burning of incense does not have an apo-

[17] See W. Wreszinski, *Atlas zur altägyptischen Kulturgeschichte*, ii (Leipzig, 1935), Pls. 36, 58, 107–9, 145 = *ANEP*, Nos. 330, 333, 334, 345. For all these pictures cf. also the important study by Keel, 'Kanaanäische Sühneriten' (above, p. 231, n. 3), 435–6, 463–7 (Appendices), where many additional representations are brought forward and classified.

tropaic significance (symbolizing the efforts made by the besieged to ward off the demonic powers which, in this case, could be identified with the enemy) then it will imply just the straightforward cultic intention of paying homage to the Pharaoh's deified image which appears opposite the city.[18] In the Old Testament, however, such an act is clearly depicted as suggesting an apotropaic meaning, when it is said of Aaron that he checked the plague by standing 'between the dead and the living', holding the censer in which the holy incense was burning (Num. 17: 12–13).

Once the practice of burning incense in censers had been absorbed into the Israelite cult, it became a priestly prerogative and was confined to the temple precincts, though on infrequent occasions the priests would certainly have performed the rite outside those precincts (just as under certain circumstances they would bear the ark or the ephod out of the temple). It is possible that in Egypt and Canaan too the ritual burning of incense in censers was regarded as the prerogative of priests.

THE ALTAR INCENSE

7

Incense could also be placed upon the altar of gold (Exod. 30: 1–10): this is the third form of the ritual use of spices mentioned in the Old Testament. All those scholars who claimed that the passage about the altar of gold and its incense belonged to a later layer of P[19] took for granted that, among other things, the same incense was referred to in both rites, which meant that the offering of incense on the altar was simply a duplication of offering it in censers. But an examination of the text leads one to believe that the incense is far from being one and the same. In actual fact, the priestly writers themselves are aware of the distinctive character of the incense offered on the altar of gold and they give expression to this awareness. They regard this incense as specific, 'inner', and different from the usual 'outer' incense which is offered in censers. According to their own view, there is a special kind of incense set apart for the interior of the temple, and for there alone.

[18] As Keel insists (art. cit. 425–30).
[19] Cf. above, p. 228, n. 26.

The 'inner' incense is distinguished from the censer-incense first of all by its composition which is specified in Exod. 30: 34–8. This fact in itself indicates the exceptional nature of this incense. In vv. 37–8 it is implied that other incense might be made (sometimes not even for an offering but simply *l*^e^*hārî*^a^*ḥ*, 'to smell', 'to use as perfume'), but then, no other incense may be 'according to the composition' of this particular one.

As indicated in the prescription, this incense has two main ingredients. The first are *sammîm*, which perhaps are not exactly spices, but substances of another kind (as some commentators have remarked) which serve to improve the mixture of spices when added to it. Three kinds of *sammîm* are mentioned here: *nāṭāp̱*, *š*^e^*ḥēlet*, and *ḥelb*^e^*nāh*. The second ingredient is pure frankincense, *l*^e^*ḇônāh*, the same spice which was added to the memorial-portions of the grain-offerings. It is only in connection with this incense and with the shewbread, both of which belong inside the tabernacle, that the priestly regulations emphasize that the frankincense must be 'pure', *zakkāh*.[20] Although some details of the preparation of this incense are not clear enough,[21] the wording of v. 34, especially the repetition there of *sammîm*, suggests that the three *sammîm* together form one ingredient which is to be added to the mixture in equal quantities with the other ingredient, the frankincense (and not that the frankincense should constitute a fourth part of the total amount of incense).[22] These two basic ingredients are then seasoned with salt.[23] The method of preparing this incense is somewhat similar to that used in preparing the anointing oil (Exod. 30: 22–3), not just because the latter contains spices too,

[20] Cf. above, pp. 208–10.

[21] Such is the Hebrew phrase *bad b*^e^*ḇad yihyeh*.

[22] Cr. U. Cassuto's commentary ad loc.

[23] S. D. Luzatto (in his Hebrew Commentary to Exodus (Padua, 1872), p. 337) argued that the *pu'al* form of the Hebrew verb in v. 35, *m*^e^*mullaḥ*, cannot mean 'seasoned with salt', since in connection with the grain-offerings the form used is in the *qal* conjugation, *timlaḥ* (Lev. 2: 13). He therefore explained the verse as follows: 'that its task, מלאכתו may be performed in purity and in holiness' (making מֶלַח cognate with מְלָאכָה). Onkelos and Rashi explained the verse as meaning that the incense should be well-mixed, just as the sailors, מַלָּחִים 'stir up the waters with their oars' (making מֶלַח cognate with מַלָּח, sailor). Cassuto accepts Luzatto's argument only to follow Onkelos and Rashi in his interpretation. Yet, this whole approach is mistaken: in the case of the grain-offerings the salt is merely sprinkled on the sacrifice, whereas in the incense-powder it is probably mixed into it. These two processes are distinguished by the use of different conjugations, in both cases the reference being to salt.

but also because both of them are made by a special process which is denoted by the same *terminus technicus*—*maʿᵃśēh rôqēᵃḥ*, 'the workmanship of the perfumer'.[24]

The inclusion of such large quantities of *sammîm* in incense was, at any rate, something exceptional. That is why this incense is associated with them and designated by the conjoint form *qᵉṭōret hassammîn*, 'the incense of *sammîm*', to distinguish it from the censer-incense which is called simply *qᵉṭōret*, without any appellative, that is, ordinary incense. The fact is that in virtually every reference to the 'inner' incense it is punctiliously described as 'the incense of *sammîm*'. Just as the incense of *sammîm* must not be put outside the tabernacle (ibid., v. 37), so 'strange incense', *qᵉṭōret zārāh*, may not be offered on the altar of gold (ibid., v. 9). The word *zārāh* does not here mean that the incense is 'idolatrous' (neither does it exactly mean 'unholy', as RSV renders it); it simply denotes incense that is 'strange' to this particular altar, i.e. that is ritually unfit to be placed upon it, since only the incense of *sammîm* is exclusively reserved for that purpose.[25] In one place the altar of gold is actually given the full epithet of 'the altar of the incense of *sammîm*' (Lev. 4: 7).

8

The unique composition of the incense of *sammîm* is much more than a matter of externals. In a way characteristic of P's method, the material uniqueness reflects the sacral–ritualistic distinctiveness of this incense.

Hence we find that, as stated above, the ordinary incense is

[24] The workmanship of *rôqēᵃḥ* is thus just another skill of artistic execution, analogous to the workmanships of *ḥôšēḇ*, *'ôrēg*, and *rôqēm* mentioned in the preparation of the tabernacle (above, pp. 160–1). We find several additional instances of this form of technical terms, which all have the substantive *maʿᵃśēh* as the *nomen rectum* and denote various types of craftsmanships: 'the work of bronze netting' (Exod. 27: 4: 38: 4), 'the workmanship of the lapidary' (ibid. 28: 11), 'the work of *ʿᵃḇôt*, cords' (ibid., vv. 14, 22; 39: 15). Such combinations are also found outside P's style: 'the workmanship of the baker' (Gen. 40: 17), 'the work of *śᵉḇāḵāh*, network', 'the work of *śaršᵉrôt*, chains' (1 Kgs. 7: 17), 'the work of *śôšan*, lily-shape' (ibid., vv. 19, 22).

[25] This is, as we saw, the peculiar significance of the term *zār* in the priestly style. Similarly, *'îš zār*, is synonymous with one who 'is not of the descendants of Aaron', and *'ēš zārāh* (Lev. 10: 1 *et al.*; cf. above, sect. 2) is 'strange, outside fire', i.e. which is ritually unfit for use on the outer altar (cf. above, p. 183).

burnt (*a*) in the court and (*b*) in censers; whereas the incense of *sammîm* is burnt inside the tabernacle and on a special altar. (*c*) The censer-incense might legitimately be offered by Nadab and Abihu or by any Aaronic priest; whereas Aaron alone is mentioned in connection with the incense of *sammîm* (Exod. 30: 7–8), and, as has been shown in Chapter XI, such a mode of wording is not incidental. The interior of the temple is regarded as a distinct sphere, in which all the cultic acts are connected with the name of, and may be performed by, the high priest alone.

(*d*) Again, the burning of incense in censers is something of an expression of a momentary, spontaneous outburst of enthusiasm, and may not even be 'statutory'. Nowhere is it mentioned as being obligatory under certain circumstances. The offering of the *sammîm*-incense, on the other hand, is a regular part of a statutory ceremonial. This incense has to be placed on the altar twice a day at the times specially appointed for all the *tāmîd* rites—in the morning and 'at the twilight'. That is why it is once given the appellation reserved for such rites: 'the incense of *tāmîd*' (Exod. 30: 8). There is only one quite exceptional occasion in the whole year when Aaron does not offer the *sammîm*-incense on the altar of gold, nor at the appointed hours of *tāmîd*, but burns it in his censer, in the same manner as the outer incense is burned: on the Day of Atonement, when he enters into the inner sanctum, he places the *sammîm*-incense on his censer, so that the cloud rising from it should screen the ark-cover (Lev. 16: 12–13), the sight of which may kill even Aaron.[26] It is clear that Aaron uses the *sammîm*-incense in his censer on this occasion only because he needs it in the innermost part of the temple, where the use of ordinary incense is forbidden. The procedure of the Day of Atonement thus merely confirms the distinctive nature of the *sammîm*-incense as the incense reserved for the interior of the temple.[27]

(*e*) There is yet a further difference between the two kinds of incense. That burnt in censers is an 'independent' offering in the

[26] Cf. above, p. 178.

[27] B. D. Eerdmans (*Alttestamentliche Studien*, iv. 29) considered that the inner altar-incense differed from the outer censer-incense only in 'function'. Determining the function of the inner incense from Lev. 16, he held that its sole purpose was to veil the presence of Yahweh. But we cannot draw any inference about the regular function of the inner incense from the ceremony of the Day of Atonement which is exceptional and irregular. As has been said, the ritual function of this incense can be explained only in relation to all the other acts performed with it at the same appointed times.

full sense of the word. It is entirely self-contained and involves no other ritual act either before or after it. In none of the instances recorded in P and in Ezek. 8 is there any mention of an animal-sacrifice or grain-offering accompanying the offering of this incense. In contrast, the *sammîm-* or *tamîd*-incense is, as has been shown in Chapter XI, no more than an inseparable part of a whole complex of acts: it is inextricably bound up with all the other inner rites of *tāmîd*. The idea that it could exist independently of all these is entirely foreign to priestly thinking.

XIII

THE SYMBOLS OF THE INNER SANCTUM

I

THERE are two trends of scholarly thought regarding the symbolic significance of the ark. One of these assumes that the ark was conceived of essentially as a chest, *Behälter*, a container for objects of the greatest holiness. But then, concealing tables of law within a closed container seemed somewhat odd to many scholars, who took it for granted that words of law engraved upon stone were surely meant to be publicly displayed. They therefore supposed that primarily the ark had held not two tables of the law but a fetish-stone, a meteorite from Mount Sinai, or a statue. The second school of thought holds that the ark was conceived of as the seat of God, as a sort of empty throne, *Thron*. The divine holiness was concentrated not inside the ark but upon it, above the wings of the cherubim, and the deity was not actually visualized but only indirectly symbolized by the empty seat. When this idea was first put forward, parallels were adduced from the ancient cultures of the Mediterranean, India, and early Christianity.[1] Subsequently examples were added from Persia and from the early stages of the history of the west European peoples. In all these the prevalent cult was aniconic, based on the notion that by placing an empty throne for the deity it was possible to influence him to be, as it were, physically present. The Yahwistic cult was assumed to be aniconic in this way.[2]

[1] W. Reichel, *Über die vorhellenischen Götterkulte* (Vienna, 1897).

[2] The most important literature is listed by Kaufmann, *THH* ii. 349. The dissertation by M. Dibelius, *Die Lade Jahves* (Göttingen, 1906) seems to be the most fundamental and careful work within the limits of the school of Wellhausen. To those holding the first opinion some scholars who preceded Reichell may be added (besides those mentioned by Kaufmann), such as L. Couard, 'Die religiös-nationale Bedeutung der Lade Jahves', *ZAW* 12 (1892), 53–90; and, e.g., R. Hartmann, 'Zelt und Lade', ibid. 37 (1917–18), 225–39; J. Morgenstern, 'The Ark, the Ephod and the Tent of Meeting', *HUCA* 17 (1942–3), 153–7, 229–66 (also in book form). Morgenstern considers the ark to have been a container, but

THE TWO SYMBOLS

2

The biblical evidence gives grounds for both these points of view. Ezekiel's description of the chariot of cherubim; the title 'who sits upon the cherubim', *yôšēḇ hakkᵉrûḇîm*, which occurs several times in the Bible and applies to God (1 Sam. 4: 4; 2 Sam. 6: 2; 2 Kgs. 19: 15; Isa. 37: 16; Ps. 80: 2; 99: 1); the common portrayal of God sitting on his throne; and lastly the ark and the *kappōret* as described in P's tabernacle, along with the explicit statement that God used to meet Moses from between the two cherubim and from above the ark-cover (Exod. 25: 22; 30: 6; Lev. 16: 2; Num. 7: 89)—all these provide sufficient proof that the cherubim were conceived as the supporters of God's seat, and hence that the ark was his throne. Yet, there is as much evidence to show that, before anything else, the ark was what its name and even its shape imply—*'ᵃrôn*, i.e. a chest made to contain something.

Indeed, whether one sees the ark as a throne or a chest, one cannot entirely exclude the alternative. Where scholars are at variance, it is only over the relative importance given to different pieces of evidence, their chronological order in relation to each other, and the assessment of the historical and factual background. Some claim that nothing is to be inferred from the evidence of P, and that the first two mentions of the title 'who sits upon the cherubim' (1 Sam. 4: 4; 2 Sam. 6: 2) are merely glosses. Others contend that the descriptions in Ezekiel and P are not pure imagination, but are the development of ancient motifs; that the idea of the ark as a chest containing the tables of the law is simply a Deuteronomistic adaptation; and that the above two passages

in his opinion the meaning of *'ᵃrôn* is not a case or a chest, but a tent. All this is assumed in the desire to find a parallel between the ark and the pre-Islamic *qubbah*. To those holding the second opinion the following scholars may be added: K. Galling, *Biblisches Reallexikon* (Tübingen, 1937), p. 343; S. A. Cook, *The Religion of Ancient Palestine in the Second Millennium B.C.* (London, 1908), pp. 21–3; G. von Rad, 'Zelt und Lade', *Kirchliche Zeitschrift* 42 (1931), 476–98 = *Gesammelte Studien zum AT* (München, 1968), pp. 109–29; idem, *Die Priesterschrift im Hexateuch* (Berlin, 1934), p. 182; W. F. Albright, *From the Stone Age to Christianity* (Baltimore, 1940), pp. 202–3, 229–30; M. Buber, *Moses* (Oxford, 1946), pp. 148, 150, 156–61, 185. Cf. also the literature listed by J. Maier, *Das altisraelitische Ladeheiligtum* (Berlin, 1965), pp. 55, 66; R. de Vaux, *Bible et Orient* (Paris, 1967), p. 264, n. 1; and especially H. J. Zobel, s.v. ארון, *ThWAT* i, cols. 391–3.

are not glosses. In fact, anyone who does not dwell overmuch on details or does not neglect the evidence contained in the sources contradicting his view, tries to discover a line of development from the concept of the chest to that of the throne, which is supposed to have started in Isa. 6: 1–5; or conversely, from the concept of the throne to that of the chest, taking the view of D as the turning point.

The opinion that the ark was considered to be a divine throne seems to have ousted others and come to the fore. However, this opinion still cannot be reconciled with the simple fact that this throne, despite its cherubim, has none the less the shape of an ordinary closed chest. Even if we allow that its shape would not prevent its being thought of as a throne, it is impossible to understand why it was called an 'ark', *'ᵃrôn*, and not a throne, *kissē'*, or some synonym for this word. This was the decisive point for all those who saw in the ark a container, *Behälter*.[3] On the other hand, although the ark was indeed conceived of as a closed chest containing the tables, yet above it there was a throne for the deity to sit on. In truth, in order to link up these two symbols adequately, we need only realize that we are really dealing here with two distinct objects: the ark and the *kappōret* (if we start for the moment from the descriptions appertaining to the tabernacle). The chest containing holy objects is the ark itself; the throne is symbolized only in its cover, the *kappōret*, on the sides of which two cherubim spread their wings.

3

That the ark and the *kappōret* constitute fundamentally separate objects is definitely shown when comparison with Solomon's temple is made. Two huge cherubim stood there, carved of olive-wood and plated with gold, and their outspread wings covered the whole width of the holy of holies. Apart from these and in no way physically linked with them, the ark was also placed there

[3] Cf., e.g., K. Budde, 'Die ursprüngliche Bedeutung der Lade Jahwe's', *ZAW* 21 (1901), 194 ff.; H. Gressmann, *Die Lade Jahve's und das Allerheiligste des salomonischen Tempels* (Berlin, 1920), p. 2; and the remark by von Rad, *Gesammelte Studien zum AT*, p. 118. Dibelius (op. cit., pp. 94–100) quoted examples of chairs from Babylonia and Egypt having the form of an ark. In the last resort, however, this argument does not solve the problem, for as it has been said, it fails to explain why this 'throne' is explicitly called *'ᵃrôn*, an 'ark'.

(1 Kgs. 6: 23–8; 8: 1–9). It is clear that the cherubim and the ark served there as two distinct symbols, even if there was (as we shall see) a certain connection between the two. It is likewise clear that the two cherubim of Solomon's inner sanctum are the exact counterpart of the two cherubim on the tabernacle's *kappōret*. This analogy is adequate demonstration of the fact that the position of the two cherubim of P on the ark-cover is rather a technical matter, and that the ark and the *kappōret* actually constitute two distinct objects.

The distinctness of these two objects can be further proved by D, who speaks of an ark and certainly assumes that no cherubim were on it—just as, during the desert period, D does not acknowledge the existence of the whole tabernacle. In one place D makes a casual mention of the shape of the ark: it is made of acacia wood, it contains the tables, the Levitical priests carry it (Deut. 10: 1–5, 8). But no mention is made there of a *kappōret* and cherubim.

Similarly, the ark in the stories of the Former Prophets has neither *kappōret* nor cherubim. To be sure, in the two passages 1 Sam. 4: 4 and 2 Sam. 6: 2 Yahweh is spoken of as one 'who sits upon the cherubim'. However, this attribute does not relate to the ark mentioned in those passages—it refers only to Yahweh and describes his nature. Moreover, it is evident that the stories of the Former Prophets assume that the ark which eventually came to rest in Solomon's temple was the ark that had been taken from the temple at Shiloh. And since it is unthinkable that Solomon's temple contained, besides the pair of large olive-wood cherubim, another pair of small golden cherubim attached to the ark-cover, we can only assume that the ark is taken there to be without the special lid of cherubim, just as it is in D. From the above two passages it is possible to prove only that the *cherubim* were conceived as the supporters of Yahweh's throne, but not that they were necessarily attached to the lid of the ark.

Ezekiel, on the other hand, describes the glorious chariot throne of God in great detail, while the ark with the tables of the law is nowhere mentioned by him. The chariot is revealed to Ezekiel not only in the vision on the river Chebar (Ezek. 1–3), but also in connection with the temple: the glory of the Lord goes forth before the destruction of Jerusalem (ibid. 8: 10), and re-enters the newly built temple (ibid. 43: 1–7). The omission of the ark in Ezekiel's prophecy can easily be explained by the simple fact that by this time the ark no longer existed (as will also be shown in Chapter XV). It can also be explained by the cosmic background of Ezekiel's vision, for the chariot which he sees wanders about the sky. The decisive point, however, is that the prophet describes a throne of cherubim without the ark at all.[4] If the ark and the cherubim had been one, he could have hardly parted them.

The fact that the *kappōret* is distinct from the ark may be demonstrated even by a stylistic examination of the passages in P dealing with these items. Two sections do indeed appear there, even though they are not indicated as such in MT: Exod. 25: 10–16, 17–22. Both begin with the customary formula: 'And they shall make', 'and you shall make'. The first speaks of the ark, the second of the *kappōret*, although at the end of this second section the ark is mentioned again. Another indication of the distinctiveness of these objects is the fact that the text gives the dimensions of each of them: two and a half cubits long and a cubit and a half across. Wherever any vessel belonging to the tabernacle is described, its dimensions appear right at the beginning of the section (that is, if there is any point in recording its size). Moreover, in the detailed lists of the tabernacle furniture (Exod. 31: 7; 35: 12; 39: 35) the ark and the *kappōret* are mentioned side by side as two separate items, just like the table, the lampstand, etc. Where the ark alone is mentioned (ibid. 40: 3), the text is brief (cf. ibid., vv. 20–1); it does not intend to include the *kappōret* as part of the ark.[5]

[4] Though in Ezek. 1–3 no mention is made of cherubim and only *ḥayyôt*, 'living creatures' are spoken of, later on the latter are explicitly identified as cherubim (9: 3; 10: 1–20 [note especially vv. 15, 20]). Such an elliptic employment of terms cannot serve as evidence for the existence of literary layers or editorial work.

[5] In connection with the view expressed here, cf. H. Torczyner (Tur-Sinai), *Die Bundeslade und die Anfänge der Religion Israels*[2] (Berlin, 1930), pp. 12–13; also his remarks in *EM* i. 539–41; and in הלשון והספר, iii (Jerusalem, 1955), pp. 22–4. None the less it is difficult to accept Tur-Sinai's assumption (*Bundeslade*, p. 14; הלשון והספר, iii. 24) that in the course of time 'ark' came to denote both objects. G. Beer and K. Galling too (*Exodus* (HAT, 1939), p. 131) and Pedersen (*ILC* iii–iv. 246–7) duly noted, as did K. Ch. W. Böhr one hundred and forty years ago (*Symbolik des mosaischen Kultus* (Heidelberg, 1837), pp. 381–2, 392 ff.), that the *kappōret* is distinct from the ark and exceeds it in importance. Most commentators are nevertheless of the opinion that the ark and the *kappōret* are one unit. A view similar to the one presented here is also expressed by H. Schmidt ('Kerubenthron und Lade', *Εὐχαριστήριον Gunkel*, i (Göttingen, 1923), pp. 131–3, 141–2, 144). However, Schmidt also believes that the expression 'He who sits upon the cherubim' in 1 Sam. 4: 4 and 2 Sam. 6: 2

P is unique in that he links the two objects physically. In the tabernacle the cherubim are made part of a *kappōret* which at the same time serves as a cover for the ark. Thus, when the ark is borne forth, the throne of cherubim is also borne forth by the Kohathites. But in the traditional cultic symbolism each of these objects must have been significant in its own right.

THE SYMBOL OF THE THRONE

4

As has been stated, there can be no doubt that P's two cherubim—like the two large cherubim of Solomon's temple and the four cherubim in Ezekiel's vision—represent nothing less than a throne for God. This emerges from the virtually explicit evidence supplied in Ezekiel's vision. It also emerges from the many descriptions relating to the temple, which conceive of God as seated on a throne; for among all the symbols in the temple there is no throne other than that formed by the cherubim. It is also obvious from the explicit epithet 'who sits upon the cherubim', which is everywhere associated with the temple.[6] And much more evidence could be brought forward. On the other hand, none of the arguments advanced against this theory and based on the form of the two cherubim, of the tabernacle, or of Solomon's temple,[7] is convincing.

Neither P nor the account in 1 Kgs. 6 specifies whether the cherubim had the form of an animal on all fours or an erect, human, upright posture on two legs. In Ezekiel's vision each cherub

is a later addition. And, in my opinion, he does not properly explain the form of the cherubim on P's *kappōret*. From among more recent publications mention can be also made of O. Keel, *Die Welt der altorientalischen Bildsymbolik und das AT* (Zürich–Neukirchen, 1972), pp. 146–50.

[6] This expression is mentioned twice in connection with the ark that was taken from Shiloh, once interwoven in the prayer of Hezekiah in the temple, and twice in Psalms (see above, p. 247). Incidentally, Psalm 99 belongs to the type called by Gunkel *Thronbesteigungslieder*. Side by side with the motif of God's kingship these psalms also contain the motif of his throne, and the two are usually associated (Ps. 47: 8; 93: 1–2; 97: 1–2; cf. also Exod. 15: 17–18). Now in Ps. 99: 1, the title 'who sits upon the cherubim' is the equivalent of the throne motif. (This title is to be understood as the subject of the second half of the verse, while the verb 'reigned' mentioned in the first half is its predicate.)

[7] See, e.g., Gressmann, op. cit., pp. 7–9, 54 ff.

has the likeness of a man with two legs standing upright, but the sole of each foot is like the sole of a calf's foot (Ezek. 1: 5, 7). Moreover, each has hands like those of a man (ibid. 1: 8; 10: 8, 21). From these descriptions one may also deduce something of the general build of the cherubim of P and of 1 Kgs. 6. Isaiah's seraphim also have a human expression and possess arms and legs. They call to each other and utter songs like human beings, and one of them even speaks to the prophet (Isa. 6: 2–3, 6–7). In any case, the seat itself is formed of the outspread wings of the cherubim; and indeed the wings of all the cherubim are spread wide, both those of the tabernacle (Exod. 25: 20; 37: 9), and Solomon's temple (1 Kgs. 6: 27), and those of Ezekiel's chariot. Each of the latter cherubim has four wings: the two upper wings are spread out in a horizontal line supporting the firmament, while the two lower ones cover their bodies like the lower wings of Isaiah's seraphim (Ezek. 1: 8–9, 11, 23). It seems, therefore, that even the cherubim of P spread their wings horizontally. The word *l^ema'lāh* in Exod. 25: 20; 37: 9 (translated in KJV 'on high', in RSV and NJPS 'above') means 'above the trunk up to the shoulders'; it does not mean above the shoulders (NEB and JB render it rightly enough: 'upwards'). The wings, spread horizontally, form the throne proper.

One may also find it said of the cherubim that they 'cover', *sôḵ^eḵîm* something with their wings: in the tabernacle they 'cover' the *kappōret* (Exod. 25: 20; 37: 9); in Solomon's temple they 'cover' the ark and its poles (1 Kgs. 8: 7). Ezekiel states that even the cherub in the garden of Eden was 'the cherub that covers', *k^erûḇ hassôḵēḵ*, and every precious stone was 'his covering', the noun *m^esukkāh* being used in the text—even though the words are rather obscure (Ezek. 28: 13–16).[8]

However, in P and in 1 Kgs. 8: 7 this verb is intended only to indicate the position of the ark in relation to the wings of the cherubim, or conversely, the way in which the wings are spread out in relation to the object beneath them. The verb *skk* used in this context should not mislead us. The symbol is not that of a

[8] Dibelius (op. cit., pp. 39–41, 72–3) states that the older view of the ark as a throne is still discernible in P. However, he believes that the declared significance attached to the cherubim in P (or the additional significance over and above the one mentioned) is that of watchmen who spread out, *sôḵ^eḵîm* their wings to protect what is beneath. Very similar is the view of von Rad (*Gesamm. Stud. z. AT*, pp. 109–22, 124). Cf. also Kaufmann, *THH* ii. 350–4.

covering but of a throne formed by the outspread wings. For cherubim cannot serve as a throne unless they spread their wings, and when the text intends to describe the way in which the wings are spread, it says that they 'cover' the ark. After all, it is not only the wings of the cherubim which 'cover', *sôḵ^e^ḵîm* the ark. There is also the *pārōḵet*-veil itself which 'screens' the ark (Exod. 40: 3, 21—expressed by the same verb, *skk*). On the other hand, Ezekiel's cherubim, those who form the throne, do not cover anything, but they too stand with outspread wings in order to support the firmament. 1 Chron. 28: 18, which mentions the cherubim, echoes the terminology of the Pentateuch and the Book of Kings and says that the wings are outspread and 'cover' the ark. However, here the text incidentally expresses the main symbolic significance of the cherubim, viz., 'the model of the chariot', *taḇnîṯ hammerkāḇāh*. The term *merkāḇāh* implies a throne which may be in motion, for Yahweh's throne in the heavens (as described in Ezekiel's vision) is not confined to one place.

5

Another apparent difficulty is to be found in 2 Sam. 22: 11 and Ps. 18: 11, where Yahweh is described as riding upon a cherub, and not as seated on a throne of cherubim.[9] This difficulty may perhaps be resolved by explaining that 'and he rode on a cherub' has the same meaning as 'and he rode in a chariot made up by a cherub'. Thus Hab. 3: 8 says: 'that thou didst ride upon thy horses upon thy chariots of victory', where the meaning is certainly not that Yahweh rides the horses—such an image is foreign to the Old Testament—but that he appears in a chariot to which the horses are harnessed. However, even if we were to assume that the passage in David's song means that Yahweh rides on the back of a cherub, this would not preclude the idea of a throne.

In fact, the cherubim in the Old Testament appear in several guises, no one of which cancels out the other. The cherubim are heavenly creatures whom, according to J's story, God placed near the garden of Eden soon after the creation (Gen. 3: 24). Ezekiel hints at a story about a cherub who dwelt in the garden of Eden (Ezek. 28: 13–14).[10] At that time God availed himself of the

[9] See, e.g., Dibelius, op. cit., pp. 72–3 (quoting R. Smend).

[10] The LXX version deals here not with the cherub himself, but with an imaginary creature, possibly the primordial man, who dwelt in the garden of

cherubim for various purposes, and he continues to be served by them perpetually. The cherubim who were placed at the east of the garden of Eden kept watch over the road to the tree of life. The cherub who dwelt in the garden of God lived and roamed in the garden and apparently also tilled it, like man before he sinned in the legend of J. And every time God wishes to descend from heaven he can avail himself of the services of one of the cherubim and ride on one, as is poetically described in the above-mentioned passage in the song of David.

The Old Testament also mentions, as is well known, many other heavenly creatures in the general category of 'cherubim': flying seraphim, 'sons of God' and Satan, horses of fire, 'stars of God', and others. All these together are called the 'host of heaven' (1 Kgs. 22: 19; cf. Ps. 148: 2). They too served God in various ways at the time of the creation and thereafter. There were also, as we know, the beasts which God fought against and defeated (Leviathan, Rahab, the fleeing serpent, the sea dragon). All these are vestigial traces of the mythological culture which preceded the emergence of Yahwism within the tribes of Israel. Out of these mostly pre-Israelite concepts the Old Testament has retained the characters of the cherubim in particular, transferring them from myth to the domain of cultic symbolism. Figures of cherubim were used as a decoration for the walls of the Jerusalem temple, and their carved images were affixed in the holy of holies. One must remember, however, that in myth the cherubim had various functions, of which the duty to form a throne for Yahweh was only one. But to the cherubim in the ritual—or at least to the specific cherubim sculptured in the inner sanctum—a sole function was assigned, perhaps the most important of all those attributed to the cherubim in myth: to form a throne for God.

THE FOOTSTOOL AND THE VARIATIONS IN THE FORM OF THE CHERUBIM

6

If the *kappōret* with its cherubim is God's throne, the ark itself is the footstool of the throne. This follows from the position of

God in the company of the cherub and was probably subordinate to him. See commentaries.

the ark under the wings of the cherubim, and indeed it is logical to assume that a throne would not lack a footstool.

From archaeological parallels it is now clear why the two tables of the law were placed within the ark. It seems that the practice of burying various books, documents, written oaths, and covenants in a special case under the images of gods in temples was common in Egypt and the Hittite kingdom—and apparently throughout the ancient Near East. In these cases the documents concerned served as a 'testimony' before the gods, which both parties would take good care to observe.[11] In the same way the tables of the law kept in the ark were a kind of 'legal' document, binding as it were upon both parties, especially the party which had taken upon itself to keep the commandments graven in the stone. The text of the tables is referred to, as we know, either as 'testimony', *'ēdût*, the term used in P, or as 'covenant', *b^{e}rît*, the term commonly used in D (and possibly in all the non-priestly sources). In the eyes of the ancients, no place could be more fitting for such a document than an ark which was the footstool of God's throne. Here P's term 'testimony' is particularly apt, for 'covenant' implies that the document only constitutes a contract between the two parties, whereas 'testimony' implies that it is a token before the throne of glory, a confirmatory evidence brought before the highest authority. The fact that this 'legal' document is written on stone is of course simply a sign of antiquity. Incidentally, D mentions that a book of *tôrāh* is also put 'by the side of the ark of the covenant of Yahweh your God, that it may be there for a witness [*l^{e}'ēd*, i.e. a testimony] against you' (Deut. 31: 26).

7

These two symbols tally well with the primary image of the temple as God's dwelling place—an image in which, as has been pointed

[11] See J. Herrmann, 'Ägyptische Analogien zum Funde des Deuteronomiums', *ZAW* 28 (1908), 299–300; Gressmann, op. cit., p. 43; Torczyner (Tur-Sinai), *Bundeslade*, pp. 37–8; idem, *EM* i. 542; idem, הלשון והספר, iii. pp. 60–1 (nevertheless, Tur-Sinai objects to the idea of the footstool; ibid., p. 7). See also the detailed discussion by R. de Vaux, *Bible et Orient*, pp. 231–59, 272–3. Something of the kind was apparently also customary in the sanctuaries of ancient Arabia. See J. A. Montgomery, *Arabia and the Bible* (Philadelphia, 1934), p. 130. Montgomery does not make clear in what part of the temple the documents were placed, but it is probable that there too they were placed beneath the feet of the gods.

out, the biblical conception of the house of God is rooted. It is only reasonable that God's house should contain a throne and that the throne should be provided with a footstool. And where God's throne and footstool are, there is his house.

As it has been shown in Chapter XI, these two symbols also fit in well with the cultic activities carried on in the outer sanctum by means of the lamps, incense, shewbread, and the ritual functions of the priestly vestments. To be sure, these two sets of symbols differ in importance. The throne and footstool indicate God's very presence in that place, and therefore constitute the essence of the house of God. Accordingly, the whole temple is sometimes designated 'throne' or 'footstool', after these two focal symbols (cf. Isa. 66: 1; Jer. 3: 16–17; 14: 21; 17: 12; Ezek. 43: 7; Lam. 2: 1; 1 Chron. 28: 2;[12] see also Ps. 99: 5: 'Exalt the Lord our God and bow down to his footstool'; cf. also Ps. 132: 7[13]). In ancient oriental temples, as in Solomon's temple as well as in P's tabernacle, the throne and footstool are kept apart in a closed room. Two special zones are thus formed within the house of God: the inner room where the deity itself is concealed, and the larger ante-chamber, where twice daily the priest carries out the prescribed ritual. Yet, despite the difference in order of importance, it is impossible to ignore the inter-connection between the two rooms, which are indeed inseparable parts of one structure.

We must again remind ourselves that even though the cherubim and the ark symbolize God's throne and footstool, the Old Testament does not 'bind' God to them, and does not for one moment

[12] The words 'and for the footstool of our God' in this verse are not parallel to the words 'for the ark of the covenant of the Lord', and do not denote the *kappōret*, but refer back to the 'house of rest'. What the text really means is this: I wish to build a house of rest for the ark, a house of rest for (i.e. that shall be) a footstool for our God. Thus the expression 'for the footstool of our God' does not denote here, as one might be led to believe, a concrete object, but is merely a designation for the whole house, in the manner of other biblical turns of speech. Cf., however, the commentaries of I. Benzinger (KHC, 1901), E. L. Curtis (ICC, 1910), and W. Rudolph (HAT, 1955), ad loc.

[13] The words 'his footstool' in the latter two verses do not refer to the ark—as many commentators have claimed—but to the entire temple. In Ps. 132: 7 it is parallel to *l^emišk^enôtāyw*, 'to his dwelling place' in its first half. The parallelism 'his dwelling place—his footstool' of this last verse should be compared with that of Ps. 5: 8: 'Thy house—thy holy temple'. It is thus clear that 'his footstool' does not signify the ark but the whole temple. In the Bible, the symbolic significance of the footstool, which is attributed to the ark, is already expressed only indirectly, being applied to the temple in general (*pace* de Vaux, *Bible et Orient*, pp. 234, 272).

assume that his place is there alone. Yahweh's chief dwelling place is imagined to be in heaven, and there on high is his throne, supported by living cherubim. It is only as an image of those heavenly cherubim that two carved cherubim are set up in the temple's innermost shrine. In other words, the throne in the holy of holies is but a model of the throne on high. The heavenly cherubim are, in the words of Ezekiel, 'living creatures' (Ezek. 1: 5, 13–15, 19 *et al.*), endowed with a will, while the cherubim over the ark are but metal statues. The heavenly cherubim are immense, while those in P are confined to the two extremes of a tablet which is two cubits and a half long and a cubit and a half broad. Nevertheless, the tabernacle's metal cherubim also form a seat. For this is the place whence Yahweh speaks to Moses (Exod. 25: 22; Num. 7: 89), and it is upon these cherubim that he 'appears in the cloud' (Lev. 16: 2). Such duality in the way in which the deity is conceived is to be found throughout the ancient world, and is particularly evident in the realm of cult. In the nature of every god there is a cosmic element, yet he is believed to 'dwell' in his temple, or temples, and to be connected with the service offered therein.[14] However, the real essence of the biblical God cannot be comprehended through external modes of behaviour and cultic symbolism. In fact, the biblical conception of God tries to free itself from mythological restrictions. Here, as in other spheres of spiritual life, the Old Testament makes use of set symbols handed down from pre-biblical mythological culture—throne, footstool, and everything else appertaining to the house of God—but within this set of symbols it postulates a God whose nature is essentially non-mythological.

8

As regards the archaeological finds pertinent to representations of cherubim, one must first distinguish between hybrid creatures in general and cherubim in particular. The ancient Near East teems with representations of hybrid creatures: bulls with human faces, lions with human faces (sphinxes), snakes with legs, four-legged beasts with bird's heads, human figures with eagle's heads, and many others—all with or without wings. It is a world in itself,

[14] Thus, one should not wonder when a psalmist exclaims in the same breath: 'Yahweh is in his holy temple, Yahweh's throne is in heaven' (Ps. 11: 4).

tortuous and varied, and the creatures that inhabit it have been given a host of names. The cherubim are but one species from this fantastic world. Obviously their place is among the winged hybrids, but it is hard to determine when an archaeological representation does depict a cherub. Scholars have long felt the Assyrian affinity of the cherubim, even before their name turned up in Assyrian texts. There were those, however, who connected them with Egypt,[15] while others considered them to be of Canaanite origin.[16]

Ezekiel, as has been indicated (above, sect. 4), describes the cherubim as a triple combination of beast (with soles 'like those of a calf's foot'), man (one pair of legs, one pair of 'arms', erect quasi-human posture), and bird (wings). It appears, however, that within these limits there were possible variations even in the biblical conception of cherubim.

Thus, in the tabernacle, each cherub definitely has only two wings (Exod. 25: 20; 37: 9), and likewise in Solomon's temple (1 Kgs. 6: 24–7). In Ezekiel, on the other hand, they are provided with four wings (Ezek. 1: 6, 8, 11, 23 *et al.*). In the tabernacle each cherub has one face (Exod. 25: 20; 37: 9: 'and their faces one to another'), whereas according to Ezekiel each cherub has four faces—those of a man, a lion, an ox, and an eagle (Ezek. 1: 10).[17] Yet in another chapter the prophet substitutes the face of a 'cherub' for the face of an ox (ibid. 10: 14), which may perhaps suggest that generally a cherub had the face of an ox. On the other hand, it should be remembered that J tells the story of man who worked and guarded the garden of Eden and was expelled from it for his sin (Gen. 2: 8–15; 3), whereas in Ezekiel's version a similar story is told about a cherub (Ezek. 28: 13–15).[18] J also relates that after the expulsion of man, God ordered the cherubim to guard the entrance to the garden of Eden (Gen. 3: 24). These analogies

[15] Gressmann, op. cit., pp. 9 ff., 70–2.

[16] W. F. Albright, 'What were the Cherubim', *BA* 1 (1938), 1–3 (basing his observations upon the bas-relief on the sarcophagus of Ahiram king of Byblos).

[17] In order to understand Ezek. 41: 18–19, where the cherub is mentioned as having only two faces, it should be remembered that here a two-dimensional picture on a flat surface, not a three-dimensional image in perspective (as in chaps. 1 and 10) is being referred to. It is well known that in general ancient Near Eastern art tends to draw figures in profile, since this is easier than drawing them *en face*. This could be why the third face is absent from the walls of Ezekiel's temple.

[18] Cf. above, n. 10.

may perhaps indicate that the cherubim of the garden of Eden had one face, and that, in the likeness of man. Moreover, Ezekiel adds to his cherubim, or at least to the creatures supporting God's chariot, several 'organs' not mentioned in earlier sources, such as the wheels full of eyes, containing within them 'the spirit of the living creature' (Ezek. 1: 15–21; 10: 9–13, 16–17).[19] All this proves that in the world of the Old Testament the cherubim's image was not fixed in every detail, but was subject, within certain limits, to variation. Furthermore, similarity of features is not in itself enough to identify the biblical cherub in archaeological remains. It is no less important to find in the Near East the creature's specific name—cherub. Now it appears that the name *kurību* has so far been found only in Assyrian texts, but they do not enable us to determine the form of the creature to which this name is assigned.[20] Its identity in Assyrian examples seems therefore to be as yet a matter of conjecture.

Even, however, if it is agreed that the biblical cherub has real parallels in Assyria—as it appears to have—this should not be taken as an indication of simple and direct dependence of Israel on Assyria in this matter. The concept of the cherub, like most of the vestigial mythological concepts connected with the 'heavenly host', certainly reached Israel indirectly, either through the nomadic tribes which, prior to their settlement in Canaan, roamed within the confines of the Mesopotamian culture, or by means of a Canaanite intermediation. Indeed, the cherub appears as early as in the story of the garden of Eden, that is to say, in that stratum of the Book of Genesis (Gen. 1–11) which is unique in its distinctively Mesopotamian stamp. The ancient cosmogonical lore which had its primary roots in Mesopotamia eventually became acclimatized to Israel. And out of all this pre-Israelite heritage the image of the cherubim succeeded in becoming the centre of the sacral–cultic symbolism of the First Temple in Jerusalem.

19 It is not the spirit of life, *rû^{a}ḥ ḥayyîm* which is contained within the wheels, but the 'spirit of the living creature', *rû^{a}ḥ haḥayyāh*, with the definite article (Ezek. 1: 20–1). This signifies that the wheels are not a mechanical fitting but are animate; their 'spirit', however, is that of the whole 'living creature' (cf. 10: 15–17). The cherubim and the wheels have one spirit.

20 Some relevant sources were quoted by R. Pfeiffer, 'Cherubim', *JBL* 41 (1922), 249–50; B. Meissner, *Babylonien und Assyrien*, ii (Heidelberg, 1925), p. 50. See also *CAD* viii, s.v. *kurību*. The word cherub has so far not been found in Phoenician or Ugaritic texts.

XIV

THE NON-PRIESTLY IMAGE OF THE TENT OF *MÔ'ĒD*

I

IN P the ark is an inseparable part of the tabernacle; it is removed from the tabernacle only when the latter is completely dismantled, to be reassembled in another place. It has already been stated that for all its journeyings P's tabernacle, by its nature, is just a temple, except that the exigencies of the march through the desert compel the Israelites to carry this imaginary temple from place to place, till they have borne it in their midst to its final resting-place at Shiloh. It is precisely the non-priestly sources that consider the ark to be a portable object, for it is their assumption that during the wanderings in the wilderness the ark was not placed as yet in a house of God.[1] However, one can hardly imagine that these sources would suppose that on their wanderings the Israelites carried the ark with them just as it was. No doubt these sources take it for granted that whenever the Israelite host halted, a special tent was set up in which the ark was placed until the next move. For usually the ark is to be found in 'the midst of the camp', *qereḇ hammaḥaneh* (Num. 14: 44). Only on the march does it travel at the head of the Israelite column accompanied by the cloud of the Lord (ibid. 10: 33–4). In the various stations this cloud presumably rests upon the tent containing the ark. It is true that the non-priestly sources nowhere mention such a temporary tent as the housing of the ark; but then, in the Pentateuch the ark itself is mentioned by these sources only rarely—once in J (Num. 10: 33–6), once in E (ibid. 14: 44), and twice in D (Deut. 10: 1–8; 31: 25–6). These brief references are insufficient to describe all the circumstances connected with the maintenance of the ark, yet the setting aside of a special tent to house it is postulated by the usual routine of life in camp. It is hardly conceivable

[1] Cf. above, pp. 65, 78 (n. 28).

that the ark should stand 'in the midst of the camp' without being covered by some kind of tent.[2]

A historical analogy for keeping the ark in a temporary tent can be found in the way in which it was housed in the city of David (2 Sam. 6: 17; 7: 2), after the decline of the house of God at Shiloh and before the building of the house of God at Jerusalem. The temporary nature of the tent set up for the ark by David stands out clearly from the recorded events of the period and we would be quite wrong to regard it, as several scholars have done, as a permanent shrine. The biblical evidence, especially 2 Sam. 7: 1–17 (as indeed Ps. 132: 2–5, 7–10, 13–14), states explicitly that David himself never intended this tent to be permanent, but that it should house the ark temporarily until he built a temple of cedar-wood for it.[3] Actually, it was left for Solomon to build the

[2] D makes no more mention than J and E of a special tent for the ark, but he too must have presupposed the existence of such. Thus, when Moses gives the book of the law to the Levites, the bearers of the ark, he commands them to put the book 'beside the ark of the covenant of the Lord your God' (Deut. 31: 26)—not in the ark, but beside it. This would imply that D envisages both the ark and the book, not as standing exposed in the open, but as covered by something, presumably by tent-curtains.

[3] It is mainly Cross who contends that P's tradition of the tabernacle rests on the tent set by David in his city; see F. M. Cross, *Canaanite Myth and Hebrew Epic* (Cambridge, Mass., 1973), pp. 72, 231, 238, 382. I am certainly prepared to share his assumption (ibid., pp. 242–3 *et al.*) that the Shiloh shrine had the form of a tabernacle, as the priestly tradition actually asserts (cf. above, pp. 201–2). However, when one comes to define the nature of David's tent one's own conjecture is not enough to outweigh the explicit evidence of the sources, and no justice is done to this evidence by disparaging it as 'later tradition' (ibid., p. 231) when no alternative evidence is available at all. Nowhere does the biblical text refer to David's tent as a *miškān*, tabernacle, but as a tent only (*miškānôt*, in the plural, in Ps. 132: 5 is a conventional application of this noun, as an epithet, to the temple; cf. above, p. 14). Moreover, it has already been emphasized that according to the priestly tradition itself Shiloh is the only place in Canaan to which the tabernacle is linked (above, p. 200). Had David's tent had something to do with the tabernacle tradition, P's story would certainly have had something to tell about Jerusalem in general and about that tent in particular. Again, the use of the verb הצג with reference to the ark, as in 2 Sam. 6: 17, is quite rare and is applied to cases of irregular, provisional placement, when the ark is visible (as opposed to its regular placement, when it is intended to be concealed). Cf. 1 Sam. 5: 2; 2 Sam. 15: 24 (the consonant ק here is substituted for ג, both of these being palatals). The verb הצג in general, even when not applied to the ark, frequently has the shade of meaning of 'exhibiting', 'displaying' an object or a person to the observer. See, e.g., Gen. 30: 38; Judg. 8: 27; Hos. 2: 5; Amos 5: 15; Jer. 51: 34 (with the preposition לפני, 'before' attached to it this verb conveys the idea of 'presenting', 'introducing'); cf. also dictionaries. Consequently, were David's tent of the category of a house of God, the text in 2 Sam. 6: 17 would certainly have applied some other verb to the ark, such as הבא (אל),

temple in the inner sanctum of which a place was found for the ark.

In this chapter our purpose is to determine whether there is any connection between the tent in which, as envisaged by the non-priestly sources, the ark should be housed temporarily and another tent—the *'ōhel môʿēd*, usually rendered by EVV as 'tent of meeting' (NEB: 'tent of presence'), which is mentioned explicitly in the non-priestly sources (as indeed, though differently, also in P). In other words, it is our purpose to consider whether, according to the non-priestly sources, the 'tent of meeting' contained the ark, or whether there was no connection between the two. The answer to this question will throw light on the true nature of *'ōhel môʿēd* and show whether it is conceived of as cultic in essence, or as an institution of an entirely different category.

THE DISTINGUISHING FEATURES OF *'OHEL MÔʿĒD*

2

Mentions of *'ōhel môʿēd* occur three times in E: in connection with the theophany on Mount Horeb (Exod. 33: 5–11), the ecstatic afflatus of the seventy elders (Num. 11: 16–29), and Miriam's leprosy (ibid. 12: 4–10). In D this tent is mentioned once, in the introductory section to Moses' Song (Deut. 31: 14–15).[4]

The most significant reference for our purpose would seem to be in the first passage (Exod. 33: 5–11). Here we are told that, following the incident of the golden calf and at God's command, the Israelites removed their ornaments (ibid., vv. 5–6). What they did with these ornaments we are apparently not told, for the next

'bring in' (cf. Exod. 26: 33; 40: 21; 1 Kgs. 8: 6), or שים, 'put in' (cf. Exod. 40: 3; 1 Kgs. 8: 21). The designation 'the tent of Yahweh' in 2 Kgs. 2: 28–30 (cf. 1: 39) is simply applied to that tent in which the ark was housed. Otherwise it will imply the temple (cf. above, pp. 14, 221) and be regarded as anachronistic in character.

[4] The first three passages all apparently belong to E, though various scholars assign one or other of them to a later layer of E (E_2) or to J. As for the fourth passage, the whole section of Deut. 31: 14–23 is considered, in the main, as not belonging to D and is commonly ascribed to JE. The possibility still exists that D himself might have absorbed into his text some fragments cited almost verbatim from an earlier source, the earlier source being E on which, in my opinion, D is dependent in general; cf. pp. 92, 334. However, the question of the exact literary identity of these four passages is of no decisive consequence to us here. Since nobody would deny their non-priestly character, it only remains to define the true nature of the *'ōhel môʿēd* referred to in all four of them.

verse continues (ibid., v. 7): 'Now Moses used to take the tent and to pitch it outside the camp, far off from the camp; and he called it *'ōhel mô'ēd*'. Most scholars suppose that this verse had originally been preceded by E's version of the preparation of the ark and that this was later excised by the redactor, because in P he already had a detailed description of the ark's construction and form. In E the ornaments taken off by the Israelites were used to prepare a magnificent ark, just like the ark of P, which was sumptuously built and overlaid with gold, and then this ark was housed in the 'tent of meeting' set up by Moses. These scholars interpret the words *nāṭāh-lô* (ibid.) to mean 'pitched for the ark'.[5]

My contention is that there is no justification whatsoever for this whole conjecture. Even if some verses have been omitted between vv. 6 and 7, it is far more probable that they described the preparation of the tent itself, not of the ark. Accordingly, the ornaments which the Israelites took off at God's command were used to embellish the *'ōhel mô'ēd* just as the parallel, priestly tradition knows to relate that the Israelites brought precious materials for the construction of the *miškān* (Exod. 25: 1–8; 35: 4–9, 20–9). The ark of E was doubtless a simple affair, like the ark of D which was made of unadorned wood (Deut. 10: 1, 3), for in any conjecture

[5] First expounded by J. Wellhausen, *Die Composition des Hexateuchs*[4] (Berlin, 1963), p. 93; to be followed by, e.g., H. Holzinger, *Exodus* (KHC, 1900), pp. 108–10, 113; S. R. Driver, *Introduction to the Literature of the OT*[9] (Edinburgh, 1913), p. 38 (cf. p. 128, note); M. Dibelius, *Die Lade Jahves* (Göttingen, 1906), pp. 45–7; C. Steuernagel, *Lehrbuch der Einleitung in das AT* (Tübingen, 1912), p. 213; H. Gressmann, *Mose und seine Zeit* (Göttingen, 1913), pp. 221, 240; E. Sellin, 'Das Zelt Jahwes', *Alttestamentliche Studien R. Kittel . . . dargebracht* (Leipzig, 1913), pp. 170–2; R. Kittel, *Geschichte des Volkes Israel*, i[5–6] (Gotha, 1923), p. 327 and n. 1; Eissfeldt, *KS* ii. 283–4; Pedersen, *ILC* ii–iv. 200; A. Bentzen, *Introduction to the OT*[2] (Copenhagen, 1952), i. 100 (cf. ii. 34); Alt, *KS* iii. 241, n. 4; W. Beyerlin, *Herkunft and Geschichte der ältesten Sinaitraditionen* (Tübingen, 1961), pp. 129–36 and many others. Beyerlin, in addition, finds logical inconsistencies within the passage Exod. 33: 7–11 and assumes it to be a revision, by the E writer, of a different, and older, version of the tradition of the tent; (cf. also the treatment of this passage by, e.g., M. Görg, *Das Zelt der Begegnung* (Bonn, 1967), pp. 151–67). The above-mentioned opinion is still maintained by R. de Vaux, in his study 'Arche d'Alliance et Tente de Réunion', *Bible et Orient* (Paris, 1967), pp. 261–76; and, for that matter, by G. Henton Davis, 'The Ark of the Covenant', *ASTI* 5 (1967), 35–7. Others, though they have conceded that the 'tent of meeting' did not contain the ark, still claim that it contained an image of God and that Moses officiated there as a priest, or that it contained the ephod and that Joshua officiated there as an intermediary of divination for the public; see I. Benzinger, *Hebräische Archäologie*[3] (Leipzig, 1927), pp. 314–15, 343–4; F. Dumermuth, 'Joshua in Exod. 33: 7–11', *ThZ* 19 (1963), 161–8.

about E's conception of the ark D should serve as a better guide than P. In the words *nāṭāh-lô* the pronominal suffix can refer to Moses. For this tent in E (and D) was specially reserved for Moses: the same passage relates that Moses used to go out to the tent alone while the people stood at the entrances to their own tents and watched him until he disappeared inside. Thus the tent was primarily intended for Moses, though everyone who sought God's presence also used to go there.[6] Even if we were to surmise that in this passage E originally related something about the preparation of the ark, it would be piling conjecture on conjecture to assume that those lost verses located the ark in the 'tent of meeting'. Such a double conjecture is utterly at variance with the actual descriptions of this tent as we find them in E and D.

3

The conjecture that E's ark was placed inside *'ōhel môʿēd* is ruled out by, for example, the explicit statement that this tent was situated 'outside the camp, far off from the camp' (Exod. 33: 7). The approach to *'ōhel môʿēd* is usually expressed in E by the verb 'to go out', *yṣ'*: Moses 'goes out' to the tent, 'everyone who sought the Lord would go out to *'ōhel môʿēd*' (ibid., vv. 7–8); Yahweh says to Moses, Aaron, and Miriam, 'Come out, *ṣᵉ'û*, you three to *'ōhel môʿēd*; and the three of them came out, *wayyēṣᵉ'û*' (Num. 12: 4). This use of the verb *yṣ'* is a further indication that, in order to approach the tent, it was necessary to go out *of the camp*. Similarly, after every communion with Yahweh in the tent, Moses 'turned again into the camp' (Exod. 33: 11). The seventy elders who assembled round the tent received the ecstatic afflatus far

[6] The particle *lô* in Exod. 33: 7 is taken by some commentators for a *dativus commodi*, against which Beyerlin (op. cit., p. 131, n. 4) remarks that according to Gesenius–Kautzsch–Cowley, *Grammar*, § 199*s* such a *dativus* occurs 'especially in colloquial language and later style', and therefore in Exod. 33: 7 the pronominal suffix should refer to the ark. Yet, it is quite possible that in Exod. 33: 7 there is no *dativus commodi* (where the particle can be removed without altering the meaning of a phrase) but just a regular use of the prepositional ל with the pronominal suffix (in which case the employment of the particle is indispensable), implying that Moses pitched the tent for himself, i.e. mainly for his own use. It should be remembered that all the instances dealt with in the *Grammar*, § 119*s* are of the reflexive use, which is not exactly the case in Exod. 33: 7. At the same time I find nothing unnatural in the fact that within two similar turns of phrase, the pronominal suffix would refer in one context to a person (Exod. 33: 7), while in another context to an object (2 Sam. 6: 17).

from the camp and the whole marvel of the occasion lay in the fact that the two men, Eldad and Medad, who had remained in the camp 'and had not gone out, *wᵉlō' yāṣᵉ'û*, to the tent' also fell into a prophetic frenzy. Moses learnt of their being divinely inspired only from a youth who ran out to him in the distant tent and brought him the news. Afterwards Moses and the elders 'returned to the camp' (Num. 11: 26–30).[7]

The place of the ark, on the other hand, was generally presumed to be 'in the midst of the camp' (Num. 14: 44). Thus, when Joshua falls prostrate before the ark (Josh. 7: 6) and when all the people of Israel stand on either side of the ark between Mount Gerizim and Mount Ebal (ibid. 8: 33), it is clearly in the midst of the people. Though the passages about the preparation of the ark are missing from the extant sections of J and E, it cannot be maintained that either of them envisaged the permanent site of the ark as being far from the camp, as E does in the case of *'ōhel mô'ēd*.[8] Only on the march did the ark travel in front of the Israelites (Num. 10: 33), and when they crossed the Jordan it went on two thousand cubits ahead of them to show them the way (Josh. 3: 4). But obviously the order of march was quite distinct from the normal order of camping.

4

For a proper understanding of the nature of *'ōhel mô'ēd* in E and D we must further note that, according to their assumption,

[7] Such, perhaps, is also the precise significance of the text in D: 'And Moses and Joshua went (i.e. went some distance from the camp) and presented themselves in *'ōhel mô'ēd*' (Deut. 31: 14).

[8] Wellhausen (*PGI*, 39, n. 1; p. 124) maintained that the 'tent of meeting', which served to house the ark, was outside the camp, just as the ancient sanctuaries were outside the city. However, to suppose that the sanctuaries (i.e. temples, houses of God) were usually located outside the city is simply to blur the difference between them and high-places. Furthermore, it is certainly inaccurate to regard the *'ōhel mô'ēd* in E as a cultic institution after the pattern of a sanctuary. Cf. the strained arguments on this problem made, for example, by Gressmann, *Mose und seine Zeit*, p. 241; and G. Beer and K. Galling, *Exodus* (HAT, 1939), pp. 158–9. S. R. Driver too, though he also made quite incisive remarks on the difference between the two categories of *'ōhel mô'ēd* (*Exodus* (CBSC, 1918), pp. 257–8, 427–8), did not refrain from stating that 'the tent of JE, like that of P, sheltered the ark' (p. 258). For the analogy between Joshua the attendant of Moses and Samuel the acolyte of Eli, which is implied in Wellhausen's remarks (loc. cit.; as well as, e.g., by Beyerlin, op. cit., pp. 132–3, 138), see below.

theophany does not occur inside the tent, but always outside, at the entrance to the tent. It is true that Moses first goes into the tent, but he does not meet God while inside. Only later does the pillar of cloud descend and stand 'at the door of the tent' (Exod. 33: 9–10). The people see the pillar of cloud from the camp and prostrate themselves, every man at his tent door, while Yahweh speaks out of the cloud to Moses who is close by. The seventy elders are made to stand 'round about the tent', i.e., outside it; Yahweh descends in the cloud, speaks to Moses, and causes some of the spirit that was upon Moses to rest upon the elders, so that they are filled with prophetic inspiration (Num. 11: 24–5). So again in the case of Moses, Aaron, and Miriam: the three of them leave the camp and presumably first of all enter the tent. Then the pillar of cloud descends and stands 'at the door of the tent'. In this case Yahweh, who is speaking from the cloud, actually calls Aaron and Miriam outside and the two of them come out of the tent. At the entrance Yahweh speaks to them and finally shows his displeasure—'and he departed, and the cloud removed from over the tent' (ibid. 12: 5, 9–10). Similarly in D: Moses and Joshua present themselves in *'ōhel môʿēd*, then the pillar of cloud descends and stands 'by the door of the tent' and Yahweh speaks his words (Deut. 31: 15).[9]

These unique descriptions of theophany prove that the interior of the tent is not considered to be the place of meeting with the deity. The interior serves merely as the place where the worshipper presents himself, as implied by the verbs *hityaṣṣēḇ* or *niṣṣaḇ* which are preferred in this context.[10] The interior is simply a place set aside for concentration and for the sharpening of the worshipper's faculties in preparation, so to speak, for the revelation of the divine presence. But the presence itself is revealed outside, at the entrance. What we have here is not a cultic institution housing the deity in its focal centre, but a tent where the solitary worshipper might receive divine inspiration from outside its empty interior—not the deity's permanent 'abode', but a place appointed for a fleeting prophetic vision.

[9] This point, as well as the analogies made in the following section, were left completely unnoticed by de Vaux in his examination of my arguments (*Bible et Orient*, pp. 265–75). Nor am I convinced by his actual proposals, where he tries to retain the thought that the ark is presumed to be housed within *'ōhel môʿēd*.

[10] Num. 11: 16; Deut. 31: 14; cf. Exod. 33: 8 and below, sect. 5.

How far the interior of such a tent is from serving as the meeting-place with the deity, can be seen from the fact that Joshua the son of Nun 'did not depart from the tent' (Exod. 33: 11). As far as one can infer from the references, Joshua, though so closely involved in all that Moses does, is not allowed to share the prophetic vision with his master. His sole task in the tent is to assist the prophet: he is his 'attendant' (ibid.), 'the servant of Moses, one of his chosen men' (Num. 11: 28).[11] Only when they present themselves in the tent for the last time, when Joshua is to be appointed by God himself as the leader of the people, does he hear the divine word in *'ōhel mô'ēd* (Deut. 31: 14–15, 23).

That this tent has nothing in common with any temple can further be seen from the fact that it is nowhere associated with priests (or Levites), still less with sacrifices or permanent rituals, or indeed with any cult in the priestly sense of the word. When Moses wishes to have the book of the law placed beside the ark, he gives an order to that effect to the Levites, who thus fulfil a priestly function (Deut. 31: 25–6), but he is never assisted by the Levites in any act of his in *'ōhel mô'ēd*. And it goes without saying that in the tent Joshua performs the office of prophet's attendant, not priestly acolyte.

5

In fact, the theophany at the non-priestly *'ōhel mô'ēd* simply reproduces, in miniature of course, the basic features of the divine revelation on Mount Sinai. The theophany at Sinai also takes place outside the camp. In preparation for it, Moses brings the people 'out of the camp to meet God' (Exod. 19: 17), and some distance from the camp (cf. ibid. 32: 19). The people 'present themselves', *mityaṣṣᵉḇîm*, at the foot of the mountain (ibid. 19: 17). Yahweh descends upon the mountain in a pillar of cloud and from out of this pillar he speaks (ibid. 19: 9; cf. Ps. 99: 7). Whenever Moses goes up to the mountain he is closely followed by his attendant, Joshua (Exod. 24: 13; 32: 17), and yet Joshua does not hear the divine word with him. In the ecstatic afflatus of the seventy elders we may find a parallel to that other occasion when,

[11] Moses, who is described in E and D as a *nāḇî'*, is thus attended by Joshua just as Elijah is attended by Elisha (1 Kgs. 19: 19–21; 2 Kgs. 2: 1–15), and the latter by Gehazi (ibid. 4: 12–15, 25–36 *et al.*).

according to J's variation of this theme, seventy elders were vouchsafed a glimpse of the God of Israel upon Mount Sinai (ibid. 24: 9–11).

Similarly, there are certain features connecting the theophanies at *'ōhel môʿēd* to the one which, in J's depiction, took place in the cleft of the rock: Moses *niṣṣāḇ*, i.e. waits reverently, on the rock and when the glory of the Lord appears he huddles in the cleft and sees only Yahweh's back (ibid. 33: 21–3). The cleft in the rock here performs for Moses the same function as the interior of *'ōhel môʿēd*, where the prophet usually hides himself, so to speak, as long as the cloud of glory stands at the entrance to the tent (unless Yahweh explicitly summons him outside). The cleft in the rock, for its part, may recall the cave on Mount Horeb where, in the narrative which displays E's traits, the prophet Elijah, having taken refuge in the cave, hears Yahweh's voice calling him outside. The prophet then goes out and stands at the entrance to the cave to 'see' Yahweh who passes before him and speaks to him (1 Kgs. 19: 9–14). To be sure, in that case Yahweh's glory is symbolized not by a cloud, but by a storm followed by 'still small voice'; nevertheless, the cave itself is for Elijah, roughly but clearly enough, what *'ōhel môʿēd* is for Moses.

A further analogy may be found in J's story of the second revelation on Mount Sinai. Moses goes up and 'presents himself', *niṣṣāḇ* or *mityaṣṣēḇ*, on the Mount and 'calls on the name of the Lord'.[12] After descending in a cloud Yahweh passes before Moses, and Moses proclaims the divine attributes. After prostrating himself in humble obeisance, Moses utters his request: 'If now I have found favour in thy sight, O Lord', etc. (ibid. 34: 2, 5–9). This may well have been the rite observed by 'every one who sought the Lord', who presented himself in the solitude of a tent like *'ōhel môʿēd*: he called on the name of Yahweh, prostrated himself and did obeisance; and, as a final stage, when the divine presence was believed to have arrived at the entrance to that tent,

[12] The root *yṣb* in the *nip'al* conjugation is further used of Samuel when he is said to be surrounded by the ecstatic prophets (1 Sam. 19: 20). It is also employed, both in *nip'al* and *hitpa'ēl*, of people in a state of expectation of a divine performance (Exod. 14: 13; 1 Sam. 12: 16; cf. Isa. 21: 8; Hab. 2: 1). The affinity between the phenomena of group ecstasy and prophets acting in companies, as they appear in connection with Samuel (1 Sam. 10: 5–6, 10–11; 19: 20–4), Elijah (2 Kgs. 2: 3–18; cf. 1 Kgs. 22: 10–12), and Elisha (2 Kgs. 4: 1, 38–44 *et al.*), on the one hand, and the case of the seventy elders (Num. 11: 16–30), on the other, is too obvious to be emphasized.

the worshipper would utter his request and might expect to hear a divine reply.

It can thus be clearly seen how essential the difference between this tent and a temple (or, for that matter, the tabernacle) is: the latter serves as a hiding-abode for the deity, while the former is basically a hiding-place from the deity. Both institutions have their origin in the notion that no human being can see God. In both of them the theophany takes the form of a cloud. But they differ fundamentally in the manner in which the cloud appears and in the place where it rests. Indeed, it can be said that this fundamental distinction is already evident in the very names of the two institutions: the word *miškān*, tabernacle indicates the place where God *šōḵēn*, dwells, i.e., his abode; whereas *'ōhel mô'ēd* (the latter noun being derived from the root *y'd*) describes the place to which he comes at an appointed time, the tent to the entrance of which he descends in response to prophetic invocation, only to leave it when the communion with him is over.[13]

Consequently, in E (and D) there are two outstanding tents existing independently of each other in the Israelite camp: one of them presumably provides the temporary covering for the ark (above, sects. 2–3), whereas the second is absolutely empty. The first is found within the camp, whereas the second is outside it and far away from it. The first serves as the temporary housing of a holy object, whereas the second is a place where men present themselves before Yahweh and receive a prophetic ecstasy. In the first, Levitical priests officiate, in the second the prophet's attendant. In short, the first is, as it were, an 'embryo' of a house of God, that is eventually to be built after the settlement in Canaan, whereas the second is a kind of permanent reflection of the revelation on Mount Sinai (or indeed vice versa, the latter being modelled after the prophetic institution).

[13] The point here is not to arrive at the primary meaning of *mô'ēd* according to extra-biblical sources, but to define how it is understood in the biblical sources themselves; contrast the position taken by F. M. Cross, *Canaanite Myth and Hebrew Epic*, p. 231, n. 52; cf. also, for that matter, R. J. Clifford, 'The Tent of El and the Israelite Tent of Meeting', *CBQ* 33 (1971), 224–7. Cross himself admits (ibid., p. 300) that in P, the term *'ōhel mô'ēd* is already understood as 'the tent of divine–human meeting', 'the tent of revelation' (cf. below, pp. 273–4), which is not its ancient Canaanite connotation. But the same meaning is actually attributed to this term in the non-priestly sources as well, fragmentary though they are. At the same time, it is highly essential to give heed to the fact that in the term *'ōhel mô'ēd* the Pentateuchal sources comprehend two institutions which are actually distinct from each other.

THE TENT OF *MÔʿĒD* AND THE TEMPLE

6

The difference between the tent of *môʿēd* and the ark is so striking that some scholars have in fact admitted that this tent was not intended as a covering for the ark and that the passage in Exod. 33: 7–11 (or rather, the verses which are missing from that passage) cannot be taken as implying that the tent contained the ark.[14] But even those scholars who have given the correct formal interpretation of the passage do not seem to be in a position to provide an accurate definition of the tent. They rightly presume that E conceived of this tent as being empty and as quite distinct from the tent which covered the ark. They regard, however, the empty tent as a cultic institution, as the one and only centre in the Israelite camp consecrated to Yahweh's worship. They therefore explain the *'ōhel môʿēd* and the ark as alternative but mutually exclusive forms of cult. Such an explanation at once becomes caught up in arguments for distinguishing various 'layers' in the same source.[15] It has even been sought to explain these alternatives in terms of historical and sociological development. The empty tent, it was argued, is a type of shrine which, though found at various levels of civilization, is most common in nomadic societies. The ark, on the other hand, is characteristic of settled communities. The empty tent was, as it were, the Yahwistic shrine of the southern tribes, while the ark was a Yahwistic emblem of the Joseph tribes. It was David who first combined the two by placing the ark in the tent.[16]

[14] See especially R. Hartmann, 'Zelt and Lade', *ZAW* 37 (1917–18), 213 and the bibliography listed there; also above, p. 263, n. 5, and the following notes.

[15] Thus, it is argued, E_1 spoke of the ark and knew of a tent which housed it, while E_2 makes no mention of the ark, since for him the tent has become of greater importance. The later period objected, as it were, to the anthropomorphic conception of God's being 'housed' in the ark, and therefore connected the theophany with the tent which is a supposedly loftier symbolism. See, e.g., B. Baentsch, *Exodus* (GHK, 1903), pp. 274–6 (on his theory, Exod. 33: 7–11 belongs to E_2 since it does not mention the ark; on exactly the same arguments, others assigned this passage to E_1 and Num. 11: 16 ff. to E_2, assuming that originally the ark had been mentioned in the first passage).

[16] See Hartmann, art. cit., 216 ff., 239–42. A similar view is held by J. Morgenstern, 'The Ark, the Ephod and the Tent of Meeting', *HUCA* 18 (1943–4), 17–18, 23–30, 32–46 (the 'tent of meeting' was the shrine of the southern tribes, like the empty *qubbah* of the pre-Islamic Arabs; the *qubbah* of the northern tribes, on the other hand, contained fetishes). It is of interest that similar ideas had been

I believe that these literary and historical speculations need no detailed refutation. Suffice it to point out that they are invalidated from the start by the simple fact that the tent of *mô'ēd* as envisaged by E and D is not a priestly institution, nor is it intended for the performance of a regular ritual, and it is therefore in no sense an alternative to the ark. The tent of *mô'ēd* and the ark are two institutions derived from different social and spiritual spheres of ancient Israelite life—prophecy (or *nābî'*ism) as against priesthood—each of which evolved its own particular symbols and rites. And the essential difference between the two is evident, at the very least, in their different positions in relation to the camp.

On the broad canvas portraying Israel's life in the wilderness, the Pentateuchal sources find room for all manner of phenomena which were in existence when the people were settled in Canaan. Some of these phenomena are described as fully as possible, while others are presented in an 'embryonic' form, or completely omitted, because of the special circumstances of life in the desert encampment. It all depends on the preconceived notions, emphasis, and particular viewpoint of the source in question. Israel's life in Canaan was varied and many-sided and, after all, this many-sidedness may well have been reflected on to the desert period. Hence the tent of *mô'ēd* and the ark represent distinct phenomena existing in historical reality: the first provides a retreat for prophetic ecstasy, removed from human habitation, the second belongs in the heart of the community. That in E and D both these two institutions have the form of tents should not mislead us: after all, the whole Israelite encampment consists of tents. The point is that not one, but two different tents are intended by these sources, both being maintained in the camp simultaneously.

7

P is unique in that it combines its tabernacle and the prophetic retreat of *'ōhel mô'ēd* into a single institution. Hence, in P, the *'ōhel mô'ēd* is not located outside the camp, nor does the divine

advanced by Morgenstern twenty-five years previously, in his article 'The Tent of Meeting', *JAOS* 38 (1918), 125–9. In this earlier article, however, it seems to me that Morgenstern hit the mark in several details. There he defined the character of *'ōhel mô'ēd* in 'J' quite correctly (Exod. 33: 7–11 was assigned by him to J) and he rightly felt that the descriptions of the prophetic revelation connected with *'ōhel mô'ēd* were essentially of the same nature as what is related of Moses in the cleft of the rock and of Elijah in the cave on Mount Horeb.

cloud descend to its entrance; instead, the *'ōhel môʿēd* is identified with the temple in the centre of the camp and its cloud becomes one with the cloud that is ever present upon the wings of the cherubim in the inner sanctum. For the priestly writers the prophetic ecstasy is virtually unknown—not even Moses is granted by them the epithet of *nāḇî'*.[17] All in all, in P the *'ōhel môʿēd* accords with the hierocentric conceptions concerning the temple and its sanctity which are central to this source. Moses enters the temple alone, while neither Joshua nor any other non-priest is permitted even to set foot inside it.

Of this single institution P uses the terms *miškān* and *'ōhel môʿēd* indiscriminately, without intending any difference in meaning.[18] Indeed, the use of the prophetic term is somehow slightly more common and even occurs in connection with matters of a purely priestly nature, as in the sections describing the sacrificial laws (Lev. chaps. 1–5; 6–7), or the two sections dealing with the installation of the priests (Exod. 29; Lev. 8–9) throughout which only the term *'ōhel môʿēd* is used. We also find the composite form *miškan 'ōhel môʿēd* (Exod. 39: 32; 40: 2, 6, 29; cf. 39: 40; similarly in 1 Chron. 6: 17). The priestly writers explain the name *'ōhel môʿēd* in the prophetic sense of the words: *'ᵃšer 'iwwāʿēd lāḵem šāmmāh*, 'where I will come to you at an appointed time' (Exod. 29: 42–3). However, the same interpretation is also applied by them to the word *ʿēdût*, as if this too had the significance of 'God's coming at an appointed time' (ibid. 30: 6; Num. 17: 19; cf. Exod. 25: 22; 30: 36). Clearly, in this case, we simply have a popular etymology based on the association of similar sounds, of the type found everywhere in the Old Testament. In fact, *ʿēdût* is derived from *ʿûd*, to bear witness, not from *yʿd*, to appoint. Hence, as it has been stated in the preceding chapter, *ʿēdût* refers to the legal 'document' deposited in the ark, that is, the tables, which serve as a witness before God and are placed under his throne; it does not refer to the appearance of the divine cloud

[17] Paradoxically enough, this epithet is applied once in P to no other than Aaron (Exod. 7: 1). But its use is somewhat different there.

[18] Alternative names employed in P for the tabernacle are *miškan hāʿēdût*, tabernacle of testimony (Exod. 38: 21; Num. 1: 50, 53; 10: 11) and *'ōhel hāʿēdût*, tent of testimony (Num. 9: 15; 17: 23; 18: 2). L. Rost ('Die Wohnstätte des Zeugnisses', *Festschrift F. Baumgärtel* (Erlangen, 1959), pp. 158–65) claims—in my opinion, for rather shaky reasons—that the former combination is extremely late, whereas the latter is not even touched on in his discussion.

which results from prophetic invocation. The roots *ʿûd* and *yʿd* though cognate in form, are different in meaning; and *ʿēdût* and *môʿēd* are two distinct conceptions. Except that in P, where the two originally distinct phenomena signified by these words have merged into a single entity, the semantic distinction between the words themselves has also become blurred.[19]

8

One must now ask how far all this corresponds to historical reality. Was the special retreat for prophetic inspiration through communion with God, as depicted in the form of E(D)'s tent of *môʿēd*, combined with the temple, as presupposed by P? What is especially remarkable here is the fact that both E (and D) and P, to all intents and purposes, agree that the divine revelation is, in some sense, bound up with permanent institutions and structures. This was no longer the case in the last stages of the First Temple period, by which time prophets could be vouchsafed the theophany

[19] The explanation given here, though in certain respects it may seem close to G. von Rad's (*Die Priesterschrift im Hexateuch* (Berlin, 1934), pp. 182–6; *Theologie des AT*, i (München, 1957), pp. 234–7; *Gesammelte Studien zum AT* (München, 1958), pp. 125–9), actually differs from it in many fundamental details. Thus, the two institutions combined into one by P are not, as von Rad thinks, the *'ōhel môʿēd* and the ark, but the *'ōhel môʿēd* and the tabernacle, of which the ark forms an inseparable part. P amalgamates the tent of *môʿēd* with the entire temple, not with one of its individual appurtenances. Von Rad finds it possible to claim that the tabernacle is in no way a retrojection of the temple (*Gesamm. Stud. z. AT*, p. 126). In fact, on this point there was much more of the truth with Wellhausen when he asserted the contrary. Again, von Rad, like many others, seems to fail to observe the essential qualities of E's tent of *môʿēd*. While he grasps the true relationship of Moses and Aaron and the difference between their function in P, he would make *Aaron* officiate primarily in the court, beside the outer altar. In fact, as has been shown in Chapter XI, the high priest's main sphere of activity was inside the temple, but without in any way infringing Moses' divining functions, which also, according to P, were performed within. — Of late, an attempt was made by B. S. Childs, *Exodus* (OTL, 1974), pp. 530–7, 'to reveal different stages in the development of the [priestly] tabernacle tradition' and to discover such stages in the literary shape of Exod. 25–31, 35–40. Childs believes that the non-priestly concept of *'ōhel môʿēd* is still discernible in, and belongs to the earliest stages of, these priestly sections—which, to my mind, is a rather too bold assumption. Incidentally, one can hardly agree that in Exod. 29: 42 the divine revelation 'is still pictured at the door of the tent of meeting' (ibid., p. 534). In this verse, the clause 'at the entrance to the tent of meeting, before the Lord' indicates the place of *ʿôlat tāmîd*, the 'regular burnt-offering' by which it is preceded. The following words, *'ᵃšer 'iwwāʿēd lāḵem*, 'where I will meet with you' etc., refer back only to the tent of *môʿēd* mentioned before; they do not point to the tent's entrance.

anywhere, even in Nineveh or on the Babylonian river Kebar. It would seem that, in this matter, both E(D) and P have preserved relatively ancient traditions.[20] But the question is whether, in those early times, the tent of *môʿēd* was an integral part of the temple or separate from it. Whose evidence is to be preferred—that of E(D) or that of P?

P's interpretation might seem to be confirmed by 1 Sam. 1–3 where the revelation to the prophet occurs inside the house of God at Shiloh. There is no possible analogy between the temple of Shiloh and the tent of *môʿēd* in E(D), or between Samuel, the attendant of Eli, and Joshua, the attendant of Moses. For, as we have seen, the tent of *môʿēd* in E(D) has nothing at all in common with a temple. Joshua is the prophet's attendant, whereas Samuel is the priest's acolyte. Samuel becomes a prophet by virtue of his own qualities and all Israel knows that 'Samuel was established to be a prophet of the Lord' (1 Sam. 3: 20), while Eli was no prophet at all. But the temple at Shiloh, as described in 1 Sam. 1–3, and P's tabernacle, the movable temple also destined eventually to be set up at Shiloh, are indeed institutions of the same order; and the presupposition that the innermost parts of both of them were also the scenes of divine communication is one of the instructive points of contact between the two.

However, the most that can really be deduced from this analogy is that, in the ancient Israelite temples, the innermost room was also believed to be a place destined for theophanies. Such undoubtedly was the historical reality in the early stages of Israelite history. At the same time, it cannot be inferred that the focal points of cultic sanctity were, in those times, the only places where the divine presence was believed to reveal itself to prophets. There must have been, in those self-same times, additional places where members of the prophetic movement were believed to receive their divine inspiration. One of these was no doubt that unique institution portrayed in E(D), the tent of *môʿēd*. The fact that this institution, as such, is ignored by P, which retains only its name as a designation of the tabernacle, follows logically from P's peculiarly hierocentric bias, which subordinates everything else to the temple. The designation of P's tabernacle as *'ōhel môʿēd*

[20] Cf. my remarks in *VT* 27 (1977), 385–97, where I maintain that, as regards this point as well as some other points, the Pentateuchal sources actually reflect a pre-classical stage of the prophetic mode of activity.

could find justification in the fact that, after all, this movable temple is also held to be a place of prophetic revelation. However, the real, historical tent of *môʿēd* was apparently quite different. Though no mention is made of it in the Former Prophets, its main features are so 'realistically', so sensibly delineated in E(D) that it is hardly possible to regard them as an arbitrary invention. We are, therefore, obliged to give priority in this matter to the evidence of E (and D).

Thus we may conclude that the real tent of *môʿēd* was an old institution of the Yahwistic religion, which took shape in prophetic circles, and that its true nature is to be found in the descriptions given by E(D). It is possible to understand how this institution came to be so completely absorbed into P's tabernacle that its original form was obliterated and only the name, *'ōhel môʿēd*, remained as an appellation of something else. Whereas, if this institution had from the first been an integral part of the temple we should be completely at a loss to explain why E(D) saw fit to remove it from there.

XV

THE EMPTYING OF THE INNER SANCTUM

I

AN air of excitement pervades the story of the exile of the ark from Shiloh and its circuitous wanderings until it is brought to the city of David (1 Sam. 4: 1—7: 1; 2 Sam. 6: 1–19). The account of its transference to Solomon's temple and its deposition underneath the wings of the cherubim is likewise distinguished by an aura of festiveness and glory (1 Kgs. 8: 1–11). From that moment onwards, silence and mystery envelop the fate of these two objects. In the list of vessels broken and carried away to Babylon by Nebuzaradan, neither the ark nor the cherubim are mentioned (2 Kgs. 25: 13–17; Jer. 52: 17–23). The question when the inner sanctum of the Jerusalem temple was emptied of its objects is of vital importance for defining correctly P's actual premises and historical setting.

The talmudic sages, on the basis of 2 Chron. 35: 3, were inclined to believe that the ark had been hidden by Josiah.[1] However, as will be shown below, this verse contains hardly any historical evidence. Talmudic sages also held that the ark was taken along into the Babylonian exile, but this too was based on nothing more than midrashic inferences.[2] At the same time, the assumption that the ark and the cherubim remained in the Jerusalem temple as long as the latter existed is also implied as a matter of course by many moderns. The latter do not necessarily interpret the absence of the ark and the cherubim from the list of vessels taken by Nebuzaradan as a case of argument *ex silentio*; they mainly base their considerations on the fact that in P's

[1] Bab. Tal. Yoma, 52*b*; Horayot, 12*a*; Jer. Tal. Sheqalim, vi. 1, and parallel passages.

[2] Bab. Tal. Yoma, 53*b*. According to 2 Macc. 2: 4–5, the ark together with the tent of meeting and the altar of incense were hidden by Jeremiah in the mountain in which Moses was buried. Cf. also the Apocalypse of Baruch 6: 7–10; Bemidbar Rabbah xv. 7.

tabernacle these two objects are to be found in the holy of holies, behind the *pārōḵet*-veil. Yet, since it is the dating of P to post-exilic times that is subject to substantiation, anyone who adduces evidence as to the Jerusalem temple from P's tabernacle is liable to be trapped in a vicious circle. While it is undoubtedly true that a great deal of information about the Solomonic temple is projected on P's tabernacle, the question still remains which particular phase in the history of this temple is really reflected therein. For the tabernacle may 'reflect' the Jerusalem temple only at the stage which actually preceded the disappearance of the inner sanctum vessels.

On the other hand, there is the evidence of foreign kings penetrating the Solomonic temple at various periods, and plundering its treasuries. There were three such invaders: Pharaoh Shishak (1 Kgs. 14: 26), Jehoash of Israel (2 Kgs. 14: 14), and Nebuchadnezzar of Babylon at the time of Jehoiachin's exile (ibid. 24: 13). Small wonder, therefore, that some scholars have linked the disappearance of the ark and the cherubim with one of these invasions, in particular with one of the first two.[3] Nevertheless, such an assumption is hardly better justified than the previous one. Shishak and Jehoash did not even enter the temple's outer sanctum, certainly not the inner one; moreover, Shishak may not have entered Jerusalem at all. In actual fact, the disappearance of the inner sanctum objects from the Jerusalem temple does not seem connected with any external event, but with internal factors within the Judean Kingdom—a unique religio-political constellation into which it passed only once in its history. This was 'the sin of Manasseh'.

THE ACTS OF MANASSEH AND THEIR IMPACT

2

Throughout the various changes that took place in the Kingdom of Judah, the temple at Jerusalem never ceased to serve exclusively as a temple of Yahweh. Even those kings who according to the Deuteronomistic editors 'did what was evil in the eyes of the

[3] Thus, S. Mowinckel ('Wann wurde der Jahwekultus in Jerusalem offiziell bildlos?' *AcOr* 8 (1930), 272–5) connects it with the invasion of Shishak. S. Loenborg, on the other hand ('Die "Silo"-Verse in Gen. 49', *ARW* 27 (1929), 376–9), connects it with the invasion of Jehoash.

Lord' never ventured to alter the basic character of the Solomonic temple. Their idolatrous acts were performed in the city, or even outside the city, while the central hallowed shrine remained untouched. There was only one single period in its history when it was temporarily deprived of its original function and for a short while ceased to serve as a temple to Yahweh (or at least exclusively so). This occurred during the reign of Manasseh and is the only happening which may explain the disappearance of the ark and the cherubim.

Solomon himself had not refrained from building, for his foreign wives, 'high-places' to the gods of Sidon, Moab, and Ammon. These, however, were built 'on the mountain east of Jerusalem', that is, outside the city (1 Kgs. 11: 5–8). There they stood for hundreds of years until they were pulled down by Josiah (2 Kgs. 23: 13–14).[4] Queen Maacah the daughter of Abishalom made an 'abominable image', *mip̱leṣet* for Asherah which her son Asa, a devoted worshipper of Yahweh, cut down and burned at the brook Kidron (1 Kgs. 15: 13). But even this image certainly did not stand within the confines of the temple.[5] During the reigns of Jehoram, Athaliah, and Ahaziah, foreign idolatry came to the fore in Jerusalem, and a special 'house', i.e. temple, was erected there for Baal, comprising altars, images, and a priest. All these were destroyed after the accession of Jehoash (2 Kgs. 11: 18). Again they had nothing to do with Solomon's temple.

Of Manasseh we are told that not only did he follow foreign gods, but also lent a foreign character to the temple itself. He built altars 'for all the host of heaven' in the two courts of the temple (2 Kgs. 21: 4–5). Further, he built altars 'on the roof of the upper chamber of Ahaz' which undoubtedly were also intended for the 'host of heaven' (ibid. 23: 12).[6] In the temple court he set up 'houses of the male cult prostitutes', 'where the women wove

[4] Cf. above, p. 138, n. 8.

[5] The word *'ᵃšērāh* signifies both the goddess of that name and a sacred tree which usually stood close to an altar. Sometimes such trees, despite being called *'ᵃšērîm*, were dedicated to Yahweh. The planting of this tree near an altar is prohibited in Deut. 16: 21, and accordingly also in the Deuteronomistic redaction of the Books of Kings (1 Kgs. 14: 15, 23; 2 Kgs. 17: 10; 23: 15). As regards Asa's mother, however, it was not just a tree that was in question, but an image of the goddess. This is also the case as regards Ahab and Manasseh, mentioned further below.

[6] Cf. above, p. 134, n. 4. With regard to the worship on roofs of the host of heaven, see Jer. 19: 13; 32: 29. Zeph. 1: 5. Cf. also J. A. Montgomery, *Kings*

hangings[7] for the Asherah' (ibid., v. 7). And on top of all this, Manasseh made a 'graven image', *pesel*, of Asherah 'as Ahab king of Israel had done' and set it up inside the house of the Lord (ibid. 21: 3, 7)—something none of the other kings of the Davidic dynasty had ever dared to do. He actually went even further than Ahab, to whom he is here compared. For Ahab at his worst set up an image of Asherah in the 'house (i.e. temple) of Baal' he built in Samaria (1 Kgs. 16: 32–3),[8] as did his daughter Athaliah in Jerusalem. Manasseh, however, introduced the image of Asherah into the very house of Yahweh, converting it into a kind of Asherah-temple. It is interesting to note that this was not all done at a stroke. It is first stated that he 'made an Asherah as Ahab' (2 Kgs. 21: 3). Subsequently the text states: 'And he set the graven image of Asherah that he had made, in the house' (ibid., v. 7). The Hebrew phrase for 'that he had made', ’^{a}*šer ‘āśāh*, in this context really has a pluperfect meaning, i.e. that he had made before. It transpires that at first the image stood somewhere outside the temple and only at some later stage did Manasseh dare to bring it inside.[9] He further placed in the temple's outer sanctum

(ICC, 1951), p. 533. Even though according to the Deuteronomistic redaction Ahaz 'did not do what was right in the eyes of the Lord his God' (2 Kgs. 16: 2), nowhere is it said of him that he set up any accessories for foreign gods; cf. above, p. 135, n. 6. The upper chamber, ‘^{a}*liyyāh*, he built was apparently connected with the steps, *ma‘*^{a}*lôt*, used also as a sundial, which are mentioned in the miracle of Isaiah (ibid. 20: 11; Isa. 38: 8). In the version of DSIsa I the text is explicitly read in this way (ibid.: במעלות עלית אחז). Cf. in this respect Y. Yadin, 'The Dial of Ahaz', *EI* 5 (1958), 92–3, 96 (Hebrew).

[7] In the MT: בתים, houses, which probably should be amended to בדים, cloths. It was customary for women in the ancient Near East to engage in spinning and weaving in the temple courts. Cf. Montgomery's comments ad loc.; and Exod. 35: 25–6.

[8] See, e.g., R. Kittel, *Könige* (GHK, 1900), pp. 242, 257. This may, however, appear doubtful. For, even after Jehu had destroyed the temple of Baal (2 Kgs. 10: 21–7), the Asherah still remained, since it is referred to in the time of his son Jehoahaz (ibid. 13: 6) and, as a sinful record, also in the recapitulation with regard to the fall of the Northern Kingdom (ibid. 17: 16). This could imply that the Asherah might have stood by itself. At any rate, it had no connection whatsoever with any temple of Yahweh.

[9] Cf. the mode of describing the deed of Maacah the daughter of Abishalom: 'because she had made, ’^{a}*šer ‘āś*^{e}*tāh*, an abominable image for Asherah' (1 Kgs. 15:13). This wording, too, refers to a distant past, to what the queen-mother had done previously. She probably made the image during the reign of Abijam, who was one of the evil-doers in the sight of the Lord (ibid. 15: 3–4). With regard to the pluperfect expressed by the subordinate clause beginning with the relative pronoun ’^{a}*šer* and proceeding with a verb in the past, cf. G. Bergsträsser, *Hebräische Grammatik*, ii (Leipzig, 1926), § 6d (b); F. R. Blake, *A Resurvey of Hebrew Tenses* (Rome, 1951), § 10, 7b.

special vessels 'made for Baal, for Asherah, and for all the host of heaven' (ibid. 23: 4).[10]

The acts of Manasseh which were detailed in the Book of the Chronicles of the Kings of Judah (ibid. 21: 17) are referred to only briefly and haphazardly within the pragmatic framework of the canonical Book of 2 Kgs. Yet, even this short reference suffices to reveal the author's feelings of disgust and repugnance. Possibly this was why he failed to dwell on them. At the same time, the introduction of the image of Asherah into the temple of the Lord is considered by him to be a climax in the long list of Manasseh's misdeeds. After mentioning it he immediately proceeds to qualify the temple as 'the house of which Yahweh said to David and to Solomon his son: In this house and in Jerusalem, which I have chosen out of all tribes of Israel, will I put my name for ever' and so forth (ibid. 21: 7). The dedication of the temple to the name of Yahweh God of Israel is mentioned emphatically by this author in connection with the occasion when Solomon carried the ark into the inner sanctum (1 Kgs. 8: 16–21), so that Manasseh's act is made to appear as its exact reversal. It is, therefore, not surprising that in the Deuteronomistic historiography these acts were deemed to have finally determined the fate of Judah and marked it for destruction (2 Kgs. 21: 10–15; 23: 26; 24: 3; Jer. 15: 4). The sins of Manasseh became a proverbial symbol of evil for a long time after his death. Some of them are reflected in the prophecy of Zephaniah (Zeph. 1: 4–9). They are dealt with in particular in the oracles of Jeremiah, where references are made to the worship of the host of heaven (Jer. 8: 1–2; 19: 13; 32: 29) and the introduction of the 'abominations' into the temple (ibid. 7: 30; 32: 34). As has already been said, even the reproofs of Ezekiel provide us with a glimpse of Manasseh's reign.[11]

3

Where was the image of Asherah placed within the temple?

According to the usual layout of temples in the ancient Near East, the appropriate place for the image of a god would be the last

[10] For the reign of Manasseh as an idolatrous period in Jerusalem cf. Kaufmann, *THH*, i. 671; ii. 234–5, 267; iii. 450; and above, p. 106. The political background to this upheaval, namely the subjection to Assyria, is a possibility which has been noted in the Histories (cf., however, above, p. 136, in n. 6).

[11] Cf. above, pp. 106–7.

room, the holy of holies. The innermost sanctum—whether it constitutes a separate room (as in Egypt, Canaan, and the Jerusalem temple) or whether it is merely a niche in the wall of a large chamber—is the place where the living presence of the god was made perceptible, usually in the form of an image. In the aniconic symbolism of the Israelite cult, this function was fulfilled by the cherubim and the ark, which, as we indicated in Chapter XIII, were held to represent a throne and a footstool. The outer sanctum, on the other hand, is the place where ritual acts in the service of the god were performed. Now we have noted that Manasseh placed special 'vessels made for Baal and Asherah' in the temple's outer sanctum (2 Kgs. 23: 4). We are therefore entitled to infer that the image of Asherah, which was introduced by him into the temple, was substituted for the ark and the cherubim. Some fifty years afterwards, when Josiah removed the Asherah from the temple and burnt it in the Kidron Valley, beating it to dust and desecrating even the dust (2 Kgs. 23: 6), the ark and the cherubim were no longer there.

4

Decisive evidence as to the absence of the ark after Manasseh's reign is found in one of Jeremiah's earliest prophecies: 'And when you have multiplied and increased in the land, in those days, says the Lord, they shall no more say, "The ark of the covenant of the Lord", it shall not come to mind, they shall not remember it or resort to it, it shall not be made again' (Jer. 3: 16). This verse follows upon words of consolation and itself contains a message of conciliation and mercy. What the prophet promises here is that in the good days to come there will no longer be any need for the ark—implying that its absence should no longer cause any grief. These words would, of course, be devoid of any significance if the ark still existed. Had it been inside the temple at the time—no one, prophet or layman, would have thought of pronouncing such 'consolations'. Any anti-cultic tendency is certainly inconceivable here, as the statements are made straightforwardly, without any intention of reproving or declaring unconventional truths.

Indeed, most modern commentators acknowledge that these words reflect a period when the ark was no longer in existence and that genuine sorrow for its absence is to be inferred from them. Only this assumption prompts them, among other apparent excuses, to connect this verse (as well as those before and after) with the period of Babylonian exile.[12] Thus they again appear to enter upon a vicious circle. There seems no adequate reason to invalidate the evidence of these verses. Granted that they do not fit well into their present context, they still by no means lack the traits of Jeremian authenticity; indeed, they are characteristic of the early stage of his prophetic activity.

5

On the other hand, there are two pieces of evidence which might appear to contradict the assumption that when Manasseh placed the image of Asherah in the temple the ark and the cherubim were removed. These are Josiah's address to the Levites (2 Chron. 35: 3), and the reference to the 'image of jealousy' in Ezek. 8: 3, 5.

As to the first, the Chronicler copied the description of Manasseh's transgressions from the Book of Kings (2 Chron. 33: 1–9). He had no intention of 'analysing' these statements so as to disclose in them evidence for the disappearance of the ark. For his part he probably assumed that as long as the Solomonic temple stood, the ark was not absent from it. He accordingly described Josiah as saying: 'Put the holy ark in the house which Solomon, the son of David, king of Israel, built; you need no longer carry it upon your shoulders' (ibid. 35: 3).[13] Can this verse be considered as historical evidence for the existence of the ark at that time? This detail was undoubtedly included in the Chronicler's description under the influence of the priestly sections of the Pentateuch. If we accept his evidence on this point, we should accept it on other points, such as, for instance, that it was not Josiah but rather Manasseh himself who cleaned out the temple and removed the

[12] See, e.g., M. Dibelius, *Die Lade Jahves* (Göttingen, 1906), pp. 27–8, 35, 126; R. Hartmann, 'Zelt und Lade', *ZAW* 37 (1917–18), 230–1; P. Volz, *Jeremiah*[2] (KAT, 1958), p. 23, as well as other commentaries ad loc.; also especially the remarks of A. W. Streane, *Jeremiah* (CBSC, 1926), p. 25; J. Bright, *Jeremiah* (AB, 1965), p. 27.

[13] The MT reads: תנו את ארון הקדש בבית . . . אין לכם משא בכתף, of which the first phrase is somewhat difficult. The best interpretation which can be provided without emending the text is that Josiah orders the Levites to return the ark to the holy of holies after it was removed from there by Manasseh. This is the view of some medieval and modern commentators; cf. for references E. L. Curtis, *Chronicles* (ICC, 1910), pp. 512–13. Others interpret תנו as 'leave it in its present place', i.e. in the holy of holies, assuming that Manasseh put the ark back there himself, though it is not directly said so in 2 Chron. 33: 15. See W. Rudolph, *Chronikbücher* (HAT, 1955), p. 326, and the references there.

'idol', *semel*, from it (2 Chron. 33: 15–16).[14] Even the proposed emendations to the text[15] may at most help in clarifying its meaning; they can hardly lend it historical reliability.

The 'image of jealousy', *sēmel haqqin'āh*, is included among Ezekiel's visions of doom (Ezek. 8–11) as placed at the northern entrance to the inner court of the temple, 'north of the altar gate' (ibid. 8: 3, 5). Some scholars assume that Manasseh's Asherah is meant thereby.[16] As the passage stands, however, it is intended to describe the situation in the sixth year of Jehoiachin's exile (ibid. 8: 1). The prophet refers not to the past, but to what his eyes are presumedly seeing at the moment. Yet, in 2 Kgs. 23: 6 there is an explicit and incontestable statement that Manasseh's image of Asherah had been destroyed some thirty years before, in the course of Josiah's reformation. Unless one accepts the eccentric view that the entire Book of Ezekiel is a mere pseudepigraph artificially attributed to the reign of Manasseh,[17] one is of necessity forced to admit that this '*sēmel* of jealousy' has nothing to do with Manasseh's Asherah, but is some imaginary statue fancied by the prophet. It should further be remembered that the plastic and detailed expression Ezekiel gives to his visions is often liable to mislead the reader. 'Men' of the godly sphere figure in the visionary chapters in question (Ezek. 8–11) which above all represent the fanciful sight of the mind's eye. Even those features in our chapters which have the appearance of realism might be no more

[14] The whole story in 2 Chron. 33: 10–19 of the deportation of Manasseh to Assyria, his repentance, and the pious restorations he made upon his return to Jerusalem is undoubtedly taken from a certain treatise of legendary material, possibly the 'Chronicles of the Kings of Israel' or the 'Chronicles of Hozai (or: of the Seers)' mentioned at the end of the section. This does not mean that such a treatise could not contain some nuclei of truth. Several scholars assume that Manasseh's involuntary journey to Assyria and the fortifications he built in Jerusalem, hinted at in this section, are historically true. See O. Eissfeldt, *Einleitung in das AT*[3] (Tübingen, 1964), p. 732; and especially Rudolph, op. cit., pp. 315–17. However, the possibility that Manasseh was the one who cleaned out the temple is utterly ruled out by Josiah's acts (cf. further on).

[15] I. Benziger, *Die Bücher der Chronik* (KHC, 1901), p. 132, reads הנה instead of תנו, i.e. 'Behold, the holy ark is now in the house', etc. Rudolph, loc. cit., reads נתנו, making up an antecedent: 'Since the holy ark was put in the house', etc.

[16] See, e.g., G. Fohrer, *Ezechiel* (HAT, 1955), pp. 50–1; also the discussion in Kaufmann, *THH* iii. 500–2, where the relevant opinions of various earlier scholars are cited.

[17] As proposed by C. C. Torrey, *Pseudo-Ezekiel and the Original Prophecy* (New Haven, 1930); cf. also his discussions with W. F. Albright and Sh. Spiegel, in *JBL* 51 (1932), 179–81; 53 (1934), 291–320; and above, p. 106, n. 29.

than realistic touches given to a fiction. The picture as a whole may well have an inkling of truth, that is to say, that at a certain time idolatrous cults really were performed in the temple courts in Jerusalem—and by that, Manasseh's reign certainly comes to mind; but there is hardly any trustworthiness in the actual situations and concrete particulars of which the picture is composed. Therefore, it cannot be accepted as a direct, historical piece of evidence.

VESSELS OF THE SANCTUMS AND OF THE TEMPLE TREASURIES

6

We must now explain why the invasions of Shishak and Jehoash and even Nebuchadnezzar's incursion into the temple at the time of Jehoiachin's exile are irrelevant to the disappearance of the objects of the inner sanctum. For this purpose we must touch again on the question of the arrangement of the temple's various groups of objects.

Vessels were kept in the Jerusalem temple not only in the court and in the sanctums, but also in the temple treasuries. These treasuries are always mentioned conjointly with 'the treasuries of the king's house' and seem to be similar in nature. The vessels in the temple treasuries were also deemed holy, though they were certainly less sacred than those in the temple sanctums. They were made of silver and gold which had been dedicated to Yahweh by the people and subsequently cast into vessels (2 Kgs. 12: 5, 14). In the days of Jehoash (the Davidite) and Josiah, it was decided that such donations should be temporarily used to repair the house of God rather than be put into the treasuries (ibid. 12: 5–16; 22: 4–7). The major proportion of the contents of the temple treasuries came, however, not so much from the donations of the people as from the Judean kings, who made votive gifts from their war loot or from other sources. Occasionally these treasuries were depleted either by foreign invaders or by the kings of Judah themselves, when they were in need of funds. The treasuries thus constantly oscillated between a state of affluence and of want.

We are told that David had already dedicated to Yahweh a large number of golden, silver, and bronze vessels out of the spoil of the peoples he had subdued (2 Sam. 8: 7–12). These were put by Solomon in the temple treasuries (1 Kgs. 7: 51).[18] During the reign of Rehoboam, Pharaoh Shishak caused the temple treasuries as well as those of the king's house to be emptied, 'and he took away everything' (ibid. 14: 26). Abijam and Asa made good this loss to some extent (ibid. 15: 15), but then Asa himself was forced to send all that was found in them to Ben-hadad king of Damascus (ibid. 15: 18–19). They were again filled up by the votive gifts of Jehoshaphat, Jehoram, Ahaziah, and Jehoash; but Jehoash in his turn was compelled to empty them in order to bribe Hazael to refrain from conquering Jerusalem (2 Kgs. 12: 19). During Amaziah's reign the treasures of both the temple and the king's house were taken away by King Jehoash of Israel, who entered Jerusalem and made a breach in its wall (ibid. 14: 14). Ahaz and Hezekiah removed their contents in order to bribe the kings of Assyria (ibid. 16: 8; 18: 14–15).[19] The contents of the treasuries were no longer in themselves sufficient for Hezekiah, who was forced to strip the gold from the doors of the temple's outer sanctum and from the doorposts (see ibid. 18: 16). The last to plunder the temple treasuries were Nebuchadnezzar, at the time of Jehoiachin's deportation (ibid. 24: 13), and probably also Nebuzaradan, at the time of the final destruction (cf. below).

The invasions of Shishak and Jehoash have, therefore, nothing to do with the temple sanctums, and it would be entirely inaccurate to associate them with the disappearance of the ark and the cherubim. These invaders did no more than what the kings of Judah sometimes ventured to do themselves.

With regard to Shishak, it should be added that his army may

[18] As an anachronistic projection 'the treasury of (the house of) the Lord' is mentioned as early as the battle of Jericho (Josh. 6: 19, 24; and above, p. 66). From this reference it may be inferred that any dedication of the *ḥērem* category was usually also put in the temple treasuries (cf. ibid. 7: 23). Indeed, the *ḥērem* is just one of the forms of dedication to the divine—the one which is liable to neither substitution nor redemption (cf. Lev. 27: 28–9; and above, p. 172, n. 50).

[19] There is no doubt that the phrase 'the house of the Lord' mentioned in connection with Jehoash (2 Kgs. 14: 14), Ahaz (ibid. 16: 8), and Hezekiah (ibid. 18: 15) is simply a shortened form of 'the treasuries of the house of the Lord'. This may be seen from the fact that 'the treasuries of the king's house' which are always contiguously mentioned with 'the treasuries of the house of the Lord' are also mentioned throughout these passages.

not even have entered Jerusalem, since the city is not mentioned in the description of his campaign in Palestine found in the temple of Amon at Karnak. From the cities listed there it may be concluded that the Egyptian army bypassed Jerusalem on the north, proceeding from Aijalon to Beth-horon and Gibeon and from there north-eastwards to Zemaraim and down into the Jordan Valley at Succoth. Shishak's campaign seems to have been mainly directed against the Northern Kingdom. Only one section of his army seems to have overrun the Negeb as far as Arad, without advancing towards the Judean hills. It is thus not impossible that the temple treasuries and those of the king's house with 'all the shields of gold which Solomon had made' were handed over to Shishak by Rehoboam himself. He thereby succeeded in diverting the Egyptian army from his land. This would be the meaning of the words 'he took away' used with reference to Shishak.[20] The story in 1 Kgs. 14: 25–6 only mentions one particular part of Shishak's route, high-lighting it as viewed from Jerusalem.

7

Nebuchadnezzar's actions were somewhat different: he entered Jerusalem and, it is stated, plundered the temple treasuries (2 Kgs. 24: 13).[21] It seems, however, that he was the first to penetrate

[20] See B. Mazar, 'The Campaign of Pharaoh Shishak to Palestine', *SVT* 4 (1957), 57–66. It should be added that even assuming (unlike Mazar's thought) that the list of Shishak is only a jumbled enumeration of geographical terms, not intended to outline the route of his campaign, the very fact that Jerusalem is not included would still prove that his armies did not enter this city.

[21] The vessels of the temple treasuries taken by Nebuchadnezzar are apparently the same vessels which Jehoiachin's contemporaries, after this exile, expected to be miraculously brought back from Babylon (Jer. 27: 16—28: 6) and the same vessels which at the return from the Exile were handed over by Cyrus to Sheshbazzar the prince of Judah (Ezra 1: 7–11). Note the names (אגרטלים, מחלפים, כפורים and 'other vessels') and the numbers (totalling 5,400; according to LXX, 5,469) given to these vessels in the latter passage. Neither the names nor the numbers fit the vessels of the sanctum. According to a late tradition found in Daniel and the Hagiographa, Nebuchadnezzar appeared in Jerusalem during the reign of Jehoiakim and took 'part of the vessels of the house of the Lord' (2 Chron. 36: 6–7; 1 Esd. 1: 40–1; Dan. 1: 1–2; cf. 5: 2–3). This tradition is not very reliable. Untenable is the statement in Dan. 1: 1 that this occurred in the third year of the reign of Johoiakim, the year preceding the battle of Carchemish and before Nebuchadnezzar even became king of Babylon. For a detailed discussion of the authenticity of this tradition, cf. J. A. Montgomery, *Daniel* (ICC, 1927), pp. 113–17. At any rate, even this tradition speaks of carrying away the vessels of the temple treasuries only.

the temple, that is, to enter the outer sanctum. Of him alone is it said that he 'cut in pieces all the vessels of gold which Solomon king of Israel had made in the *hêkāl* (i.e. the outer sanctum; EVV: the temple) of the Lord' (ibid.).[22] Thus the vessels of the treasuries were taken by him as they were, while those of the *hêkāl* underwent deformation, their precious metal only serving as war booty.[23] Nebuchadnezzar's entry into the temple's sanctum is regarded by the biblical writer as a precursory fulfilment of earlier prophecies; in his words: 'as the Lord had said' (ibid.). It was a threatening omen of the final destruction.

Since Nebuchadnezzar had destroyed the vessels of the outer sanctum, they are not mentioned in the list of Nebuzaradan's spoils, just as no mention is made in this list of the ark and the cherubim. We have two parallel versions of the list at the end of the Books of Kings (2 Kgs. 25: 13–17) and at the end of Jeremiah (Jer. 52: 17–23). The list omits in the *hêkāl* the tables and the altar of incense, both of which had already been 'cut in pieces' eleven years before. It seems likely that Nebuzaradan took only the vessels of the temple court (the bronze vessels enumerated in the list) and those of the temple treasuries (the gold and silver vessels mentioned therein). Even the lampstands referred to in Jer. 52: 19 (and omitted from the parallel version in 2 Kgs. 25: 15) apparently belonged not to the sanctum, but to the temple treasuries. In this respect they should not be associated with the lampstands mentioned among the inner furnishings in 1 Kgs. 7: 48–50.[24]

This supposition also accords with the fact that the tables and the lampstands as well as the ark and the cherubim are absent

[22] For the narrower sense of the term *hêkāl*, implying in this case, in fact, only the temple's outer sanctum, cf. above, p. 14.

[23] For 'cut in pieces' (JB, NEB: 'broke up') the MT has *wayᵉqaṣṣēṣ* which bears the meaning not only of cutting off, but also of stripping an overlaid object of its metal plates. Cf. 2 Kgs. 18: 16 (said of the temple doors); possibly also ibid. 16: 17.

[24] In Jer. 52: 19 the lampstands are lumped together with small bowls, censers, pots, dishes, and other kinds of minor utensils, while in 1 Kgs. 7: 49 they are related to the incense-altar and the tables of gold. It should be pointed out that only when discussing the bronze utensils of the outer altar mentioned in the list of Nebuzaradan's spoil it is said that they were 'used in ministration' (2 Kgs. 25: 14; Jer. 52: 18), while neither of the parallel versions of the Books of Kings and Jeremiah make any similar statement with regard to the gold and silver vessels. This may serve to strengthen the argument that the gold and silver vessels taken by Nebuzaradan did not appertain to the outer sanctum, but were simply votive gifts deposited in the temple treasuries.

from the visionary temple of Ezekiel (Ezek. 40–3). Of all the inner furniture of the temple only the inner altar remained there, and this is described as 'an altar of wood' (ibid. 41: 22) indicating that it was no longer overlaid with gold. It is only metaphorically designated there as 'table' (ibid.). It seems reasonable to suppose that this altar remained in the outer sanctum because, unlike the tables, it was attached to the floor, or because of its comparatively heavy weight it was preserved even after being stripped of its gold at Nebuchadnezzar's command. Indeed, Ezekiel's descriptions of his visionary temple are based mainly on the actual temple at Jerusalem as it was in its last years of existence, that is, after Jehoiachin's exile. The prophet's vision does not change it except so as to make the areas of its courts more symmetrical and rectangular and in order to satisfy certain demands of the priestly school.[25]

8

To sum up: Shishak and Jehoash did no more than empty the temple treasuries. It was Manasseh who set up vessels for Baal and Asherah in the outer sanctum and introduced the image of Asherah into the inner sanctum of the temple, and it was probably through him that the ark and the cherubim were removed. When Josiah came to cleanse the temple, the ark and the cherubim were no longer there. Many decades after the 'sin of Manasseh', Nebuchadnezzar entered the outer sanctum of the temple and 'stripped' its vessels of their gold overlay, thus actually destroying them (and also plundered the temple treasuries). When the fateful moment of final destruction arrived, eleven years after the exile of Jehoiachin, the temple was already deprived at least of most of its inner accessories. This sequence of events serves, among other things, to substantiate one of the present inquiry's central contentions, which, as has been shown, has much other evidence in its favour, that the state of affairs underlying P's Utopia, belongs historically to the stage which preceded Manasseh, that is, to about the times of Ahaz and Hezekiah.

[25] Cf. above, pp. 45–6, 95 (also my discussion in *EM*, v. 353–5).

XVI

PILGRIM-FEASTS AND FAMILY FESTIVALS

I

THE etymology of the biblical noun *ḥag*, a technical term for a most conspicuous sort of sacred occasions, has not yet been satisfactorily explained. Certain lexicographers still assume that it is related to the noun *ḥûg*, 'circle', and associate it with the idea of dancing in a circle, on the grounds that originally this was the main feature of the celebration of a *ḥag* (as Wellhausen put it: 'the holy circle').[1] However, the objection has already been raised that the verb *ḥwg* in biblical Hebrew (Job 26: 10) as well as in Syriac means only 'to make a circle', 'to go round in a circle'; one cannot force into it the meaning 'to dance'. The Aramaic root *ḥng* (from which the noun חנגא, dance, comes) is quite different, and should not be confused with *ḥwg*. It was Nöldeke who pointed out almost a century ago that the only meaning that can be extracted from the word *ḥag* in the Semitic languages is that of 'festal, joyful gathering',[2] which, incidentally, should also have the connotation of making a pilgrimage. Indeed, wherever the word occurs in the Old Testament, this meaning, with its two or three defining components, emerges quite clearly: the gathering of large numbers of people; rejoicing, which, in the words of Amos 5: 23, might find its expression in 'noise of songs and melody of

[1] See the dictionaries of Gesenius–Buhl and Koehler–Baumgartner, s.v. חגג; cf. J. Wellhausen, *Reste arabischen Heidentums*[2] (Berlin, 1927), pp. 110, 141. Qimḥi and the eighteenth-century Hebrew commentator Y. H. Altschuler (the author of *Meṣûdôt*), in their remarks on 1 Sam. 30: 6, also explained the word thus.

[2] Th. Nöldeke, *ZDMG* 41 (1887), 719. Cf. S. R. Driver, *Notes on the . . . Books of Samuel*[2] (Oxford, 1913), p. 223; and in Brown–Driver–Briggs' dictionary, s.v. חג (where Wellhausen's explanation is not accepted). Those who adopted the former view tried to rely on Ps. 107: 27: יָחוֹגּוּ ינועו כשכור, but the word here has another meaning, and some actually read here: יָחֻגּוּ. Cf. M. Z. Kaddari, *Thesaurus of the Language of the Bible*, iii (Jerusalem, 1968), s.v. חגג. It is worth noting that this root has not turned up in the Canaanite and the Ugaritic *corpora*.

harps' (in fact, possibly, but not necessarily, in dancing too); and that, in the context of a pilgrimage (see, e.g., Deut. 16: 14–15; Isa. 30: 29; Amos 5: 21–3; 8: 10).

However, even this threefold meaning still does not convey the full sense of the term in biblical Hebrew; for though the etymology is not as yet entirely certain, the actual meaning of the word, as employed by biblical writers, is nevertheless quite clear. A public gathering, albeit connected with pilgrimage and accompanied by heightened expressions of joyfulness, will never be considered a *ḥag*—unless it is associated with a temple. In other words, a *ḥag*-pilgrimage cannot be made to any holy site or to any place of worship, but has to be connected with a visit to God in one of his houses, and its actual background is the temple court, 'before Yahweh'.[3] In this context, we must recall the essential, institutional difference between an altar and a house of God.[4] Thus, for the purpose of celebrating a *ḥag*, an Israelite did not usually stay in his own town, even if there was an altar there, but had to make a pilgrimage to one of the temple cities (except when there was a temple in his own town). In point of fact, the *ḥag*-pilgrimage was just a reflection on a cultic-religious level of the prevalent ancient Near Eastern notion, that a suzerain's vassals are expected to acknowledge his sovereignty by regularly appearing before him at his residence.

THE THREE PILGRIM-FEASTS

2

To realize the fundamental connection between the *ḥag* and the temple, it is enough to note that wherever a *ḥag* is mentioned, it is specifically against the background of a temple. The *ḥag* described in Judg. 21: 19–23, with the dances of the girls, took place in Shiloh, one of the prominent temple cities. Similarly the prophet describes 'the night when a holy *ḥag* is observed' as a time of

[3] One could therefore happily accept the suggestion of NEB, which invariably renders *ḥag* as 'pilgrim-feast', if only its specific association with the temple were more obviously implied in the English equivalent. At the same time it is certainly better than to render *ḥag* as simply a 'feast' (as other EVV do).

[4] Cf. above, pp. 15–16.

song and 'gladness of heart', 'when one sets out to the sound of the flute to go to the mountain of the Lord, to the Rock of Israel' (Isa. 30: 29). Similarly the psalmist says that 'a multitude keeping *ḥag*' is seen by him as a throng making its way 'to the house of God with shouts of exultation and thanksgiving' (Ps. 42: 5).[5] Only once is the root-word developed to suggest an apparently different meaning. This is when David's men overtook the Amalekites who had raided Ziklag and the settlements of the Negeb. The Amalekites are described as 'eating and drinking and *ḥôgᵉgîm*' (1 Sam. 30: 16). One must infer, however, that what the text here means to imply is simply that they were behaving like people celebrating a *ḥag*.[6] We also find that the concept of *ḥag* is applied in three places in the Exodus narratives without any association with a temple (Exod. 5: 1; 10: 9; 32: 5–6). But the truth of the matter is that in those places the idea of *ḥag* is employed in an anachronistic way, and the narratives even project temple scenes back on to the desert period, as will be shown below (sects. 6–7); hence these instances do not disprove the general rule.

Of all the holy days in the year's cycle, the term *ḥag* is used in the Old Testament of only three: the *ḥag* of Unleavened Bread, the *ḥag* of Weeks, and the *ḥag* of Booths. This is an additional positive indication that the essential point of a *ḥag* is that it involves a pilgrimage to a temple. Neither the New Year nor the Day of Atonement, still less the New Moon or the Sabbath, is called a *ḥag*, which clearly demonstrates that they did not involve the obligation of pilgrimage, though in the priestly terminology most of them came under *miqrāʾê qōdeš*, that is, 'holy proclamations' (rather than 'holy convocations' or 'assemblies', as RSV, JB, NEB have it, or 'sacred occasions' as rendered by NJPS), and work was forbidden on them (Lev. 23; Num. 29: 1, 7).[7] Indeed, the text states explicitly that the duty to 'come and

5 The use of the word *ḥag* in Ps. 118: 27 is very obscure: 'bind a *ḥag* [RSV: the festal procession] with branches, up to the horns of the altar'. Some explain that this refers to the sacrifice of the *ḥag*. However, even in this psalm the background of the temple and the procession passing through its gates can be clearly perceived, when it says: 'Open to me the gates of righteousness, that I may enter through them and give thanks to the Lord; this is the gate of the Lord . . . Blessed be he who enters in the name of the lord, we bless you from the house of the Lord' (ibid., vv. 19–20, 26).

6 Cf. Driver, loc. cit.

7 This is the simple reason for the fact that neither the New Year ('the first day of the seventh month' as it is termed in P) nor the Day of Atonement is

appear before Yahweh' applies to the three *ḥaggîm* only. This had already been pronounced in the Book of the Covenant: 'Three times in the year you shall keep a *ḥag* to me . . . Three times in the year all your males shall appear before the Lord God' (Exod. 23: 14, 17). This injunction also occurs, with slight variations, in the Minor Book of the Covenant (ibid. 34: 23), and is again included in D's instructions (Deut. 16: 16). In all three codes a further demand is made: 'None shall see my face empty-handed'. In explanation of this D adds: 'every man shall give as he is able, according to the blessing of Yahweh your God which he has given you' (ibid., v. 17). That is to say, it was not considered proper to pay a visit to God at one of his temples on one of the pilgrim-feasts, without offering him an oblation.

One should not too readily infer from these statements that no Israelite ever had occasion to come to a temple except on the *ḥaggîm*. On the contrary, it was quite usual for people to visit the temple and prostrate themselves before the Lord there on all the holy days all the year around (Isa. 1: 12–15; Ezek. 36: 38; Lam. 1: 4; 2: 7 *et al.*), including the New Moons and Sabbaths (Isa. 66: 23; Ezek. 46: 1–3); as we shall see further on, whole families would even assemble in local sanctuaries at special times specifically appointed for them. But then, such visits and gatherings in the temples were held to be optional, whereas pilgrimage and

mentioned in the non-priestly sources. Prevalent critical thought tends to infer that at the time of the early sources these two holidays did not yet exist in Israel's life, as they are the products of the post-exilic period. However, one should remember that the codes of J, E, and D (just as that of P) are not systematic bodies of laws in the western sense, but merely eclectic compilations of rules in which there are more 'gaps' than testimonies and many aspects of life are left entirely unilluminated. Even a cursory examination suffices to make one sense that the central interest of the relevant pericopes in Exod. 23: (13) 14–19; 34: 18–26; Deut. 16: 1–17 is the matter of feast-pilgrimage; but, as it has been said, neither the New Year with the Day of Atonement, nor the New Moon with Sabbath, appertains to this subject. In just the same way, had the New Year and the Day of Atonement not fallen under the category of 'holy proclamations' and had no additional sacrifices been ordained for them, even P would not have mentioned them in the lists of Lev. 23; Num. 28–9 (and thus, the very existence of 'the first day of the seventh month' as a festal day would not have come to light). On the other hand, no-one can doubt the antiquity of the New Moon and the Sabbath in Israel's life, yet a mention of the new Moon is nowhere made in the Pentateuch by the non-priestly sources, and the Sabbath is not referred to in D's code (although is included in the ten commandments). Cf., also, for instance, the case of circumcision—definitely an ancient custom but mentioned only incidentally, not in codes but in narratives, in J (Exod. 4: 24–6) and E (Gen. 34: 14–26), and not at all in D.

worship on the *ḥaggîm* were considered obligatory—a religious and national obligation, since by their very nature the *ḥaggîm* were events of national significance.

3

The obligation to appear before Yahweh three times a year was incumbent primarily on the men alone, as the text has it: יֵרָאֶה כל זכורך 'all your males shall appear' (Exod. 23: 17; 34: 23). Apparently, this emphasis on the males is not merely a legal formula, that may be ascribed to the dominance of the man's position, but must rather be taken literally. Thus the talmudic sages were to expound this injunction: זכורך—להוציא את הנשים, '"your males"—this excludes the women'.[8] However, time and circumstances served to weaken the limits of this obligation, so that whole families did in fact take part in the *ḥag* pilgrimages. This is actually the state of affairs reflected in D, for he repeats the injunction concerning the duty of the males to appear before Yahweh on the three pilgrim-feasts (Deut. 16: 16), and yet describes the whole family participating in the visit to the temple and in the rejoicings on those occasions (ibid., vv. 11, 14; 31: 11–12 *et al.*).

It is not impossible that the very demand to abolish the high-places and to centralize the cult (Deut. 12: 5–19) also affected D's understanding of the *ḥaggîm*. For unless all the members of the family were allowed to participate in the *ḥag* pilgrimages to the chosen place, there would scarcely have been an opportunity for them to partake of the sacrifices and the holy gifts. With the cult centralized, there would have been no question of restricting opportunities for families to take part in sacrifices solely to optional visits to the temple or of excluding women and children from those who celebrate the *ḥag*. It seems that P also takes for granted that the entire family participates in the feast-pilgrimage, since he too demands the concentration of the cult.[9] Nevertheless,

[8] Bab. Tal. Ḥagigah, 4*a*; Qiddushin, 34*b et al.*

[9] To be sure, the participation of entire families in the pilgrim-feasts is not stated explicitly by P; however, it is not unusual for the priestly writers to make assumptions about rules or practises without ever expressly stating their undoubted existence (cf. above, p. 211). At any rate, we also do not find in P the ancient rule that the obligation to appear before Yahweh is incumbent only on males.

the extension of the *ḥag* pilgrimage to the whole family does not concern only D and P. Permitting all the family to take part in the *ḥag* does not spring only from reformist demands to centralize the cult. As it will be explained later (sects. 6–7) even J and E admit indirectly that whole families take part in the *ḥaggîm*—though the injunction in the Books of the Covenant formally applies only to the males. This means that even in the early period, when the houses of God were still standing in their places and the cult-sites outside Jerusalem had not yet all been wiped out, the feast pilgrimage used to be practically an affair for the whole family.

Another question is the extent to which the *ḥag* pilgrimages were conscientiously observed. It is hard to imagine that these pilgrimages, whether they were considered mandatory only for the men or actually customary for the women and children too, were carried out strictly and purposefully. It is certainly inconceivable that during the feasts all the settlements in the country were completely emptied of their inhabitants, or even of only their adult male population, and that the entire people streamed to the temple cities. If anyone thinks that such a mass exodus from the settlements is a possibility, I would simply say that the small temple cities did not even have sufficient area to accommodate such vast masses. The Minor Book of the Covenant had already seen fit to speak of this matter in a persuasive tone: 'For I will cast out nations before you . . . neither shall any man desire your land, when you go up to appear before Yahweh your God three times in the year' (Exod. 34: 24). From this tone one can infer that there were in reality certain decisive obstacles to fulfilling this obligation and that the *ḥag* was far from being fully observed. There is no doubt that, in point of fact, the *ḥag* pilgrimages to the temples, with all the formal obligation they involved, were mainly regarded as praiseworthy manifestations of piety and fear of God. Even in the latter part of the Second Temple period, long after the canonization of the Pentateuch, when pilgrimage on the three feasts was considered an explicit precept of the Law, and huge crowds would flock to Jerusalem, the total number of pilgrims constituted only a small part of the people.[10] How much more would this have been the case in earlier ages.

[10] Cf. S. Safrai, העליה לרגל בימי הבית השני (Tel-Aviv, 1965), pp. 24–6.

4

Of the three feasts which are the appointed seasons for pilgrimage, the Feast of Unleavened Bread is the one of the barley harvest (cf. Lev. 23: 9–11) and occurs in the month of *'Āḇîḇ* (Exod. 13: 4, 5; 23: 15; 34: 18 *et al.*), that is, the month in which the barley ripens (cf. ibid. 9: 31; Lev. 2: 14). The Feast of Weeks is the one of the wheat harvest (Exod. 34: 22; cf. 23: 16). The period between these two feasts was regarded as a continuous season of harvest (cf. 2 Sam. 21: 9–10; Jer. 5: 24; Ruth 2: 3–23). The harvest season was thus bounded at both ends: The Feast of Unleavened Bread marked its beginning, the Feast of Weeks its end. The Feast of Weeks, therefore, appears as both an extension and a terminating point of the Feast of Unleavened Bread. Its dependence on the former finds expression even in the way its date was fixed, namely, by counting seven weeks from the Feast of Unleavened Bread, as is explained in H (Lev. 23: 15–16; cf. Jer. 5: 24: '. . . and keeps for us the weeks appointed for the harvest'), and hinted at briefly in P (Num. 28: 26) and in D (Deut. 16: 9–10). Since the substantive 'weeks', *šāḇu'ôt*, in the plural, is associated with the name of this feast not only in P, H, and D, but also in the Minor Book of the Covenant (Exod. 34: 22), there should be no doubt that the text of the latter refers to the same counting of seven weeks, considers it as self-evident, and simply for the sake of brevity did not trouble to give information on how the counting should be done. The dependence of the Feast of Weeks on the preceding Feast found expression also in the terminology of the talmudic sages, who called it, after the term employed in Lev. 23: 36; Num. 29: 35, *'ᵃṣeret*[11] or עצרת של פסח, 'the *'ᵃṣeret* of Passover (Feast)',[12] just as the eighth day following the Feast of Booths is called in the Law *'ᵃṣeret* (loc. cit.).

Unlike the first two *ḥaggîm*, which are inter-connected harvest feasts, the third *ḥag* stands on its own and in the early sources is called *ḥag hā'āsîp̄*, '(Pilgrim-)Feast of Ingathering', because it comes at the time when the produce of the field is brought in from the threshing-floor and the produce of the vineyard from the wine-press (Exod. 23: 16; 34: 22; cf. Lev. 23: 39; Deut. 16: 13). The Holiness Code explains the special custom connected

[11] Mishnah Shebi'it i. 1; Bab. Tal. Megillah, 4*a*; Rosh Hashshanah, 4*b*; Menaḥoth, 65*b*; cf. Josephus, *Antiquities*, iii. 10. 6.

[12] Shir Hashshirim Rabbah vii. 2 *et al.*

with this feast, namely, the use of the four species and the dwelling in booths (Lev. 23: 39–43), whence it is also called the Feast of Booths—but it is given this designation only in P (ibid., v. 34) and in D (Deut. 16: 13).

5

The third feast was more highly esteemed than the first two. Careful attention to the wording of the text shows clearly that though the eating of unleavened bread during the Feast of the Barley Harvest is supposed to continue for seven days, and though according to P both the first and seventh days are regarded as 'holy proclamations' (Exod. 12: 16; Lev. 23: 6–8; Num. 28: 18, 25), the attribute *ḥag* is applied only to one of these two days, and thus on only one of them is a pilgrimage supposed to be made—either on the first or on the seventh. It is highly probable that this was the actual state of affairs in pre-exilic times. According to P, the *ḥag* falls only on the first day, the fifteenth of the first month (Exod. 12: 14; Lev. 23: 6; Num. 28: 17); the seventh day, at the end of the week of eating unleavened bread, is not called a *ḥag* in P.[13] Similarly, according to D, the Passover sacrifice is brought to the chosen place in the evening and eaten during the night, and on the next day the Israelite returns home. Afterwards, he eats unleavened bread for six more days, which would imply that during these days he remains in his own town. On the seventh day, according to D, an *'aṣeret*, 'solemn assembly' (NEB: 'closing ceremony') is held, when work is forbidden (Deut. 16: 6–8), but *'aṣeret* is not a *ḥag*, neither does it involve a pilgrimage to the temple.[14] It is indeed quite difficult to assume that just a few days

[13] In Ezekiel's code, however, the distinctive character of the first day as the *ḥag* day has become blurred. See Ezek. 45: 21; and especially ibid., v. 23: 'And on the seven days of the *ḥag* he shall provide a burnt-offering to the Lord', etc. It seems highly plausible that the wording of these verses, as well as of other passages in Ezekiel's code, is quite loose, and that no inference should be drawn from it as to the actual meaning of the priestly text in the Pentateuch. He who so wishes can find even in this detail just an indication (to which many more can be added) of the secondary character of Ezekiel's code, which, as has been stated, is only an epigonic growth of the priestly school. A much sounder and more genuine 'reading' of Ezek. 45: 21 emerges in Num. 28: 16–17, as a comparison of the two texts would easily show (yet, this does not mean that Ezekiel's words were copied directly from the P text as it appears in the Book of Numbers).

[14] From the way in which the noun *'aṣeret* is used in the Bible, one can deduce that it implies 'gathering, mass assembly', and that, not necessarily for the purpose of rejoicing (cf. 2 Kgs. 10: 20; Jer. 9: 1; Joel 1: 14; 2: 15–16). The natural

after the Israelite has returned from the temple D would find fit to oblige him to go all the way back. In a fragment of E, on the other hand, it is explicitly stated that it is the seventh day of the week when unleavened bread is eaten that is the *ḥag* (Exod. 13:6).[15] As for the Feast of Weeks it goes without saying that it involves but one day (Lev. 23: 16–21; Num. 28: 26–31; cf. Deut. 16: 9–10).

It is also worth noting that nowhere do H and P apply the term *ḥag* to (the Feast of) Weeks. They call it 'the day of *bikkûrîm*, firstfruits [of wheat harvest]' (Num. 28: 26; cf. Lev. 23: 16–21), which means that, according to their conception, this feast, though labelled as a 'holy proclamation' and a day on which no work can be done, does not involve the obligation of making a pilgrimage to the temple. This is the only possible explanation for the absence of the *ḥag* of Weeks from Ezekiel's list (Ezek. 45: 21–5) and can substantiate our contention that Ezekiel's code is posterior to P, being just an epigonic growth of the priestly school. Were Ezekiel anterior to P, it would have been difficult to explain why the latter saw fit to reinstitute the Feast of Weeks in the form of

place for such a gathering would be the temple court (see the verses in Joel; likewise, according to 2 Kgs. 10: 20–1 the gathering is held in the Baal temple). But the *ʿaṣeret* differs from the *ḥag* in that it did not necessarily involve merry-making (on the contrary, it may be synonymous with fast, as in Joel), nor does it involve the obligation of pilgrimage and 'appearing before Yahweh'. In fact, therefore, such a gathering can be a local affair (as is also implied by the felicitous rendering of this word by the Targums—כנישתא, 'assembly'). In practice, the term *ʿaṣārāh*, *ʿaṣeret* could be used as a parallel of *ḥag* (Amos 5: 21) or of New Moon and Sabbath (Isa. 1: 13; at the end of this verse one should read with LXX: צום ועצרה, instead of MT: און ועצרה, since צום, 'fast' is really coupled with עצרה in biblical Hebrew). Yet, parallel words are not identical in their meaning; even heaven and earth serve, as we know, as parallel terms in biblical Hebrew.

[15] It must be admitted that E's language in Exod. 13: 3 ff. may be brief and elliptical, and, consequently, according to him the first day is also considered a *ḥag*. Further on (pp. 341–8) we shall see that the paschal sacrifice, which was performed in the night before the beginning of the Feast of Unleavened Bread, was indeed one of the temple sacrifices. This means that according to E, and possibly also according to J, the Israelite had to come to the house of God twice in the week of unleavened bread: on the eve of the first day (to sacrifice the Passover offering and to celebrate the first day as a *ḥag*), and on the seventh day (which, at least according to E, is also a *ḥag*). At the same time one must not forget that these sources are not based on cult centralization, and, with a good few temples still in existence, it would be quite possible for a person to make a pilgrimage even twice in one week, each time for one day. But the conditions would be entirely different according to P and D, who recognize the legitimacy of only one temple. It is no surprise, therefore, that they found it necessary to abolish the *ḥag* on the seventh day and to replace it by an *ʿaṣeret*, or allowed it to remain only a 'holy proclamation'.

'the day of firstfruits'. The secondary importance attributed to the Feast of Weeks can also be taken as a further proof that it was regarded only as an extension of the Feast of the Barley-Harvest.

The Feast of Booths, however, lasts for seven consecutive days, as is clearly explained in the sources subsequent to the Books of the Covenant. The priestly legislation states that an eighth day is added to this feast as an *ʿᵃṣeret*, and both the first day and this additional day are considered *miqrāʾê qōdeš*, 'holy proclamations'—yet, at the same time, the *ḥag* itself continues for all seven of the main days (Lev. 23: 33–6, 39, 41; Num. 29: 12, 35). Similarly, D points out that all seven days of the Feast of Booths constitute the *ḥag* (Deut. 16: 13, 15). For the seven days of this *ḥag* P even specifies public sacrifices on a very large scale, far more than are allotted to the seven days of the Feast of Unleavened Bread and to the Day of Firstfruits (Num. 29: 12–34). This is why it is called *heḥāg*, 'the Feast (of pilgrimage)', with the definite article and without any qualification (1 Kgs. 8: 2, 65; 12: 32–3; Ezek. 45: 25; Neh. 8: 14), that is, the most significant among the three *ḥaggîm*, the *ḥag par excellence*.[16] Indeed, the harvest season is not a convenient time for lengthy celebrations. The farmer is very busy and would certainly not take time off to make a pilgrimage to the temple, except for a very brief stay—at the beginning of the season and at its end. But after the ingathering, when the rainy season starts, and the crops have been brought in, he can well reward himself for his exertions, celebrating for seven consecutive days.

In H this great *ḥag* is called the '*ḥag* of Yahweh' (Lev. 23: 39), and from the context it transpires that the designation '*ḥag* of Booths' was applied to it later, when the former name possibly became less prevalent and its usage decreased.[17] It seems that it is

[16] The same designation, *heḥāg*, with just the definite article, is also attached to this feast in the mishnaic Hebrew (Bikkurim i. 6. 10; Sheqalim iii. 1 *et al.*).

[17] Lev. 23 belongs to P, but it contains two H fragments: vv. 9–22 and 39–43. The latter fragment deals with the Feast of Booths: it describes the four species and the peculiar duty to stay in booths for seven days. It is easy to understand why this fragment was inserted here: this description the details of which are not specified anywhere else was important to the writer of this section. In order to expound the features of the feast and make them clear, the priestly writer used crystallized literary material, quoting it, as it were, to his reader. Now within this fragment the feast is called, not 'the *ḥag* of Booths', but 'the *ḥag* of Yahweh'—even though it explains the practices which are apt to *give* it the name '*ḥag* of Booths'. This name had already been used in v. 34 by the priestly writer himself, the writer who introduced the H fragments into this section but the reason for the name comes out only in what follows, in the fragment cited from H.

this Feast that is meant when the biblical writer puts into the mouth of the Israelites the claim: 'we must hold the *ḥag* of Yahweh' (Exod. 10: 9; cf. below), and when the prophet speaks of the '*ḥag* of Yahweh' (Hos. 9: 5). It is likewise probable that this same Feast is meant in the narrative of Judg. 21: 19–23 which speaks of the '*ḥag* of Yahweh', that used to be held in Shiloh and one of the customs connected with it was the dance of the girls. The dance was not performed in the vineyards at all, but, presumably, in the temple's environs, or in the outskirts of the city. All that the narrative tells us is that the *Benjaminites* lay in wait in the vineyards and that when the girls came out to dance, the Benjaminites appeared from the vineyards and caught 'every man his wife' (ibid., vv. 20–1).[18] This narrative has nothing to do with a vintage festival, nor is there any sound reason to connect it with the story of the leaders of Shechem, who went out into the field 'and gathered the grapes from their vineyards, trod them, and held *hillûlîm*' (Judg. 9: 27). The case of the leaders of Shechem has no connection whatsoever with a *ḥag*. Theirs was simply a merry-making of *hillûlîm* (and all that can be found in it is an indirect allusion to the law of Lev. 19: 23–4, where the same term *hillûlîm* is employed). It is said that the *ḥag* of Shiloh was held 'from year to year' (Judg. 21: 19), that is, once a year, but this should not be taken as implying that there were no other *ḥaggîm* in Israel at that time.[19] The only inference which can be drawn from such a statement is that the '*ḥag of Yahweh*' was a unique event in the year, all the more so since the narrative tends to attribute to that *ḥag* a distinct local colouring, one of its characteristic features being the fact that it was accompanied by the dance of the girls; such a *ḥag*, indeed, took place but once a year and only in Shiloh.

[18] This point has already been commented upon by M. H. Segal, in his own manner; see his article 'The Song of Songs', *Tarbiẓ* 8 (1937), 135; and in מבוא המקרא, iii (Jerusalem, 1947), p. 684. However, in his posthumously published volume, *The Pentateuch* (Jerusalem, 1967), p. 237, he retracted his former opinion.

[19] Such was the conclusion drawn by Wellhausen (*PGI*, 89–90), who was followed by many scholars, all of whom also concurred with his argument that the merry-making of the leaders of Shechem resembled the *ḥag* in Shiloh. See, e.g., G. F. Moore, *Judges* (ICC, 1895), p. 450; K. Budde, *Richter* (KHC, 1897), p. 141; I. Benzinger, *Hebräische Archäologie*[3] (Leipzig, 1927), p. 387; H. J. Kraus, *Gottesdienst in Israel*[2] (München, 1962), p. 204. Most of these also describe the feast in Shiloh as a vintage festival, and state that the dance of the girls took place in the vineyards.

Nowhere in the Old Testament do we find support for the claim that at any early period in the life of Israel there was only one *ḥag*. Not only do all the Pentateuchal codes of law, even the earliest of them, speak explicitly of three *ḥaggîm*, but the earliest of the prophets also speak only of *ḥaggîm* in the plural (Amos 5: 21; 8: 10; Isa. 29: 1; similarly in Hos. 2: 13 the singular is used in a collective sense). But it is true that the '*ḥag* of Yahweh', which bore a few additional names and was the great feast of the autumn season, surpassed the harvest feasts in splendour and popularity and was regarded as the most conspicuous of the *ḥaggîm*. This is how it is portrayed from the earliest times right down to the end of the First Temple period (cf. Deut. 31: 10–13; Zech. 14: 16–19) and to some extent even down to the Second Temple times.

THE *ḤAG* AND THE EXODUS STORIES

6

In three places in the accounts of the Exodus do we find that mentions are made of the term *ḥag* (Exod. 5: 1; 10: 9; 32: 5). This seems to invalidate our contention that association with the temple is one of the essential distinctive marks of the *ḥag*. However, this contradiction is only apparent, since all three references are no more than anachronistic retrojections, that is, features taken from life in the land of Israel and used to lend colour and liveliness to an account of an earlier period, after the customary manner of the biblical narratives. In this case, the anachronistic texture is even broader in scope than it appears at first sight, since several additional, unnoticed details are involved in it, and these are apt to render the atmosphere of a pilgrimage more perceptible and to make some phenomena connected with the *ḥag* more comprehensible. And as it has been said, these details also serve to prove that all members of the family joined in the pilgrimages and rejoicing of the *ḥaggîm*, though in principle the duty to appear before Yahweh applied only to males. It is even logically demonstrable that the tumult and gaiety which the celebrants enjoyed, especially in the seven consecutive days of the great *ḥag*, were not limited to the males only, and that their dependants were not deprived of the jubilations.

According to E's account, Moses and Aaron appeared before Pharaoh and demanded of him in the name of Yahweh: 'Let my people go, that they may hold a *ḥag* to me in the wilderness' (Exod. 5: 1). The claim that they have to hold a *ḥag* is merely an excuse to enable them to escape from Egypt: Pharaoh will then discover that Israel have fled, and will try to bring them back by force (ibid. 14: 5 ff.). Now the claim that they have to hold the *ḥag* in the desert and nowhere else seems to accord with the position of the Hebrews in Egypt, as their 'natural' place is considered to be the desert, and it is only fitting, as it were, that they should celebrate their *ḥag* there. But at the same time the narrative here is enmeshed in anachronistic assumptions founded on sedentary conditions of life in Israel. For it seems to forget, for a moment, that the period here dealt with actually preceded the settlement, and that the Hebrews had as yet neither temples nor priests nor even the *ḥag* itself in its biblical sense; and the narrative goes on to describe the *ḥag* performed in Egypt as like that customary in the land of Israel.

Thus, it was certainly quite usual for a pilgrim to adorn himself with jewellery and put on his best clothes. If he was poor and simple, as most of the people were, he probably did not hesitate to borrow some finery from his neighbours. This detail, undoubtedly a prevalent popular custom, is also ascribed by the narrative to those who went out of Egypt. And it is indeed noted that they did not go empty-handed. For before they went out to celebrate their *ḥag*, they asked of the Egyptians, 'each woman of her neighbour, and of her who sojourns in her house', 'every man of his neighbour and every woman of her neighbour', jewellery of silver and gold as well as fine garments, and they put them 'on their sons and on their daughters'; furthermore, Yahweh gave the people favour in the sight of the Egyptians, so that the latter did not refuse to lend to them and were left despoiled (Exod. 3: 21–2; 11: 1–3; 12: 35–6). The naïvety and moral crudeness of a folk-story, as embodied in this detail, are a separate matter. No little embarrassment did this detail cause to earlier and later expositors, who in various ways made efforts to take the sting out of it, yet it would seem that, in this respect, the actual meaning of the story rather evaded them. Incidentally, however, we are informed that it was quite usual for women and children too to be included among the pilgrims.

7

Such a detail, that on going out to hold the feast in the wilderness the Israelites borrowed jewellery and garments from their Egyptian neighbours, could not be mentioned by J, for unlike E (cf. Exod. 1: 15—2: 10 *et al.*), he assumes that the Israelites did not live among the Egyptian population, but were concentrated in a special area of their own, in the Land of Goshen (Gen. 45: 10–11; 46: 28–34; 47: 1–6, 27*a*).[20] The pretext, according to J, for Israel's going out into the wilderness differs somewhat from that in the parallel source. Throughout most of J's account, the Israelites do not wish to hold a *ḥag* in the desert, but merely to sacrifice there, that is, to offer regular sacrifices not necessarily connected with a pilgrim-feast. As they say to Pharaoh: 'let us go, we pray, a three days journey into the wilderness, that we may sacrifice to Yahweh our God' (Exod. 3: 18; cf. 8: 4, 21–5), 'lest he fall upon us with pestilence or with the sword' (ibid. 5: 3). And as Moses frequently pronounces in the name of Yahweh: 'Let my people go that they may serve me, *w^eya'abdûnî*' (ibid. 7: 16, 26; 8: 16; 9: 1, 13; 10: 3), where the 'service' (from the root *'bd*) in reference to God, after the invariable biblical usage, implies offering sacrifices: peace-, burnt-, or grain-offerings—but these could be offered on occasions other than pilgrim-feasts.

None the less, in one instance, in J too Moses lets slip a reference to a *ḥag*, that is, to an image of a pilgrim-feast. Before the plague of locusts, Pharaoh entreats Israel saying: 'Go, serve Yahweh your God; but who are to go?' (ibid. 10: 8). To this Moses answers: 'We will go with our young and our old, we will go with our sons and with our daughters . . . for we must hold the *ḥag* of Yahweh' (ibid., v. 9). Thus we see again that it was quite usual for all members of a family to take part in a pilgrim-feast. Interesting enough is Pharaoh's reaction to Moses' answer: 'The Lord be so with you, when I let you and your little ones go [for this expression, יהי כן יהוה עמכם, cf. Amos. 5: 14; it means: 'the Lord be with you, as *you* believe'—but the one who says so does not believe himself; why Pharaoh does not believe that Yahweh will be with Israel, he goes on to explain]; look, you have some evil purpose in mind [since you plot to run away; and he who is

[20] The priestly narrative also holds that, while living in Egypt, the Israelites were concentrated in their own special area, 'in the best of the land, in the land of Rameses' (Gen. 47: 6*a*, 11).

planning to do evil, Yahweh will not be with him—this is the key to understanding the rest of what he says]. Oh no! [לא כן, i.e. you ought not to take your children with you] Go, the men among you, and serve Yahweh . . . for that is what you want [If you want to hold a *ḥag*, then the obligation to perform the pilgrimage falls on the males only—for the rest of the family it is merely optional[21]]' (ibid., vv. 10–11). Thus it turns out that the pretext of the *ḥag* becomes a stumbling block for Moses, and only plays into Pharaoh's hands. After the plague of darkness, however, Pharaoh hastens to consent to let the little ones of Israel go too (ibid., vv. 24–6), and after the slaying of the firstborn, he does not even refuse to let all their flocks and herds go with them (ibid. 12: 31–2).

Needless to say, there is no lack of popular naïvety in this narrative either. The exchanges of words between Pharaoh and Moses are all depicted with the simplicity of a popular legend, and are far from portraying the complex historical circumstances or the actual procedure followed at the Egyptian court. The negotiation between the two figures is itself conceived entirely in terms of the way of life in Israel and is infused with Israelite concepts, so much so that in the story such concepts are even used in the arguments put into Pharaoh's mouth. But then, we are incidentally given the opportunity to observe some aspects of Israelite life, as reflected in the narrative, and especially to comprehend the concept of *ḥag*, as employed by the narrator.

Similarly, Aaron's proclamation: 'Tomorrow shall be a *ḥag* to Yahweh' (Exod. 32: 5) is nothing more than the retrospective application of a concept borrowed from life in biblical Israel. Nor should there be any doubt that several details in the narrative of the golden calf are calculated to bring to mind features of a pilgrim-feast as performed in a temple court: the sacrificing of burnt- and peace-offerings, accompanied by eating, drinking, and public gaiety (ibid., v. 6), the clamour of the people, heard from afar as 'the sound of singing' (ibid., vv. 17–18), and the frenzied dances around the image (ibid., v. 19). Here, again, one can incidentally deduce that women and children took part in the celebrations (ibid., v. 2).

[21] It would seem that H. Holzinger (KHC, 1900), S. R. Driver (CBSC, 1918), and G. Beer and K. Galling (HAT, 1939), in their commentaries on Exodus, may have had such an explanation in mind, in their remarks ad loc. It is also possible that Naḥmanides anticipated them.

THE YEARLY FAMILY SACRIFICE

8

Of Elkanah, Samuel's father, it is related that his custom was to go up from his city to worship and sacrifice in the temple of Shiloh (1 Sam. 1: 3). During one of these visits Hannah, his wife, made a vow in supplication for a child, which Yahweh granted her and after weaning her son, she brought him to the temple along with a thanksgiving offering (ibid., v. 24). There Eli afterwards blessed Elkanah and his wife (ibid. 2: 20), whereupon his blessing was fulfilled and Hannah became a fruitful woman. When reading this story one usually thinks of the three annual pilgrim-feasts. Were Elkanah's visits to Shiloh really occasioned by these feasts?

Several medieval exegetes have, indeed, favoured this interpretation.[22] However, a cursory perusal of the story suffices to convince one that the text refers to only one annually recurring trip. The expression *miyyāmîm yāmîmāh*, 'from year to year' employed in 1 Sam. 1: 3 actually denotes an event that recurs only once a year (cf. Exod. 13: 10; Judg. 11: 40; 21: 19). The self-same expression is found again in the narrative, where it reads: 'And his mother used to make for him a little robe and take it to him from year to year', *miyyāmîm yāmîmāh* (1 Sam. 2: 19), that is, she used to make him a new robe just once a year. In other passages as well the text makes it quite clear that Elkanah's trip to Shiloh was observed only once a year (see, e.g., 1 Sam. 1: 7, 20–1).

The question thus arises, why are Elkanah's trips taken to have occurred only once a year?[23] The fact itself is not disputed by the

[22] Thus, Targum Jonathan translates the phrase ועלה האיש ההוא מימים ימימה (1 Sam. 1: 3) as follows: וסליק גברא ההוא מקרתיה מזמן מועד למועד. The words ויהי היום (ibid., v. 4) are rendered by him: והוה יום מועדה (as if the definite *h* of the word היום were pointing to a well-known day, a feast day). A *midrash* of the talmudic sages also assumes that Elkanah's visits to Shiloh were occasioned by the great seasonal pilgrim-feasts (Yalqut Shimʿoni, ad loc.; Qohelet Rabba v. 26).

[23] In his remarks on 1 Sam. 1: 3 the fourteenth-century Jewish Italian exegete R. Isaiah di Trani, for his part, claims that Elkanah took a special vow to make an annual pilgrimage to Shiloh *in addition* to the three seasonal pilgrimages prescribed by the Law. He finds proof of this view in the text's statement that Elkanah with his family 'went up to offer to the Lord the yearly sacrifice and to pay his vow' (ibid., v. 21). However, apparently only the yearly sacrifice is taken to be regularly connected with Elkanah's pilgrimages (cf. ibid. 2: 19). The vow seems to be the one uttered by Hannah (ibid. 1: 11) and as Elkanah acknowledged it, it also devolved upon him as is somewhat similarly ordained by the priestly law in Num. 30: 7–8, 14–15; cf. H. W. Hertzberg, *I & II Samuel* (OTL, 1964), p. 28.

moderns and they too posit the view that these trips were occasioned by one of the pilgrim-feasts, and to their mind, by the Feast of Ingathering, the annual pilgrim-feast *par excellence*.[24] Some have even suggested that our narrative contradicts the Pentateuchal laws and reflects an earlier stage when a pilgrim-feast was made only once a year, before the introduction of the harvest feasts into Israel's life, or at least before the latter became obligatory.[25]

This supposition, however, will not stand up under closer examination either. The narrative nowhere suggests that the occasion of Elkanah's visits was a pilgrim-feast, nor does it ever employ the term *ḥag* or the verb *ḥgg*. It merely states that Elkanah went up to Shiloh *lᵉhištaḥᵃwôt*, i.e. to prostrate himself before Yahweh, and also to offer the yearly sacrifice and to pay his vow (1 Sam. 1: 3, 21; 2: 19). There is no allusion to a gathering of festal celebrants or to scenes of popular rejoicing, as the pilgrim-feast is depicted in the Old Testament. It is evident that what is happening here is a 'private', personal pilgrimage by Elkanah and his household alone. Even the statement in 1 Sam. 2: 14: 'So they did at Shiloh to all the Israelites who came there' does not argue against the personal character of Elkanah's pilgrimage. This verse, which some scholars believed indicated that Elkanah's pilgrimage occurred upon a *ḥag*, describes the attitude of Eli's sons towards worshippers who pay visits to Shiloh the year around and is part of a parenthetic description of the priests' corruption. The thread of the main story is not resumed until 2: 18, where the text makes a *Wiederaufnahme* (a resumptive repetition) from 2: 11 and reverts to Elkanah's own trips to Shiloh.

I therefore believe that in Elkanah's case the text describes neither a pilgrim-feast nor anything else of this category, but rather a solemn occasion of another sort which, following the turn of phrase used in 1 Sam. 1: 21; 2: 19, may actually be termed *zeḇaḥ hayyāmîm*, 'the yearly sacrifice'. The nature of this occasion may be deduced from accidental details provided by the narrative.[26] It

[24] Cf. above, p. 299, n. 19. See also, e.g., R. de Vaux, *Les Institutions de l'aT*, ii (Paris, 1960), p. 398; W. Beyerlin, *Herkunft und Geschichte der ältesten Sinaitraditionen* (Tübingen, 1961), pp. 139, 141; and W. Nowack, *Bücher Samuelis* (GHK, 1902), p. 3; M. H. Segal, ספרי שמואל (Jerusalem, 1956), p. ד; H. W. Hertzberg, op. cit., pp. 23–4; H. H. Rowley, *Worship in Ancient Israel* (London, 1967), pp. 89–90.

[25] Cf. above, p. 299, n. 19; also, e.g., H. P. Smith, *Samuel* (ICC, 1899), p. 5.

[26] Of the scholars who I know have dealt with the subject, only Pedersen,

is a family or clan feast, confined to the family and celebrated by all its members, women and children included. It has no public or national significance whatsoever. Like any festive occasion it first of all finds expression in sacrifice and this involves the consumption of choice food and drink, to wit, meat as well as wine (cf. 1 Sam. 1: 4–9, 13–14). Since this sacrifice is deemed very special it is considered fitting that it be offered up in a house of God; if one did not exist in their own city, the family would journey to another city which did have one.[27] Thus, it is the custom of Elkanah and his family to travel annually to Shiloh for this purpose. During their visit to the temple they observe some other rites which are considered appropriate to a holy place: they pray, make and pay their vows, and prostrate themselves before Yahweh upon their arrival and before departure (cf. ibid., v. 19). This annual sacrifice does not seem to have a definite date, unlike the pilgrim-feasts, which, being in character national occasions, have their dates fixed (according to the system prescribed in P) either on the day of the full moon, the Canaanite *kese*', that is, on the fifteenth day of a given month or by an exact reckoning of weeks. Unlike the national *ḥaggîm*, this festivity is not occasioned by the sanctity of the very day on which it is performed. There is no inherent 'objective' holiness of time in this case, but rather a holiness of practice and conditions only. Being what it is, it need not recur more than once a year.[28] The observance of this custom, however, may have been restricted in accordance with local practice to a certain season or period of the year.

Consequently, Elkanah's custom does not conflict with the ancient Pentateuchal laws neither does it attest to an earlier historical stage. It belongs to another category of feasts, the observance of which was understood as a kind of 'option' and as a custom particular to and kept by all the members of a given family. This custom finds no mention in the Pentateuchal codes precisely because it was a familial institution. The Pentateuchal laws are concerned with promulgating and enjoining the observance

ILC, 376–82, 385 seems to come close to the view taken here. However, our approaches and observations differ in certain respects, some of them important.

[27] Cf., however, below, sect. 10.

[28] Hence its designation *zebaḥ hayyāmîm*, 'the yearly sacrifice', a sacrifice that is held once annually. For *yāmîm* meaning 'year' cf. Lev. 25: 29–30; Judg. 17: 10; 19: 2 (a *wāw* copulative should be added before the next word); see further 1 Sam. 27: 7; 29: 3 *et al.*; *pace* F. S. North, *VT* 11 (1961), 446–8.

of feasts which have only a general application, which the entire people, as a party to Yahweh's covenant, are bound to keep. The annual family sacrifice may not have been practised in all parts of Israel. If it did become a widespread custom it is still doubtful whether its date was ever fixed and common to all. Furthermore, it can be taken for granted that local colourings and variations were predominant in such an institution.

9

This custom is referred to in yet another narrative in the Book of Samuel. David plans to absent himself from Saul's table on the New Moon day and asks Jonathan to explain his absence thus: 'David had earnestly asked leave of me to run to Bethlehem, his city, for there is *zeḇaḥ hayyāmîm* there for all the *mišpāḥāh*, family' (1 Sam. 20: 6). Saul does not comment on David's absence on that day (ibid., vv. 24–6), but when the latter fails to appear on the following day, Jonathan hastens to explain that David has entreated him: 'Let me go, for we have a *zeḇāḥ mišpāḥāh* in the city' (ibid., vv. 28–9). This wording implies, then, that *zeḇāḥ hayyāmîm* is also styled *zeḇaḥ mišpāḥāh*, 'the family (or clan) sacrifice'. The latter term describes the character of this custom no less remarkably. Unlike Elkanah and his household, however, Jesse and his clan do not need to journey to another city, for apparently there was a temple in Bethlehem itself.[29] At the same time, though the annual family sacrifice in Bethlehem is held, according to the story, on the New Moon day, it should not be understood as basically connected with the New Moon, for as an excuse for David's absence it is also employed on the second day of the month (ibid. 20: 27 [cf. LXX], 34).

In Bethlehem the *zaḇeḥ hayyāmîm* was held in the clan's city of residence, whereas Elkanah, who was wont to observe the custom in Shiloh, was of Mount Ephraim and is referred to as an 'Ephraimite', אפרתי (1 Sam. 1: 1).[30] Now the name אפרת or אפרתה is used in the Old Testament as an appellative of the city of Bethlehem

[29] See above, p. 34.

[30] At the end of this verse LXX reads: *ἐν Νασ(ε)ιβ Ἐφράιμ*, implying בנציב (>בנצוב) (>בנצוף) אפרים (with ב as preposition) in place of MT: בן צוף אפרתי. A city by the name of נציב was, indeed, found in Judah (Josh. 15: 43; cf. Eusebius, *Onomasticon*, p. 136, l. 21), but, Wellhausen's opinion on this point notwithstanding, the MT offers the more acceptable reading, as most scholars agree.

(Gen. 35: 16, 19; 48: 7; Mic. 5: 1; Ruth 4: 11 *et al.*), whereas the gentilic form is employed to denote either a member of the tribe of Ephraim (Judg. 12: 5; 1 Kgs. 11: 26) or an inhabitant of Bethlehem (1 Sam. 17: 12; Ruth 1: 2). It is therefore quite possible that in the case of Elkanah, too, the attribute אפרתי is used in that latter sense, viz., that Elkanah was of Bethlehemite stock rather than an 'Ephraimite', though he did dwell in the hill country of Ephraim (such a gentilic appellation can actually denote a person's place of origin, not his present place of residence). Accordingly, Elkanah's way of celebrating the yearly sacrifice would constitute a further link between him and the people of Bethlehem. When viewed in this light, the attempt of Elkanah's son, Samuel, to conceal the real object of his visit to Bethlehem by saying that he has 'come to sacrifice to Yahweh' (1 Sam. 16: 2–5) becomes all the more comprehensible. It would be natural for a person to come to his ancestral city to offer up sacrifices, especially if the city boasted a temple, as Bethlehem probably did—and it could be a perfectly plausible reason to give. Thus it transpires that Samuel's clan was not necessarily Ephraimite, but of Bethlehemite origin, that is, of the tribe of Judah.[31]

In any case, some supplementary indications could at least hint at connections between Bethlehem and the settlements of Mount Ephraim. The young Levite from Bethlehem finds his way to the house of Micayehu in the hill country of Ephraim and settles there (Judg. 17: 7–12). Another Levite who dwells in Ephraim takes a concubine from Bethlehem (Judg. 19: 1–19). The old Ephraimite who lives in Gibeah accepts the Levite's story that he went to Bethlehem in Judah as a matter of course, and unlike the local inhabitants, the Benjaminites, brings him to his house (ibid., vv. 16–20). Consanguineous and marriage relationships apparently formed particular ties between the populations settled on the opposite sides of Benjamin's territory, and the term *'Eprāt* (which seems to be cognate to Ephraim) as an epithet of Bethlehem (or one of its quarters) as well as the appellation *'Eprātî*, shared by both the Ephraimites and Bethlehemites, may betoken those ties.[32]

[31] If this inference is correct, and Samuel, the last judge, who became David's patron and supporter was indeed of the tribe of Judah, it may well have some bearing on our understanding of certain occurrences of contemporary Israelite history.

[32] The name אפרתה also occurs in the genealogies of the Book of Chronicles as the name of one of the wives of Caleb the son of Hezron. She bore him several

The relationship between the populations of Mount Ephraim and Bethlehem on the one hand, and the appearance of an annual family sacrifice in both these areas on the other, may suggest that the custom, as described in both narratives, was observed mainly in and about these regions. It seems very likely that the narratives reflect the local, specific manifestation of this family institution, whereas in other regions it may have had significant variations.

10

It must further be remembered that the biblical concept of *mišpāḥāh* is rather flexible and at any rate includes more than the narrow circle of the immediate family. Since the observance we are discussing is called the sacrifice of the *mišpāḥāh* it may embrace a kinship group of considerable size. The passage referring to the Bethlehemite observance does not, indeed, state that the sacrifice was held by Jesse and his household alone. On the contrary, David's excuse that 'there is a yearly sacrifice there for *all* the *mišpāḥāh*', 'for our *mišpāḥāh* holds a sacrifice *in the city*' (1 Sam. 20: 6, 29), implies that the entire city population was in fact expected to participate in the celebration. It is not unusual in the East for an entire city-community to become interrelated through marriage so that it actually turns into a single clan. In such a case, a topo-geographical term also serves to denote a tribal unit.

Once this is observed, we can add one other narrative to our data, and once again Samuel figures in it. Arriving at Samuel's city, Saul and his servant are told by the maidens that the seer 'has come just now to the city, because the people have a sacrifice today on the high-place' (1 Sam. 9: 12). Although here the sacrifice is not described as the yearly or the clan sacrifice it is nevertheless possible that the story refers to an analogous custom, for it is said that the entire city-community is taking part in the celebration. At any rate, there is no Pentateuchal law ordering all the inhabitants of a city to take part in a special sacrifice, nor is

sons, said to be the ancestors of various clan-cities, among them Bethlehem, but also Kiriath-jearim, Beth-gader, Netophah, Atroth-beth-joab, the clans of Zor'ah and Eshta'ol, and other settlements. See 1 Chron. 2: 19, 24, 50–4; 4: 4 and commentaries. However, it is extremely doubtful whether these genealogical combinations have any real bearing on the geographical conditions of the period of the monarchy. For another view see S. Klein, 'Studies in the Genealogical Lists of the Book of Chronicles', מאסף ציון, iii (1929), 7–8 (Hebrew).

there any allusion in the narrative to the effect that the occasion was a pilgrim-feast. The next part of the maidens' conversation tells us of the eating procedure and the role of the prophet in the ceremony: 'For the people will not eat till he comes, since he must bless the sacrifice; afterward those eat who are invited' (ibid., v. 13). The 'invited persons', *haqqᵉrūʾîm* who sit and partake of the sacrificial repast in a special chamber, *liškāh*, are about thirty in number (ibid., v. 22). This group does not only consist of guests from outside the city. Apparently it also includes prominent citizens and heads of families from the city proper. From other biblical passages too we can gather that it was customary for *qᵉrūʾîm*, specially invited persons, to partake of the sacrificial meal (see Zeph. 1: 7; 1 Sam. 16: 3–5; 2 Sam. 15: 11–12; 1 Kgs. 1: 9–49 *passim*; cf. Exod. 34: 15; Num. 25: 2).[33] Thus, the procedure for eating the sacrificial meal which Saul and his servant chanced upon would consist of the following stages: first the seer blesses the sacrifice, then the 'invited persons' partake of the sacrifice, finally the rest of the people join in the meal. The latter evidently have to content themselves with the remnants of the food and their participation in the meal may simply be symbolic. At the same time, though it is said that the entire community takes part in the sacrifice, the town maidens find time to fetch water from outside the city. However, their act may be connected with the feast.

This sacrifice may differ in certain respects from the ones observed by Elkanah and in Bethlehem. Thus, the person who blesses the sacrifice and apparently also sits at the head of the table in the chamber is here a seer, a man of God. However, without any doubt, a similar man of God present at the 'clan sacrifice' in Bethlehem would also have undertaken the same role. Furthermore, the narrative probably also considers Samuel, who appears to be distinguished here by old age, to be the leader and patriarchal chief of his townsmen, although his importance as a soothsayer is more salient and takes precedence over his patriarchal prominence.[34] This becomes all the more probable, as Samuel's city is said in this narrative to be in the land of Zuph (1 Sam. 9: 5),

[33] The same virtually obtained with respect to non-sacrificial meals in which meat and wine would be served (Prov. 9: 2–5. 14–18).

[34] The particular emphasis on Samuel's divining quality is prompted here by, among other things, the structure and object of the narrative, in which Saul, while searching for lost asses, must meet the diviner who will inform him of the word of God and anoint him king over Israel.

and Zuph is the eponym of Elkanah's family (1 Sam. 1: 1). It follows, then, that here Samuel is held to be dwelling among his own kinsfolk.[35] Consequently, we may suppose that the yearly sacrifice at Bethlehem was not unlike the sacrifice made by Samuel's townspeople and that the components of the latter were not absent from the former: 'specially invited persons', *qᵉrûʾîm* and a 'chamber', *liškāh*[36] as well as one who blesses the sacrifice on behalf of all the city folk.

The sacrifice of Samuel's townspeople differs in yet another respect, in that it is held on a high-place, not in a temple, as was Elkanah's yearly sacrifice and, apparently, Bethlehem's. Nevertheless, even this difference is not cogent in this instance. For it is inconceivable that an entire population would leave its own city simply to hold a sacrifice in another city. Moreover, it has already been pointed out that an eminent high-place could be superior to a provincial, modest temple, though formally, in terms of cultic institutions the temple is of a higher category.[37] The high-place of Samuel's city which looms impressively in the background throughout the narrative (1 Sam. 9: 13–14, 19, 25) appears to have been a pre-eminent place of this type. In certain circumstances, then, there could be no strictures against performing the yearly sacrifice at some important high-place, even though from the qualitative point of view a temple could be deemed preferable.

[35] At the same time, although head and leader of his townsmen, his influence extends over the neighbouring region too. Usually he lives in his own city (1 Sam. 9: 6); yet, just before Saul and his servant arrive, Samuel returns to the city to bless the sacrifice (ibid., v. 12). Before that he was away from the city (ibid., v. 23), apparently on a visit to another town or to some other high-place (cf. S. R. Driver, *Notes on . . . the Books of Samuel*², p. 72). The same state of affairs is reflected in the parallel narrative: 'And he went on a circuit . . . to Bethel, Gilgal and Mizpah. . . . Then he would come back to Ramah, for his home was there' (ibid. 7: 16–17). There is no convincing reason to doubt the homogeneity and continuity of the narrative in 1 Sam. 9 as some scholars asserted (W. Caspari, H. W. Hertzberg *et al.*; see also H. J. Stoebe, 'Noch Einmal die Eselinnen des *Ḳîš*', *VT* 7 (1957), 363–5). The narrative seems to assume that Samuel left the city immediately after the sacrifice had been made and returned at the time appointed for the meal. For when Samuel enters the chamber he reminds the cook that he had instructed him to set aside a special portion (ibid. 9: 23). Hence it appears that Samuel returned to the city only to begin the meal. This also implies that the sacrificial meal is blessed immediately before eating begins, as the text has it: 'For the people will not eat till he comes, since he must bless the sacrifice' (ibid., v. 13).

[36] It is worth noting that in LXX a *liškāh*, *κατάλυμα* also finds mention in the narrative on Elkanah (1 Sam. 1: 18); cf. also above, p. 24, n. 20.

[37] See above, p. 25.

II

In the Karatepe inscription, Azitawadda King of the Danunites boasts that, among other things, he built his city and placed in it the statue of Baal-*Krntryš*, and ordained that certain cultic acts be performed there. The inscription then reads: *wylk zbḥ lkl hmskt zbḥ ymm ʾlp 1 wb*[*ʿt ḥ*]*rš ś 1 wbʿt qṣr ś 1* (Text A, ii, 19–iii, 2; cf. Text C, iv, 2–6). That is, I offered (or: established, or fixed; or: there was offered or established) a sacrifice (sacrificial order) for all the molten images: for *zbḥ ymm* one ox, and at the time of ploughing one sheep, and at the time of harvesting one sheep. What is of importance for us is the meaning of the words *zbḥ ymm* in this context.

Ever since scholars began to decipher this inscription, many have interpreted *zbḥ ymm* as *zeḇaḥ yāmîm*, citing the biblical verses in which this expression is found.[38] The meaning of this part (as well as of other parts) of the text is not clear enough. Yet, it is *a priori* difficult to suppose that the monumental royal inscription would refer to the very custom of which the narratives in the Book of Samuel speak. 'The Yearly sacrifice', mentioned incidentally as it is in the Old Testament, is a popular, folk institution, its background, tradition, and its setting, the closed circle of the clan. It hardly seems the sort of thing that would be described in a royal inscription, or counted among the undertakings of a king seeking to exalt his name for all time. Furthermore, it is difficult to suppose that *zeḇaḥ hayyāmîm* in its Old Testament definition would be considered a fitting sacrifice 'to all the images' of the gods in the royal temple. Again, if we suppose that *zbḥ ymm* refers here to a sacrifice (of one ox) made once a year, one might well wonder why it is considered more important than the seasonal sacrifices at ploughing and harvest times, when only one sheep is offered.

[38] See R. Marcus and I. J. Gelb, *JNES* 8 (1949), 119; A. M. Honeyman, *PEQ* 81 (1949), 27; R. T. O'Callaghan, *Orientalia*, 18 (1949), 179; F. Rosenthal, *ANET*, p. 500; Donner-Röllig, *KAI* ii, pp. 37, 42. N. H. Tur-Sinai, הלשון והספר, i[2] (Jerusalem, 1954), p. 79, renders it in the same way; as does E. Olavarri, *EsBi* 29 (1970), 311–12, 320–4. The latter, moreover, identifies the 'time of harvesting', *ʿt qṣr*, of the inscription with the Feast of Weeks. Tur-Sinai suggests dividing the words of the text and explaining them in an unusual way (op. cit., pp. 72–3). Of late, cf. also B. A. Levine, *In the Presence of the Lord* (Leiden, 1974), pp. 132–5, by whose arguments I have not been convinced. Attempts made, hesitantly by A. Alt (*WdO* 1 (1949), 283), and without hesitation by C. H. Gordon (*JNES* 8 (1949), 111), to read 'a sacrifice of one-thousand days', have not been accepted.

It is probable, therefore, that those who rendered *zbḥ ymm* as *zebaḥ yômām*, 'a daily sacrifice' were right.[39] The daily sacrifice of an ox, then, is mentioned here as the king's sacrifice (not that of families, who are not referred to in the royal inscription and can have had no part to play), while at ploughing and harvest times an offering of a sheep is *added* to it.[40] At any rate, it has been shown that the phrase *zebaḥ hayyāmim* does not serve as a technical, specific term, but is rather a vague description of a familial observance, which can be styled in another way (or other ways) too. It is hardly conceivable that such a designation, which has about it a certain 'casualness' and arises from a certain literary style, would be applied as a definitive, authoritative term in a royal inscription. This is to say that even if we concede that the inscription does speak of *zebaḥ yāmîm* and not of *zebaḥ yômām*, it still should not lead us into thinking that the *zebaḥ yāmîm* means the same thing in the inscription and in the Book of Samuel. They would only appear to share a common wording.

THE YEARLY BANQUET AND OTHER FAMILY FEASTS

12

Something analogous to the yearly sacrifice as described in the Book of Samuel may be referred to in the opening narrative of the Book of Job. The seven sons of Job, it is related, used to hold a drinking banquet, *mišteh*, 'in the house of each on his day', where they would be joined by their three sisters. The sisters were, in point of fact, the 'invited guests' to the banquet (Job. 1: 4). When the days of feasting had come to an end Job would summon all his sons (and daughters) to him, would 'sanctify' them, that is, cleanse them of ritual contamination,[41] and offer a

[39] J. Leveen and C. Moss, *JJS* (1948), 192.

[40] J. Pedersen, *AcOr* 21 (1953), 40–1, 54, recognized that the sacrifice of an ox cannot here be taken to be an annual event, for the sacrifices at ploughing and harvest times are also annual (yet are only of one sheep). Nevertheless, he assumes that *zbḥ ymm* refers to *zebaḥ hayyāmîm* and interprets *yāmîm* as denoting an indefinite period of time. Accordingly, he rendered *zbḥ y(ā)m (î)m* as 'regular' or 'ordinary sacrifice'. It seems to be inaccurate, both thus to interpret the term *yāmîm* (which in the Old Testament stands for the precise period of one year), and to read the biblical concept *zebaḥ hayyāmîm* into the inscription.

[41] This is the obvious meaning of the verb *qdš* (used in the verse) when employed in the 'strong' conjugations (that is, *pi'ēl* or *hitpa'ēl*) in the terminology typical of the non-priestly sources—that is, to purge or purify (a person or an

burnt-offering for each of them, for fear that they might have sinned unwittingly. 'Thus did Job do *kol hayyāmîm*, all the days' (ibid., v. 5). Though the text calls the occasion a 'drinking banquet', *mišteh*, it tells us that the brothers and sisters also indulged in eating (ibid., vv. 13, 18): no doubt assuming that choice food was served, that is, meat, which may even have been sacrificial meat.[42] The family meal is called a *mišteh*, then, only to highlight the gaiety characterizing it, or just because there is no specific term for such an occurrence in biblical idiom.[43]

How long did the feast last? Some scholars contend that it was held every day of the week in the house of each brother in turn, so that the weeks of the year were spent in an incessant round of feasting. The expression *kol hayyāmîm* in 1: 5 would, accordingly, denote 'the year around', 'during the year'.[44] A more plausible view, however, is that the feast was held only once a year for seven days, the usual period of time devoted to elaborate feasting (cf. Gen. 29: 27–8; Judg. 14: 12–18; 1 Kgs. 8: 66; Esther 1: 5 *et al.*).[45] The expression *kol hayyāmîm* would denote 'all the years',

object or oneself) from uncleanness. This act is an essential prerequisite for participating in a sacral ceremony or partaking of a sacrificial meal. Cf. Exod. 19: 10, 22–3; Josh. 3: 5; 1 Sam. 16: 5; 2 Sam. 11: 4; 1 Kgs. 8: 64 *et al.* In the style of the priestly school the verb also denotes the positive, active sense of imparting or acquiring the quality of holiness. Cf. my comments in *EM* iv. 494–5.

42 The question whether or not the meat was sacrificial begs the question whether non-sacrificial slaughter was considered to be legitimate. There are various indications that even in the pre-Josianic times non-sacrificial slaughter was practised and had to be put up with although fundamentally considered unlawful (cf. my comments in *EM* iv. 550–1). However, even if we agree with G. Fohrer, *Hiob* (KAT, 1963), p. 77, that the narrative refers to a non-sacrificial meal we may still be justified in seeing it as analogous to a sacral meal. Sacrificial repasts, which included wine-drinking, were also sometimes the occasion for exuberant gaiety (even when they were made within sacred precincts).

43 For the use of the term *mišteh* in the sense of meal cf. Gen. 19: 3; 26: 30; 1 Kgs. 3: 15; Isa. 25: 6; Jer. 16: 8 *et al.*; also N. H. Tur-Sinai, *The Book of Job* (Jerusalem, 1957), p. 7.

44 This is the view of Ibn-Ezra and the author of *Meṣudôt*; among moderns, of B. Duhm (KHC, 1897), A. B. Davidson (CBSC, 1918), G. Hölscher (HAT, 1952), G. Fohrer, and others. This interpretation has already been advanced by LXX which translates בית איש יומו—καθ' ἑκάστην ἡμέραν. Another possible interpretation would be that the feast was held on seven separate occasions during the year, each time in the house of a different brother. The text would then leave unspecified the period of time the feast lasted on each occasion and would only indicate that each brother had a particular day during the year on which the feast resumed at his home.

45 Such is more or less the view expounded in the commentaries of A. Dillmann (KEH, 1891), K. Budde (GHK, 1913), S. R. Driver and G. B. Gray

viz., 'every year, yearly'.[46] This interpretation appears to be sustained by a closer examination of the phrase בית איש יומו (Job 1: 4), where both the words איש יומו are used in the singular, which implies that the festivity held in the house of each brother in turn lasted no longer than one day. The phrase כי הקיפו ימי המשתה, 'when the *days* of feasting had run their course' (ibid., v. 5) can refer, then, only to the conclusion of the period of time in which the festivity was held 'in the house of each brother *on his day*' as stated in the previous verse.

Thus, once again we meet with an annual feast celebrated by the entire family. There are, of course, noteworthy differences between the feast of Job's sons and the yearly sacrifice observed by Elkanah and the people of Bethlehem (and of Samuel's town), but certain considerations may render them less forcible than they appear:

(*a*) True, Job, the head of the family, does not take part in the banquet. Nevertheless, when the days of feasting are over, he summons his sons to him, offers burnt-offerings for them, and only then does the feasting formally come to an end.

(*b*) The family congregates for the feast in the brothers' homes, not in a temple (nor even in a high-place). However, this is because of the actual nature of the society portrayed in the Book of Job, a society totally unacquainted with temples. This society, ethnically related to the tribes of Qedem, is similar to that of the Genesis stories and its way of life is similar to that of the Patriarchs. It has no recourse either to temples or to priesthood, and all priestly functions are performed in it by the head of the family. The people of Qedem as well as the early Hebrew tribes are described as mainly occupied in, and living on, cattle-raising and the absence of temples with a priestly class is apparently connected with the semi-nomadic conditions of their existence.[47] Yet, for our purposes

(ICC, 1921; with hesitation), N. H. Tur-Sinai, M. Pope (AB, 1965) and others.

[46] Cf. above, p. 306, n. 28.

[47] Scholars have long noted the marked resemblance between the Book of Job, particularly its prose narrative, and the Patriarchal stories. At the same time, it seems to me that the resemblance does not prove a common historical–chronological setting but merely common social conditions and mode of life. That is to say, Job is not considered a contemporary of the Patriarchs but only as one living in similar circumstances (his mode of life points to somewhat more sedentary agricultural conditions). One must not overlook the fact that we are dealing with two distinct ethnic groups here: among Israel's ancestors the

it is quite sufficient that there is a certain basic resemblance between the feast of Job's sons and the custom of yearly sacrifice, for we have already noted that from the start one may expect to meet with significant variations in the features of such an institution according to its diffusion in various places and periods.

13

In three narratives in the Book of Samuel we have encountered a family custom, not mentioned in any of the Pentateuchal codes, which was observed once a year, but not on a fixed date. The non-national character of the custom (in that each clan was wont to observe it in its own way and at its own time) makes it likely that there would be noticeable variations from place to place. Another example of this custom, or of a related one, appears in the introductory narrative to the Book of Job.

In point of fact, these customs are only examples of the category of cultic–familial, non-national observances that were prevalent in biblical times and found no mention in the Pentateuchal codes. Just another case in point is the sheep-shearing festival which despite its connection with farming had nothing to do with the agricultural pilgrim-feasts. This too was essentially a family observance and was the occasion for elaborate eating and drinking (1 Sam. 25: 4–36; 2 Sam. 13: 23–28; cf. Gen. 31: 19; 38: 12–17).[48] One can surely assume that there were several additional festal observances of this sort which took place outside the temple limits and they should by no means be mistaken for the *ḥaggîm.*

semi-nomadic mode of life ended with the settlement in Canaan, whereas the people of Qedem, to which Job belongs (Job 1: 3), continued to live thus until later times (cf. Jer. 49: 28–9; Ezek. 25: 4–5 *et al.*). Now this mode of life is unfamiliar with temples, but altars are indeed found there, as they are also mentioned in the Patriarchal stories (cf. above, pp. 17–18). It has already been noted that the yearly family sacrifice could also be performed at a venerated altar or high-place. If, however, in the case of Job's sons we have an instance of a non-sacrificial meal (cf. above, p. 314, n. 42) it may still be regarded as a secular transformation of an otherwise sacral feast.

48 On this festival cf. Pedersen, *ILC* iii–iv. 397–8. It should be noted that the setting of this family festival, unlike that of the yearly sacrifice of Elkanah and in Bethlehem, was from the outset entirely removed from the temple precincts. Only an oblation of the first fleeces was brought to the priest (Deut. 18: 4).

XVII

THE PASSOVER SACRIFICE

I

THE paschal sacrifice is mentioned indirectly in all the Pentateuchal sets of laws: in the Book of the Covenant (Exod. 23: 18) and the Minor Book of the Covenant (Exod. 34: 25)—as will be demonstrated later on; within the framework of P—in the calendar of the 'holy proclamations' (Lev. 23: 5) and in the register of public sacrifices made during the year (Num. 28: 16); also in D's code, where a number of details of this sacrifice are cited (Deut. 16: 1–7). However, the actual features of the offering are precisely specified in 'narrative' passages constituting a part of the story of the Exodus. There are two of these: a detailed P passage (Exod. 12: 1–20; with the appendix at the end of this chapter, vv. 43–50) and a J passage (ibid., vv. 21–7).

The talmudic sages understood the two latter passages to refer mainly to the Passover sacrifice made in Egypt, as distinct from the permanent Passover referred to in other sections,[1] and they were followed by the medieval commentators and a number of moderns. Indeed one cannot deny that these two passages are set in Egypt and that the performance of the sacrifice is here inseparable from the story of the deliverance itself. As the story has it, the signs on their doorways of blood from the sacrifice caused Yahweh to pass over the houses of the Israelites, when he smote all the first-born of man and beast on the eve of the Exodus (Exod. 12: 12–13, 23). This also explains the name of the sacrifice—פסח הוא ליהוה, 'It is the Passover [sacrifice] to Yahweh', because on that night he passed over (Heb. *pāsaḥ 'al*) the houses of the Israelites (ibid., vv. 11, 27).[2] The offering of the first Passover

[1] Mekhilta to Exod. 12: 3; Bab. Tal. Pesaḥim 96*a et al.*

[2] The phrase פסח [הוא] ליהוה occurs in this form in all the sources (see further Exod. 12: 48; Lev. 23: 5; Num. 9: 10, 14; 28: 16; Deut. 16: 1–2; 2 Kgs. 23: 21, 23). It perhaps contains an intimation of the pagan origin of the ceremony. We find similar locutions such as חג המצות ליהוה, 'the Feast of Unleavened Bread to Yahweh' (Lev. 23: 6; cf. Exod. 12: 14; 13: 6); חג הסכות ליהוה . . ., 'the Feast of Booths to Yahweh' (Lev. 23: 34; cf. ibid., v. 41; Num.

sacrifice therefore in itself rescued the Israelites from the catastrophe and also enabled them to leave Egypt (cf. Num. 33: 3). Nevertheless, there can be no doubt that the first sacrifice presumably serves as a model for the future and that in every generation the details of the sacrificial rite have to be repeated in exactly the same manner. There is no indication that any distinction should be made between the Egyptian Passover and that of future generations. Express notes concerning the validity of the sacrifice for the ages to come are even appended to the P (Exod. 12: 14, 17) and J (ibid., vv. 24–7) passages. Similarly it is stated in the continuation of the P passage that just as the first night was 'a night of vigil for Yahweh' so it must remain one of vigil 'for all the people of Israel throughout their generations' (ibid., v. 42). This means that the account of the preparation of the first sacrifice becomes a statute, or, conversely, the presentation of the law against the background of the Exodus story furnishes the broad aetiological explanation for the dramatic features of the sacrifice. Needless to say, the two passages are only parallel literary formulations of a single theme.

A mention should further be made of the P statute on the duty of observing the Second Passover, incumbent upon anyone who was 'defiled by a corpse or on a long journey' at the proper time. This law, too, is prescribed in a narrative framework (Num. 9: 1–14).

DISTINGUISHING FEATURES AND SUPPOSED ORIGIN

2

The following are the features that characterize the paschal offering and the dramatic gestures connected with its preparation.

According to the P passage (Exod. 12: 1–14) this sacrifice is to be made on a specific day in the year, namely, the fourteenth of the first month, and the offering is to be slaughtered at twilight (on this detail cf. Lev. 23: 18; Num. 9: 3; 28: 16). The offering

29: 12); חג שבעות ליהוה אלהיך, 'the Feast of Weeks to Yahweh your God' (Deut. 16: 10); cf. also Exod. 32: 5. It is quite possible that the pilgrim-feasts, being bound up with agriculture and settled conditions of life, also had pagan origins.

is held in readiness from the tenth of the month, and is eaten by all the members of the household together, or by them and their neighbours. It must be brought from the flock only, of the sheep or of the goats, and the animal must be without blemish, a male, and a year old.[3] Its blood must be smeared on the two doorposts and on the lintel of the house. It is to be eaten at night, after the sacrifice has been roasted on the fire, 'its head, legs, and entrails'—it must not be eaten raw or cooked with water—and should be accompanied by unleavened bread and bitter herbs. None of it should be left over until morning. It must be eaten hurriedly and in an atmosphere of drama, with loins girded, sandals on the feet, a staff in the hand. In the appendix to this passage further instructions are added: only the circumcised may partake of the Passover; none of its flesh may be taken outside the house; not a bone of the offering may be broken (Exod. 12: 43–9; cf. Num. 9: 11–12).

The J passage (Exod. 12: 21–7) in no way contradicts the priestly descriptions. In a number of particulars it totally agrees with them: the Passover offering is to be brought from the flock, it must be prepared on a family basis, and its blood applied to the two doorposts. On the other hand it contains several details which are not specified in the priestly passage: only here is it explained that the blood of the sacrifice is to be collected in a basin,[4] and that a bunch of hyssop is to be used to daub blood on the entrance of the house,[5] and that no one may go out of the door of the house till morning (in the parallel account we find only a prohibition against leaving any part of the sacrificial flesh until morning). It appears that if we are to extract as many details as possible of the drama of the paschal sacrifice, we must combine the two accounts.

[3] According to P (Lev. 22: 23) 'an ox or a sheep with a limb extended or contracted' might be sacrificed as a free-will offering, but not for a vow (and *a fortiori* not for a thanksgiving or a public sacrifice). At any rate, the status of the Passover is higher than that of a free-will offering,

[4] Hebrew: *sap*, a vessel for holding liquids (cf. 2 Sam. 17: 28; 1 Kgs. 7: 50; 2 Kgs. 12: 14 *et al.*). But the LXX understood the word in the sense of the threshold of the door, rendering it in Exod. 12: 22: *παρὰ τὴν Θύραν*.

[5] We also find hyssop used in purifying against leprosy, for sprinkling blood (Lev. 14: 4–7, 49–52), and in purifying against defilement by the dead, for the sprinkling of the water of lustration (Num. 19: 6, 18–19), while the psalmist declares: 'Purge me with hyssop and I shall be clean' (Ps. 51 : 9). On its botanical identity see M. Zohary, *EM*, i. 185–6. Its identification with the plant called in Arabic زعتر or صعتر was already suggested by Saadia Gaon; cf. Y. Kapaḥ, פירושי רס״ג על התורה (Jerusalem, 1963), ad loc. and Ibn-Ezra on Exod. 12: 22.

Both refer to the same happening, but neither of them has all the details, which means that they actually complement one another.

These aspects jointly produce a most 'strange' and extraordinary pattern. Suffice it to point out that eating at night is itself a complete reversal of customary procedure in biblical times (even with regard to secular slaughtering). And of all the various categories of sacrifice, there is not a single oblation that must be eaten at night-time, save the Passover—just as there is not a night in the whole year on which it is obligatory to eat sacrificial flesh except the one that begins (according to P's specification) on the fourteenth of the first month at twilight. How much more so is the entire picture strange, eating at night being only one feature of a unique complex of ritual peculiarities.

3

The dramatic embellishments of the Passover point clearly to its nomadic origin. The indications are: the collective participation in the preparation and consumption of the sacrifice; the choosing of the offering specifically from the flock, not from the herd; the eating at night, which is when nomads are used to eat; eating the sacrificial flesh roasted, not raw or boiled with water; the emphasis given to the role of blood and the particular use made of it in connection with this sacrifice; the hurried eating of the meal and the atmosphere of drama in which it is eaten.[6]

It was once suggested that this sacrifice originally had a purificatory significance, and that the use of hyssop in applying blood to the lintel and doorposts also points to such origins. On the other hand, a number of scholars, basing their argument particularly on J's evidence in Exod. 12: 21–7, state that this was primarily an apotropaic rite: blood was applied to the lintel and doorposts for protection against plagues without a sacrifice or the consumption of flesh (which are not mentioned in the J passage).[7] Now the

[6] The arguments of, for instance, I. Engnell, *Critical Essays on the OT* (London, 1970), p. 190, against the nomadic origins of this sacrifice are not convincing.

[7] The interpretation of the Passover as a purificatory sacrifice was put forward by H. Ewald, *Die Alterthümer des Volkes Israel*[3] (Göttingen, 1866), pp. 460–1. It is based on the premise that the P sections of the Pentateuch are not late (in contradiction to the view subsequently accepted by the Wellhausen school). The theory that the Passover was an apotropaic ritual, merely of smearing blood, was advanced, e.g., by K. Marti, *Geschichte der israelitischen Religion*[4] (Strasburg, 1903), pp. 40–1; and I. Benzinger, *EB*, iii. 3594–5. More recently H. J. Kraus has adopted an interpretation akin to this (*Gottesdienst in Israel*[2] (München, 1962), p. 62), and he, too, relies principally on Exod. 12:

paschal ritual as a whole certainly does contain an apotropaic element. Nevertheless, we should not give undue emphasis to one detail, or seek to base our argument on a single piece of evidence, ignoring other evidence, namely that of P, which parallels and complements it. If we wish to gain a clear perspective on the question, it is better to look at the entire picture as reflected in all the sources and to concede that there are indications of the Passover's nomadic origin, and possibly also of its basic connection with this season of the year (as well as with the day of the full moon), without making further speculations.[8] The basic connection between the Passover offering and nomadic conditions of life differentiates it from the Feast of Unleavened Bread, which had its place only in settled conditions of life. The link between the sacrifice and the feast is the result of circumstances, not of intrinsic similarities.

A number of authentic characteristics of the Passover have been excised from D's account of it. True, even according to D the Passover is prepared at night (Deut. 16: 1, 4, 6–7) and eaten before morning (ibid., v. 4), but it is brought from the flock and the herd (v. 2), and is boiled (v. 7). Boiling is the way in which settled peoples usually cook their meat (cf. Judg. 6: 19; 1 Sam. 2: 13; Ezek. 46: 24 *et al.*). D's description of the sacrifice is therefore flatter and more even than that given in the other sources.[9] In addition, D does not fail to emphasize that the Passover must be presented only at the chosen place (Deut. 16: 5–7).

4

With regard to the Passover celebrations mentioned in the historical books one can remark briefly that the account of the

21–7. Views similar to these two, in a somewhat confused form, were already expressed by W. J. Moulton, *DB*, iii. 688–9. The apotropaic element in the Passover sacrifice is also pointed out by S. E. Loewenstamm, *The Tradition of the Exodus in its Development* (Jerusalem, 1965), pp. 84–8, 93–4 (Hebrew); of late also, e.g., by P. Laaf, *Die Paschafeier Israels* (Bonn, 1970), pp. 154–8, 167–9.

[8] One of the most recent scholars to use the evidence of P is actually L. Rost, *Das kleine Credo und andere Studien zum AT* (Heidelberg, 1965), pp. 101–6. Rost describes the Passover as an apotropaic celebration of nomadic herdsmen which took place before they started out on their annual journey. The celebration, accompanied with a sacrifice, was held at the beginning of the year, at full moon, at the time when the nomads used to move camp from the desert to settled areas. Kraus (loc. cit.) seems to accept Rost's explanation as well.

[9] On the excision of some ancient features of the Passover in D's portrayal cf. also M. Weinfeld, *Tarbiẓ* 31 (1962), 5.

Israelites' Passover at Gilgal, the evening before manna ceased (Josh. 5: 10–11), is P's. Josiah's Passover was kept, as it has been said, in the spirit of D, after this king's reforms and as a climax to them, and in the Book of Kings a number of Deuteronomistic expansions were added to the account of this Passover (2 Kgs. 23: 21–3).[10] But the parallel description in 2 Chron. 35: 1–19 is a synthesis with elements from both D and P: the sacrifice is offered up from the flock and the herd, but is handled by the priests and the Levites (the latter prepare it for themselves and for the priests, as well as for the singers and gate-keepers). The Chronicler's note: 'And they cooked, *wayᵉḇaššᵉlû* the Passover lamb *with fire* according to the ordinance' (ibid., v. 13), is simply an attempt to combine the two expressions: 'You shall boil it, *ûḇiššaltā* and eat it' (Deut. 16: 7) and the emphatic injunction to roast it over *the fire* (Exod. 12: 8–9). This account probably reflects the way the Passover was prepared during the Chronicler's own time, when the Pentateuch had already been canonized in its entirety, but the midrashic tradition that was to take shape in the rabbinic interpretation had not yet emerged.[11]

A similar observation may be made about Hezekiah's Passover. Priests and Levites take part in its preparations, and because the priests and the people were ritually unclean and many people did not come to Jerusalem at the proper time, the Passover was kept on the fourteenth of the second month (2 Chron. 30: 1–20), in complete accord with the law of Num. 9: 1–14. In the case of Josiah's Passover (2 Chron. 35: 12–13) and in the case of Hezekiah's (ibid. 30: 5, 16, 18) the Chronicler bases himself expressly on 'Scripture'—'as it is written in the book of Moses', and in 'the law of Moses the man of God', 'according to the ordinance'. Similarly, the Passover that, according to Ezra 6: 19–21, was kept

[10] Cf. above, p. 133.

[11] Talmudic legislation is based on Exod. 12: 3–5, 21 only and ordains that the Passover sacrifice—both that of Egypt and the regular Passover—should be chosen from the flock alone (Mekhilta ad loc.; Jer. Tal. Pesaḥim viii. 3 *et al.*). The legislation underlying the Pseudepigrapha also rules thus (Jubilees 49: 3). In commenting on the mention of the herd in Deut. 16: 2 the talmudic sages state that it refers to the *ḥᵃgîgāh*, the festal sacrifice (Sifre ad loc.; Mishnah Pesaḥim vi. 3–4), or to מותר הפסח, 'the remainder of the Passover' (i.e. the lamb that was set aside to be a Passover sacrifice, was lost and not recovered until after another had been sacrificed in its stead), which is presented as a peace-offering (Bab. Tal. Pesaḥim, 70*b*). Cf., however, H. L. Ginsberg's observation in 'The Brooklyn Museum Aramaic Papyri', *JAOS* 74 (1954), 155.

by those who had returned from captivity to Zion conformed to the Chronicler's idea of what was correct practise and belongs to the same category.

THE PROBLEM OF THE PASSOVER'S ANTIQUITY

5

Is the Passover mentioned in the sources preceding D (and P)?

On this matter Wellhausen expressed a most surprising opinion, one which has had a continuing influence on scholarship to this day. He argued that D was the first of the Pentateuchal sources to recognize the paschal sacrifice and the first in which the word *pesaḥ*, 'Passover' itself was mentioned. In Exod. 34: 25 (which, in the opinion of many scholars, including Wellhausen, is part of the 'Cultic Decalogue') the Passover is not mentioned, because the correct reading of this verse is that given in Exod. 23: 18 (where, in truth, the word *pesaḥ* does not occur).[12] The verse Exod. 23: 18 cannot itself be an allusion to the Passover (without specifically mentioning the name) because the Book of the Covenant, in which this verse occurs, recognizes the law of the first-born (Exod. 22: 28–9) and in Wellhausen's view the offering of the firstlings is the ancient form of the Passover.[13] As for the difficulty presented by Exod. 12: 21–7, Wellhausen tends to resolve it by arguing that this is a late addition to JE, or to the P passage preceding it.[14]

The Passover, Wellhausen claims, is only a later development of the offering of the firstlings of the cattle, which is one of the most ancient institutions of the biblical cult. According to biblical tradition Abel himself, the first shepherd in the world, sacrificed the firstlings of the flock (Gen. 4: 4). Wellhausen posits that before leaving Egypt the Israelites asked permission to go and slaughter the first-born of the sheep. The Egyptians did not accede to this request, and therefore their own first-born were killed. The fact that according to Exod. 13: 11–16 (apparently an E section) the obligation to sacrifice the firstlings was not imposed upon the Israelites until they left Egypt Wellhausen would dismiss with the

[12] Wellhausen, *PGI*, 82–5.

[13] Cf. ibid. 88.

[14] See idem, *Die Composition des Hexateuchs*[4] (Berlin, 1963), pp. 73–5. At about the same time K. Budde argued against Wellhausen on this point; see his article 'Die Gesetzgebung der mittleren Bücher des Pentateuchs', *ZAW* 11 (1891), 197–200.

claim that the passage has undergone Deuteronomistic revision.[15] As for the verses Exod. 13: 1–2, where it is again stated that the practice of sacrificing the firstlings was established only when the Israelites left Egypt, there is apparently no need to pay heed to them, since they belong to P, which is taken to be late. Until the appearance of D there were, then, only firstlings, which were sacrificed during the month of Abib. In Wellhausen's view this sacrifice was fundamentally a nomadic, not an agricultural institution; the fact that in principle it was also incumbent on human first-born he would explain as one of the later distortions of this institution. D was the first to call this sacrifice *pesaḥ*, and when he speaks of the Passover that is to be offered 'from the flock or the herd' (Deut. 16: 2), he is actually referring to the firstlings of the flock or the herd. D was also the first to connect this oblation with the Feast of Unleavened Bread and to make it a memorial to the Exodus. In P the practice was still further removed from its authentic sources, but remained connected with the Feast of Unleavened Bread and linked to memories of the departure from Egypt.[16]

6

The contrived nature of this hypothesis is quite evident. It is entirely based on the supposition that J and E do not recognize or mention the Passover but only the sacrifice of the firstlings. However, the truth is that Exod. 12: 21–7 is not a later addition, and most scholars cannot but admit that essentially the passage belongs to J or to E (the arguments in favour of J appear stronger), and we have already seen that it is a simple parallel to P's narrative.[17] Moreover, it will be shown further on that even the Books

[15] Wellhausen, *PGI*, 84.

[16] See ibid. 82–9, 97–8. Wellhausen's view was echoed, in particular, by W. Robertson Smith, *The Religion of the Semites*² (London, 1894), pp. 464–5.

[17] The most that can be said is that traces of Deuteronomic nuances may be found in the second half of this passage: from 'You shall observe this rite' onwards (vv. 24–7*a*). This will undoubtedly be contested by those scholars, including Wellhausen, who claim that there was Deuteronomistic editing of the Tetrateuch, that is, of JE there. See, e.g., H. Holzinger, *Einleitung in den Hexateuch* (Freiburg, 1893), pp. 485, 492; idem, *Exodus* (KHC, 1900), p. 34. But it can still be argued that this is an example of a 'proto-Deuteronomic' style, indications of which are discernible here and there in the body of J and E (to be sure, much more in E than in J); on this point cf. below, pp. 345–6, n. 45. At all events, not even such nuances can be found in the first half of this passage (vv. 21–3).

of the Covenant, the law codes of J and E, recognized the Passover, and since alongside this oblation J and E also acknowledge the existence of the offering of the firstlings, there can be no doubt that these are two different sacrifices. The flocks and herds give birth usually in the spring time, and hence the firstlings are mentioned in the same context as the Passover and the Feast of Unleavened Bread; but the sacrifice of the firstlings as such does not take place at a fixed time and may even occur outside its season. This is actually stated in Exod. 22: 29 with regard to the first-born oxen and sheep: 'Seven days it shall be with its dam; on the eighth day you shall give it to me'.[18] Compared with this, the Passover sacrifice, as can also clearly be seen in J's account in Exod. 12: 21–7, is different in kind and in all its aspects.

Furthermore, assuming that there is a direct and continuous line of development from the sacrifice of the first-born to the Passover one fails to understand why the separation between the Passover and the firstling occurred in P, that is, why the first-born sacrifice was preserved as a discrete offering (Exod. 13: 1–2; Lev. 27: 26–7; Num. 18: 15–18), just as it is distinguished from the Passover in D too (Deut. 12: 6, 17; 14: 23; 15: 19–23), and, in point of fact, even in J and E themselves (although Wellhausen

[18] It had been argued that this verse is a late addition in accordance with Lev. 22: 27 and dates from the time when the Passover sacrifice and the offering of the first-born had already been separated from each other; see, e.g., W. Nowack, *Lehrbuch der hebräischen Archäologie*, ii (Freiburg, 1894), p. 147. But this view is quite groundless, apart from the dubious conjecture concerning a genetic relationship between the first-born and the Passover. Exod. 22: 29 speaks of firstlings of cattle, while Lev. 22: 27 refers to every sacrifice brought from the cattle. In other words, even though Exod. 22: 29 sets no fixed time for the sacrifice of the firstling, there must be no undue delay in its offering after its eighth day. In D, on the other hand, there is no such demand and it seems to be assumed that the Israelite will simply sacrifice the first-born of his cattle when he comes to the chosen place (Deut. 15: 19–20). Likewise in P and in H there is no such demand concerning the firstling (for Lev. 22: 27 specifies the minimum time which must elapse after its birth before any beast may be sacrificed, but there is not necessarily any obligation to sacrifice it). The reason is that the views of D and P (as well as of H) are based on the centralization of the cult, and in these circumstances the Israelite could not be obliged to make the tiring journey to the temple every time a firstling calf was born; it is better that he should sacrifice it when he comes there for a pilgrim-feast. But the Book of the Covenant can impose such a duty, for when there are many temples available, the sacrifice can be made without undue difficulty; cf. S. R. Driver, *Exodus* (CBSC, 1918), ad loc. Thus the humanitarian law of letting the calf or lamb remain 'with its mother' for eight days after its birth, came to be integrated into the Book of the Covenant and P (or H) in various ways, as a common legal heritage apparently related to prevailing custom.

would not admit the latter). If the sacrifice of the first-born did evolve into the Passover, we should expect it to be absorbed by the new sacrifice and not to continue to exist as a distinct institution. In all the disparaging remarks about the logical failures and historical shortcomings of P's descriptions of the Passover,[19] I have found no answer to this question. The assumption that the sacrifice of the first-born was originally a nomadic institution, which only in one of its later transformations was expanded to include human first-born, is also a mere hypothesis.

7

To be sure, not all scholars have agreed with Wellhausen's peculiar view, for most concede that Exod. 12: 21–7 is part of one of the non-priestly sources. Nevertheless, there are many who allow the existence of the paschal offering in J, namely, in Exod. 12: 21–7, but are not prepared to admit that this sacrifice is also mentioned in Exod. 23: 18 (that is, in the Book of the Covenant) and in Exod. 34: 25 (that is, in the Minor Book of the Covenant). Only one of these two verses (Exod. 34: 25) speaks explicitly of *ze̱baḥ ḥag happāsaḥ*, 'the sacrifice of the Feast of the Passover'; hence it is possible to claim that the parallel verse (Exod. 23: 18) does not refer to this sacrifice but to any ordinary sacrifice.[20] Further, the law that occurs in both these verses is divided into two injunctions; consequently, it may be claimed that only the second injunction ('Neither shall the sacrifice of the Feast of the Passover be left until the morning') and not the whole of Exod. 34: 25 refers to the Passover.[21] Some scholars do indeed maintain that the whole of Exod. 34: 25 refers to the Passover,[22] and others give this interpretation to Exod. 23: 18 too. But this is because they prefer the recension of Exod. 34: 25 (the reverse of Wellhausen's argument)

[19] Wellhausen, *PGI*, 97–8.

[20] See, e.g., the remarks in the commentaries to Exodus by A. Dillmann (KEH, 1897), S. R. Driver, U. Cassuto (Jerusalem, 1967), M. Noth (ATD, 1959), B. S. Childs (OTL, 1974), ad loc.

[21] Driver and Noth, for example, made this assumption in their commentaries to Exodus. But before this Driver was apparently inclined to the opinion that both verses in their entirety refer to Passover and the Feast of Unleavened Bread. See S. R. Driver, *Deuteronomy* (ICC, 1902), pp. vii, 190; cf. also H. H. Rowley, *Worship in Ancient Israel* (London, 1967), pp. 49, 117.

[22] This is admitted in, for example, the commentaries to Exodus by H. Holzinger (KHC, 1900), B. Baentsch (GHK, 1903), G. Beer and K. Galling (HAT, 1939), ad loc.

or consider Exod. 34: 25 to be the earlier source from which Exod. 23: 18 (together with the adjacent verses) was, as it were, derived.[23]

I, for one, am prepared to maintain that the connection as well as the difference between the two above-mentioned verses, and similarly between the pericopes Exod. 23: 14–19 and 34: 18–26 as a whole, is not to be explained by clerical dependence, by the assumption that the one might have been copied from the other. They are two parallel and independent literary formulations of the same material. None of the divergences between the two texts can be explained as a copyist's error. What we are confronted with, rather, are the works of two scribes who committed to writing fixed dicta that had already been given their form by oral inculcation. The two parallel formulations are still close, therefore, to the language in which this material was recited and taught, and the purport of the two verses is, to all intents and purposes, the same. In truth, both refer to the paschal sacrifice, as we shall see below. This means that even the collections of laws earlier than D recognize this offering definitely enough. Furthermore, they already recognize it as an adjunct of the Feast of Unleavened Bread and as one of the sacrifices made in temples.

THE ANCIENT INJUNCTIONS CONCERNING THE PASSOVER

8

The following are the two verses which appear in parallel forms in the Books of the Covenant, and each one of them is divided into two instructions:

Exod. 23: 18: I לא תזבח על חמץ דם זבחי II ולא ילין חלב חגי עד בקר

Exod. 34: 25: I לא תשחט על חמץ דם זבחי II ולא ילין לבקר זבח חג הפסח

[23] See especially the view held by Beer and Galling, in their commentary, ad loc. Indeed, all who regard Exod. 34: 17–26 as a 'Cultic Decalogue' (not as the Minor Book of the Covenant, which it really is) must prefer it to Exod. 23: 14–19, because according to this premise Exod. 34: 18 ff. constitutes a part of the Decalogue, the continuity of which must not be broken. R. de Vaux, *Les Institutions de l'aT*, ii (Paris, 1960), p. 386, concedes that Exod. 23: 18 and likewise Exod. 34: 25 must refer to the paschal sacrifice, but he finds in them Deuteronomic editing. Kraus makes a somewhat similar admission (op. cit., p. 62).

The sense of the first injunction is: You shall not offer (or, You shall not slaughter) my sacrifice (i.e. the Passover sacrifice) while there is still leavened bread in the house. This point is expressed in the priestly section Exod. 12: 1–20: From the moment the paschal lamb has been slaughtered, unleavened bread must be eaten and there must be no *ś^e'ōr*, leaven left over in the houses (ibid., vv. 15, 18). The Passover sacrifice itself is eaten with unleavened bread and bitter herbs (ibid., v. 8; Num. 9: 11). This premise undoubtedly underlies the injunction in the Books of the Covenant and is also stated explicitly in Deut. 16: 3–4. This is how the verse was also explained by the talmudic sages: You shall not slaughter the paschal lamb while unleavened bread still exists,[24] and they were followed by the medieval commentators, who here hit on the real meaning of the text.

Critical commentators, asserting that this instruction covers all sacrifices, believe that here the verse is referring to the grain-offering which accompanies animal sacrifice and which must not be leavened.[25] This is explained in the priestly regulation (Lev. 2: 11; 6: 10), though the priestly regulation is somewhat more lenient in the case of loaves of thanksgiving-offering, which do include cakes of leavened bread (ibid. 7: 13). However, a small detail seems to have been left unnoticed by moderns, namely, that the grain-offering accompanying the animal sacrifice is subsidiary to it, and if the verses Exod. 23: 18; 34: 25 had referred to that grain-offering, the text ought to have read: You shall not burn (or put, or bring) unleavened bread *on* [the blood of] my sacrifice. With regard to the two loaves of 'the Day of Firstfruits', which are of primary importance, the burnt-offerings being subsidiary to them, the text reads: 'You shall offer up with [literally, *on*] the bread seven lambs a year old without blemish . . . And the priest shall wave them with [literally, *on*] the bread of the firstfruits' etc. (Lev. 23: 18–20).[26] Had the verses Exod. 23: 18; 34: 25

[24] Mekhilta to Exod. 23: 18; Bab. Tal. Pesaḥim, 63*a et al.*

[25] Cf. above, p. 326, n. 20. Cassuto regards this as an anti-Canaanite trend, since he assumes that the Canaanites did not consider unleavened bread to be holy.

[26] No argument can be inferred from the statement on the loaves of the thanksgiving offering: 'With [literally, *on*] cakes of unleavened bread he shall bring his sacrifice' (Lev. 7: 13), since that verse speaks of bringing, הקריב (not slaughtering, שחט or sacrificing, זבח) and the reference is to cakes and wafers of unleavened bread, which are placed *upon* the leavened loaves. The order of offering in the case of peace-offerings of thanksgiving, as explained in the text

referred to the grain-offering which is subsidiary to the sacrifice, they would not have been formulated as they are: 'You shall not offer/slaughter *upon* leavened bread'. Furthermore, the context of the verses and the juxtaposition of their members incline one to contend that, just as the second member speaks of the Passover (see further on), so the first member refers to that offering, even though it is not specifically named.

The phrase דם זבחי, 'blood of my sacrifice', is, for its part, intrinsically difficult, and all the commentators have been hard put to it to suggest a solution, for we do not find 'blood' as the object of the verbs זבח, 'offer' and שחט, 'slaughter'. The best suggestion one can make is that the noun in the construct has adjectival force here, and hence the meaning of the expression would be 'blood sacrifice'.[27] But even this suggestion is open to doubt.

9

The sense of the second injunction is: You shall not delay the Passover sacrifice till morning (that is, finish it during the night). We are able to deduce that this injunction refers specifically to the Passover, *inter alia* from the express mention of the name *pesaḥ* in one of the two parallel versions (Exod. 34: 25).[28] True, this verse reads: זבח חג הפסח, 'the sacrifice of the (Pilgrim-) Feast of Passover', and nowhere else in the Old Testament is the term *ḥag*, 'pilgrim-feast' applied to the Passover, for the feast is only 'the (Pilgrim-)Feast of Unleavened Bread'. Nevertheless, as we shall see later, the mention of the Passover is original in this verse. The obligation to finish eating the flesh of the Passover before morning is stated explicitly in P's passage (Exod. 12: 8, 10)

is as follows: the cakes and wafers of unleavened bread are offered על זבח התודה, 'upon the sacrifice of thanksgiving', or, more exactly, על חלות לחם חמץ, 'on the cakes of leavened bread' that were placed upon the sacrifice of the thanksgiving. In other words, the unleavened bread is offered on the leavened bread, and the leavened bread on the sacrifice (see ibid., vv. 12–13).

[27] Thus we find רע מעלליכם (Isa. 1: 16)—'your evil doings'; קומת ארזיו (ibid. 37: 24)—'its tall cedars'. Cf. Cassuto's commentary to Exodus, ad loc.

[28] Among those who interpreted this law in a general sense (not as referring specifically to the Passover) there were some who argued that it was formulated at a time when the Passover was the principal sacrifice of Israelite worship (see Driver's commentary, p. 245). But this argument is altogether improbable.

and in D (Deut. 16: 4, 7), and indirectly, but indubitably, even in the section of J (Exod. 12: 22). It is this duty that underlies this injunction, as some early expositors, who grasped the plain meaning of the text here, correctly understood.[29]

The precept not to delay the Passover until the morning finds expression in the two parallel instructions with slight verbal variations: in Exod. 23: 18 there is an injunction not to delay the burning of the fat parts of the festal offering, that is, of the Passover; thereby expression is given to the obligation to eat the sacrifice in the course of the night, for the sacrificers are not allowed to begin eating until the fat has been burnt on the altar (cf. 1 Sam. 2: 15–16). Nor should one suppose that, although the fat has to be burnt, the eating may be postponed to the following day, for there is no reason to keep the flesh once its consumption is permitted. This implies that, if the dictum enjoins the Israelites not to hold up the disposal of the fat of the sacrifice during the night, it does so on the strict understanding that the sacrificers must eat the offering in the course of that night. Exod. 34: 25, on the other hand, speaks of the sacrifice itself and states that, as a whole, the burning of the fat and the consumption of the offering must not be held over until morning. Consequently, although there are verbal variations they do not involve a substantive difference of meaning, and both formulations refer in effect to the same thing.

Those who claim that the instruction in Exod. 23: 18 refers to all the sacrifices, interpret it to mean that the burning of the fat (and by implication, the consumption of the flesh) may not be postponed until the following day, so that the sacrifice should not become invalidated after it has been slaughtered. They find it possible to liken it to the priestly law that ordains that the sacrifice of the thanksgiving must be eaten 'on the day that he offers his sacrifice' and no part of it may be left 'until morning' (Lev. 7: 15; 22: 29–30).[30] It appears that the expression 'until morning', which occurs both in the formulation of Exod. 23: 18 and in the laws of Lev. 7:15; 22: 30, led those scholars to suppose that the same subject was being dealt with in both cases. But upon examination it becomes evident that there is no room here for analogy.

[29] This is the interpretation given by Rashbam and S. D. Luzzatto. Others (Rashi, Ibn-Ezra, Naḥmanides) explained this injunction as referring to the burnt- and peace-offerings of all the holydays.

[30] See, e.g., Driver's commentary, p. 246; cf. A. Dillmann, *Exodus*[3] (KEH, 1897), p. 279.

First of all it must not be forgotten that the priestly law itself is lenient in respect of votive and free-will offerings: they may be eaten in the course of two days and do not become 'foul' until the third day (Lev. 7: 16–18).[31] One might wonder, therefore, why the non-priestly law of Exod. 23: 18 saw fit to demand something not even required by P, which as a rule is the more stringent in such matters. Nor is it to be supposed that the law of Exod. 23: 18 is referring to what are called sacrifices of thanksgiving in P, for even then we would have found a more lenient ruling outside P (especially as the actual distinction between votive and free-will offerings and sacrifices of thanksgiving does not exist outside P's legislation).

Furthermore, even with regard to the thanksgiving offering, which is to be eaten in one day, P's law prescribes: ביום קרבנו ... יֵאָכֵל, '[And the flesh . . .] shall be eaten *on the day* of his offering, he shall not leave any of it until morning'; ביום ההוא ... יֵאָכֵל, 'It shall be eaten *on the* same *day*, you shall leave none of it until morning' (Lev. 7: 15; 22: 30). When referring to the votive and free-will sacrifices, which are eaten in the course of two days, the text expresses itself similarly: ביום הקריבו את זבחו יֵאָכֵל וממחרת ..., 'It shall be eaten *on the day* that he offers his sacrifice, and on the morrow . . . but what remains of the flesh of the sacrifice on the third *day* shall be burned with fire; if any of the flesh of his sacrifice of peace-offering is eaten on the third *day*, he who offers it shall not be accepted' etc.; ביום זבחכם יֵאָכֵל וממחרת, 'It shall be eaten *the* same *day* you offer it, or on the morrow' etc. (Lev. 7: 16–18; 19: 6–7). The reason for this is clear: all the sacrifices (except the Passover) must be eaten during the day, and the text enjoins that their consumption must not be delayed till the next day. The nights are not taken into account, for the night was not a time for eating. But the injunction in Exod. 23: 18; 34: 25 states ולא ילין לבקר, לא ילין . . . עד בקר, 'shall not be left lying [literally, *not spend the night*] until morning'. The root לין employed in the verses clearly attests that the action takes place *at night* and must not be postponed till the morning. It is also clear that circumstances, as reflected in the linguistic divergences, are different—namely, that the sacrifice dealt with

[31] Lev. 19: 5–8 likewise refers to votive and free-will offerings, for it says they may be eaten till the third day, even though they are termed here indefinitely *zeḇaḥ šelāmîm*, 'sacrifice of peace-offerings'. The employment of the general term here is based on the fact that most of the peace-offering sacrifices were presented as votive or free-will offerings.

here, unlike the regular peace-offerings, is made in the evening (in D's terminology כבוא השמש, 'at the sunset'; P's term is בין הערבים, 'at the twilight') and eaten at night; hence it was proper to enjoin that its fat and flesh should not be held over until morning. Unlike the votive, free-will, and thanksgiving peace-offerings, which are mentioned in the priestly legislation, unlike all the sacrifices offered throughout the year, here a night sacrifice is implied. But there is only one such sacrifice in the year, and that is the Passover. It may, therefore, be said that the expression לא ילין, 'shall not be left lying through night', betrays the particular character of the sacrifice alluded to in these verses: that it is specifically a night sacrifice.

In other words, this injunction refers to exactly the same point that is discussed in the priestly accounts in connection with the Passover offering: it is not to be left lying until morning—that is to say, it must be eaten at night, none of it is to be left over till morning, and anything that is left over must be burnt by fire, all as prescribed in Exod. 12: 8, 10; Num. 9: 12. Scholars seem to have been prevented from realizing this because, *damnosa hereditas*, the consensus holds that P is exceedingly late. On the surface J's account seems not to specify that the paschal lamb must be eaten by morning, but only that one may not go out of the door of one's house until morning (Exod. 12: 22); yet, the palpable similarity of the two statements cannot be doubted.[32] This being so, it lends additional weight to the contention that the first injunction refers only to *eating* the leavened bread, which is forbidden from the moment the paschal lamb is slaughtered—a point which is also expressed, as has been said, in P's descriptions (ibid., vv. 15, 18).

[32] It might be suggested, even more precisely, that the expression לא תשחט, 'You shall not slaughter' (Exod. 34: 25) corresponds to J's expression in Exod. 12: 21 ושחטו הפסח, 'and slaughter the Passover', and P's expression in Exod. 12: 6 ושחטו אותו כל קהל עדת ישראל, 'and all the aggregate community of the Israelites shall slaughter it'. Furthermore, in both sources the text immediately proceeds to speak of the use to which the blood is to be put (ibid., vv. 7, 22), and it is not impossible that it has a certain connection with the idiom דם זבחי, 'the blood of my sacrifice' in the Books of the Covenant. Similarly, the statement זבח פסח הוא ליהוה (ibid., v. 27), 'It is the Passover sacrifice to Yahweh' may be analogous to the designations זבחי, 'my sacrifice', . . . זבח הפסח, 'sacrifice . . . of Passover' in Exod. 23: 18; 34: 25. This might mean that the wording of the ancient injunctions still reverberates, albeit quite vaguely, in J's, and perhaps even in P's, narratives about the institution of the Passover (cf. also below, n. 37).

10

If the evidence given so far is not sufficient to demonstrate the true significance of the injunctions in Exod. 23: 18; 34: 25, additional and decisive testimony is further provided in D.

It is a common feature of D that he does not use an entirely new phraseology or only his own specific diction for his laws (or for the narrative portions of his discourses). His statements are frequently based on an ancient nucleus, on a verbal foundation found ready to hand, to which D adds his own particular contribution—special emphases due to differences of view, or didactic and parenetic statements in his own manner and style. We are often able to remove the embellishments and reveal the succinct, ancient kernel of the law, since this kernel appears in a similar form, and at times even in entirely identical words, in other legal sections, which are earlier than D. Thus, the law of the slave is built in Deut. 15: 12–18 on three verses of the ancient statute cited in the Book of the Covenant, namely, the opening verse and the two closing verses (Exod. 21: 2, 5–6). The nucleus of the law of Deut. 16: 18–20 concerning the appointment of judges and the maintenance of justice occurs with literal exactness in the Book of the Covenant (Exod. 23: 6, 8). The injunctions 'None shall see my face empty-handed', 'Three times in the year all your males shall appear before the Lord God', which are found in Exod. 23: 15, 17; 34: 20, 23, also appear verbatim and in the same context in D, but in the reverse order and with a number of expansions (Deut. 16: 16). On the other hand, the prohibition 'You shall not boil a kid in its mother's milk', which is mentioned in Exod. 23: 19; 34: 26, reappears in D without any expansions, but divorced from the context of the pilgrim-feasts and in connection with an entirely different theme—that of forbidden foods (Deut. 14: 21). This nucleus is cited, then, without additions, but before it found its way into D it was removed from its original context and placed in another.

Many scholars consider such verbal similarities prove that D derived most of his laws directly from the earlier codes, particularly from the Book of the Covenant (Exod. 20: 23—23: 33).[33]

[33] One of the first to give comprehensive expression to this view was A. Kuenen, *Historisch-kritische Einleitung in die Bücher des AT*, i (Leipzig, 1887), pp. 159–61. Subsequently it recurs frequently in the writings of scholars. Cf. Holzinger, *Hexateuch*, pp. 302–3 and the references there.

This opinion is linked to a broader view that postulates that J and E were available to the author of D, and just as he drew upon those sources for the composition of the 'historical'-narrative reviews incorporated in his discourses (Deut. 1: 6—3: 29; 9: 8—10: 11), so he based his legislation on the collections of laws contained in those sources. However, in this form the theory does not do justice to all the facts. Repeated examinations of the relevant material have confirmed in me the belief that, though both J and E are certainly older than D, only E was actually used by the author of D,[34] and, since the Book of the Covenant is the law code of E, it is not impossible that it, too, was known to the author of D. And yet, it is difficult to suppose that D's author drew his legal material directly from the Book of the Covenant. It is obviously true that many laws found in the Book of the Covenant, which disclose no particular trend, are not cited in D's code, and, contrariwise, many regulations which are cited in the latter and which are also undoubtedly founded on ancient nuclei, have no basis or root in the statutes incorporated in the Book of the Covenant. Moreover, there is so great a difference between the two codes with regard to the arrangement of the legal material, that it does not make sense to argue that D's code was compiled by direct recourse to the Book of the Covenant. It would be much more to the point to say that D had his own access to the legal material that was preserved and transmitted by a long tradition, the material which, in part, and in an older literary crystallization, is also found in the Book of the Covenant.[35] Accordingly, D's author availed himself of E's narrative framework in constructing a number of sections in the discourses of Moses, but his approach to the legal material that was embedded, in part, in the heart of this framework was his own. He needed this new approach in order to point out the distinct character of the Second Covenant, which, in his view, Yahweh made with Israel in the steppes of Moab east of the Jordan, 'in addition to the covenant which he had made with them at Horeb' (Deut. 28: 69; cf. 1: 5).

[34] Cf. above, pp. 92, 262.

[35] This view is in fact held by, e.g., C. Steuernagel, *Deuteronomium*² (GHK, 1923), p. 40, except that in his opinion several expansions to D led to verses similar to those of the Book of the Covenant being interpolated in D. A somewhat similar view is held by Kaufmann, *THH*, i. 54–8, who speaks of 'a rich legal literature' that was current among the Israelites (he does not resort to the concept of tradition in this context).

Thus, it was not from the Book of the Covenant that D extracted the ancient kernels of his laws, but from that very source that at an earlier stage furnished the Book of the Covenant itself with its basic material (even in the Book of the Covenant those nuclei are sometimes slightly embellished). But this does not alter the actual fact that brief verbal and largely identical nuclei of those laws are sometimes cited in D's code (wrapped up in additional phrases) and in the Book of the Covenant (much more disclosed). This fact will help us to confirm the meaning of the instructions with which we are concerned, in the form which they take in Exod. 23: 18; 34: 25, since they, too, are incorporated in D.

II

The passage in D which is devoted to the Passover and the Feast of Unleavened Bread (Deut. 16: 1–8) can be divided into three segments: an introduction, which enjoins the presentation of the Passover in the month of Abib (v. 1); a hurried description of how to sacrifice the Passover and to link to it the eating of unleavened bread for seven days (vv. 2–4); an instruction to sacrifice the Passover only in the chosen place, and the repeated command to eat unleavened bread for the six days after returning home (vv. 5–8). Now the second segment is just an expansion and an 'inflation' of the two injunctions recurring in Exod. 23: 18; 34: 25. The compressed and laconic wording of those verses lies at the heart of this segment and actually constitutes the foundation for its ordinances. The passages need only be compared for us to observe the real source of D's material:

לא תזבח על חמץ דם זבחי ולא ילין חלב חגי עד בקר

'*You shall not offer* [the blood of] my sacrifice so long as anything leavened exists [literally, *on anything leavened*]; and the fat of my feast [festal sacrifice] *shall not be left lying until morning*' (Exod. 23: 18)

לא תשחט על חמץ דם זבחי ולא ילין

וזבחת פסח ליהוה אלהיך צאן ובקר... לא תאכל עליו חמץ שבעת ימים תאכל עליו מצות לחם עני . . . ולא ילין מן הבשר אשר תזבח בערב ביום הראשון לבקר

'*You shall offer up* the Passover for Yahweh your God from the flock or the herd . . . You shall *not* eat *anything leavened* with it [literally, *on it*]; seven days you

לבקר זבח חג הפסח

'*You shall not* slaughter [the blood of] my sacrifice so long as anything leavened exists [literally, *on anything leavened*]; and the *offering* of the Feast of Passover *shall not be left lying until morning*' (Exod 34: 25)

shall eat unleavened bread with it, bread of distress . . . and *none* of the flesh of what you *offer up* on the evening of the first day *shall be left lying until morning*' (Deut. 16: 2–4)

D's dependence, in this passage, on the ancient injunctions cited in the Books of the Covenant is shown not only by the verbal pattern formed by the verses, but also by the fact that the excerpt from D states no more than is contained in those injunctions, except for some slight elaborations, which are called for, in part, by D's particular viewpoint. This, then, is the essential content of the second segment in the D passage: the Passover offering must be made from the flock or the herd in the chosen place—nothing leavened may be eaten with it, only unleavened bread for seven days—and its flesh must not be left lying until morning. The last two points correspond to the two above-mentioned injunctions, while the preceding point (v. 2) serves as a preamble to them. The third segment in the D passage (vv. 5–8) is primarily intended to emphasize the strict obligation to offer up the Passover specifically in the chosen place, and the matter is mentioned only in order to reiterate D's constant demand for the centralization of the cult. The brief statement concerning the chosen place, contained in v. 2, was apparently not enough for the writer, so that when he had discharged the task of citing the main law and dealing with it (vv. 3–4), he found it necessary to come back to the centralization of worship and to urge it at length (vv. 5–8).

For the sake of exactness it must immediately be mentioned that besides the verbal pattern discernible in the second segment of the D excerpt (vv. 2–4), which resembles the ancient injunctions in Exod. 23: 18; 34: 25, there are a number of stereotyped phrases throughout the passage, which also have parallels in the sources that preceded D, namely, in the Book of the Covenant and in the E passage Exod. 13: 3–7. The following references will illustrate the point:

1. את חג המצות תשמר ··· למועד חדש האביב כי בחדש האביב יצאת ממצרים '*You shall observe* the Feast of Unleavened Bread . . . at the set time of *the month of Abib*, *for in the month of Abib you came out from Egypt*' (Exod. 34: 18; cf. 23: 15)	שמור את חדש האביב ועשית פסח··· כי בחדש האביב הוציאך יהוה אלהיך ממצרים לילה '*Observe the month of Abid* and keep the Passover . . . *for in the month of Abib* Yahweh your God *brought you out of Egypt* by night' (Deut. 16: 1)
2. שבעת ימים תאכל מצות כאשר צויתיך למועד חדש האביב כי בו יצאת ממצרים '*Seven days you shall eat unleavened bread* as I have commanded you, at the set time in the month of Abib, *for in it you came out of Egypt*' (Exod. 23: 15; cf. 34: 18; also 13: 3–4, 7)	שבעת ימים תאכל עליו מצות לחם עני כי בחפזון יצאת מארץ מצרים '*Seven days you shall eat* it with *unleavened bread*, bread of distress —*for you came out of* the land of *Egypt* hurriedly' (ibid., v. 3)
3. זכור את היום הזה אשר יצאתם ממצרים '*Remember this day*, in which *you came out from Egypt*' (Exod. 13: 3)	למען תזכר את יום צאתך מארץ מצרים כל ימי חייך 'That all the days of your life you may *remember the day when you came out of* the land of *Egypt*' (ibid., v. 3)
4. מצות יֵאָכֵל את שבעת הימים ולא יֵרָאֶה לך חמץ ולא יֵרָאֶה לך שאור בכל גבולך 'Unleavened bread shall be eaten *for seven days*; no leavened-bread shall be seen with you, *and no*	ולא יֵרָאֶה לך שאור בכל גבולך שבעת ימים '*No leaven shall be seen with you in all your territory for seven days*' (ibid., v. 4)

leaven shall be seen with you in all your territory' (ibid., v. 7)	
5. שבעת ימים תאכל מצות וביום השביעי חג ליהוה	ששת ימים תאכל מצות וביום השביעי עצרת ליהוה אלהיך
'Seven *days you shall eat unleavened bread, and on the seventh day* there shall be a pilgrim-feast *to Yahweh*' (ibid., v. 6)	'Six *days you shall eat unleavened bread, and on the seventh day* there shall be a solemn assembly *to Yahweh* your God' (ibid., v. 8)

Note that in the first set of parallels, while the verse in the Book of the Covenant speaks of the Feast of Unleavened Bread, the corresponding verse in D refers to the Passover sacrifice, and yet the same expressions are employed in both. In the second set of parallels, the statement about the month of Abib evolves in D into one containing an adverb—instead of 'for in it (in the month of Abib) you came out of Egypt' we find 'for you came out of the land of Egypt hurriedly', but the essential verbal pattern is preserved. In the fifth set of parallels 'seven days' are changed to 'six days'; this is due to D's emphatic requirement that the Israelites go to the chosen place on the first day and offer up the Passover there alone (vv. 5–7). Thus, when the man returns home, he has six days left during which unleavened bread should be eaten.[36] These variations prove that in D's language the stereotyped phrases are put to 'living' use, and that he uses them to put across his own ideas too.[37]

[36] This is the simple explanation of the six days of eating unleavened bread mentioned in Deut. 16: 5, although several verses earlier the same passage refers to seven days of eating unleavened bread (ibid., v. 3). Critical exegetes have experienced difficulty—but quite needlessly—in understanding D's wording here; while the talmudic sages adopted an exposition of their own (Bab. Tal. Pesaḥim, 120*a*; Ḥagigah, 18*a*; Menaḥot, 66*a*).

[37] For the verbal parallels in Deut. 16: 1–8 as a whole cf. the critical commentaries and especially that of S. R. Driver. In a number of instances echoes of these old stereotyped expressions even found their way into the style of P. With the sentence שבעת ימים תאכל מצות, 'Seven days you [sing.] shall eat unleavened bread' (Exod. 13: 6; 23: 15; 34: 18; cf. Deut. 16: 3, 8) compare שבעת ימים מצות תאכלו, 'Seven days you [pl.] shall eat unleaved bread' (Exod. 12: 15; Lev. 23: 6). With its variant מצות יֵאָכֵל את שבעת הימים, 'Unleavened bread shall be eaten for the seven days' (Exod. 13: 7) compare שבעת ימים מצות יֵאָכֵל, 'For seven days unleavened bread shall be eaten' (Num. 28: 17). With the phrasing of the sentences ...שבעת הימים...ולא יֵרָאֶה לך שאור בכל

Now although throughout this passage D's language is replete with set expressions found ready to hand, the second segment (Deut. 16: 2–4) is nevertheless built principally on the two ancient injunctions cited in the Books of the Covenant. As stated above, not only does the verbal pattern of these injunctions form the foundation of this segment, but with regard to the paschal oblation it does not state (at least in vv. 3–4) more than is to be found in these injunctions. The only additional point is to be found in v. 2, the preamble to the segment, which states that the Passover must be of the flock or the herd and sacrificed at the chosen place. The other stereotyped phrases that found their way into this segment, and into the entire passage Deut. 16: 1–8, are connected with the duty to eat unleavened bread and most of them are used here to express this obligation, which remains valid for seven consecutive days (and is a continuation of the sacrifice).

We may, therefore, conclude that if D already understood the two injunctions which occur in the Books of the Covenant to refer to Passover, and based his own instructions regarding this sacrifice on them, then this may fairly be assumed to be their meaning; all the more so since, as has already been shown (above, sects. 8–9), this is the only meaning which transpires from what is stated in the injunctions themselves.

12

It is also possible to consider the exact wording of the ancient injunctions on the paschal sacrifice as they were known to the author of D.

The wording of the first injunction undoubtedly conformed with that of Exod. 23: 18: לא תזבח על חמץ, not with that of Exod. 34: 25: לא תשחט על חמץ. Although the verb שחט ('slaughter') is applied specifically to the Passover in other passages,[38] we find that underlying the text of Deut. 16: 2–3 is the combination וזבחת . . . לא . . . על(יו) חמץ which corresponds

גבולך, 'For seven days . . . and no leaven shall be seen with you in all your territory' (Exod. 13: 7), likewise ולא יֵרָאֶה לך שאור בכל גבולך שבעת ימים, 'No leaven shall be seen with you in all your territory for seven days' (Deut. 16: 4) compare שבעת ימים . . . תשביתו שאור מבתיכם, 'Seven days . . . you shall remove leaven from your houses', שבעת ימים שאור לא יִמָּצֵא בבתיכם, 'For seven days no leaven shall be found in your houses' (Exod. 12: 15, 19).

[38] Cf. above, p. 332, n. 32.

to the wording of the Book of the Covenant in Exod. 23: 18 (above, sect. 11).

On the other hand, the version of the second injunction that was known to D conformed in the main with the wording of Exod. 34: 25: . . . ולא ילין לבקר זבח, for in Deut. 16: 4 the phrasing is: ולא ילין . . . תזבח . . . לבקר. Furthermore, it seems that the word הפסח mentioned at the end of Exod. 34: 25 was also included in the formulation available to D, for if we continue from the second segment to the beginning of the following verse, the verbal pattern of the second injunction is completed to the end: ולא ילין . . . (תזבח) . . . לבקר . . . לזבח . . . הפסח . . . (Deut. 16: 4–5). This means that the phraseology of the ancient injunction exerted an associative influence on the author of D and apparently furnished him with the key words when he proceeded to voice, in the context of Passover, his demand for the centralization of the cult. Hence it may be posited that the word הפסח is an original part of Exod. 34: 25, and should not be omitted as a later addition, as a number of scholars think.[39]

Consequently, the text of the directions in the form which was known to D and which became the basis of his rulings with regard to the Passover sacrifice was as follows: לא תזבח על חמץ . . . ולא ילין לבקר זבח הפסח, without the word חג, which is not mentioned in any part of the D passage. In truth, in such a context the word חג has no place, for it has already been stated that the combination חג הפסח, 'the (Pilgrim)-Feast of Passover' in Exod. 34: 25 is improper and has no parallel anywhere in the Old Testament, for the Passover is a *zebaḥ*, not a *ḥag*. At the same time, the 'divided' character of the formulation known to D—being partly like Exod. 23: 18 and partly like Exod. 34: 25—confirms the assumption that the writer of D did not extract these injunctions from one of those passages, nor did he copy them, like a scribe, from one of them. They reached him in a form quite independent of either of those given to them in Exod. 23: 18 and 34: 25, and, as already stated, directly from the source from which they reached (at an earlier stage) the Books of the Covenant themselves.

[39] See, e.g., Wellhausen, *PGI*, 82 (note); idem, *Die Composition des Hexateuchs*[4], p. 334; Benzinger, op. cit. (above, p. 320, n. 7), cols. 3590, 3593; W. R. Arnold, 'The Passover Papyrus from Elephantine', *JBL* 31 (1912), 9; H. G. May, 'The Passover and the Unleavened Cakes', ibid. 55 (1935), 66. To be sure, the phrase *ḥag happesaḥ*, 'the Pilgrim-Feast of Passover' is impossible in biblical Hebrew, but the solution is not to remove the word *pesaḥ*. See further.

Now although the word חג was apparently not included in the formulation of the injunctions as they were known to D, it would be unduly hasty to erase it from the text of Exod. 34: 25. True, it is not impossible that it crept in there by mistake and is a kind of prolonged dittography of the word זבח preceding it.[40] However, the analogy with the text of Exod. 23: 18 suggests that the word חג may play a more organic role in this context and point to one of the two versions that were grafted together in Exod. 34: 25: זבח חגי (with the omission of the י) and זבח הפסח. This seems probable.

The ancient injunctions on the Passover thus appear in a number of linguistic forms—all of them variant wordings of the same legal rules, the preservation of which, on the periphery of literature, called for inculcation by repetition and declamation.

The variants of the first injunction are, then, as follows:

לא תזבח על חמץ דם זבחי	(Exod. 23: 18; synthesized in Deut. 16: 2–3)
לא תשחט על חמץ דם זבחי	(Exod. 34: 25)

The variants taken by the second injunction are as follows:

ולא ילין חלב חגי עד בקר	(Exod. 23: 18)
ולא ילין לבקר זבח חגי	(incorporated in Exod. 34: 25)
ולא ילין לבקר זבח הפסח	(incorporated in Exod. 34: 25; synthesized in Deut. 16: 4–5)

THE PASSOVER AS A TEMPLE SACRIFICE

13

The study of both the wording of the verses Exod. 23: 18; 34: 25 and the connection between these verses and Deut. 16: 2–5 led us to the inevitable conclusion that the dramatic ceremony of Passover, as it is described, somewhat fully in P (Exod. 12: 1–14) and rather briefly in J (Exod. 12: 21–7), is already found in a succinct and allusive form in the two ancient injunctions of Exod. 23: 18; 34: 25. In the priestly account, and partly also in J's account, an

[40] That is, the letter *ḥ* that comes at the end of this word was duplicated and a *g* attached itself to it making it a separate word.

effort to expose this ceremony in a concrete, visualized form is discernible, as is a wish to emphasize certain aspects of it (and, needless to say, the literary formulation of these accounts is later than that of the Books of the Covenant), but so long as no explicit contradiction between the testimonies can be found it would not be fair to assume that they are not fundamentally in accord. This conclusion appears to be important enough in itself, at least as a key to a correct understanding of the verses in the Book of Exodus. But it also leads to two decisive corollaries.

First, that all the biblical sources already recognized the Passover sacrifice as linked to the Feast of Unleavened Bread. This connection is even expressed explicitly in the injunctions of Exod. 23: 18; 34: 25, for they forbid the offering of the Passover while anything leavened exists, that is, it is there regarded as a prelude to the Feast of Unleavened Bread. In one of the formulations the Passover is actually designated זבח חג, that is to say, the special sacrifice (night sacrifice) that is attached to the *ḥag*, the pilgrim-feast (namely, the Feast of Unleavened Bread). Consequently, it cannot be argued that the connection of the Passover sacrifice with the Feast of Unleavened Bread is an innovation made by D.[41] In the J passage (Exod. 12: 21–7) there is no mention of the Feast or of Unleavened Bread simply because its main aim is to describe the rite of sprinkling the blood of the Passover sacrifice after it has been slaughtered. This passage says almost nothing about other aspects of the sacrifice, and no inferences should be drawn from silence.

The second corollary is that according to all the biblical evidence the Passover is regarded as a temple sacrifice, that is to say, a sacrifice that has to be offered up at one of the houses of God, not on a solitary altar. As for D and P it goes without saying that they would not permit the sacrifice of the Passover anywhere but in the one temple, in which, according to their system, the entire cult is concentrated (see also below). But even the injunctions in Exod. 23: 18; 34: 25 place this sacrifice in a temple context—for they consider the Passover to be a *ḥag*-sacrifice and connect it with the Feast of Unleavened Bread, which, as has been pointed out, can be observed only by pilgrimage to one of the temples. There-

[41] There is even less reason to argue, with de Vaux (op. cit., 386), that the actual amalgamation of the Passover with the Feast of Unleavened Bread is first discernible only in Ezek. 45: 21 and in P.

fore, it cannot be doubted that the paschal offering's attachment to the temples was, just like its relationship to the Feast of Unleavened Bread, established at an early stage in Israel's history. At any rate, this connection preceded the injunctions prescribed in the Books of the Covenant.

Scholars who (contrary to Wellhausen) argue in favour of the Passover's antiquity, consider that in the ancient Israelite times the Passover was a family sacrifice, in the sense that it was offered up on a high-place, or on a solitary altar, or even within the house. They draw their proof from D's prohibition: 'You may not offer the Passover sacrifice in any of your towns that Yahweh your God gives you' (Deut. 16: 5), from which one may infer that this was actually what they were doing until D transferred it to the chosen place. These scholars could ostensibly find support in J's account of Exod. 12: 21–7, where the Passover sacrifice is described as if it were offered within the family home, its participants not going out of the door of the house until morning. In this manner it is portrayed even in P's account of Exod. 12: 1–14, although as the consensus holds that P is extremely late, proponents of this theory cannot set particular store by its testimony.[42]

14

Do those arguments really prove that in biblical times the Passover offering was ever regarded as a sacrifice to be made in the home or an oblation of the high-places?

[42] Kaufmann, too, holds that according to P the Passover sacrifice 'is offered up outside the temple and not by a priest'; *inter alia* Kaufmann uses this argument to prove that the idea of cult centralization is absent from P and hence that P belongs to 'the code for the worship at high-places' (*THH*, i. 122–3; cf. above, p. 7, n. 8). Somewhat similar was W. W. Baudissin's argument when he touched on this point (*Die Geschichte des Alttestamentlichen Priesterthums* (Leipzig, 1889), p. 93). J. B. Segal, on the other hand, uses it to show that according to P there was no connection between the Passover sacrifice and the temple, and in all good faith he believes that the evidence to undermine the entire documentary theory is here provided (*The Hebrew Passover* (London, 1963), pp. 74–5). The argument that P's description of the Passover 'represents a purely domestic rite, having nothing to do with priest or temple or pilgrimage' was also voiced by, e.g., W. W. Cannon, *Expositor* 19 (1920), 226. I find, however, that the latter made incidental but quite incisive remarks on this matter. Thus, he rightly sensed that P's description 'displays the oldest form of Passover rite' (loc. cit.) and that 'if we are to think of it as a new Passover ordinance fashioned by priests in exile or later, it throws the whole history of the rite into confusion; it cannot be reconciled either with the other documents or with the facts' (p. 232). Only 'if it is viewed as what it really is, an old document older than Deut. 16 . . . everything falls into its place' (p. 233).

It has already been stated that the J passage Exod. 12: 21–7 does not in any way try to encompass the whole complex of details connected with the Passover. This passage speaks only of the slaughter (mentioned here in one word), of a number of rites relating to the sprinkling of the blood, and of the participant's duty to remain in the house till morning. The writer felt these details deserved mention and emphasis in order to convey something of the extraordinary character of the paschal sacrifice, but they do not by any means describe the sacrifice exhaustively, not even just its ceremonial–dramatic aspects. The actual eating of the flesh is not even mentioned here. Yet, the writer tells us the Passover is *zeḇaḥ leYahweh*, 'a sacrifice to the Lord' (v. 27), thereby expressing the self-evident premise that the flesh of the Passover is destined to be eaten and the pieces of fat to be burnt on an altar. It is inconceivable that he intended to tell his readers that the fat should be eaten by the participants, or burnt within the house, although according to his express statement it is the participants' duty to stay indoors until morning. Perforce we must suppose that he assumes that before the participants put the blood on the lintel and the doorposts and proceed to eat the flesh in the house (staying there until morning), they will have to ensure that the pieces of fat are burnt and the blood sprinkled on an altar, as the ritual requires in the case of every properly-offered-up *zeḇaḥ*. In Exod. 23: 18 there is an explicit prohibition against leaving the fat of the feast (festal offering) until morning and here, too, the text undoubtedly assumes that the pieces of fat will be burnt, not in the house, but on an altar. As a matter of fact, just because of the unusual character of this sacrifice—the fact that it was slaughtered at the beginning of the evening and consumed in the course of the night without anyone leaving the house—there was good reason for this injunction: the participants should have to attend to the separation of the pieces of fat for the altar without delay, before shutting themselves up in their houses to eat the flesh.[43]

Yet, on which altar does the text presume the Passover fat will be burnt at the beginning of the evening? Is it a high-place or one of the provincial altars? Since we have already concluded that

[43] Note that P's law intimates that the one who brings the peace-offering must deliver the pieces of fat to the priest with his own hands (Lev. 7: 29–31). Cf. Lev. 3: 3–5, 9–11, 14–16: the owner of the peace-offering presents the pieces of fat and the priest burns them.

there is, at all events, an inevitable connection between the Passover sacrifice and the nearby altar, the solitary altar is not, from the outset, preferable in this regard to the altar adjoining the temple. It is entirely natural that the scene of the ceremonial drama of the sacrifice should be near the temple and that the house in which the participants remain for the night should be one of the chambers in the temple courts.[44] Now the injunctions laid down in Exod. 23: 18; 34: 25 show clearly that the altar that is to hold the fat of the Passover, as well as the site of the sacrifice itself, must be in the same place as the *ḥag*.

Another allusion to the connection, in J's own opinion, between the paschal offering and the temple is to be found in the special didactic phrasing that marks J's account of this sacrifice and includes the direction to explain and teach the nature of the ceremony to the children, when they would ask what it means (Exod. 12: 24–7*a*). Similar statements appear in E in connection with the eating of unleavened bread on the Feast of the month of Abib (Exod. 13: 5–10) and with regard to the sacrifice of the first-born (ibid., vv. 11–16). In D this type of phraseology was elaborated and perfected until it became a distinctive feature of the source, but here it still appears in a somewhat restrained form. And although *au fond* this phraseology is common to all the three subjects under discussion, certain slight variations are nevertheless noticeable between J's account of the Passover sacrifice and E's account of the Feast of Unleavened Bread and the first-born. That is to say, the fact that these are two distinct writers making use of the same style is the cause of the difference—slight but quite perceptible—in the niceties of their diction and modes of expressions.[45]

Now the similar didactic phraseology, which, in this instance, links the three subjects and the two sources together, testifies to

[44] For the 'chambers', *l*^{e}*šāḵôt* which were found in the Jerusalem temple courts, cf. above, pp. 24 (n. 20), 193.

[45] The citations given below will demonstrate the similarity in form and features between the parallel 'proto-Deuteronomic' passages as well as palpable differences in their expressions.

J on the Passover (Exod. 12: 24–27*a*)	*E on the Feast of Unleavened Bread* (Exod. 13: 5–10) *and the first-born* (ibid., vv. 11–16)
1. ושמרתם את הדבר הזה לחק לך ולבניך עד עולם (24).	ושמרת את החקה הזאת למועדה מימים ימימה (10).

a common background and environment, because all three cultic scenes are marked by unusual features, all three are interrelated—and, most probably, all three appertain to the temple precincts. Had the Passover been regarded by J as fundamentally a non-temple sacrifice, it is hardly conceivable that he would have applied to it the same sort of terminology as did E when describing the Feast of Unleavened Bread and the first-born. Indeed, it is difficult to imagine that the Passover could be considered to be of lower status than the sacrifice of the firstlings, or even of lower

2. והיה כי תבאו אל הארץ אשר יתן יהוה לכם כאשר דבר׳ ושמרתם את העבדה הזאת (25)	והיה כי יביאך יהוה אל ארץ הכנעני והחתי והאמרי והחוי והיבוסי אשר נשבע לאבותיך לתת לך... ועבדת את העבדה הזאת בחדש הזה (5) והיה כי יביאך יהוה אל ארץ הכנעני כאשר נשבע לך ולאבותיך ונתנה לך (11)
3. והיה כי יאמרו אליכם בניכם מה העבדה הזאת לכם׳ ואמרתם	והגדת לבנך ביום ההוא לאמר בעבור זה עשה יהוה לי בצאתי ממצרים (8) והיה כי ישאלך בנך מחר לאמר מה זאת׳ ואמרת אליו
and then the text proceeds to narrate the events of the Exodus, which is the aetiological background of the ceremony (vv. 26–27*a*)	and the text proceeds to recount the events as above. The aetiological character of the passage is also noticeable in the wording of the continuation: על כן אני זובח ליהוה כל פטר רחם הזכרים ‘*Therefore* I am sacrificing to Yahweh every first male issue of the womb’ (vv. 14–15)

On examining the passages it will be seen that those concerning the Feast of Unleavened Bread and the first-born resemble each other more closely than that which deals with the Passover. In the former two there also occurs a similar instruction with regard to the sign and the frontlets (vv. 9, 16), which does not appear in the passage relating to the Passover. Furthermore, the phraseology that is subsequently to become—as it is, or with slight changes—a distinctive mark of D is much more noticeable in these two passages than in the J passage (because E, not J was lying before D; cf. above, p. 334). However, this is not as yet precisely D's style. The argument that Exod. 12: 24–27*a*; 13: 3–16 contain neither D nor Deuteronomistic redaction, but only a ‘pre- or proto-Deuteronomic’ style has already been propounded by N. Lohfink, *Das Hauptgebot, Eine Untersuchung literarischer Einleitungsfragen zu Dtn 5–11* (Rome, 1963), p. 121. He was followed in a painstaking examination particularly by M. Caloz, ‘Exode 13: 3–16 et son rapport au Deutéronome’, *RB* 75 (1968), 5–62.

status than an ordinary free-will sacrifice, both of which were offered up only in temples.[46]

15

The priestly passage Exod. 12: 1–14 is longer and more detailed than the J passage, but it too is elliptical in character and does not exhaust all the aspects of the Passover ceremony. This passage, too, aims only to discuss certain facets of the ritual and to point them out as a matter of particular interest. These are: the method of preparing the lamb, the slaughter, the sprinkling of the blood, and the rites that accompany the consumption of the sacrifice. Here too there is no doubt that P himself assumes that the burning of the fat precedes the eating of the flesh, especially as this order of procedure is accepted even by the non-priestly sources (1 Sam. 2: 15). But the burning of the fat is possible only on the one altar beside the tabernacle, which is the sole place of worship in the camp of Israel. If we strip away from P the idea of cult centralization, the palpable reality underlying his account will be at most as follows: that the Passover was offered up and eaten in temple cities, and in order to make the sacrifice families would make a pilgrimage to those cities; they did not offer it up on the solitary altars in the provinces. The priestly writer himself states that as 'an ordinance for ever' the Israelites must celebrate the day after Passover and observe it as 'a *ḥag* to Yahweh' (Exod. 12: 14), which implies that the Passover was offered up only on a pilgrim-feast. The priestly writers further relate that in the second year after the Exodus the Israelites offered up the Passover in the camp after the tabernacle had been erected (Num. 9: 1–5), and there they expressly call it 'the Lord's offering' (ibid., vv. 7, 13). It is inconceivable that the Lord's offering, *qorbān* could be offered up in the camp without recourse to the altar adjoining the tabernacle and that this oblation could be eaten without the pieces of fat first having been burnt on the altar.

But then, both the J and P passages describe the first paschal sacrifice as being made in Egypt, before the tabernacle itself was erected, or before the Israelites reached Canaan and their temples established. These accounts involve the appearance of a non-temple sacrifice, even of a sacrifice made in the home, but this is

[46] On the firstling and the free-will offering as temple sacrifices cf. my remarks in *EM*, iv. 42; v. 324, 784 (and above, pp. 16–17).

only an 'optical' illusion. It is the attempt by biblical tradition to link the Passover with the Exodus from Egypt that has caused a certain tension in the description of this particular offering ('the Passover of Egypt'), which, in fact, was momentarily removed from its real setting and portrayed as if it were by itself, totally unconnected with the temple. This tension was unavoidable because of the aetiological load weighing on the writers, by which J and P were compelled to fit this sacrifice into anachronistic circumstances, into a period when a temple was not yet in existence.[47] However, there is no difference in principle between these accounts and other biblical narratives in which an anachronistic element is manifest.[48] The projection of the regular paschal observance, customary and familiar, on the image of 'the Passover of Egypt', thus somewhat distorted the true nature of the sacrifice from some points of view. Every anachronistic projection is liable to impair the optimal features of an institution, but the real character of the latter should not be construed from its reflection alone.

Consequently, of the injunction in Deut. 16: 5 one can say only that it is directed against the possibility of offering up the Passover in one of the temples (as distinct from the solitary altars) outside the chosen place. D's writer apparently has this in mind when he employs here his usual expression 'in one of your towns', since in his view all places outside the chosen place, whether temples or altars only, are to be regarded as 'towns' (literally, 'gates'). He does not refer, in this context, to solitary altars.

[47] Needless to say, according to this interpretation the historical–national motivation of the Passover offering, that is, its connection with remembering the Exodus from Egypt, is not an innovation by D. Such motivation already exists in J (it also appears independently in P). It may be conjectured that E, too, shared their view on this point, except that E's account of the preparation of the Passover has not been preserved.

[48] The narratives of J and P about manna, for example, state in all innocence that when the Israelites received their bread from heaven—at a time when they had not yet reached Mount Sinai—they were already obliged to keep the Sabbath (Exod. 16: 22–30) and even placed a jar of manna 'before the Lord . . . before the testimony to be kept' (ibid., vv. 32–4), that is, in the holy of holies. E's narrative, moreover, describes the Exodus from Egypt as a trip to observe a pilgrim-feast (cf. above, pp. 300–1).

GLOSSARY OF BIBLICAL TERMS AND PHRASES

THIS glossary lists only biblical terms and phrases, and only those that are referred to in this book—either, as in the majority of cases, in their Hebrew form, or, as occasionally, in their English equivalent. The entries are arranged in alphabetical order of the actual forms, not by roots (no account is taken, however, of the definite article in this arrangement). The tetragrammaton is abbreviated to *h* throughout.

Each entry contains the following elements:

(1) Indication of part of speech, where necessary.

(2) Categorization of the term into one of the following classes:
[P] = 'priestly', characteristic of P or exclusively limited thereto. Note that terms occurring in H, or in Ezekiel's diction (which was influenced by D as well), but not in P proper, have not been included in this category. Several terms, however, which occur only in Ezekiel or in Chronicles, but whose dependence on priestly patterns can be considered incontestable, are put under this category with the symbol italicized: [*P*].
[N] = 'non-priestly', never found in P.
Where no symbol is given = found within P and outside, common to priestly and non-priestly styles.

(3) Reference to the main discussion of the term (mainly where it is mentioned in its Hebrew form).

(4) Translation of the term, or the interpretation given it, or ascribed to it, in this book. Italicized words will be found in the Subject Index, where additional references are given.

(5) Cross references, or additional remarks explaining the categorization of the term, or its place in one of the later groups.

It should also be noted that a fair number of terms classified as belonging to Groups II and III are basically non-cultic and secular, but were employed in cultic or religious contexts. In addition, the categorization is at times based on rather a limited scope, and one cannot be certain that words of infrequent occurrence outside P were not known to P's writers too, or that words appearing occasionally only within P were not known also outside P.

1. Non-Cultic

אביב	[N] 294; 'ripe barley' [for the month by this name see *Ābîb*]
אהל	(verb) [N] 196; 'dwell in a tent'
אֹהֶל	(noun) 14, 195, 201 n. 21; 'tent'
אהל מועד I	[N] 2, 260–71, 273–4; '*tent of meeting*' (or 'communion'), as a prophetic–oracular institution [cf. II אהל מועד in III]
אזרח	[P] 11 n. 11; 'citizen', 'free tribesman'
אחֻזה	[P] 116, 118, 127; 'possession (of land)'
אחֻזת הלויים	[*P*] 127; 'the possession of the Levites' [Ezekiel's adaptation of a term found in P]
אחֻזת עולם	[P] 118; 'perpetual (untransferable) possession'
אחֻזת העיר	[*P*] 117, 127; 'the possession of the city (residents)' [Ezekiel's adaptation of a term found in P]
אפרת, אפרתה	[N] 307, 308 n. 32; an appellative of *Bethlehem* (+name of a wife of Caleb)
אפרתי	[N] 307–9; 'Ephraimite' *or* 'Bethlehemite'
ארגמן	159–61; '*purple* (wool) cloth'
אֲרֻחַת תמיד	[N] 207 n. 2; 'regular allowance (of food)'. See also תמיד (II)
בּוּץ	[N] 160 n. 24; 'fine linen', byssus, βύσσος
בית אב	87; 'a father's house', 'family'
בית הפקֻדות	[N] 97 n. 15; 'house of oversight' (= prison)
בכל אות נפשו	[N] 61, 62 n. 6; 'with all the desire of his soul'
במה I	[N] 18, 19 n. 9; 'mountain, hill, height'
במה II	[N] 19 nn. 8, 9; 'trunk, torso, back (of an animal)'. See also III במה (II)
בעל פקידות	[N] 97 n. 15; 'sentry', 'guardsman'
בִּשֵּׁל	(verb) 322; 'boil, seethe (meat) in liquid'
גְּאֻלָּה	[P] 118 n. 10; '*redemption*' [within the Pentateuch used only in P]
גְּאֻלַּת עולם	[P] 118; 'perpetual (right of) redemption'
גדר	123 n. 18; 'fence'
גור, גֵּר	88; '*sojourn*(*er*)'
דרור	[N]123–4 n. 20; 'liberty, release' = (*an*)*durâru* [mentioned once in H, Lev. 25: 10, and outside the Pentateuch]

היכל [N] 13–14; 'palace, big house' [cf. היכל ה׳ in II]

חוג (verb and noun) [N] 289 n. 2; '(make a) circle'
חומה 123 n. 18; '(heavy) wall' (of a fortress or a city). See also קיר; קיר החומה
חמץ 327–9, 335–7, 339–41; 'leavened (*bread*)'
חֲמִשִּׁית [N] 190 n. 3; 'pentagonal' (doorpost? door-frame?)
חצר(ים) 117–18; (implying) 'village(s), hamlet(s)' [non-P reference in Deut. 2: 23]

ימים 306 n. 28; (as a designation of) 'a year'
(מ)ימים ימימה [N] 299, 304; 'from year to year'
(יצג), הציג [N] 261 n. 3; (in the meaning of) 'to exhibit, display'

כוס [N] 216 n. 13, 223 n. 22; 'cup'
כל הימים [N] 314–15; 'the year around' *or* 'all the years (= yearly)'
כֶּסֶא [N] 306, 321; 'day of the full moon' [mentioned only in Ps. 81: 4; Prov. 7: 20]

לחם תמיד [N] 207 n. 2; 'regular (daily) meal' [for a counterpart in P's style see in II]. See also תמיד (II)
לין (verb) [N] 331–2; 'spend (= to be left lying during) the night' [occurs once in H, Lev. 19: 13, and elsewhere; never in P]

מגרש (העיר) [P] 112–13, 117–20, 121 n. 14, 123, 128 n. 26; 'pasture (common) land', 'open space' (round a city). See also ערי מגרש; שדה מגרש
מחנה See קרב המחנה
מלאכה 191 n. 4, 243 n. 23; '(mainly skilful) work, occupation'
מְסֻכָּה, מְסֻכָה [N] 252; 'covering' [in Ezek. 28: 13]
*מִסְכֶּנֶת [N] 51 n. 15; 'a storage-house'
מעלות [N] 279 n. 6; 'steps'
מעשה אופה [N] 243 n. 24; 'workmanship of the baker'
מעשה שבכה [N] 243 n. 24; 'the work of interlacement'
מעשה שׁוֹשַׁן [N] 243 n. 24; 'the work of lily-shape'
מעשה שַׁרְשְׁרוֹת [N] 243 n. 24; 'the work of chains'. See also s.v. מעשה (III)
משכן (משכנות, משכנים) 14 n. 3, 195–6 n. 12; '*tabernacle(s)*' (as a habitation of nomads) *or* 'abode, dwelling place'. See also משכן (III); אהל ומשכן (II) אהל מועד; (III) משכן ה׳; (II) משכן כבודו/שמו; (III) משכן העד(ו)ת; (II) משכנות (ה׳); שכן
משפחה 307, 309; 'family', 'clan'

משתה [N] 313–14; 'drinking *banquet*'
משתה תמיד [N] 207 n. 2; 'regular (daily) banquet' [only in Prov. 15: 15]. See also **תמיד** (II)

נביא 267 n. 11, 271–2; '(ecstatic) *prophet*'
נגד השמש [N] 36 n. 41; 'in face of the sun' (= on a hill)
נגף 188; 'plague'
(נוס), נס 121–2 n. 15; 'to flee' (as used of an inadvertent murderer)

סכך 216 n. 13, 252–3; 'to cover'

עבד(י) ה' [N] 65 n. 9; 'the Lord's slave(s)' or 'servant(s)' (as a prophetic epithet)
עוד, (העיד) 255, 272–3; 'to bear witness' [found in P only in the form of the substantive **עדות**; cf. in II]
עטרה [N] 170; 'crown'
עיר 14 n. 1; 'a city'. See also **קיר העיר; שדה (ה)עיר**
עיר הכהנים [N] 120 n. 14; 'the city of the priests'
עליה [N] 279 n. 6; 'an upper chamber'
ערי מגרשים [*P*] 119–20 nn. 11, 14; 'cities that have pasture (common) lands' [only in 1 Chron. 13: 2, based on P's term]

פאר 170; 'cap'. See also **פארי מגבעות** (III)

צדה (verb) 121 n. 15; 'lie in wait' (= act with intent, said of deliberate murderer)

קיר 123 n. 18; '(relatively thin) wall' (usually of a house or a room) [cf. **חומה**]
קיר החומה [N] 123 n. 18; 'the (upper) surface of (= the wall of a dwelling-room built on) the (city-) wall'
קיר העיר [P] 123 n. 18; 'the built-up area' (of a city)?
קצף (verb and noun) 188; '(to be) wrath(ful)'
קִצֵּץ (verb) 167, 287 n. 23; 'cut in pieces', 'deform' (*or* 'cut into')
קר(ו)אים [N] 24, 310–11, 313; '(specially) invited persons' (to a meal)
קרב המחנה [N] 260–1; 'the midst of the camp'

(ה)רֹאֶה [N] 309–10; 'seer'
רְבֻעִית [N] 190 n. 33; 'square', perhaps 'rectangular' (doorpost? doorframe?)
(רוח), הריח (קטרת) 242; 'to smell' (burnt incense), 'to use it as perfume'
רוח חיים [P] 259 n. 19; 'the spirit of life' [Gen. 6: 17; 7: 15, (22); cf. Ezek. 37: 5–6, 14]
רֵעֶה המלך [N] 72, 81 n. 30; 'the king's friend'
רקמה 161 n. 25; 'variegated fabric' [in P only the form **רֹקֵם**]

שְׂאֹר 328, 337–9; *'leaven'*

שָׂדֶה 120; 'field'

שְׂדֵה מגרש [P] 118, 120; 'the field(s) of the pasture (common) land (or of the open spaces)' (round a city)

שְׂדֵה (ה)עיר [P] 120; 'the field(s) of (= the cultivable land round) the city'

שכן (verb) 53 n. 17, 196, 269; 'dwell (mainly in a tabernacle)'

שש 160 n. 24, 163 n. 29; '(fine Egyptian) *linen*' [in non-cultic context mentioned in Gen. 41: 42; Ezek. 16: 10, 13 *et al.*]. See also שש משזר (III)

תכלת 160–2; '*blue* (wool) cloth' [in non-cultic context mentioned in Jer. 10: 9; Ezek. 23: 6 *et al.*]. See also כליל תכלת (III)

II. Used in the Context of Cult or Temple

אהל (ה׳) [N] 14, 221, 262 n. 3; '(the Lord's) tent' (designation of the temple)

אהל ומשכן [N] 195–6, 201 n. 21; (hendiadys implying) 'movable structure' (typical of nomadic life)

אוב(ות) וידעוני(ם) [N] 135–6; '*medium(s)* and wizard(s)', 'ghosts (or necromancers) and familiar spirits' [mentioned in H, D, and outside the Pentateuch]

אוצר(ות) (בית) ה׳ [N] 284–8; treasure(s), or treasury (treasuries), of the *temple*

אוּרים ותֻמים 4, 67; *urim and thummim* (mantic implements, literal meaning unknown)

אות ברית [P] 143 n. 12; 'sign of (practically divine) promise, obligation'

אזכרה [P] 230, 233 n. 6; '*memorial* (token) *portion*' (= the part of the grain-offering which is burnt on the altar) [cf. Isa. 66: 3]

(ה)אחד לחדש השביעי [P] 2, 291 n. 7; 'the first (day) of the seventh month' (= the civil New Year)

אֲחֻזת ה׳ [P] 39; 'the Lord's possession'

איש זר [P] 183, 239, 244 n. 25; 'an outside person' (= non-priest)

אל אלהי ישראל [N] 49; 'El, the God of Israel' (designation of an altar by Shechem)

אל בית אל [N] 52; 'El of Bethel' (designation of an altar by Bethel)

אלהי זהב [N] 29 n. 28; '*god* (= *image*) *of gold*'

אלון בכות [N] 52; 'the *oak* of weeping', by Bethel

אלון מעוננים [N] 50 n. 12; 'the *terebinth* of soothsayers', close to Shechem

אלון מֻצָב [N] 50 n. 12; 'the *oak* of the pillar (?)', near Shechem

אלילים [N] 105; 'false, worthless gods' (images) [occurs in H and outside the Pentateuch]

אמנה [N] 9; 'pact' (concluded under Ezra's leadership)

אפוד 166–8; *ephod* (priestly vestment)

ארון (אדני) ה׳/אלהים [N] 79, 246–8; 'the *ark* of the Lord God'

ארון (ה)ברית (ה׳, האלהים) [N] 142, 199 n. 16, 247–8, 255, 281; 'the ark of (= containing the tables with the words of) the covenant (of the Lord, God)' [cf. ארון העד(ו)ת in III]

אש זרה [P] 183 n. 18, 188, 232, 244 n. 25; 'strange (outside) fire' (= not belonging to the altar)

אש תמיד [P] 207 n. 2, 232 n. 4; 'permanent (perpetual) fire' (of the outer altar)

אשי ה׳ 61–2, 210 n. 8; 'offerings to Yahweh made by (= in principle destined to be consumed by) fire' [outside P mentioned in D, Dtr, and 1 Sam. 2: 28]

אשם 184–5; 'guilt-*offering*' [outside P mentioned as presented in the form of money, i.e. silver or golden objects, rather than in that of farm-products: 1 Sam. 6: 3–17; 2 Kgs. 12: 17]

אשרה (אשרים) [N] 30, 48, 57, 105, 134, 278 n. 5; '(sacred tree of) *Asherah*' (pl. *Asherim*)

אשרה [N] 278; Asherah (Canaanite goddess by this name)

בין הערבים [P] 207–8, 332; 'at the *twilight*' (lit. 'between the two evenings')

בית אל/בעל ברית [N] 50–1; 'the house of El-/Baal-berith' (a Canaanite temple in Shechem)

בית אלהים [N] 13, 221; 'house of God', the descriptive term for *temple*

[N] 28 n. 26, 52; designation of a pillar-stone by Bethel

בית במות [N] 25, 28 n. 27, 82–3; 'house (temple) of *high-places*'

בית ה׳ [N] 13, 34, 38 n. 45; 'house of Yahweh', the descriptive term for *temple* [does not occur in P, nor in H]

בית זב(ו)ל [N] 14, 189; 'lofty house' (designation of the Jerusalem temple)

בית (ה)מקדש [N] 15; 'house of holiness' (designation of the temple)

במה III [N] 19–25; '*high-place*' (a special kind of altar). See also בית במות; (I) במה I, II; כהנ(י) (ה)במות

ברית [N] 142–3, 255; '*covenant*' (and the words expressing it). See also ארון (ה)ברית; ספר הברית

[P] 143 n. 12; (connoting practically divine) 'promise', 'obligation'. See also אות ברית; (קום) הקים ברית

ברית כהֻנת עולם [P] 143 n. 12; '(covenanted) promise of perpetual priesthood'

ברית מלח [P] 143 n. 12; (lit. 'covenanted promise of salt', apparently meaning) 'unyielding, everlasting promise'

גלולים [N] 104–6, 135; '*idols*' [occurs in H, D, and outside the Pentateuch]

דביר [N] 141 n. 11, 190 n. 2; the inner *sanctum*, *holy of holies* [etymology uncertain]

דם זבחי [N] 329, 332 n. 32; 'blood of my sacrifice' (= my blood sacrifice?)

הד(ו)ם (רגלי ה׳) [N] 223 n. 22, 256–7; '(the Lord's) footstool' (the *ark*'s symbolic significance and an appellation of the temple)

(ה)היכל, היכל הבית [N] 14, 178 n. 5, 287; (designating) 'the outer sanctum', 'the ante-chamber'

היכל ה׳ [N] 13–14, 27, 201; 'the palace of Yahweh'

הלולים [N] 299; 'praisegiving', 'rejoicing'

הר ה׳ [N] 36 n. 43; 'the mountain of Yahweh' (title of the Jerusalem temple *mount*)

הר הקדש [N] 14; 'holy hill' (title of the temple mount)

זב(ו)ל See בית זב(ו)ל

זבח (verb) 138 n. 8, 328 n. 26; 'offer up a(n animal) sacrifice (to be eaten mainly by the sacrificer)' [incidentally also occurs in Lev. 9: 4, P]

זִבֵּחַ (verb) [N] 23–4, 234, 235 n. 9; 'offer up a(n animal) sacrifice (to other gods, or in illegal worship to Yahweh)' [exceptions: 1 Kgs. 8: 5 = 2 Chron. 5: 6; 2 Chron. 30:22, indicating abundance of sacrifices]

זבח(ים) 24, 61 n. 4, 329, 344; '*offering*(*s*) from the flock or the herd (the flesh of which is to be eaten mainly by the sacrificer)' [occasionally also used by P: Lev. 17: 8; 23: 37; Num. 15: 3 *et al.*]. See also שלמים

זבח חג(י) [N] 329, 341–2; 'the (special) sacrifice of (= joined to) the (or my) pilgrim-feast' (possibly an indirect designation of the paschal offering)

זבח הימים [N] 305–7, 312–13; 'the *yearly* sacrifice'

זבח משפחה [N] 307; 'the family (clan) *sacrifice*'

זבח פסח [N] 332 n. 32, 340–1, 344; 'the *Passover* sacrifice'. See also פסח

זבח שלמים See שלמים

זבח תודה [P] 16, 328–31; 'thanksgiving-*offering*' [within the Pentateuch used only in P]

זכ(ה) [P] 164 n. 30, 208–10, 242; 'pure'. See also לבונה זכה; שמן זית זך

זר(ה)	[P] 183, 187, 243–4; (denoting) 'strange, unauthorized (person or material)', not belonging to the priestly circle. See also **איש זר; אש זרה; קטרת זרה**
זרק (דם)	216 n. 13; 'throw, toss, dash (blood)'
החג	[N] 298 n. 16, 300; 'the (great) Pilgrim-Feast (of the autumn season)'
חג(ים)	289–90, 299–303; '*pilgrim*(*age*)-*feast*(*s*)' [cf. **החג** with the definite article]
חג האסיף	[N] 295; 'the Pilgrim-*Feast* of Ingathering'. See also **החג**
חג ה׳	[N] 298–300, 302; 'the Pilgrim-Feast of Yahweh' (designation of the autumn pilgrim-feast)
חג המצות	294–5, 317 n. 2, 335–8; 'the (Pilgrim-)*Feast of Unleavened Bread*'
חג הסֻכות	140, 291, 295, 297–8; 'the (Pilgrim-)*Feast of Booths*'
חג הקציר	[N] 294–5; 'the (Pilgrim-)Feast of (Wheat) Harvest' (designation of the *Feast of Weeks*) [cf. Exod. 23: 16]
חג השבֻעות	[N] 294–5, 318 n. 2; 'the (Pilgrim-)*Feast of Weeks*'
חגג	(verb) 290–1; 'celebrate a pilgrim-feast'
חדש	See **ראש חדש**
חטאת	46, 184–5, 231 n. 3; 'sin-offering' [outside P mentioned as given in the form of money: 2 Kgs. 12: 17; cf. **אשם**; the relevance of Hos. 4: 8 here is doubtful]
חלות לחם חמץ	[P] 329 n. 26; 'cakes of leavened bread' (accompanying the thanksgiving offering)
חמנ(ים)	[N] 105, 237 n. 14; 'incense stand(s)', 'incense altar(s)' [in H and outside the Pentateuch]
חצר(ות) בית ה׳	[N] 192–3; 'the *court*(*s*) of the house of the Lord'
(ה)חצר הגדולה	[N] 192; 'the greater *court*' (of the temple)
החצר החדשה	[N] 193 n. 7; 'the new court'
חצר הכהנים	[N] 186; 'the court of the priests'
החצר העליון	[N] 193 n. 7; 'the upper court'
החצר הפנימית	[N] 192 n. 6; 'the inner *court*'
חרם	16, 31, 172 n. 50, 285 n. 18; 'strictly devoted (irredeemable) thing'
ידעונים	See **אובות וידעונים**
יום הבכורים	[P] 297–8; 'the *Day of* the *Firstfruits*'
יום הכפורים	[P] 178–9, 291–2 n. 7; 'the *Day of Atonement*'
(יעד) נועד (ל...)	[P] 269, 272–3; 'come to (meet) somebody at an appointed time (by appointment)'
(יצב), נִצַּב, הִתְיַצֵּב	[N] 50 n. 11, 266–8; 'present oneself (in reverent expectation)'
(יקע), הוקיע	[N] 36 n. 41; '*impale*'
י(ו)שב הכרובים	[N] 247–51; 'he who sits upon the cherubim'

כבוא השמש	[N] 332; 'at the sunset' [basically non-cultic]
כהנ(י) (ה)במות	[N] 99–101; 'priest(s) of (the) *high-places*'
הכהן הגדול	93; 'the high (pre-eminent) priest' [occurrences in P: Num. 35: 25, 28; cf. Lev. 21: 10 and Josh. 20: 6]
(ה)כהן (ה)משיח	[P] 177, 180; 'the anointed (high) priest'
כהנ(י) הַמִּשְׁנֶה	[N] 93–4, 96 n. 13, 97; 'priest(s) of the second order'
כהן הראש	[N] 93; 'the chief priest'
הכהנים הלויים/בני לוי	[N] 62, 78, 83, 147; 'the priests the *Levites*' ('the Levitical priests'), '. . . the sons of Levi'
(ה)כהנים (ה)משוחים	[P] 177, 180; 'the anointed (ordinary) priests'
(כהנים) שומרי הסף	[N] 94, 96 n. 13; '(priests) that keep the threshold'
כונ(ים)	[N] 234; 'sacrificial (crescent) cakes' (for the 'queen of heaven') [=*kamânu*]
כיור	156, 186, 189; 'laver', 'basin' [basically non-cultic container; cf. 1 Sam. 2: 14]
כלאים	[N] 160–2, 164–7, 170–4, 211–12; '*mixture* of two kinds' (as *of wool and linen*) [mentioned only in H and D]
כליל	[N] 68 n. 13; 'whole (burnt-) offering'
כמרים	[N] 134 n. 4; 'illicit (spurious, heathen) priests'
כסא (ה׳)	[N] 248, 256; '(Yahweh's) *throne*' (designation of the temple, based on the cherubim's symbolic significance)
כרוב(ים)	246–54, 256–9, 281–2, 287–8; '*cherub*(*im*)'
לבונה	230, 233, 235, 242; '*frankincense*', λίβανος, λιβανωτός [basically non-cultic]
לבונה זכה	[P] 164 n. 30, 208, 210, 242; 'pure frankincense'
לחם אלהים	[P] 17, 219; '*God*'s food (bread)'
לחם התמיד	[P] 210; 'regular (weekly) bread' [for the same compound in secular usage see in I]
לפני האלהים	[N] 50 n. 11; 'before God' [cf. לפני ה׳]
לפני ה׳	26, 198, 215, 273 n. 19, 292–4, 296 n. 14; '*before the Lord*'
לפני העד(ו)ת	[P] 26 n. 24; '*before the testimony*'
לרצון להם	[P] 215; 'acceptable for them (to Yahweh)'
לשכה, לשכות	[N] 24, 193, 310–11, 345; 'chamber(s)' [basically non-cultic]
מזבח	20 n. 12, 24 n. 21, 48–50, 52–4, 56–7, 100; '*altar*'. See also מזבח (העולה, הנחשת) (III); מזבח (הקטרת, הזהב) (III)
מכון (לשבת ה׳)	[N] 14; 'fixed place (for Yahweh's sitting)'
מלא יד	(verb) 67; 'fill one's hand' (= consecrate him for priesthood)
(מֶלַח), תִּמְלַח, מְמֻלָּח	[P] 243 n. 23; ('salt'), 'will season with salt', 'blended with salt'

מנורה (מנורות) 16, 153 n. 8, 156, 189, 287–8 ;'*lampstand(s)*' [basically non-cultic]

מִנְחָה 24, 100, 132, 185 n. 21, 234 n. 8; (as a technical term for) 'grain-*offering*'

מנחה ונסך [N] 234; 'grain- and drink-offerings' (as the two forms of modest oblation)

מנחת התמיד [P] 172 n. 50, 182 n. 17; 'daily (regular) grain-offering' (apparently referring to the loaves of bread set inside the tabernacle; in Lev. 6: 13 another oblation is dealt with) [cf. **לחם התמיד**]

מעונ(ה), מעון ביתו/קדשו [N] 14; 'habitation', 'habitation of his (Yahweh's) house', 'his holy habitation'

מעשר 109, 116–17 n. 8, 127–8; '*tithe*'

מפלצת [N] 278, 279 n. 9; 'monstrous object', 'abominable image (of idolatry)'

מצבה [N] 48, 50, 53, 56; 'stone-*pillar*'

מצות 100 n. 20, 328–9; 'unleavened *bread* (or cakes)' [basically non-cultic]

מקדש 14–15, 20, 50, 60, 172 n. 50, 177 n. 4, 182 n. 17; 'sacred place or object(s)', 'holiness'. See also **בית (ה)מקדש; מקדש הקדש**

מקדש הקדש [P] 15; (literally:) 'the holy (place, section) of sanctity' (= the inner sanctum)

מקום קדוש [P] 184–5, 233 n. 6; 'a holy place' (within the court)

מקטרת [N] 157 n. 18, 238, 240; '(apparently upright) censer' [cf. **מחתה** in III]

מקרא קדש [P] 291–2, 296–7; 'holy proclamation'

מרכבה See **תבנית המרכבה**

מרכב(ו)ת השמש [N] 134 n. 4; 'the sun *chariot*(s)'

משכי(ו)ת [N] 145 n. 16; 'figure(d stones, objects)'

משכן כבודו/שמו [N] 14; 'where his glory (his name) dwells'

משכנות (ה׳) [N] 14; 256 n. 13, 261 n. 3; '(the Lord's) tabernacles, dwelling place' (as the temple's epithet) [cf. **משכן** in I]

משמרת (המשכן, ה׳, המקדש) [P] 60, 181–2; 'the guard of (the tabernacle, Yahweh, the sanctity)'

משמרת הבית [*P*] 60, 94; 'the guard of the house (temple)' [Ezekiel's adaptation of a concept appearing in P]

משמרת המזבח [*P*] 60, 94, 186 n. 26; 'the guard of the altar' [Ezekiel's adaptation of a concept appearing in P]

משרת(י) ה׳ 64–5 n. 9, 218–19; 'the Lord's servant(s)' or 'attendant(s)' (as a priestly epithet)

משרתי הבית [*P*] 61, 96; 'the servants of the house (temple)' (as a Levitical non-priestly epithet in Ezekiel's usage) [apparently based on P's diction: cf. Num. 1: 50; 8: 26 *et al.*]

נגיד See **פקיד נגיד**

נדבה 16, 117 n. 8, 331; 'free-will *offering*'

נדר 16, 116 n. 8, 119, 127 n. 25; '*vow* (votive) *offering*'

נוה (ה') [N] 14; '(Yahweh's) abode' (epithet of the Jerusalem temple)

נְוֵה צדק [N] 14; 'abode of righteousness' (epithet of the Jerusalem temple)

נְוֵה שאנן [N] 14; 'quiet abode' (epithet of the Jerusalem temple)

נחלת ה' [N] 39, 41; 'the Lord's heritage'

נחש (הנחשת), נחשתן [N] 133, 234 n. 7, 235 n. 9; the bronze serpent

נסך 32, 41 n. 47, 216–17; 'drink offering', 'libation'

(נסך), הסיך נסכ(ים), יֻסַּךְ (verbs) 216, 234; 'pour libation(s)', 'will be poured out (as a libation)'

נר תמיד [P] 208; 'lamp (possibly lamps, as a cluster) that burns regularly'

(סור), סר, הסיר (הבמות) [N] 23, 139; 'be removed', 'remove' (said of high-places)

סֶמֶל (סֶמֶל הקנאה) [N] 282–3; 'idol', 'image' ('of jealousy', 'of lust')

סף [N] 319 n. 4; 'basin', 'goblet'

ספר הברית [N] 134, 136–7, 142, 143 n. 12; 'the book of (= in which one finds the words of) the covenant', i.e. document on which a covenant is said to be based and the kind of which is mentioned in 2 Kgs. 23: 2–3, 21 [for Exod. 20:22—23:33 cf. *Book of the Covenant*]

עבד את ה' [N] 302; 'serve the Lord (by offering sacrifices)'

עבודה (עבודת המשכן) [P] 60–1, 181–2; '(the non-priestly, Levitical) work (at the tabernacle)'

עד(ו)ת [P] 142, 272–3; '*testimony*' (denoting the words on the tables) [cf. **ברית**]. See also **אהל** (III) **העד(ו)ת**; (III) **ארון העד(ו)ת**; **לפני העד(ו)ת**; (III) **משכן העד(ו)ת**

עוֹלָה 46, 61, 63, 68 n. 13; 'burnt- (whole) offering'

עולת תמיד [P] 273 n. 19; 'regular (daily) burnt-offering'

העזרה [N] 186; 'the temple's outer court' [only in 2 Chron. 4: 9; 6: 13]

ע(ו)מד לפני ה' [N] 199 n. 16; '(to) stand(s) before the Lord'

עצבים [N] 105; 'images', 'idols'

עצרה, עצרת 295–7; '(solemn) gathering', 'mass assembly'

ערך (verb) 210; 'set in order' [basically non-cultic]

פסח 317–18, 319–48; '(sacrifice of) *Passover*', 'paschal offering'

פסל [N] 279; 'graven image', 'statue'

פסל ומסכה [N] 35 n. 39; (hendiadys implying) 'a statue poured from a single casting'

פְּקֻדָּה, פְּקֻדּוֹת 96, 97 n. 15; 'oversight', 'charge' *or* 'group of overseers performing their task together' [basically secular term]. See also **בית** (I) **הפקֻדות**; (I) **בעל פקידות**; **פקיד(ים)**

פקיד(ים) [N] 94, 96–7; ‘officer(s)’, ‘overseer(s)’ (in the temple court or elsewhere) [basically secular term]

פקיד נגיד [N] 96–7; ‘chief officer’ (in the temple court)

פתח אהל מועד [P] 184, 198; ‘(at) the entrance to the tent of meeting’

צבא השמים [N] 134 n. 4, 254; ‘*host of heaven*’

קדש (verb) 160 n. 25, 176; ‘become holy’, ‘contract holiness’

קִדֵּשׁ, הִתְקַדֵּשׁ [N] 313–14 n. 41; ‘purge, purify (person, object, oneself) from uncleanness’ (being the condition for any sacred act) [in P means also ‘make holy’]

(ה)קדש [P] 172 n. 50, 182 n. 17; ‘sacred place (section) or object(s)’, ‘holiness’

קדש לה׳ 169, 215; ‘holy to Yahweh’ (as a cultic formula)

קדש קדשים [P] 172 n. 50; ‘exceedingly (or irreversibly) holy place or object’

קדשים 16 n. 5; ‘sacred things (donations)’

(קום), הקים ברית [P] 143 n. 12; ‘to fulfil a (practically divine) promise’

קְטוֹרָה See קְטֹרֶת

(קטר), הקטיר 230–1, 233; ‘burn (sacrifice, possibly incense, or sacrificial portions) on the altar’ (if incense, also in censer)

קִטֵּר, מְקַטְּרִים [N] 23–4, 100, 132 n. 1, 233–4; ‘offer (burn) grain-offering (mainly to other gods, or in illegal worship to Yahweh)’

קִטֵּר (noun) [N] 234; ‘grain-offering’ (apparently in the form of kneaded dough)

קְטֹרֶת (קְטוֹרָה) 230–1, 233–5, 243; ‘*incense*’, also ‘fragrance of (burning) sacrifice’

קטרת זרה [P] 183 n. 18, 243–4; ‘strange (unauthorized) incense’ (= not belonging to the gold altar)

קטרת תמיד [P] 208, 244–5; ‘regular (regularly, daily burnt) incense’

קנה (הטוב) [N] 235; ‘sweet cane’ [cf. קנה בשם in III]

(קרב), הקריב [P] 328 n. 26; ‘bring, present (a sacrifice to God)’

קרבן [P] 347; ‘offering, oblation’

קָרְבַּן העצים [N] 10 n. 10; ‘wood offering’ [only in Neh. 10: 35; 13: 31]

(ראה), יֵרָאֶה את פני ה׳ [N] 291–4, 296 n. 14, 333; (all your males) ‘shall appear (present themselves) before Yahweh’

ראש (ה)חדש [P] 2, 224, 291–2 n. 7; ‘the beginning of the month’, ‘the *New Moon* (*day*)’ [in P with ראש in the construct state, outside the Pentateuch חדש alone]

רוח החיה [*P*] 259 n. 19; 'the spirit of the living creature' (of Ezekiel's vision) [reminiscent of P's style; cf. רוח חיים in I]

ריח ניחוח 230–1; 'pleasing odour' [non-P reference in Gen. 8: 21]

שבת 2, 224, 291–2 n. 7; *Sabbath*

(שחה), השתחוה [N] 305–6; 'prostrate oneself' (before God in temple) [also used in non-cultic context]

שחט (verb) 328–9, 332 n. 32, 339; 'slaughter (beast for sacrifice)'

שלמים 46, 61, 331 n. 31; 'peace- (well-being? communion?) offering'; practically the same as זבח [in P the compound זבח שלמים predominates; other works have mostly שלמים or זבח alone]

שמן זית זך [P] 164 n. 30, 208; 'pure (clear) olive oil'

שמר (כהֻנה) (verb) [P] 183–4; 'guard (= observe the prohibitions of) (the priesthood)'

שמר משמרת See משמרת

שעטנז [N] 160 n. 25; 'a cloth mixed of wool and linen' [another term for cloth of כלאים; mentioned only in H and D]

שֶׁקֶץ (שִׁקֻּץ), שוצים 104–5, 135; 'detestable thing(s)', 'abomination(s)' [in P occurs only in the sing. שקץ]

שְׂרָפִים [N] 252, 254; 'seraphim' (fiery serpents)

תא(ים) [N] 96; 'cell(s)', 'guard-room(s)' (in the temple)

תבנית המרכבה [N] 253; 'the model of the chariot', 'of the (movable) throne' [designation of the cherubim-throne in 1 Chron. 28: 18]

תודה See זבח תודה

תורה, תורות 143–4, 255; '(divine) law(s), instruction(s) (usually kept in scrolls)' [secular equivalent is known in Proverbs]

תמיד 207, 213–14, 217–18, 244–5; 'regularly repeated', 'regular repetition' [basically non-cultic]. See also אֳרֻחת תמיד; אש תמיד; (I) לחם התמיד; מנחת התמיד; (I) משתה תמיד; נר תמיד; עולת תמיד; קטרת תמיד

תנופה [P] 59, 184; 'wave offering'

תֹּפֶת [N] 25; *topheth* (apparently name of a site where the Moloch cult was practised)

תרומה [P] 209 n. 6; 'gift-offering', 'contribution'

תרומת יָדֶךָ [N] 16 n. 5; 'contribution of your hand(s)'

תרפים [N] 35; *teraphim* (implement of divination)

III. Used in the Tabernacle Pericope

All of the following terms are found in P, though some also occur outside. Many of them are basically common and secular rather than cultic in character, and were only applied to the tabernacle and its accessories (cf. above, p. 349).

אבנט 162 n. 27, 169, 170 n. 47; '*girdle*'

אבני זכרון 213; 'stones of reminder'

אבני מִלֻּאִים 168; 'stones for setting'

אבני שהם 168 n. 43, 213; '*onyx stones*' (cornelians, *lapis lazuli*)

אדנ(ים) 151, 153; '*socket(s)*'

אהל מועד II 179, 184–5, 262, 271–5; '*tent of meeting*', as another designation of the tabernacle [cf. אהל מועד I in I]

אהל העד(ו)ת 272 n. 18; 'tent of the testimony'

אורים ותמים See in II

אילים See עורות אילים

אפוד See in II

א(ו)רג See מעשה א(ו)רג

ארון העד(ו)ת 142, 199 n. 16, 247–8, 255; 'the *ark* of the testimony'. See also עד(ו)ת (II)

בגדי הקדש 173–4; 'the (remarkably) holy garments'

בגדי (ה)שְּׂרָד 172–3; 'the (sumptuous? stitched?) garments (of ritual officiation?)'

בד 174, 183; 'plain linen'

בדים 156, 158; 'poles'

בריח(ים) 151; '*bar(s)*' (for joining the planks)

ווים 152, 157; '*hooks*'

זהב טהור 163–4, 169; 'pure *gold*'. See also המנורה הטהורה; השלחן הטהור

חוברת See מחברת

חלבנה 242; galbanum, χαλβάνη

(ה)חצר 153–5; 'the *court*'

חֵשֶׁב 166, 167 n. 39; 'the part (of the ephod) where the artistry of *ḥôšēḇ* is shown'

ח(ו)שב See מעשה ח(ו)שב

חֹשֶׁן 168, 213; 'the *breastpiece*'

חש(ו)קים 164; 'bands'

טבעות 156, 163, 168; 'rings'

ידות 151, 'tenons'

יעים 157; 'scrapers', 'shovels'

יריעות (לאהל, האהל) 152, 162, 180; '(outer) *curtains* (for a tent)'. See also יריעות עזים

יריעות (המשכן) 151, 161–2; '(lower) *curtains* (of the tabernacle)'

יריעות עזים 160, 162–3; 'curtains of (hair of) *goats*'

יתדות 152, 155; '*pegs*'

כלי הקדש 157; 'the holy utensils' (implying the minor articles)

141 n. 11; 'the holy vessels'

כלי שמן 157; 'oil utensils (implements)'

כלי (ה)שרת	156; ‘the utensils (implements) of officiation’
כליל תכלת	158, 164 n. 30, 168; ‘pure (complete) blue’
כפות	156; ‘ladles’
כַּפֹּרֶת	153, 158, 178, 248–51; a(n unexplained) technical term for the *ark-cover* [in LXX ἱλαστήριον]
כרובים	See in II
כתנ(ו)ת	169–70, 172; ‘*tunic*(*s*)’
כתפות	166; ‘shoulder-pieces’ or ‘-straps’ (of the ephod)
לבונה	See in II
לוחות	See נבוב לוחות
לֻלָאוֹת	151, 152 n. 5; ‘*loops*’
מגבעות	170, 210; ‘*caps*’. See also פארי מגבעות
מוט	156; ‘carrying bar’
מזבח (העולה, הנחשת)	155–6, 159, 176–7; ‘the (tabernacle's *outer*) *altar* (of burnt-offering, of bronze)’
מזבח (הקטרת, הזהב)	153, 156–7, 159, 242–5; ‘the (tabernacle's inner) *altar* (*of incense*, of gold)
מזלגות	157; ‘forks’
מזרק(ות)	157, 216 n. 13; ‘basin(s)’, ‘container(s) for throwing a liquid’
מַחְבֶּרֶת, חוֹבֶרֶת	166; ‘joining’, ‘connecting line’ (of cloths)
מחתה, מחתות	156–7, 238, 241; ‘(apparently long-handled) *censer*(*s*)’ [cf. מקטרת in II]
מיתרים	152, 155; ‘*cords*’
מכנסים (מכנסי בד)	170–1, 174; ‘*breeches*’ (‘breeches of plain linen’)
מלקחים	156; ‘tongs’
מנורה	See in II
(ה)מנורה (ה)טהורה	163; ‘the pure (= of pure gold) lampstand’
מנקיות	156, 216 n. 13; ‘*jars*’
מסך לפתח האהל	153–5, 162–5; ‘a *screen* for the entrance of the tent’ (the outer veil)
מסך לשער החצר	153–5, 185–6; ‘a *screen* for the gate of the court’ (the court's screen)
מעיל האפוד	168, 180; ‘the *ephod's robe*’
מעשה אֹרֵג	160–1, 168–9; ‘the workmanship of the (simple) weaver’
מעשה חרש אבן	243 n. 24; ‘the workmanship of the lapidary’
מעשה ח(ו)שב	160–1, 165, 167–8; ‘the workmanship of the (highly) ingenious weaver’
(מעשה) מקשה	See מקשה
מעשה עבות	243 n. 24; ‘the work of cords’
מעשה רוקח	243; ‘the workmanship of the perfumer’
מעשה רֹקֵם	160–2, 165, 170–1; ‘the workmanship of the variegator (skilful weaver)’
מעשה רשת נחשת	243 n. 24; ‘the work of the bronze netting’
מצנפת	170, 210–11; ‘*turban*’ (of the high-priest)
מִקְשָׁה	156, 159, 167; ‘hammered work’
משזר	See שש משזר

משכן אהל מועד 272; 'the tabernacle of the tent of meeting'
משכן (ה') 14 n. 3, 140, 179, 196, 221, 261 n. 3, 263, 269, 272; 'the *tabernacle* (of the Lord)'
משכן העד(ו)ת 272 n. 18; 'the tabernacle of the testimony'

נבוב לוחות 151 n. 2, 156 n. 14; 'hollow (made) of boards'
נזר 169, 214–16; '*diadem*'. See also **ציץ**
נָטָף 242; a kind of myrrh-oil (stacte?; LXX *στακτή*)
נר(ות) 156, 208 n. 4, 209 n. 5; '*lamp*(*s*)'

סירות 157; 'pails'
סַמִּים 208, 242–5; 'substances serving to improve an incense (sorts of spices?)'. See also **קטרת (ה)סמים**

עגלות צב 150–1; '*covered wagons*' [cf. Isa. 66: 20]
עורות אילים 162–3; '(tanned) *skins of rams*'
עור(ות) תחש(ים) 152, 162–3, 180 n. 12; '*skin*(*s*) *of goat*(*s*)'?
עזים See **יריעות עזים**
עמודים 153–4, 157–8; '*pillars*' (*of the tabernacle*)

פארי מגבעות 170; head-dresses (for ordinary priests). See also **פאר** (I) **מגבעות;**
פעמון(ים) 168–9, 214; '*bell*(*s*)'
פרכת 152–3, 161–2; term for the *veil* which shuts off the inner sanctum
פתח אהל מועד See in II

ציץ 169, 214–16; 'frontlet', 'plate' (indicating the high-priest's *diadem*). See also **נזר**

קטרת See in II
קטרת (ה)סמים 208, 243–5; 'the *incense of* (spices?)'. See also (II) **קטרת זרה;** (II) **קטרת תמיד**
קלעים 154–5, 162; '*hangings*' (of the tabernacle's court)
קנה בשם 235; 'sweet cane', *κάλαμος ἀρωματικός*
קערות 156; 'bowls'
קרסים 151, 152 n. 5; '*clasps*'
קרשים 150–1, 163; '*planks*'
קְשָׂוֹת 156, 216 n. 13; '*jugs*'

רמון(ים) 169, 171; '*pomegranate*(*s*)' (as a decoration of the ephod's robe)
רֹקֵם See **מעשה רקם**

שחלת 242; one of the substances improving the altar-incense (identity uncertain; LXX *ὄνυξ*)
שֻׁלְחָן 153, 159, 210; '*table*'

(ה)שֻׁלחן (ה)טהור	163; 'the pure (= of pure gold) table'
שמן המאור	164 n. 30, 182 n. 17; 'the *oil for lighting*'
שמן המשחה	4 n. 3, 59, 243; 'the oil of *anointing*'
שני תולעת	See תולעת שני
שְׂרָד	See בגדי שרד
שש מָשְׁזָר	160 n. 24, 169 n. 44, 173 n. 52, 174 n. 54; 'fine twined (or twisted) *linen*'
תולעת שני	159 n. 21, 160; '*crimson* (or scarlet) cloth (of wool)'
תחש	See עור(ות) תחש(ים)

SUBJECT INDEX

In this index, whether the item referred to appears in the body of the text or in the notes, only the page number is indicated.

INDEX OF BIBLICAL REFERENCES

Parentheses round the number of a note indicate that the biblical passage is treated only in that note. Where the note is given without parentheses, the reference is both to the page-text and to the note.